A HISTORY OF THE
COUNTY
CRICKET
CHAMPIONSHIP

Robert Brooke

A HISTORY OF THE
COUNTY
CRICKET
CHAMPIONSHIP

Robert Brooke

GUINNESS PUBLISHING

ABOUT THE AUTHOR

ROBERT BROOKE was born, brought up and schooled in the area
which is now called 'West Midlands', but would still describe himself as
'of Warwickshire'. He supplements his meagre earnings from
cricket writing with the proceeds of his early morning newsstand at a
commuter station in Solihull.
He has written a number of cricket books, either as sole or co-author,
and contributed to many others. For a number of years he has written
a monthly column for *The Cricketer* and is a member of the team which
produces *Wisden Cricketers' Almanack*. A founder of The Association of Cricket
Statisticians in 1973, he still produces book reviews and the occasional
pamphlet for that body. He is also a member of the Cricket Writers' Club,
The Cricket Society, and Warwickshire County Cricket Club.

Editor: Charles Richards
Text design and layout: Kathy Aldridge
Cover design: David Roberts
Picture editor: Alex Goldberg

Copyright © Robert Brooke 1991

The right of Robert Brooke to be identified as the Author of
this Work has been asserted in accordance with the
Copyright, Design & Patents Act 1988.

Published in Great Britain by Guinness Publishing Ltd,
33 London Road, Enfield, Middlesex

Typeset in Century Schoolbook by
Ace Filmsetting Ltd, Frome, Somerset

Printed and bound in Great Britain by
The Bath Press, Bath

'Guinness' is a registered trademark of
Guinness Publishing Ltd

British Library Cataloguing in Publication Data
Brooke, Robert
  A history of Cricket's County Championship.
  1. England. County cricket, history
  I. Title
  796.35863

ISBN 0-85112-919-6

CONTENTS

INTRODUCTION

The County Championship, currently sponsored by Britannic Assurance plc, attracts smaller day-by-day spectatorship than any other major English county competition, and, since it has long been the 'bread and butter' competition of English cricket, remarkably few headlines. Yet in its official form it is one of the oldest cricket competitions in the world, and certainly, in the view of this writer, the most stimulating.

Although I sometimes allow myself to suffer Test matches, and when my own county, Warwickshire, is involved I might even attend limited-overs matches and there enjoy the camaraderie among the supporters of winning – and sometimes even non-winning – counties, I am in reality a full-time watcher, supporter and aficionado of the County Championship. Therefore, as the centenary of its official establishment in 1890 approached, I was delighted when Guinness agreed to publish a statistically-based history of the recognised county competition, and I set to work with a will.

By September 1989, a large proportion of my work had been completed and I took the opportunity afforded by the annual Cricket Writers' Club dinner and the Nat West Trophy final taking place in London on successive days to check some references at the Newspaper Library in Colindale. Accompanying me to London was a briefcase containing almost all of my copious notes for the County Championship history.

This briefcase I last saw in the hands of two fleeing flowers of young British manhood scurrying down an alley in central London. Threats, and some well-aimed kicks, had persuaded me to gift them my money, credit cards and jacket; my request that they leave my case, which contained material of 'no value or interest' were ignored, and countless hours work went down the drain – or, in the view of the Police, probably onto the nearest rubbish dump when the contents had been examined! My barely legible calligraphy would have been dismissed as the jottings of a mad professor or Russian spy, and I feared, rightly, that my notes were lost forever.

Simon Duncan, my editor at Guinness Publishing, gave me a sympathetic hearing when I begged to be excused my deadline and I was grateful when some time later he suggested the deadline be extended a year and I try again.

Now you have the result; the sheer depression arising from the knowledge that most of the work had already been done, and lost, made it the most difficult book I have ever written. In fact there were times, early on, when I found it almost impossible to continue but regular calls from Simon kept me at it, and I only hope my final offering will prove all the effort, and heartbreak, to have been worthwhile.

The book itself is divided into several sections, the major one devoted to a season-by-season resumé of the Championship. The opening chapter consists of a short general history of county cricket, and here I am grateful to the then editor of *The Cricket Statistician* for enabling me to extract certain information from an early issue of that learned journal. There is a short 'records' section for each county, and in these – and in the general records section – most space has been allocated to career records of batting and bowling, since these are, so far as I am aware, not available from any other source.

Should the pessimistic conclusion to my postscript, 'Qualification and Other Matters', upset or annoy any readers, they have my apologies. I hope I am mistaken in my beliefs, and that fifty years from now there will still be a County Championship with records to be updated. The 1991 season marks the start of the 11th decade of the official County Championship. Eleven is the ultimate cricket number, it means our team, our line-up, is complete!

Finally my thanks again to Simon Duncan, to Alex Goldberg for searching out the photographs, and to Guinness Publishing for showing so much patience.

Robert Brooke
January 1991

ABBREVIATIONS

COUNTIES

Derbys . . . . Derbyshire
Glam . . . . Glamorgan
Gloucs . . . . Gloucestershire
Hants . . . . Hampshire
Lancs . . . . Lancashire
Leics . . . . Leicestershire
Middx . . . . Middlesex
Northants . . . . Northamptonshire
Notts . . . . Nottinghamshire
Som . . . . Somerset
Sx . . . . Sussex
Warwicks . . . . Warwickshire
Worcs . . . . Worcestershire
Yorks . . . . Yorkshire

OTHER

Inns . . . . Innings
Wkts . . . . Wickets
Mdns . . . . Maiden overs
Avge . . . . Average
* . . . . Not out
NO . . . . Number of 'Not out' innings
HS . . . . Highest Score
ct . . . . caught
st . . . . stumped

GROUNDS

BL . . . . Bramall Lane, Sheffield
D . . . . Dore, Sheffield
AR . . . . Aylestone Road, Leicester
GR . . . . Grace Road, Leicester

1

COUNTY CRICKET AND THE CHAMPIONSHIP

Genesis and Early History

On 16 December 1889, the Secretaries of the main cricketing counties met at Lord's to agree the fixture list for the following season; on the same day, a private meeting attended by representatives of Gloucestershire, Kent, Lancashire, Middlesex, Nottinghamshire, Surrey, Sussex and Yorkshire agreed upon a method of deciding the order of merit among the 'first-class' counties the following season, 1890. The majority decision was that in matches between their counties, one point should be awarded for a win, one deducted for a defeat, with draws ignored.

The decision on points-scoring was not nearly so important as the convening of the meeting in the first place. For the first time, the major counties were acknowledging that a county championship was desirable, and confirming this recognition by working out a means of deciding which was the top county each season, a decision previously made by the cricket press!

It may be thought that the introduction of so far-reaching and revolutionary a scheme would have been greeted with clashing of cymbals and blowing of trumpets; in fact the response both in the news media and among the spectators was low key almost to the point of non-existent. When Gloucestershire entertained Yorkshire at Bristol on 12–14 May, the progress of the match was reported in some detail but nowhere have I traced any mention of the game being the first in the new 'official'

championship. Be this as maybe, Yorkshire – probably at full strength, except that eternal 12th man Lees Whitehead was given the nod over the youthful Robert Moorhouse – won comfortably, and by lunch on the third day they were the first leaders of the County Championship.

In view of their subsequent record (only recently have they established themselves as one of the weakest county sides) this first result was eminently appropriate, but in this first season Yorkshire hadn't the depth to prevent Surrey taking the title, though they did finish a creditable equal third.

In fact the monumental press indifference hid what was an interesting battle for honours. At the end of June, Nottinghamshire, Surrey and Yorkshire shared top spot, while Sussex (−3) and Gloucestershire (−6) languished way behind the rest and seemingly out of their class. Yorkshire and Notts both faded in the run in and it was left to Lancashire to mount a late, but vain challenge.

They needed to beat Surrey at The Oval in late August to stay in contention, but were swept away by the home side who thus made sure of the title with two games remaining. The fact that they lost these last two games suggests that the new championship perhaps meant more than the press coverage, or lack of it, seemed to indicate. At the other end, five wins in their last six matches took Gloucestershire to sixth place, above Middlesex and poor Sussex who, five points adrift, were undeniably worthy of the first 'wooden spoon'.

Surrey would be known for all time as the first official champion county, but if this would seem to imply that inter-county cricket, or even the idea that one county should be thought of as 'champion', was of comparatively recent vintage, nothing could have been further from the truth. Inter-county matches had been taking place since the early 18th century and the oldest surviving reference appeared in *The Postman* newspaper on 25 June 1709, when readers were informed: 'On Wednesday, the 29th instant will be play'd a famous match of cricket on Dartford Brimpth for £50 by Kent and Surrey.'

That this was a representative county match seems most unlikely; certainly no county *clubs* are known to have existed at the time, and they were probably two teams of players gathered together from the two counties by a couple of wealthy patrons. This is not claimed to be the first ever 'inter-county' match, simply the earliest for which contemporary evidence survives; even then, nothing is known about the play, nor the result.

In the years that followed, a number of similar inter-county matches are known to have taken place, but it is almost certain that others were played of which no record now survives. In 1728 a Swiss traveller in England is reported to have mentioned the popularity of county cricket, with large crowds attending the games; yet up to that time, only about half a dozen games which by the most loose criteria could be termed 'county matches' are known about. The sad conclusion must be that much has been lost forever.

The 'higher orders' continued their sponsorship of inter-county matches throughout the 18th century, but they were comparatively few in number. Not until 1773 do we know of an alleged inter-county match for which something like a proper scorecard survives. This was Surrey v Kent at Laleham Burway in June of that year.

The first definite reference to a county cricket *club* seems to have been in 1790, the members of the 'Essex Cricket Club' meeting fortnightly at the Green Man in Navestock during that summer. The reference to 'Oxfordshire Cricket Club' on an engraving inscribed 1788 is not accepted (though it *may* be authentic), since another copy of the print is dated 1825.

Nothing is known of the early Essex club and it had little relevance in the general history of county cricket. Indeed, at around this time the very concept seemed to be dying and from August 1796, when Middlesex played Surrey, until June 1825, when Sussex and Kent met at Brighton, not a single important inter-county

match is recorded.

Matters now started to develop apace, however, and although it was still many years before a proper championship was even visualised, in 1837 Kent defeated Nottinghamshire at Town Malling in a game described by the *Maidestone Journal* thus: '. . . the approaching match may be considered as a contest for the championship.'

The first ball of the first 'official' County Championship match was appropriately faced by WG Grace. 'The Doctor', best known of all English cricketers, was 41 at the time and fully held his own into his late forties (Mary Evans Picture Library)

So, were Kent the first County Champions? Possibly, yet in 1827 *Bell's Life in London*, the leading sporting newspaper of the day, states that if Sussex should win (against 'England'!) their players shall wear the belt. This is clearly a reference to real or imaginary championship belts, so one could equally claim that Sussex, who won five out of six 'important' games in this season, were the first champion county. Late in the season they beat Kent twice, thus perhaps confirming their top ranking. Records also show that in the previous season Sussex twice beat a combined Hampshire–Surrey side, though in the Kent v Sussex contests honours were even. Sussex are now acclaimed by some sources as champions for that season, but one feels the evidence to be inconclusive.

The list below was compiled for the December 1980 edition of *The Cricket Statistician* and based on the research of various people brought together by Peter Wynne-Thomas. It is probably as authentic as any list could be.

UNOFFICIAL LIST OF COUNTY CHAMPIONS – to 1863	
1826 Sussex	1845 Sussex
1827 Sussex	1846 –
1828 Kent	1847 Kent
1829 –	1848 Sussex
1830 Surrey	1849 Kent
1831 Surrey	1850 Surrey
1832 –	1851 Surrey
1833 Sussex	1852 Notts & Sussex
1834 –	1853 Notts
1835 –	1854 Surrey
1836 –	1855 Sussex
1837 Kent	1856 Surrey
1838 Kent	1857 Surrey
1839 Kent	1858 Surrey
1840 –	1859 –
1841 Kent	1860 –
1842 Kent	1861 –
1843 Kent	1862 Notts
1844 –	1863 –

County cricket in the middle of the 19th century continued with Middlesex, Kent, Surrey and Sussex always involved, with occasional, and usually inconsequential, interjections from the North in the form of Nottinghamshire, Lancashire and Yorkshire. Yet its progress with regard to organisation and popularity was somewhat desultory. For many years the sporting press had selected this county or that as the season's champions, but it was not until the 1870s that some sort of merit table was introduced. Again, the press was the instigator; but there was little consistency with regard to the methods of calculating the champions, or even over which matches should be included. Too much notice should not therefore be taken of the lists of 'champions' which were reproduced in cricket publications, some of them starting as early as 1864.

The table below, covering seasons 1864–69, gives possible county champions for this period; but in quoting seven different, reputable sources, it is possible to illustrate the considerable difficulties encountered when any attempt is made to list official county champions before 1890.

	Bowen	Wisden	John Lillywhite	James Lillywhite	Cricket	WG Grace	Holmes
1864	Surrey	—	—	—	—	Surrey	—
1865	Nottinghamshire	—	Nottinghamshire	—	—	Nottinghamshire	—
1866	Middlesex	—	Middlesex	—	—	MIddlesex	—
1867	Yorkshire	—	Yorkshire	—	—	Yorkshire	—
1868	Nottinghamshire	—	—	—	Nottinghamshire	Yorkshire	—
1869	Notts/Yorkshire	—	Notts/Yorkshire	—	Notts/Yorkshire	Nottinghamshire	—
1870	Yorkshire	Yorkshire	Yorkshire	—	Notts/Yorkshire	Yorkshire	—
1871	Nottinghamshire	Nottinghamshire	Nottinghamshire	Nottinghamshire	Notts/Yorkshire	Nottinghamshire	—
1872	Nottinghamshire	—	Nottinghamshire	Nottinghamshire	Notts/Yorkshire	Surrey	—
1873	Gloucs/Notts	Nottinghamshire	Gloucestershire	Gloucs/Notts	—	Gloucs/Notts	Gloucs/Notts
1874	Gloucestershire	—	Gloucestershire	Gloucestershire	—	Gloucestershire	Derbyshire
1875	Nottinghamshire	Nottinghamshire	Nottinghamshire	Nottinghamshire	—	Nottinghamshire	Nottinghamshire
1876	Gloucestershire	—	Gloucestershire	Gloucestershire	—	Gloucestershire	Gloucestershire
1877	Gloucestershire	—	Gloucestershire	Gloucestershire	—	Gloucestershire	Gloucestershire
1878	—	—	—	—	Middlesex	Nottinghamshire	Middlesex
1879	Lancashire/Notts	Nottinghamshire	Lancashire/Notts	Lancashire/Notts	—	Lancashire/Notts	Lancashire/Notts
1880	Nottinghamshire	Nottinghamshire	Nottinghamshire	Nottinghamshire	—	Nottinghamshire	Nottinghamshire
1881	Lancashire	Lancashire	Lancashire	Lancashire	—	Lancashire	Lancashire
1882	Lancashire/Notts	Lancashire/Notts	Lancashire/Notts	Lancashire/Notts	Lancashire	Lancashire/Notts	Lancashire/Notts
1883	Nottinghamshire	Yorkshire	Nottinghamshire	Nottinghamshire	Notts/Yorkshire	Yorkshire	Nottinghamshire
1884	Nottinghamshire	Nottinghamshire	Nottinghamshire	Nottinghamshire	Nottinghamshire	Nottinghamshire	Nottinghamshire
1885	Nottinghamshire	Nottinghamshire	—	Nottinghamshire	Nottinghamshire	Nottinghamshire	Nottinghamshire
1886	Nottinghamshire	Nottinghamshire	—	Nottinghamshire	Surrey	Nottinghamshire	Nottinghamshire
1887	Surrey	Surrey	—	Surrey	Surrey	Surrey	Surrey
1888	Surrey	Surrey	—	Surrey	Surrey	Surrey	Surrey
1889	Lancs/Notts/Surrey	Lancs/Notts/Surrey	—	Lancs/Notts/Surrey	Lancs/Notts/Surrey	Lancs/Notts/Surrey	Lancs/Notts/Surrey

The table includes the opinions of the four major cricketing publications of the 1880s and that of the greatest cricketer of the period.

KEY:
Bowen — Rowland Bowen – cricket historian.
Wisden — *Wisden Cricketers' Almanack.*
John Lillywhite — John Lillywhite's *Cricketers' Companion* (incorporating Frederick Lillywhite's *Guide to Cricketers*).
James Lillywhite — James Lillywhite's *Cricketers' Annual.*
Cricket — *Cricket* magazine. The details for 1868–72 are as listed in *Baily's Magazine.* The 1878 entry is from *Cricket & Football Times.*
WG Grace — List published in 1903 in *Cricket,* edited by HG Hutchinson.
Holmes — Rev RS Holmes – his list was first published in *Cricket* 1894. From 1901 until Bowen's revision in 1959 this was accepted as the 'official' list of champions.

The 'championship' seems to have been awarded in the main to the team with fewest defeats, but in the 1880s a points system was gradually preferred. Right up to 1889 the press was responsible for deciding the champions; that season saw a triple tie involving Nottinghamshire, Lancashire and Surrey, who each gained 10.5 points on the basis of one for a win, half for a draw. Interestingly, had the old 'least lost' method been used, the final table would have been unchanged.

The meeting in December 1889 changed all the speculation; the counties at last decided to recognise their own championship and take responsibility for the means used to calculate positions in the table.

The experiment of playing 2-day county matches, in 1919, certainly suited Nottinghamshire's George Gunn, as he achieved his best ever season's average (Hulton Picture Company)

2

CHAMPIONSHIP MILESTONES

Points, Prize Money and Other Conditions

890 Gloucestershire, Kent, Lancashire, Middlesex, Nottinghamshire, Surrey, Sussex and Yorkshire contest the inaugural Championship. The number of losses deducted from the number of wins gives a side's overall points total; draws are ignored. The side with the most points are the Champions.

891 Somerset are promoted.

895 Derbyshire, Essex, Hampshire, Leicestershire and Warwickshire are promoted.

Until 1895 each county played a maximum of 16 games, with most sides playing each other twice. With the addition of these five counties, the Rule was made that each side played a *minimum* of 16 games.

With some sides only able to arrange the bare minimum of matches, whereas Surrey and Yorkshire each arranged 26, a change in the method of reckoning was decided upon. While the points system remained the same the *number of* points *per finished game* (ie excluding draws) now determined the final placings.

The old rule was in fact retained for 1895 (when the two systems would in any case have produced the same leading position) but when the new method was brought in for 1896, although Champions Yorkshire would still have finished first under the old system, Surrey would have

been runners-up instead of 4th had the old method been retained.

1899 Worcestershire are promoted.

1905 Northamptonshire are promoted.

1910 New method of reckoning introduced, as an experiment for one season. Teams were now placed according to their *percentage of wins* in *all* matches played, including draws. The new rule was proposed by Lancashire, who suffered most. Placed 4th that season, they would have been second under the previous method. Kent would have been Champions, and Somerset last, under any method used to that date.

1911 Another new method of points-scoring, put forward by Somerset; 5 points were awarded for a win, 3 points for a first innings lead in a drawn game, and 1 point was scored by a side behind on first innings in a drawn game. The percentage of points won to possible points determined the placings. Kent, runners-up, would have won the title under all previous systems.

1919 Two-day matches introduced as an experiment, with longer hours of play. Method of reckoning reverts to percentage of wins in matches played. Worcestershire did not compete in the Championship for financial reasons.

1920 Two-day matches abandoned; return to three days. In a new method of points-scoring, 5 were awarded for a win, and 2 for a first innings lead in a drawn match. Placings again decided by percentage of points to possible points. Worcestershire returned.

1921 Glamorgan promoted.

1922 Each side to undertake at least 11 home and 'out' fixtures. 2.5 points awarded to each side for a tie.

1924 Method of scoring reverts to 5 points awarded for an outright win, 3 points for first innings lead in drawn match, 1 point for first innings loss in drawn match. Matches with no first innings result are ignored. Placings still decided on percentage of points obtained to points possible. In seasons with no Test series, each county to play at least 12 home and out matches.

1927 New method of scoring: 8 points for a win, 5 points for first innings lead in drawn match, 3 points for first innings deficit in drawn match; 4 points awarded to each side for a tie, *and for 'no result' where six hours' play was possible*. Matches with no result and under six hours' play ignored. Placing system unchanged.

1929 Every county to play 28 matches, percentages therefore dropped. Team with most points will now be Champions.

1931 Method of scoring changed: 15 points for an outright win, 7.5 points each side for match finishing with scores level. In a drawn match, the side with first innings lead gets 5 points, the other side 3 points. Where the scores were equal on first innings in a drawn match, each side gets 4 points. In the case of no result or no play at all, 4 points to each side.

1932 If no play is possible on the first two days, the game is played under one-day Laws. The winning side in these circumstances gets 10 points, the losers 3 points.

1933 Each county now to play at least 24 matches, but can arrange up to 32. Championship therefore decided once again on percentage of points won to points possible.

1938 New method of points-scoring: a win secures 12 points; if scores finish level, 6 points each side. For a side that secures a first innings lead but fails to win, 4 points; 2 points each side if level on first innings. Match ignored if no play or no result on first innings. If no play on first two days, one-day Laws apply, the winning side getting 8 points. Total of championship points gained is divided by total of matches played. The team with the highest average is the champion county.

1946 Each team to play 26 matches; the side gaining most points wins the title.

1950 Each side to play 28 matches.

1953 Where the scores finish level in a drawn game, only the side batting is awarded 6 points; the bowling side gets no points other than those already awarded for first innings.

1957 Bonus points are introduced for fast scoring. Where a side leading on first innings scores faster (by runs per over), 2 bonus points are awarded; but points for first innings lead alone are reduced from 4 to 2. When there is no play in the first two-thirds of a match which subsequently is not taken further than first innings, the side leading on first innings is awarded 8 points.

1958 Bonus points rule amended; the 2 points are awarded only if the side attaining a first innings lead has a faster scoring rate *at the time of passing the opponents' total*. In the event of sides finishing level on points, the number of wins will separate them; if still equal, the side with most bonus points finishes highest.

1960 With each county given the choice of 28 or 32 matches, the Championship is once more to be decided on average number of points gained per match. In the event of a tie, the side with the greater percentage of wins will be Champions; if still level, the side with the greater average of bonus points per match prevails.

1961 Where a side is batting last in a drawn match, 6 points are awarded unless an innings has been forfeited, in which case only 2 points are awarded. Experiments introduced this season include abolition of the follow-on, to give sides batting second a better chance. At the same time it was stated that teams were free to *forfeit* their second innings, but none did.

1963 Points system amended: 10 points for an outright win, 5 points each for a tie; when scores finish level in a drawn match, the side batting score 5 points, the fielding side no points other than any first innings points gained; 2 points are awarded for first innings lead, 1 point each for tie on first innings. If there is no play in the first two-thirds of a match and the match is decided on first innings, the side scoring most runs gains 6 points. If the scores finish equal in such a match, the side batting second scores 3 points. With each side playing 28 matches, the team with most points are the Champions.

1966 As an experiment, the first innings of 102 matches, out of a total of 238 played, are restricted to 65 overs. This applies to the first 12 games played by each county on a home and away basis. Normal conditions resume in the return matches, and also where counties met only once during the season. Scoring changes: first innings points to be awarded whatever the ultimate result of the match. The side leading on first innings to score 2 points; 1 point each in the event of a first innings tie.

1967 The experimental 65-overs rule is discarded after one season. A new points system is introduced:

Overseas players were allowed to play in the County Championship from 1968. One of the first to make an impression was the West Indian all-rounder Keith Boyce, who joined Essex (Hulton Picture Company)

Winning side awarded 8 points plus any scored in first innings; in the event of a tie, each side scores 4 points, plus first innings points; if scores finish level in drawn match, the side batting gets 4 points, plus any scored in first innings.

Four points scored for first innings lead, 2 points each for first innings tie; if scores are equal in first innings of drawn match where the first innings of the side batting second is not completed, only that side scores 2 points; first innings points are retained whatever the outcome of a match.

Two points each awarded for a draw, plus first innings points; games with no play or no first innings results are still included in the final table as 'matches played', though no points scored.

The side with most points is the champion county. In the event of sides finishing level on points, the side with most wins prevails.

1968 Ten points to be awarded for an outright win, with 5 each for a tie; if scores are level in a drawn match, the side batting gets 5 points plus any points scored in the first innings. Bonus points re-introduced for first time since 1962, as follows:

First innings points awarded for first 85 overs on each first innings, and retained whatever the final result. *Batting*: For each 25 runs above 150 scored in the first 85 overs, 1 point awarded; i.e. 175 runs – 1 pt, 200 – runs 2 pts, 225 runs – 3 pts, etc. *Bowling*: For each 2 wickets taken by bowling side in first 85 overs, 1 point awarded. i.e. 2 wickets – 1 pt, 4 wickets – 2 pts, 6 wickets – 3 pts, 8 wickets – 4 pts, 10 wickets – 5 pts.

For the first time, each county was able to register immediately, without qualification, one overseas player. No other player could be thus engaged for 3 years after, nor could the player appear for another county for 3 years.

1969 Due to the new Sunday League, each side to play 24 matches, instead of 28.

1972 Matches reduced to 20 each, due to another new limited-overs competition, the Benson & Hedges Cup.

1973 Changes made to batting bonus points: 75 runs in first 25 overs – 1 point, 150 runs in first 50 overs – 2 points; for every subsequent 25 runs, in first 85 overs, a further point. Bowling bonus points unchanged.

For the first time, monetary rewards were introduced in the County Championship. £3000 to the Champions, £2000 the runners-up, £1000 for 3rd place, £500 for 4th place. £500 each to the sides with the highest run-rate and best bowling strike-rate throughout the season. Lord's Taverners' trophy presented for the Champions.

1974 The two first innings limited to a total of 200 overs, with the side batting first limited to 100 overs. Any overs up to 100 not used by the side batting first could be added to the overs of the side batting second. First innings bonus points altered. *Batting*: 150 runs – 1 point, 200 runs – 2 pts, 250 runs – 3 pts, 300 runs – 4 pts. *Bowling*: 3 wickets – 1 point, 5 wickets – 2 pts, 7 wickets – 3 pts, 9 wickets – 4 pts.

1975 Bowling bonus points amended: 3–4 wickets – 1 point, 5–6 wickets – 2 points, 7–8 wickets – 3 points, 9–10 wickets – 4 points. Still first innings only.

1977 Each team to play 22 matches, increased from 20. Twelve points awarded for an outright win. *Prize money*: 1st place – £4000, 2nd – £2500, 3rd – £1250, £100 to winner of each match, £1 for each bonus point. Cadbury-Schweppes become the first sponsors of the County Championship. They were to plough £260,000 into the competition over three years.

1978 *Prize money*: 1st place – £8000, 2nd – £2500, 3rd – £1250, for each win – £100, for each bonus point – £5.

1979 Six points awarded for a tie, and to the side batting in a drawn match where scores finish equal, both increased from 5. *Prize money*: 1st place – £8000, 2nd – £3500, 3rd – £1750, for each win – £120, for each bonus point – £5.

1980 *Prize money*: 1st place – £9000; 2nd – £4000; 3rd – £2000; 4th – £1000; winner of each match – £150; for each bonus point – £5.

1981 *Prize money*: 1st place – £12,000; 2nd place – £6000; 3rd place – £3000; 4th place – £1500; for each win – £150; for each bonus point – £5. Now 16 points for a win, 8 points each for a tie; first innings points unchanged. The 200 overs limit for first innings is discontinued.

1982 *Prize money*: 1st place – £13,000; 2nd – £6500; 3rd – £3250; 4th – £1650.

1983 *Prize money*: 1st place – £14,000; 2nd – £7500; 3rd – £3500; 4th – £1750. Each side to play 24 matches.

1984 The Britannic Assurance Company replace Cadbury-Schweppes as sponsors.

Prize money: 1st place – £15,000; 2nd – £7500; 3rd – £3500; 4th – £1750.

1985 *Prize money*: 1st place – £20,000; 2nd – £10,000; 3rd – £5000; 4th – £2500; 5th – £1250. £250 for winner of each match.

1986 *Prize money*: 1st place – £22,000; 2nd – £10,500; 3rd – £5250; 4th – £2750; 5th – £1375; £210 for winner of each match. £500 for Championship player of year (PAJ DeFreitas, Leics). £750 for county of the month, £250 for player of the month.

1987 *Prize money*: 1st place – £25,000; 2nd – £12,500; 3rd – £6500; 4th – £3500; 5th – £2000. All other awards unchanged. Player of season – RJ Hadlee (Notts).

1988 Matches reduced to 22 per team, from 24. Six 4-day matches arranged, for first time ever. *Prize money*: 1st place – £35,000; 2nd – £17,500; 3rd – £10,000; 4th – £5000; 5th – £2500. Other awards unchanged. Player of season – FD Stephenson (Notts).

1989 *Prize money*: 1st place – £37,000; 2nd – £18,500; 3rd – £10,500; 4th – £5250; 5th – £2625; £220 for winners of each month. Other awards unchanged. Player of season – PA Neale (Worcs), winning £500.

1990 Conditions unchanged. Player of season – DL Haynes (Middx)

The new Brittanic Assurance Championship trophy
(KBMD)

3

THE CHAMPIONSHIP SEASONS

Mordecai Sherwin, the heavyweight Nottinghamshire wicket-keeper, was outstanding in the early years of the championship (Mary Evans Picture Library)

1890

FINAL TABLE

	P	W	L	D	Pts
1 Surrey	14	9	3	2	6
2 Lancashire	14	7	3	4	4
3 Kent	14	6	3	5	3
Yorkshire	14	6	3	5	3
5 Nottinghamshire ..	14	5	5	4	0
6 Gloucestershire .	14	5	6	3	−1
7 Middlesex	12	3	8	1	−5
8 Sussex	12	1	11	0	−10

Points total represents losses deducted from victories, as decided at meeting of County Secretaries, December 1889.

BEST INDIVIDUAL SCORES

267 A Shrewsbury, Notts v Sussex, Trent Bridge
196 W Gunn, Notts v Sussex, Trent Bridge
171 F Butler, Notts v Sussex, Hove
156 W Quaife, Sussex v Gloucs, Hove

BEST INNINGS ANALYSES

9–41 AW Mold, Lancs v Yorks, Huddersfield
8–27 JW Sharpe, Surrey v Gloucs, Oval
8–32 W Attewell, Notts v Sussex, Hove
8–38 AW Mold, Lancs v Yorks, Old Trafford

BEST MATCH ANALYSES

14–87 JW Sharpe, Surrey v Gloucs, Oval
14–97 WA Woof, Gloucs v Notts, Clifton
13–54 GA Lohmann, Surrey v Lancs, Old Trafford
13–76 AW Mold, Lancs v Yorks, Huddersfield

LEADING BATSMEN

	Inns	NO	Runs	HS	Avge
WH Patterson (Kent)	8	2	302	123*	50.33
A Shrewsbury (Notts)	24	2	1082	267	49.18
R Abel (Surrey)	19	1	704	151*	39.11
WG Grace (Gloucs)	25	2	832	109*	36.17
J Cranston (Gloucs)	24	1	793	152	34.47
W Gunn (Notts)	23	2	693	196	33.00
F Ward (Lancs)	10	2	237	145	29.62
GA Lohmann (Surrey)	19	3	464	57	29.00
WW Read (Surrey)	20	1	539	80	28.36
JR Painter (Gloucs)	24	1	652	119	28.34

LEADING BOWLERS

	Runs	Wkts	Avge
GP Harrison (Yorkshire)	214	21	10.19
EA Nepean (Middlesex)	268	26	10.30
W Attewell (Notts)	870	73	11.91
J. Briggs (Lancs)	740	62	11.93
JW Sharpe (Surrey)	1232	102	12.07
GA Lohmann (Surrey)	1431	113	12.66
R Peel (Yorkshire)	1165	91	12.80
WA Woof (Gloucs)	720	55	13.09
A Watson (Lancs)	982	71	13.83
F Martin (Kent)	1272	88	14.45

LEADING ALL-ROUNDERS

No one approached the 1000 runs–100 wickets 'double'. Best all-round figures:

	Runs	Avge	Wkts	Avge
GA Lohmann (Surrey)	464	(29.00)	113	(12.66)
WG Grace (Gloucs)	832	(36.17)	45	(19.06)

LEADING WICKET-KEEPERS

	Dismissals		Total
M Sherwin (Notts)	33ct	4st	37
D Hunter (Yorks)	18ct	15st	33

1891

FINAL TABLE

		P	W	L	D	Pts
1	Surrey	16	12	2	2	10
2	Lancashire	15	8	4	3	4
3	Middlesex	16	8	5	3	3
4	Nottinghamshire.	14	5	4	5	1
5	Kent.	15	4	5	6	−1
	Somerset	12	5	6	1	−1
7	Sussex	14	4	7	3	−3
8	Yorkshire.	16	5	10	1	−5
9	Gloucestershire .	16	2	10	4	−8

Lancs v Kent, Liverpool: no play.

LEADING BATSMEN

	Inns	NO	Runs	HS	Avge
R Abel (Surrey)	22	1	916	197	43.61
W Gunn (Notts)	20	2	780	161	43.33
A Shrewsbury (Notts)	19	0	794	178	41.78
TC O'Brien (Middx)	23	2	735	113	35.95
G Bean (Sussex)	26	3	773	145*	33.60
LCH Palairet (Som't)	19	1	560	100	31.11
AE Stoddart (Middx)	22	1	645	215*	30.71
JM Read (Surrey)	20	1	577	135	30.36
W Barnes (Notts)	14	2	363	104	30.25
A Ward (Lancs)	24	1	678	185	29.47

BEST INDIVIDUAL SCORES

215* AE Stoddart, Middx v Lancs, Old
     Trafford
197 R Abel, Surrey v Sussex, Hove
185 A Ward, Lancs v Kent, Gravesend
178 A Shrewsbury, Notts v Kent, Trent
     Bridge

LEADING BOWLERS

	Runs	Wkts	Avge
JT Hearne (Middx)	1219	118	10.33
GA Lohmann (Surrey)	1407	132	10.65
AW Mold (Lancs)	1386	112	12.37
JT Rawlin (Middx)	827	65	12.72
WH Lockwood (Surrey)	540	42	12.85
J Briggs (Lancs)	1154	89	12.96
F Martin (Kent)	1284	98	13.10
JW Sharpe (Surrey)	1156	88	13.13
E Wainwright (Yorks)	948	67	14.14
W Attewell (Notts)	1074	73	14.71

BEST INNINGS ANALYSES

9–32 JT Hearne, Middx v Notts, Trent Bridge
9–47 JW Sharpe, Surrey v Middx, Oval
8–22 JT Hearne, Middx v Lancs, Lord's
8–31 G Bean, Sussex v Yorks, Dewsbury

LEADING ALL-ROUNDERS

	Runs	(Avge)	Wkts	(Avge)
GA Lohmann (Surrey)	579	(26.31)	132	(10.65)
R Peel (Yorks)	588	(24.50)	66	(17.16)

BEST MATCH ANALYSES

15–131 AW Mold, Lancs v Somerset, Taunton
14–65   JT Hearne, Middx v Yorks, Lord's
14–95   AW Mold, Lancs v Gloucs, Bristol
14–97   JW Sharpe, Surrey v Middx, Oval

LEADING WICKET-KEEPERS

	Dismissals		Total
D Hunter (Yorks)	25ct	10st	35
AT Kemble (Lancs)	19ct	12st	31

1892

FINAL TABLE

		P	W	L	D	Pts
1	Surrey	16	13	2	1	11
2	Nottinghamshire .	16	10	2	4	8
3	Somerset	16	8	5	3	3
4	Lancashire	16	7	5	4	2
5	Middlesex	16	7	6	3	1
6	Yorkshire.......	16	5	5	6	0
7	Kent..........	16	2	9	5	−7
	Gloucestershire .	16	1	8	7	−7
9	Sussex	16	1	12	3	−11

LEADING BATSMEN

	Inns	NO	Runs	HS	Avge
A Shrewsbury (Notts)	24	2	920	212	41.81
WW Read (Surrey)	27	5	896	196*	40.72
HT Hewett (Somerset)	27	1	1047	201	40.26
WH Patterson (Kent)	14	1	511	114	39.30
SW Scott (Middx)	27	5	861	224	39.13
WG Grace (Gloucs)	25	3	802	99	36.77
LCH Palairet (Som't)	21	1	659	146	32.95
A Hearne (Kent)	21	2	626	116*	32.94
W Gunn (Notts)	24	2	714	98*	32.45
AE Stoddart (Middx)	29	1	848	130	30.28

BEST INDIVIDUAL SCORES

224 SW Scott, Middx v Gloucs, Lord's
212 A Shrewsbury, Notts v Middx, Lord's
201 HT Hewett, Somerset v Yorks,
    Taunton
196 WW Read, Surrey v Sussex, Oval

LEADING BOWLERS

	Runs	Wkts	Avge
W Attewell (Notts)	1241	97	12.79
R Abel (Surrey)	347	27	12.85
WH Lockwood (Surrey)	1510	114	13.24
J Briggs (Lancs)	1158	85	13.62
AW Mold (Lancs)	1425	104	13.70
GA Lohmann (Surrey)	1415	102	13.87
A Watson (Lancs)	741	52	14.25
W Flowers (Notts)	802	53	15.13
GB Nichols (Somerset)	789	51	15.47
WC Hedley (Somerset)	570	36	15.83

BEST INNINGS ANALYSES

9–29 AW Mold, Lancs v Kent, Tunbridge
    Wells
9–33 EJ Tyler, Somerset v Notts, Taunton
8–42 GA Lohmann, Surrey v Sussex, Hove
8–50 AW Mold, Lancs v Middx,
    Old Trafford

LEADING ALL-ROUNDERS

	Runs (Avge)		Wkts (Avge)	
E Wainwright (Yorks)	641	(27.86)	77	(16.22)

BEST MATCH ANALYSES

15–96 EJ Tyler, Somerset v Notts, Taunton
14–107 GA Lohmann, Surrey v Yorks, Leeds
14–159 AW Mold, Lancs v Sussex, Hove
13–85 W Attewell, Notts v Somerset, Trent
    Bridge

LEADING WICKET-KEEPERS

	Dismissals		Total
M Sherwin (Notts)	37ct	2st	39
AT Kemble (Lancs)	19ct	11st	30

THE FIRST CHAMPIONS

The 1890 transition from 'unofficial' to 'official' championship has to be accepted as little more than an 'on paper' metamorphosis. In fact, until possibly the last game or two, there is little evidence that either clubs or players noticed there was anything different.

It is therefore highly appropriate that this absence of any sense of change extended to the cricket itself and that Surrey, undisputed, albeit unofficial, champions in 1887 and 1888 and joint-winners in 1889, won the title in 1890, the first time that the participants had admitted such a thing existed. They went on to retain the title, with a fair degree of comfort, in the two following seasons, and since they were first again in 1894, 1895 and 1899, and runners-up in 1897, one would find few takers for any theory that they were not 'the' team of the first decade of the County Championship.

A statistical examination bears out their champion status though not, perhaps, so resoundingly as expected. Due to differing methods of calculating points and positions, it is hard to compile an acceptable statistical analysis of the decade, but taking the method operative during the first six seasons of the Championship – deducting losses from wins and ignoring draws – Surrey finished the 1890s with a total of 88 points, followed by Yorkshire, champions three times and runners-up once, with 68 and Lancashire, winners only once but runners-up on five occasions, on 53. Interestingly the first decade also saw three of the most celebrated 'old' counties, Kent, Gloucestershire and Sussex, building up hefty minus totals, despite the intervention of several 'new' counties after 1894.

The secret of Surrey's success is relatively easy to discover. Bobby Abel led the batting throughout and despite suspect eye-sight, eccentric technique against pace and lack of size, 'The Guv'nor', with 12 420 runs (average 43.88) was leading run-scorer for the county. Early on he gained most support from Walter and Maurice Read; they were adequately replaced by William Brockwell and Tom Hayward, top-class batsmen who could also bowl.

Not that such versatility was usually needed. In the early 1890s John Sharpe and the great George Lohmann usually took most of the necessary wickets, and when the effects of their hard work and ill health respectively took their toll, Bill Lockwood and then Tom Richardson were ready to make their mark. For the rest of the decade these two marvellous pace bowlers dominated the Surrey attack, accepting whatever support occasionally became necessary. Oddly enough, despite the mainly contemporaneous nature of their careers they rarely operated well as a 'pair'. Had they been at their best opposite each other, one would find it hard to contemplate Surrey ever losing during the period.

As it was, Richardson took an astounding 1116 wickets for an average of 15.83, with a quite miraculous return of 666 wickets at 14.46 over three seasons from 1895–97. When the strain began to tell, Lockwood re-emerged from the comparative shadows to establish himself as top bowler for the remainder of the decade. Lockwood, 639 wickets; Brockwell, 7773 runs and 245 wickets; Hayward, 7229 runs and 299 wickets; Lohmann, 480 wickets at 12.94. No wonder Surrey were the first great side of the official County Championship, and no wonder little was heard of the captains, John Shuter and KJ Key. It was clearly too easy a job!

Opening batsman Bobbie Abel twice topped the averages in the 1890s as his high scoring helped Surrey to six Championship wins (Hulton Picture Company)

1893

FINAL TABLE

	P	W	L	D	Pts
1 Yorkshire........	16	12	3	1	9
2 Lancashire	16	9	5	2	4
3 Middlesex	16	9	6	1	3
4 Kent...........	16	6	4	6	2
5 Surrey	16	7	8	1	−1
6 Nottinghamshire.	16	5	7	4	−2
7 Sussex	16	4	7	5	−3
8 Somerset	16	4	8	4	−4
9 Gloucestershire .	16	3	11	2	−8

LEADING BATSMEN

	Inns	NO	Runs	HS	Avge
AE Stoddart (Middx)	26	1	1178	195*	47.12
W Gunn (Notts)	27	1	1223	156	47.03
W Rashleigh (Kent)	12	1	443	101*	40.27
A Ward (Lancs)	29	2	1035	140*	38.33
A Shrewsbury (Notts)	28	2	976	164	37.53
WL Murdoch (Sussex)	31	4	965	96	35.74
JA Dixon (Notts)	21	0	748	139	35.61
G Bean (Notts)	26	0	924	186	35.53
FH Sugg (Lancs)	27	2	858	169*	34.32
HT Hewett (Somerset)	22	1	669	120	31.85

BEST INDIVIDUAL SCORES

195 AE Stoddart, Middx v Notts, Lord's
186 G Bean, Sussex v Lancs, Old Trafford
169 FH Sugg, Lancs v Sussex, Old Trafford
164 A Shrewsbury, Notts v Sussex, Hove

LEADING BOWLERS

	Runs	Wkts	Avge
W Hearne (Kent)	545	46	11.84
E Wainwright (Yorks)	1130	90	12.55
J Briggs (Lancs)	1485	108	13.75
W Brockwell (Surrey)	719	51	14.09
R Peel (Yorkshire)	922	65	14.18
T Richardson (Surrey)	1420	99	14.34
AW Mold (Lancs)	1754	117	14.99
JT Hearne (Middx)	2198	137	16.04
GH Hirst (Yorks)	963	59	16.32
WA Humphreys (Sussex)	2005	122	16.43

BEST INNINGS ANALYSES

9–47 T Richardson, Surrey v Yorks, Sheffield
9–54 RJ Mee, Notts v Sussex, Trent Bridge
8–19 J Briggs, Lancs v Yorks, Leeds
8–29 JT Rawlin, Middx v Gloucs, Clifton

LEADING ALL-ROUNDERS

	Runs	(Avge)	Wkts	(Avge)
JT Rawlin (Middx)	600	(25.00)	82	(19.82)

BEST MATCH ANALYSES

15–114 W Hearne, Kent v Lancs, Old Trafford
15–154 JT Hearne, Middx v Notts, Trent Bridge
15–193 WA Humphreys, Sussex v Somerset, Taunton
14–145 T Richardson, Surrey v Notts, Trent Bridge

LEADING WICKET-KEEPERS

	Dismissals		Total
HR Butt (Sussex)	22ct	22st	44
D Hunter (Yorks)	29ct	9st	38

1894

FINAL TABLE

		P	W	L	D(T)	Pts
1	Surrey	16	13	2	0(1)	11
2	Yorkshire	15	12	2	1	10
3	Middlesex	16	8	5	3	3
4	Kent	15	6	6	3	0
	Lancashire	16	7	7	1(1)	0
6	Somerset	16	6	7	3	—1
7	Nottinghamshire .	16	4	8	4	—4
8	Sussex	16	3	11	2	—8
9	Gloucestershire .	16	2	13	1	—11

Yorks v Kent, Bradford: no play (rain).

LEADING BATSMEN

	Inns	NO	Runs	HS	Avge
W Gunn (Notts)	24	1	851	121*	37.00
TC O'Brien (Middx)	14	3	384	110*	34.90
W Brockwell (Surrey)	24	2	754	107	34.27
W Rashleigh (Kent)	15	0	514	95	34.26
GR Baker (Lancs)	25	4	619	96	29.47
FH Sugg (Lancs)	28	3	717	157*	28.68
FS Jackson (Yorks)	25	2	659	145	28.65
A Street (Surrey)	11	2	258	68	28.66
WW Read (Surrey)	23	2	597	161	28.42
TW Hayward (Surrey)	25	3	618	142	28.09

BEST INDIVIDUAL SCORES

161 WW Read, Surrey v Yorks, Oval
157* FH Sugg, Lancs v Somerset, Taunton
145 FS Jackson, Yorks v Notts, Leeds
142 TW Hayward, Surrey v Kent, Oval

LEADING BOWLERS

	Runs	Wkts	Avge
E Wainwright (Yorks)	987	97	10.17
R Peel (Yorks)	882	79	11.16
ATA Newnham (Gloucs)	226	20	11.30
T Richardson (Surrey)	1358	120	11.31
AW Mold (Lancs)	1636	144	11.36
Alfred Shaw (Sussex)	516	41	12.58
GH Hirst (Yorks)	731	56	13.05
F Parris (Sussex)	760	57	13.33
FS Jackson (Yorks)	336	25	13.44
JT Hearne (Middx)	1670	119	14.03
FE Smith (Surrey)	814	58	14.03

BEST INNINGS ANALYSES

8-28 F Parris, Sussex v Gloucs, Bristol
8-34 WH Lockwood, Surrey v Kent, Catford
8-45 F Martin, Kent v Lancs, Tonbridge
8-50 JT Rawlin, Middx v Yorks, Sheffield

LEADING ALL-ROUNDERS

	Runs	(Avge)	Wkts	(Avge)
WH Lockwood (Surrey)	591	(24.62)	92	(14.11)

BEST MATCH ANALYSES

15-87 AW Mold, Lancs v Somerset, Old Trafford
15-98 F Parris, Sussex v Gloucs, Bristol
13-38 E Wainwright, Yorks v Sussex, Dewsbury
13-60 AW Mold, Lancs v Somerset, Old Trafford

LEADING WICKET-KEEPERS

	Dismissals		Total
D Hunter (Yorks)	32ct	16st	48
H Wood (Surrey)	39ct	3st	42

1895

FINAL TABLE

		P	W	L	D	Pts
1	Surrey	26	17	4	5	13
2	Lancashire	21	14	4	3	10
3	Yorkshire	26	14	7	5	7
4	Gloucestershire .	18	8	6	4	2
5	Derbyshire	16	5	4	7	1
6	Middlesex	18	6	6	6	0
	Warwickshire ...	18	6	6	6	0
8	Essex	16	5	7	4	−2
	Somerset	17	6	8	3	−2
10	Hampshire	16	6	9	1	−3
11	Sussex	18	5	9	4	−4
12	Leicestershire ...	16	3	10	3	−7
	Nottinghamshire	18	3	10	5	−7
14	Kent	18	3	11	4	−8

Lancs v Somerset, Old Trafford: abandoned without a ball bowled.

BEST INDIVIDUAL SCORES

424 AC MacLaren, Lancs v Somerset,
    Taunton
288 WG Grace, Gloucs v Somerset, Bristol
257 WG Grace, Gloucs v Kent, Gravesend
219 W Gunn, Notts v Sussex, Trent Bridge

BEST INNINGS ANALYSES

10–32 H Pickett, Essex v Leics, Leyton
10–49 EJ Tyler, Somerset v Surrey, Taunton
9–22 R Peel, Yorks v Somerset, Leeds
9–39 GA Davidson, Derbys v Warwicks,
      Derby

BEST MATCH ANALYSES

17–119 W Mead, Essex v Hants, Southampton
16–111 AW Mold, Lancs v Kent, Old Trafford
16–122 CL Townsend, Gloucs v Notts, Trent
       Bridge
15–50 R Peel, Yorks v Somerset, Leeds

LEADING BATSMEN

	Inns	NO	Runs	HS	Avge
AC MacLaren (Lancs)	20	0	1162	424	58.10
R Abel (Surrey)	39	4	1787	217	51.05
WG Grace (Gloucs)	29	1	1424	288	50.85
A Shrewsbury (Notts)	14	1	630	143	48.46
LCH Palairet (Som)	25	1	1159	165	48.29
A Ward (Lancs)	35	2	1446	116	43.81
KS Ranjitsinhji (Sx)	34	1	1364	110	41.33
TC O'Brien (Middx)	25	3	883	202	40.13
A Street (Surrey)	16	3	504	161*	38.76
Walter Quaife (Sussex)	33	2	1156	105	37.29

LEADING BOWLERS

	Runs	Wkts	Avge
CL Townsend (Gloucs)	1561	124	12.58
AW Mold (Lancs)	2497	182	13.71
T Richardson (Surrey)	3294	237	13.89
WC Hedley (Somerset)	669	48	13.93
GA Lohmann (Surrey)	838	60	13.96
R Peel (Yorks)	2013	136	14.80
FS Jackson (Yorks)	777	52	14.94
TW Hayward (Surrey)	573	38	15.07
J Briggs (Lancs)	1797	119	15.10
JR Painter (Gloucs)	412	27	15.25

LEADING ALL-ROUNDER

	Runs (Avge)		Wkts (Avge)	
GA Davidson (Derbys)	641	(26.70)	89	(15.69)

LEADING WICKET-KEEPERS

	Dismissals		Total
C Smith (Lancs)	51ct	25st	76
JH Board (Glos)	52ct	23st	75

1896

FINAL TABLE

	P	W	L	D	Pts	F/G	%
1 Yorkshire	26	16	3	7	13	19	68.4
2 Lancashire	22	11	4	7	7	15	46.6
3 Middlesex	16	8	3	5	5	11	45.4
4 Surrey	26	17	7	2	10	24	41.6
5 Essex	12	5	4	3	1	9	11.1
6 Nottinghamshire	16	5	5	6	0	10	0
7 Derbyshire	16	4	6	6	−2	10	−20.0
8 Hampshire	16	5	8	3	−3	13	−23.1
9 Kent	18	5	9	4	−4	14	−28.6
10 Gloucestershire .	18	5	10	3	−5	15	−33.3
11 Somerset	16	3	7	6	−4	10	−40.0
12 Warwickshire ...	18	3	8	7	−5	11	−45.5
13 Leicestershire...	14	2	8	4	−6	10	−60.0
14 Sussex........	18	2	9	7	−7	11	−63.6

F/G – Finished Games (ie excluding draws)
Positions decided by points as a percentage of finished games.

BEST INDIVIDUAL SCORES

301 WG Grace, Gloucs v Sussex, Bristol
292 LCH Palairet, Somerset v Hants,
　　 Southampton
274 GA Davidson, Derbys v Lancs, Old
　　 Trafford
268 EG Wynyard, Hants v Yorks,
　　 Southampton

BEST INNINGS ANALYSES

9–75 W Mead, Essex v Leics, Leyton
8–33 AW Mold, Lancs v Surrey, Old Trafford
8–34 E Wainwright, Yorks v Essex, Bradford
8–35 S Haigh, Yorks v Hants, Harrogate

BEST MATCH ANALYSES

15–113 T Richardson, Surrey v Leics, Oval
14–77　 E Wainwright, Yorks v Essex,
　　　　 Bradford
14–122 EJ Tyler, Somerset v Gloucs, Bristol
14–132 W Mead, Essex v Leics, Leyton

LEADING BATSMEN

	Inns	NO	Runs	HS	Avge
KS Ranjitsinhji (Sx)	33	4	1698	165	58.55
W Storer (Derbys)	22	3	1091	142*	57.42
AC MacLaren (Lancs)	15	2	713	226*	54.84
WG Grace (Gloucs)	32	3	1565	301	53.96
EG Wynyard (Hants)	14	0	705	268	50.35
LCH Palairet (Som)	26	2	1204	292	50.16
WN Roe (Somerset)	10	2	388	105	48.50
W Gunn (Notts)	19	2	785	207*	46.17
JT Brown (Yorks)	41	7	1556	103	45.76
GA Davidson (Derbys)	24	2	953	274	43.31

LEADING BOWLERS

	Runs	Wkts	Avge
W Attewell (Notts)	1259	86	14.63
TW Hayward (Surrey)	1202	81	14.83
S Haigh (Yorks)	1085	71	15.28
GA Lohmann (Surrey)	1122	73	15.36
T Richardson (Surrey)	2953	191	15.46
FG Bull (Essex)	1094	70	15.62
A Hearne (Kent)	1058	63	16.79
E Smith (Yorks)	376	22	17.09
AW Mold (Lancs)	2236	130	17.20
AW Hallam (Lancs)	1010	58	17.41

LEADING ALL-ROUNDERS

	Runs	(Avge)	Wkts	(Avge)
R Peel (Yorks)	1135	(35.46)	97	(19.07)
T Hayward (Surrey)	1182	(36.93)	81	(14.85)
E Wainwright (Yorks)	817	(25.53)	90	(18.72)
GH Hirst (Yorks)	1018	(32.83)	80	(23.91)

LEADING WICKET-KEEPERS

	Dismissals		Total
H Wood (Surrey)	51ct	10st	61
D Hunter (Yorks)	44ct	13st	57

1897

FINAL TABLE

	P	W	L	D	Pts	F/G	%
1 Lancashire	26	16	3	7	13	19	68.4
2 Surrey	26	17	4	5	13	21	61.9
3 Essex	16	7	2	7	5	9	55.5
4 Yorkshire	26	13	5	8	8	18	44.4
5 Gloucestershire .	18	7	5	6	2	12	16.6
6 Sussex.........	20	5	6	9	−1	11	−9.0
7 Warwickshire...	18	3	4	11	−1	7	−14.2
Middlesex......	16	3	4	9	−1	7	−14.2
9 Hampshire	18	4	7	7	−3	11	−27.2
10 Nottinghamshire	16	2	5	9	−3	7	−42.8
11 Somerset	16	3	9	4	−6	12	−50.0
12 Kent	18	2	10	6	−8	12	−66.6
13 Leicestershire...	14	1	10	3	−9	11	−81.8
14 Derbyshire	16	0	9	7	−9	9	−100

BEST INDIVIDUAL SCORES

311 JT Brown, Yorks v Sussex, Sheffield
268* JA Dixon, Notts v Sussex, Trent Bridge
250 R Abel, Surrey v Warwicks, Oval
244 AC MacLaren, Lancs v Kent, Canterbury

BEST INNINGS ANALYSES

9–23 FG Bull, Essex v Surrey, Oval
8–36 A Hearne, Kent v Middlesex, Lord's
8–39 J Briggs, Lancs v Hants, Old Trafford
8–40 FG Roberts, Gloucs v Kent, Maidstone

BEST MATCH ANALYSES

15–123 FG Roberts, Gloucs v Kent, Maidstone
15–154 T Richardson, Surrey v Yorks, Leeds
14–102 T Richardson, Surrey v Kent,
Beckenham
14–176 FG Bull, Essex v Lancs, Leyton

LEADING BATSMEN

	Inns	NO	Runs	HS	Avge
AC MacLaren (Lancs)	19	2	879	244	51.70
R Abel (Surrey)	39	3	1833	250	50.91
W Gunn (Notts)	23	3	987	230	49.35
WG Quaife (Warwicks)	27	6	983	178*	46.80
JA Dixon (Notts)	24	1	1030	268*	44.78
JT Brown (Yorks)	36	3	1431	311	43.36
KS Ranjitsinhji (Sx)	36	5	1318	170	42.51
AJ Turner (Essex)	17	3	590	111	42.14
HW Bainbridge (Warwicks)	26	2	998	162	41.58
FGJ Ford (Middx)	14	1	524	150	40.30

LEADING BOWLERS

	Runs	Wkts	Avge
T Richardson (Surrey)	3387	238	14.23
C Heseltine (Hants)	600	38	15.78
J Briggs (Lancs)	2294	140	16.38
WR Cuttell (Lancs)	1813	102	17.77
AW Mold (Lancs)	1571	88	17.85
AW Hallam (Lancs)	1651	90	18.34
JT Hearne (Middx)	1890	102	18.52
AJL Hill (Hants)	594	31	19.16
GL Jessop (Gloucs)	1113	58	19.18
TW Hayward (Surrey)	1757	91	19.30

LEADING ALL-ROUNDERS

	Runs (Avge)		Wkts (Avge)	
TW Hayward (Surrey)	1045	(34.83)	91	(19.30)
FS Jackson (Yorks)	1089	(33.00)	62	(20.48)
CL Townsend (Gloucs)	643	(25.72)	88	(24.92)

LEADING WICKET-KEEPERS

	Dismissals		Total
C Smith (Lancs)	45ct	20st	65
H Wood (Surrey)	50ct	3st	53

1898

	P	W	L	D	Pts	F/G	%
FINAL TABLE							
1 Yorkshire	26	16	3	7	13	19	68.4
2 Middlesex......	18	10	3	5	7	13	53.8
3 Gloucestershire .	20	9	3	8	6	12	50.0
4 Surrey.........	24	11	4	9	7	15	46.6
5 Essex	20	10	6	4	4	16	25.0
6 Lancashire	26	9	6	11	3	15	20.0
7 Kent	20	5	6	9	−1	11	−9.0
8 Nottinghamshire	16	1	2	13	−1	3	−33.3
9 Derbyshire	15	2	6	7	−4	8	−50.0
Warwickshire...	17	2	6	9	−4	8	−50.0
Sussex.........	20	3	9	8	−6	12	−50.0
12 Hampshire	18	2	8	8	−6	10	−60.0
13 Somerset	16	1	10	5	−9	11	−81.8
Leicestershire...	16	1	10	5	−9	11	−81.8

BEST INDIVIDUAL SCORES

315* TW Hayward, Surrey v Lancs, Oval
300 JT Brown, Yorks v Derbys, Chesterfield
243 J Tunnicliffe, Yorks v Derbys,
Chesterfield
236* W Gunn, Notts v Surrey, Oval

BEST INNINGS ANALYSES

9-48 CL Townsend, Gloucs v Middx, Lord's
9-68 JT Hearne, Middx v Lancs, Old
Trafford
9-128 CL Townsend, Gloucs v Warwicks,
Cheltenham
8-21 S Haigh, Yorks v Hants, Southampton

BEST MATCH ANALYSES

16-114 JT Hearne, Middx v Lancs, Old
Trafford
15-83 T Richardson, Surrey v Warwicks,
Oval
15-116 GA Davidson, Derbys v Essex, Leyton
15-132 CL Townsend, Gloucs v Middx, Lord's

LEADING BATSMEN

	Inns	NO	Runs	HS	Avge
WG Quaife (Warwicks)	28	8	1219	157*	60.95
CB Fry (Sussex)	31	4	1604	179*	59.40
R Abel (Surrey)	34	2	1832	219	57.25
AE Stoddart (Middx)	22	3	1005	157	52.89
A Shrewsbury (Notts)	27	6	1076	154*	51.23
W Storer (Derby)	25	3	1113	109	50.59
W Gunn (Notts)	28	5	1107	236*	48.13
WG Grace (Gloucs)	28	4	1141	168	47.54
TW Hayward (Surrey)	31	2	1373	315*	47.34
J Tunnicliffe (Yorks)	38	5	1538	243	46.60

LEADING BOWLERS

	Runs	Wkts	Avge
W Rhodes (Yorks)	1745	126	13.84
E Wainwright (Yorks)	802	56	14.32
JT Hearne (Middx)	1846	125	14.76
FS Jackson (Yorks)	1217	80	15.21
GA Davidson (Derbys)	1020	65	15.69
CJ Kortright (Essex)	1480	88	16.81
WH Lockwood (Surrey)	1860	109	17.06
H Baldwin (Hants)	911	53	17.18
AE Trott (Middx)	1825	102	17.89
W Mead (Essex)	1452	81	17.92

LEADING ALL-ROUNDERS

	Runs (Avge)		Wkts (Avge)	
CL Townsend (Gloucs)	1072	(38.28)	130	(19.96)
WR Cuttell (Lancs)	908	(26.70)	107	(20.39)

LEADING WICKET-KEEPERS

	Dismissals		Total
HR Butt (Sussex)	44ct	11st	55
FH Huish (Kent)	48ct	3st	51

1899

FINAL TABLE

	P	W	L	D	Pts	F/G	%
1 Surrey	26	10	2	14	8	12	66.6
2 Middlesex	18	11	3	4	8	14	57.1
3 Yorkshire	28	14	4	10	10	18	55.5
4 Lancashire	25	12	6	7	6	18	33.3
5 Sussex	22	7	5	10	2	12	16.6
6 Essex	20	6	6	8	0	12	0.0
7 Warwickshire . . .	20	4	5	11	−1	9	−11.1
8 Kent	19	6	8	5	−2	14	−14.2
9 Gloucestershire .	20	5	8	7	−3	13	−23.0
10 Nottinghamshire	16	2	4	10	−2	6	−33.3
Hampshire	20	4	8	8	−4	12	−33.3
12 Worcestershire .	12	2	5	5	−3	7	−42.8
13 Somerset	16	2	8	6	−6	10	−60.0
Leicestershire . . .	18	2	8	8	−6	10	−60.0
15 Derbyshire	18	2	9	7	−7	11	−63.6

Lancs v Kent, Old Trafford, 22–24 May: abandoned without a ball bowled.

LEADING BATSMEN

	Inns	NO	Runs	HS	Avge
RM Poore (Hants)	16	4	1399	304	116.58
KS Ranjitsinhji (Sx)	35	5	2285	197	76.16
R Abel (Surrey)	36	3	2134	357*	64.66
TW Hayward (Surrey)	29	1	1798	273	64.21
FL Fane (Essex)	12	0	733	207	61.08
A Shrewsbury (Notts)	22	2	1130	175	56.50
CL Townsend (Gloucs)	34	4	1694	224*	56.46
WG Quaife (Warks)	35	8	1480	207*	54.81
AO Jones (Notts)	23	1	1185	250	53.86
W Gunn (Notts)	24	1	1147	150	49.86

BEST INDIVIDUAL SCORES

357* R Abel, Surrey v Somerset, Oval
304 RM Poore, Hants v Somerset, Taunton
273 TW Hayward, Surrey v Yorks, Oval
250 AO Jones, Notts v Gloucs, Bristol

LEADING BOWLERS

	Runs	Wkts	Avge
W Rhodes (Yorks)	2021	129	15.66
AE Trott (Middx)	2291	146	15.69
W Mead (Essex)	1918	112	17.12
CM Wells (Middx)	377	22	17.13
JT Brown, jnr (Yorks)	951	54	17.61
WM Bradley (Kent)	2103	112	18.77
JR Mason (Kent)	1491	79	18.87
A Paish (Gloucs)	2367	125	18.93
WH Lockwood (Surrey)	1872	98	19.10
AW Mold (Lancs)	2089	108	19.34

BEST INNINGS ANALYSES

10–48 CHG Bland, Sussex v Kent, Tonbridge
9–28 W Rhodes, Yorks v Essex, Leyton
9–104 EF Field, Warwicks v Leics, Leicester
9–105 WH Lockwood, Surrey v Gloucs, Cheltenham

BEST MATCH ANALYSES

15–154 HI Young, Essex v Warwicks, Edgbaston
15–184 WH Lockwood, Surrey v Gloucs, Cheltenham
14–127 W Mead, Essex v Yorks, Leyton
14–196 A Paish, Gloucs v Surrey, Cheltenham

LEADING ALL-ROUNDERS

	Runs (Avge)	Wkts (Avge)	
WH Lockwood (Surrey)	1110 (42.69)	98	(19.10)
W Brockwell (Surrey)	1220 (39.35)	81	(25.16)
JR Mason (Kent)	1089 (36.30)	79	(18.87)

LEADING WICKET-KEEPERS

	Dismissals		Total
FH Huish (Kent)	70ct	4st	74
HR Butt (Sussex)	47ct	8st	55

(Above): *CB Fry, topline athlete and footballer as well as classical batsman, at his peak at the turn of the century with Sussex. His later life was sadly imbued with feelings of frustration and failure* (Hulton Picture Company)

(Insert): *Lord Hawke, who played a big part in Yorkshire's first 'official' title win in 1893. A legendary skipper, with some enlightened views on the welfare of county professionals* (Hulton Picture Company)

1900

FINAL TABLE

	P	W	L	D	Pts	F/G	%
1 Yorkshire	28	16	0	12	16	16	100.0
2 Lancashire	28	15	2	11	13	17	76.4
3 Kent	22	8	4	10	4	12	33.3
Sussex	24	4	2	18	2	6	33.3
5 Nottinghamshire	18	7	4	7	3	11	27.2
6 Warwickshire . . .	18	3	2	13	1	5	20.0
7 Middlesex	22	9	7	6	2	16	12.5
Gloucestershire .	22	9	7	6	2	16	12.5
Surrey	28	9	7	12	2	16	12.5
10 Essex	22	4	6	12	−2	10	−20.0
11 Somerset	16	4	11	1	−7	15	−46.6
12 Worcestershire .	22	3	10	9	−7	13	−53.8
13 Derbyshire	18	2	7	9	−5	9	−55.5
14 Leicestershire . . .	22	3	11	8	−8	14	−57.1
15 Hampshire	22	0	16	6	−16	16	−100.0

BEST INDIVIDUAL SCORES

275 KS Ranjitsinhji, Sussex v Leics, Leicester
246 JHG Devey, Warwicks v Derbys, Edgbaston
229 CB Fry, Sussex v Surrey, Hove
223* WG Quaife, Warwicks v Essex, Leyton

BEST INNINGS ANALYSES

10–42 AE Trott, Middx v Somerset, Taunton
10–55 J Briggs, Lancs v Worcs, Old Trafford
9–40 W Mead, Essex v Hants, Southampton
9–94 WH Lockwood, Surrey v Essex, Oval

BEST MATCH ANALYSES

14–66   W Rhodes, Yorks v Hants, Hull
14–68   W Rhodes, Yorks v Essex, Harrogate
14–127 WH Lockwood, Surrey v Essex, Oval
14–185 T Richardson, Surrey v Essex, Leyton

LEADING BATSMEN

	Inns	NO	Runs	HS	Avge
KS Ranjitsinhji (Sx)	34	4	2563	275	85.43
CB Fry (Sussex)	30	1	1830	229	63.10
R Abel (Surrey)	34	2	1880	221	58.75
WG Quaife (Warwicks)	26	7	1102	223*	58.00
JR Mason (Kent)	33	2	1662	147	53.61
S Kinneir (Warwicks)	26	6	1005	156	50.25
TW Hayward (Surrey)	40	3	1850	193	50.00
TL Taylor (Yorks)	18	3	740	147	49.33
PF Warner (Middx)	30	0	1335	170	44.50
GL Jessop (Gloucs)	41	2	1733	179	44.43

LEADING BOWLERS

	Runs	Wkts	Avge
W Rhodes (Yorks)	2532	206	12.29
CM Wells (Middx)	468	36	13.00
AW Mold (Lancs)	1354	97	13.95
S Haigh (Yorks)	2054	145	14.16
S Webb (Lancs)	1102	72	15.30
W Mead (Essex)	1885	122	15.45
J Briggs (Lancs)	2094	120	17.45
GL Jessop (Gloucs)	1533	86	17.82
C Blythe (Kent)	2106	114	18.47
S Santall (Warwicks)	702	37	18.97

LEADING ALL-ROUNDERS

	Runs (Avge)		Wkts (Avge)	
WH Lockwood (Surrey)	1102	(30.61)	115	(19.84)
GL Jessop (Gloucs)	1733	(44.43)	86	(17.82)

LEADING WICKET-KEEPERS

	Dismissals		Total
D Hunter (Yorks)	34ct	26st	60
HR Butt (Sussex)	49ct	9st	58

1901

FINAL TABLE

	P	W	L	D	Pts	F/G	%
1 Yorkshire	27	20	1	6	19	21	90.4
2 Middlesex......	18	6	2	10	4	8	50.0
3 Lancashire	28	11	5	12	6	16	37.5
4 Sussex.........	24	8	4	12	4	12	33.3
5 Warwickshire ...	16	7	4	5	3	11	27.2
6 Surrey	27	7	6	14	1	13	7.6
7 Kent	21	7	7	7	0	14	0.0
Hampshire	18	6	6	6	0	12	0.0
9 Nottinghamshire	19	5	6	8	−1	11	−9.0
10 Essex	21	4	5	12	−1	9	−11.1
11 Worcestershire .	21	7	10	4	−3	17	−17.6
12 Leicestershire...	19	4	10	5	−6	14	−42.8
Somerset	17	4	10	3	−6	14	−42.8
14 Gloucestershire .	24	3	10	11	−7	13	−53.8
15 Derbyshire	20	0	13	7	−13	13	−100.0

Surrey v Yorks, Oval; Essex v Leics, Leyton; Notts v Kent, Trent Bridge; Worcs v Somerset, Worcester: all abandoned without a ball bowled.

LEADING BATSMEN

	Inns	NO	Runs	HS	Avge
KS Ranjitsinhji (Sx)	31	4	2067	285*	76.55
CB Fry (Sussex)	34	2	2382	244	74.43
G Brann (Sussex)	10	3	518	130	74.00
JT Tyldesley (Lancs)	47	4	2605	221	60.58
TW Hayward (Lancs)	41	6	2039	181	58.25
LCH Palairet (Som't)	30	1	1637	194	56.44
WG Quaife (Warwicks)	22	4	1007	177	55.94
S Kinneir (Warwicks)	23	1	1220	215*	55.45
RE Foster (Worcs)	37	1	1957	136	54.36
AO Jones (Notts)	35	2	1718	249	52.06

BEST INDIVIDUAL SCORES

285* KS Ranjitsinhji, Sussex v Somerset, Taunton
273 W Gunn, Notts v Derbys, Derby
249* JG Greig, Hants v Lancs, Liverpool
249 AO Jones, Notts v Sussex, Hove

LEADING BOWLERS

	Runs	Wkts	Avge
W Rhodes (Yorks)	2664	196	13.59
GH Hirst (Yorks)	2262	135	16.75
EE Steel (Lancs)	818	44	18.59
T Soar (Hants)	415	22	18.86
A Bird (Worcs)	781	40	19.52
FW Tate (Sussex)	2520	126	20.00
JR Mason (Kent)	1736	86	20.18
TW Hayward (Surrey)	510	25	20.40
AW Mold (Lancs)	1097	53	20.69
RD Burrows (Worcs)	2015	94	21.43

BEST INNINGS ANALYSES

9–77 J Sharp, Lancs v Worcs, Worcester
9–87 WM Bradley, Kent v Hants, Tonbridge
8–17 TG Wass, Notts v Derbys, Welbeck
8–29 JR Mason, Kent v Somerset, Taunton

LEADING ALL-ROUNDERS

	Runs (Avge)		Wkts (Avge)	
GH Hirst (Yorks)	1174	(33.54)	135	(16.75)
J Vine (Sussex)	963	(27.51)	95	(28.96)
JR Mason (Kent)	1272	(37.41)	86	(20.18)
JR Gunn (Notts)	1090	(36.33)	82	(21.93)
LC Braund (Somerset)	1064	(35.46)	78	(29.50)

BEST MATCH ANALYSES

15–161 J Vine, Sussex v Notts, Trent Bridge
15–187 AE Trott, Middx v Sussex, Lord's
14–109 A Bird, Worcs v Hants, Southampton
14–119 FW Tate, Sussex v Kent, Tonbridge

LEADING WICKET-KEEPERS

	Dismissals		Total
F Stedman (Surrey)	57ct	14st	71
C Smith (Lancs)	54ct	13st	67

1902

FINAL TABLE

		P	W	L	D	Pts	F/G	%
1	Yorkshire	25	13	1	11	12	14	85.7
2	Sussex.........	24	7	3	14	4	10	40.0
3	Nottinghamshire	20	6	3	11	3	9	33.3
4	Surrey.........	28	8	5	15	3	13	23.0
5	Lancashire	23	7	5	11	4	12	16.1
6	Warwickshire ...	18	6	5	7	1	11	9.0
7	Kent	22	8	8	6	0	16	0.0
	Somerset	18	7	7	4	0	14	0.0
9	Worcestershire .	22	5	6	11	−1	11	−9.0
10	Derbyshire	16	4	5	7	−1	9	−11.1
11	Leicestershire...	19	2	4	13	−2	6	−33.3
12	Middlesex......	17	3	7	7	−4	10	−40.0
13	Essex	20	2	5	13	−3	7	−42.8
14	Gloucestershire .	20	3	9	8	−6	12	−50.0
15	Hampshire	16	2	10	4	−8	12	−66.6

Leics v Yorks, Leicester; Middlesex v Lancs, Lord's: both abandoned without a ball bowled.

BEST INDIVIDUAL SCORES

234* KS Ranjitsinhji, Sussex v Surrey, Hastings
230 KS Ranjitsinhji, Sussex v Essex, Leyton
180 J Douglas, Middx v Essex, Leyton
179 R Abel, Surrey v Sussex, Hastings

BEST INNINGS ANALYSES

9-41 LC Braund, Somerset v Yorks, Sheffield
9-59 WH Lockwood, Surrey v Essex, Leyton
9-73 FW Tate, Sussex v Leics, Leicester
9-91 TG Wass, Notts v Surrey, Oval

BEST MATCH ANALYSES

15-68 FW Tate, Sussex v Middx, Lord's
15-71 LC Braund, Somerset v Yorks, Sheffield

14-99 S Hargreave, Warwicks v Lancs, Old Trafford
14-126 B Cranfield, Somerset v Lancs, Old Trafford

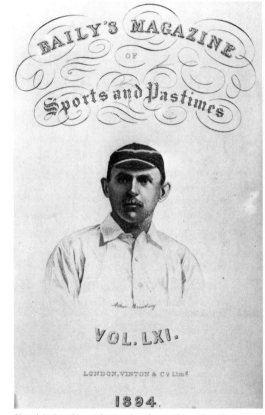

Notts' Arthur Shrewsbury enjoyed something of an 'Indian summer' in 1902, aged 46. Feeling that age and infirmity would prevent him from playing any more cricket, he committed suicide at the start of the following season (Hulton Picture Company)

LEADING BATSMEN

	Inns	NO	Runs	HS	Avge
KS Ranjitsinhji (Sx)	15	2	866	234*	66.61
A Shrewsbury (Notts)	29	7	1153	127*	52.40
RE Foster (Worcs)	11	2	450	109	50.00
R Abel (Surrey)	39	6	1570	179	47.57
EM Ashcroft (Derby)	19	1	843	162	46.83

J Douglas (Middx)	10	0	466	180	46.60
TL Taylor (Yorks)	31	3	1276	142*	45.57
JT Tyldesley (Lancs)	32	3	1291	165	44.51
WG Quaife (Warwicks)	23	3	852	153*	42.60
CB Fry (Sussex)	27	1	1072	159*	41.23

LEADING BOWLERS

	Runs	Wkts	Avge
S Haigh (Yorks)	1475	123	11.99
S Webb (Lancs)	243	20	12.15
W Rhodes (Yorks)	1748	140	12.48
FW Tate (Sussex)	2185	153	14.28
FS Jackson (Yorks)	525	36	14.58
JR Mason (Kent)	1097	73	15.02
TG Wass (Notts)	2115	138	15.32
C Blythe (Kent)	1728	111	15.56

S Hargreave (Warwicks)	1551	97	15.98
S Santall (Warwicks)	754	47	16.04

LEADING ALL-ROUNDERS

	Runs	(Avge)	Wkts	(Avge)
EG Arnold (Worcs)	989	(29.96)	95	(19.25)
CB Llewellyn (Hants)	626	(26.08)	94	(17.67)
WH Lockwood (Surrey)	675	(24.10)	87	(19.11)

LEADING WICKET-KEEPERS

	Dismissals		Total
JH Board (Gloucs)	44ct	11st	55
FH Huish (Kent)	36ct	12st	48

1903

FINAL TABLE

	P	W	L	D	Pts	F/G	%
1 Middlesex	16	8	1	7	7	9	77.7
2 Sussex	23	7	2	14	5	9	55.5
3 Yorkshire	26	13	5	8	8	18	44.4
4 Lancashire	26	10	5	11	5	15	33.3
5 Nottinghamshire	20	6	4	10	2	10	20.0
6 Worcestershire	20	8	6	6	2	14	14.2
7 Warwickshire	18	5	4	9	1	9	11.1
8 Kent	20	7	6	7	1	13	7.6
Essex	20	7	6	7	1	13	7.6
10 Somerset	17	6	6	5	0	12	0.0
11 Surrey	27	7	11	9	−4	18	−22.2
12 Derbyshire	16	4	7	5	−3	11	−27.2
13 Gloucestershire	20	3	10	7	−7	13	−53.8
14 Leicestershire	20	1	10	9	−9	14	−81.8
Hampshire	15	1	10	4	−9	11	−81.8

Surrey v Hants, Oval; Middlesex v Essex, Lord's; Somerset v Hants, Bath; Kent v Sussex, Tonbridge; Essex v Hants, Leyton; Middlesex v Kent, Lord's; all abandoned without a ball bowled.

BEST INDIVIDUAL SCORES

296 AO Jones, Notts v Gloucs, Trent Bridge
294 JR Gunn, Notts v Leics, Trent Bridge
286 GL Jessop, Gloucs v Sussex, Hove
248 JT Tyldesley, Lancs v Warwicks, Liverpool

BEST INNINGS ANALYSES

9–35 S Hargreave, Warwicks v Surrey, Oval
9–67 C Blythe, Kent v Essex, Canterbury
8–15 A Hearne, Kent v Gloucs, Tonbridge
8–39 B Cranfield, Somerset v Gloucs, Gloucester

BEST MATCH ANALYSES

15–76 S Hargreave, Warwicks v Surrey, Oval
15–115 W Mead, Essex v Leics, Leyton
14–59 SF Barnes, Lancs v Derbys, Derby
14–70 SF Barnes, Lancs v Essex, Leyton

LEADING BATSMEN

	Inns	NO	Runs	HS	Avge
CB Fry (Sussex)	36	6	2413	230	80.43
KS Ranjitsinhji (Sx)	29	5	1394	204	58.08
CM Wells (Middx)	11	4	360	82*	51.42
J Iremonger (Notts)	31	1	1380	210	46.00
JT Tyldesley (Lancs)	41	5	1618	248	44.94
AO Jones (Notts)	33	2	1388	296	44.77
PA Perrin (Essex)	36	4	1428	170	44.62
JR Gunn (Notts)	33	2	1369	294	44.16
GH Hirst (Yorks)	34	3	1367	153	44.09
G Brann (Sussex)	13	0	571	135	43.92

LEADING BOWLERS

	Runs	Wkts	Avge
J Hallows (Lancs)	273	24	11.37
S Hargreave (Warwicks)	1498	123	12.17
GH Hirst (Yorks)	1510	118	12.79
C Blythe (Kent)	1788	137	13.05
W Ringrose (Yorks)	485	36	13.47
T Langford (Hants)	586	42	13.95
CJ Kortright (Essex)	398	28	14.21
W Mead (Essex)	1665	114	14.60
W Rhodes (Yorks)	2105	143	14.72
FG Roberts (Gloucs)	1263	79	15.98

LEADING ALL-ROUNDERS

	Runs (Avge)	Wkts (Avge)
GH Hirst (Yorks)	1367 (44.09)	118 (12.79)
JR Gunn (Notts)	1369 (44.16)	104 (18.06)

LEADING WICKET-KEEPERS

	Dismissals		Total
H Strudwick (Surrey)	57ct	15st	72
HR Butt (Sussex)	56ct	10st	66

Percy ('Peter') Perrin had his usual fine season for Essex. He remains top scorer for the county in the Championship and his unbeaten 343 is the highest championship score made for a losing side. He became a Test selector, though incompetence in the field had precluded a Test career as a player (Hulton Picture Company)

1904

FINAL TABLE

	P	W	L	D	Pts	F/G	%
1 Lancashire	26	16	0	10	16	16	100.0
2 Yorkshire	27	9	2	16	7	11	63.6
3 Kent	21	10	4	7	6	14	42.8
4 Middlesex......	18	9	4	5	5	13	38.4
5 Nottinghamshire	20	7	4	9	3	11	27.2
6 Sussex.........	24	5	4	15	1	9	11.1
7 Leicestershire...	20	6	6	8	0	12	0.0
Warwickshire...	16	5	5	6	0	10	0.0
9 Gloucestershire .	18	5	6	7	−1	11	−9.0
10 Derbyshire	18	5	8	5	−3	13	−23.0
11 Surrey.........	28	6	12	10	−6	18	−33.3
12 Somerset	18	5	11	2	−6	16	−37.5
13 Worcestershire .	18	3	8	7	−5	11	−45.4
14 Essex	20	3	10	7	−7	13	−53.8
15 Hampshire	18	2	12	4	−10	14	−71.4

Yorks v Kent, Harrogate: match declared void on 2nd day, owing to the wicket having been tampered with.

LEADING BATSMEN

	Inns	NO	Runs	HS	Avge
CB Fry (Sussex)	32	2	2376	229	79.20
KS Ranjitsinhji (Sx)	22	4	1330	207*	73.88
JT Tyldesley (Lancs)	37	5	2237	225	69.90
WG Quaife (Warwicks)	27	5	1398	200*	63.54
AO Jones (Notts)	31	4	1648	187	61.03
J Iremonger (Notts)	31	1	1812	272	60.40
FH Gillingham (Essex)	11	1	550	201	55.00
PA Perrin (Essex)	31	4	1421	343*	52.62
GH Hirst (Yorks)	39	3	1848	157	51.33
TW Hayward (Surrey)	43	2	2074	188*	50.58

LEADING BOWLERS

	Runs	Wkts	Avge
JT Hearne (Middx)	1334	83	16.07
JN Crawford (Surrey)	715	44	16.25
WC Smith (Surrey)	1051	62	16.95
E Humphreys (Kent)	458	26	17.61
J Hallows (Lancs)	2021	108	18.71
EG Dennett (Gloucs)	2381	123	19.35
C Blythe (Kent)	2346	121	19.38
A Hearne (Kent)	408	21	19.42
W Rhodes (Yorks)	2070	104	19.90
WR Cuttell (Lancs)	1992	100	19.92

BEST INDIVIDUAL SCORES

343* PA Perrin, Essex v Derbys, Chesterfield
273* EG Hayes, Surrey v Derbys, Derby
272 J Iremonger, Notts v Kent, Trent Bridge
229 CB Fry, Sussex v Yorks, Hove

BEST INNINGS ANALYSES

9–30 C Blythe, Kent v Hants, Tonbridge
9–31 WC Smith, Surrey v Hants, Oval
9–34 HJ Huggins, Gloucs v Sussex, Bristol
9–37 J Hallows, Lancs v Gloucs, Gloucester

BEST MATCH ANALYSES

15–76   C Blythe, Kent v Hants, Tonbridge
15–93   JT Hearne, Middx v Somerset, Lord's
15–96   EG Dennett, Gloucs v Middx, Bristol
15–122 AR Warren, Derbys v Notts, Welbeck

LEADING ALL-ROUNDERS

	Runs (Avge)		Wkts (Avge)	
J Hallows (Lancs)	1058	(40.69)	108	(18.71)
GH Hirst (Yorks)	1848	(51.33)	105	(21.81)
W Rhodes (Yorks)	1082	(32.78)	104	(19.90)
JR Gunn (Notts)	1051	(36.24)	105	(24.70)

LEADING WICKET-KEEPERS

	Dismissals		Total
D Hunter (Yorks)	54ct	7st	61
FH Huish (Kent)	47ct	5st	52

1905

FINAL TABLE

	P	W	L	D(T)	Pts	F/G	%
1 Yorkshire	28	18	3	7	15	21	71.4
2 Lancashire	25	12	3	10	9	15	60.0
3 Sussex.	28	13	4	11	9	17	52.9
4 Surrey	27	14	6	6(1)	8	20	40.0
5 Leicestershire . . .	22	8	5	9	3	13	23.1
6 Kent	22	10	7	4(1)	3	17	17.4
7 Warwickshire . . .	22	5	4	13	1	9	11.1
8 Worcestershire .	18	5	5	8	0	10	0.0
Gloucestershire .	18	8	8	2	0	16	0.0
10 Nottinghamshire	20	6	7	7	−1	13	−7.6
11 Middlesex	18	4	7	7	−3	11	−27.2
12 Essex	20	3	10	7	−7	13	−53.8
13 Northamptonshire	12	2	8	2	−6	10	−60.0
14 Derbyshire	20	3	14	3	−11	17	−64.7
15 Somerset	18	1	10	7	−9	11	−81.8
16 Hampshire	20	1	12	7	−11	13	−84.6

BEST INDIVIDUAL SCORES

341 GH Hirst, Yorks v Leics, Leicester
277 CP McGahey, Essex v Derbys, Leyton
255* WG Quaife, Warwicks v Surrey, Oval
250 JT Tyldesley, Lancs v Notts, Trent Bridge

BEST INNINGS ANALYSES

9-47 W Brearley, Lancs v Somerset, Old Trafford
9-81 WS Lees, Surrey v Sussex, Eastbourne
9-89 GC Gill, Leics v Warwicks, Edgbaston
9-126 B Tremlin, Essex v Derbys, Leyton

BEST MATCH ANALYSES

17-137 W Brearley, Lancs v Somerset, Old Trafford
15-142 GA Wilson, Worcs v Somerset, Taunton
13-105 GJ Thompson, Northants v Leics, Leicester
13-109 WS Lees, Surrey v Notts, Oval

LEADING BATSMEN

	Inns	NO	Runs	HS	Avge
RE Foster (Worcs)	10	3	644	246*	92.00
CB Fry (Sussex)	24	2	1912	233	86.90
WG Quaife (Warwicks)	38	11	1785	255*	66.11
GH Hirst (Yorks)	35	7	1713	341	61.17
JG Greig (Hants)	16	2	724	187*	51.71
EW Dillon (Kent)	25	1	1268	141	50.72
HK Foster (Worcs)	22	1	1015	180	50.00
AJL Hill (Hants)	15	2	647	124	49.76
CJB Wood (Leics)	36	3	1567	200*	47.48
CP McGahey (Essex)	35	2	1550	277	46.96

LEADING BOWLERS

	Runs	Wkts	Avge
S Haigh (Yorks)	1429	97	14.73
AE Bailey (Somerset)	444	29	15.31
W Rhodes (Yorks)	1986	126	15.76
GJ Thompson (Northants)	1268	75	16.90
WS Lees (Surrey)	2785	169	17.01
W Brearley (Lancs)	2256	121	18.64
GH Hirst (Yorks)	1618	88	18.38
WC Smith (Surrey)	740	40	18.65
W Cook (Lancs)	726	38	19.10
EG Dennett (Gloucs)	2553	131	19.48

LEADING ALL-ROUNDERS

	Runs	(Avge)	Wkts	(Avge)
W Rhodes (Yorks)	1117	(36.03)	126	(15.76)
EH Killick (Sussex)	1241	(27.57)	101	(20.28)

LEADING WICKET-KEEPERS

	Dismissals		Total
HR Butt (Sussex)	66ct	15st	81
D Hunter (Yorks)	48ct	16st	64

1906

FINAL TABLE

	P	W	L	D	Pts	F/G	%
1 Kent	22	16	2	4	14	18	77.7
2 Yorkshire	28	17	3	8	14	20	70.0
3 Surrey	28	18	4	6	14	22	63.6
4 Lancashire	26	15	6	5	9	21	42.8
5 Nottinghamshire	20	9	4	7	5	13	38.4
6 Warwickshire ...	20	7	4	9	3	11	27.2
7 Essex	22	9	6	7	3	15	23.0
8 Hampshire	20	7	9	4	−2	16	−12.5
9 Gloucestershire .	20	6	10	4	−4	16	−20.0
10 Sussex.........	24	6	12	6	−6	18	−33.3
11 Somerset	18	4	10	4	−6	14	−42.8
Middlesex......	18	4	10	4	−6	14	−42.8
Northamptonshire	16	4	10	2	−6	14	−42.8
14 Worcestershire .	20	2	8	10	−6	10	−60.0
15 Leicestershire...	22	3	14	5	−11	17	−64.7
16 Derbyshire	20	2	17	1	−15	19	−78.9

BEST INDIVIDUAL SCORES

295* JT Tyldesley, Lancs v Kent, Old Trafford
240 RH Spooner, Lancs v Somerset, Bath
225 CJB Wood, Leics v Worcs, Worcester
219 TW Hayward, Surrey v Northants, Oval

BEST INNINGS ANALYSES

10–40 EG Dennett, Gloucs v Essex, Bristol
 9–35 JEBBPQC Dwyer, Sussex v Derbys, Hove
 9–36 W Huddleston, Lancs v Notts, Liverpool
 9–44 F Harry, Lancs v Warwicks, Old Trafford
 9–44 JEBBPQC Dwyer, Sussex v Middx, Hove

BEST MATCH ANALYSES

16–69 TG Wass, Notts v Lancs, Liverpool
16–100 JEBBPQC Dwyer, Sussex v Middx, Hove
15–70 F Harry, Lancs v Warwicks, Old Trafford
15–88 EG Dennett, Gloucs v Essex, Bristol

LEADING BATSMEN

	Inns	NO	Runs	HS	Avge
TW Hayward (Surrey)	47	7	2814	219	70.35
CJ Burnup (Kent)	19	3	1116	179	69.75
KL Hutchings (Kent)	25	4	1358	176	64.66
J Iremonger (Notts)	37	6	1650	200*	53.22
PA Perrin (Essex)	39	3	1767	150	49.08
EG Arnold (Worcs)	35	3	1541	166	48.15
EW Dillon (Kent)	13	2	528	85	48.00
JT Tyldesley (Lancs)	43	3	1873	295*	46.82
FH Gillingham (Essex)	17	2	679	102	45.26
AO Jones (Notts)	37	3	1483	105	43.61

LEADING BOWLERS

	Runs	Wkts	Avge
W Huddleston (Lancs)	613	50	12.26
S Haigh (Yorks)	1868	138	13.53
WR Cuttell (Lancs)	909	67	13.56
GH Hirst (Yorks)	2701	182	14.84
AW Hallam (Notts)	1600	91	17.58
WR Grayson (Lancs)	428	24	17.83
TG Wass (Notts)	1614	90	17.93
EG Dennett (Gloucs)	2876	160	17.97
W Bestwick (Derbys)	2019	111	18.18
NA Knox (Surrey)	2139	117	18.28

LEADING ALL-ROUNDERS

	Runs (Avge)		Wkts (Avge)	
GH Hirst (Yorks)	1771	(43.19)	182	(14.84)
JN Crawford (Surrey)	1064	(29.55)	111	(19.54)
JR Gunn (Notts)	1154	(37.22)	105	(20.65)

LEADING WICKET-KEEPERS

	Dismissals		Total
J Humphries (Derbys)	60ct	7st	67
H Strudwick (Surrey)	66ct	1st	67

1907

FINAL TABLE

		P	W	L	D	Pts	F/G	%
I	Nottinghamshire	19	15	0	4	15	15	100.0
2	Worcestershire .	18	8	2	8	6	10	60.0
	Yorkshire	26	12	3	11	9	15	60.0
4	Surrey	28	12	4	12	8	16	50.0
5	Middlesex	20	8	4	7	4	12	33.3
6	Lancashire	26	11	7	7	4	18	22.2
7	Essex	22	10	7	5	3	17	17.6
8	Kent	26	12	9	5	3	21	14.2
9	Warwickshire . . .	19	6	5	8	1	11	9.0
10	Gloucestershire .	22	8	12	2	−4	20	−20.0
11	Leicestershire . . .	20	6	10	4	−4	16	−25.0
12	Hampshire	24	6	11	7	−5	17	−29.4
13	Sussex	26	7	13	6	−6	20	−30.0
14	Somerset	18	3	12	3	−9	15	−60.0
15	Northamptonshire	20	2	12	6	−10	14	−71.4
16	Derbyshire	20	2	17	1	−15	19	−78.9

Yorks v Derbys, Sheffield; Derbys v Warwicks, Derby; Yorks v Notts, Huddersfield: all abandoned without a ball bowled. Middlesex v Notts: abandoned on 2nd day due to pitch having been damaged.

BEST INDIVIDUAL SCORES

240 GL Jessop, Gloucs v Sussex, Bristol
210 RR Relf, Sussex v Kent, Canterbury
209 JT Tyldesley, Lancs v Warwickshire, Edgbaston
204 Jas Seymour, Kent v Hants, Tonbridge

BEST INNINGS ANALYSES

10–30 C Blythe, Kent v Northants, Northampton
9–38 JA Cuffe, Worcs v Yorks, Bradford
9–41 FA Tarrant, Middx v Gloucs, Bristol
9–45 GH Hirst, Yorks v Middx, Sheffield

BEST MATCH ANALYSES

17–48 C Blythe, Kent v Northants, Northampton
15–21 EG Dennett, Gloucs v Northants, Gloucester
15–97 EG Dennett, Gloucs v Northants, Northampton
12–63 GH Hirst, Yorks v Leics, Hull

LEADING BATSMEN

	Inns	NO	Runs	HS	Avge
CB Fry (Sussex)	27	3	1157	187	48.20
PF Warner (Middx)	33	4	1353	149	46.65
TW Hayward (Surrey)	37	3	1570	161	46.17
GN Foster (Worcs)	15	3	593	78	45.61
AJL Hill (Hants)	17	1	705	116	44.06
RE Foster (Worcs)	19	1	753	174	41.83
HK Foster (Worcs)	29	3	1085	152	41.73
JB Hobbs (Surrey)	48	6	1717	166*	40.18
JT Tyldesley (Lancs)	44	2	1597	209	38.02
Jas Seymour (Kent)	40	1	1483	204	38.02

LEADING BOWLERS

	Runs	Wkts	Avge
S Haigh (Yorks)	898	78	11.51
AW Hallam (Notts)	1803	153	11.78
TG Wass (Notts)	1969	145	13.07
JT Newstead (Yorks)	278	21	13.23
W Huddleston (Lancs)	941	71	13.25
FA Tarrant (Middx)	1749	115	15.20
GH Hirst (Yorks)	2130	140	15.21
F Harry (Lancs)	1165	75	15.53
JN Crawford (Surrey)	1715	110	15.59
EG Dennett (Gloucs)	2881	184	15.65

LEADING ALL-ROUNDERS

	Runs (Avge)		Wkts (Avge)	
GH Hirst (Yorks)	1032	(34.40)	140	(15.21)
FA Tarrant (Middx)	1034	(33.35)	115	(15.20)

LEADING WICKET-KEEPERS

	Dismissals		Total
FH Huish (Kent)	50ct	22st	72
JH Board (Gloucs)	35ct	30st	65

Tom Wass, shown here (left) with his Nottinghamshire colleague George Anthony, was a pace bowler at his best on damp wickets. He reached his peak this season as with Albert Hallam he bowled Notts to the title (Hulton Picture Company)

1908

FINAL TABLE

	P	W	L	D	Pts	F/G	%
1 Yorkshire	28	16	0	12	16	16	100.0
2 Kent	25	17	3	5	14	20	70.0
3 Surrey	29	13	4	12	9	17	52.9
4 Middlesex	19	6	3	10	3	9	33.3
5 Sussex	28	6	4	18	2	10	20.0
6 Worcestershire .	18	6	5	7	1	11	9.1
7 Lancashire	25	10	9	6	1	19	5.3
8 Nottinghamshire	20	6	7	7	−1	13	−7.7
9 Hampshire	22	7	9	6	−2	16	−12.5
10 Gloucestershire .	24	8	11	5	−3	19	−15.8
11 Essex	22	5	7	10	−2	12	−16.7
12 Warwickshire . . .	21	5	9	7	−4	14	−28.6
13 Leicestershire . . .	21	4	8	9	−4	12	−33.3
14 Derbyshire	22	5	13	4	−8	18	−44.4
15 Northamptonshire	22	3	14	5	−11	17	−64.7
16 Somerset	20	2	13	5	−11	15	−73.3

Surrey v Lancs, Oval; Kent v Middlesex, Tunbridge Wells; Warwicks v Leics, Coventry: all abandoned without a ball bowled.

BEST INDIVIDUAL SCORES

243 JT Tyldesley, Lancs v Leics, Leicester
232 JN Crawford, Surrey v Somerset, Oval
230 CP McGahey, Essex v Northants, Northampton
215 HK Foster, Worcs v Warwicks, Worcester

BEST INNINGS ANALYSES

9-78 JT Hearne, Middlesex v Yorks, Bradford
8-23 GR Cox, Sussex v Gloucs, Hove
8-29 TG Wass, Nottinghamshire v Essex, Trent Bridge
8-44 S Santall, Warwicks v Somerset, Leamington Spa
8-44 JW Hitch, Surrey v Kent, Oval
8-44 JR Badcock, Hants v Sussex, Portsmouth

BEST MATCH ANALYSES

16–103 TG Wass, Notts v Essex, Trent Bridge
14–75   AE Relf, Sussex v Derbys, Hove
14–111 W Brearley, Lancs v Essex, Old
        Trafford
14–161 AE Lewis, Somerset v Warwicks,
        Leamington Spa

Spy

LEADING BATSMEN

	Inns	NO	Runs	HS	Avge
KS Ranjitsinhji (Sx)	13	2	716	200	65.09
CB Fry (Sussex)	10	0	598	214	59.80
PF Warner (Middx)	26	2	1298	120	54.08
HK Foster (Worcs)	20	1	999	215	52.57
BJT Bosanquet (Middx)	15	2	661	135	50.84
FA Tarrant (Middx)	28	3	1206	157	48.24
TW Hayward (Surrey)	40	0	1874	175	46.85
GN Foster (Worcs)	19	1	815	154	45.27
FH Gillingham (Essex)	23	1	967	194	43.95
JT Tyldesley (Lancs)	37	2	1522	243	43.48

LEADING BOWLERS

	Runs	Wkts	Avge
S Haigh (Yorks)	860	71	12.11
GH Hirst (Yorks)	1941	156	12.44
WC Smith (Surrey)	806	56	14.39
JT Newstead (Yorks)	1700	115	14.78
W Brearley (Lancs)	2261	148	15.27
EC Kirk (Surrey)	384	24	16.00
C Blythe (Kent)	2753	167	16.48
W Rhodes (Yorks)	1295	78	16.60
FR Foster (Warwicks)	397	23	17.26
W East (Northants)	974	56	17.39
W Huddleston (Lancs)	974	56	17.39

LEADING ALL-ROUNDERS

	Runs (Avge)		Wkts (Avge)	
GH Hirst (Yorks)	1332	(40.36)	156	(12.44)
AE Relf (Sussex)	1130	(27.56)	109	(19.11)

LEADING WICKET-KEEPERS

	Dismissals		Total
FH Huish (Kent)	47ct	28st	75
JH Board (Gloucs)	39ct	23st	62
HR Butt (Sussex)	49ct	13st	62

*(Left): BJT (Bernard) Bosanquet gained fame as an early
purveyor of the 'googly', but was also a fine batsman, as
evidenced by his record in this season for Middlesex. His son
Reggie became a TV personality* (Mary Evans Picture
Library)

1909

FINAL TABLE

	P	W	L	D	Pts	F/G	%
1 Kent	26	16	2	8	14	18	77.8
2 Lancashire	24	14	4	6	10	18	55.6
3 Yorkshire	26	12	4	10	8	16	50.0
4 Sussex	26	7	3	16	4	10	40.0
5 Surrey	30	16	7	7	9	23	39.1
6 Middlesex	21	6	5	10	1	11	9.0
7 Northamptonshire	18	9	8	1	1	17	5.9
8 Hampshire	22	7	7	8	0	14	0.0
9 Worcestershire .	20	8	8	4	0	16	0.0
10 Nottinghamshire	19	6	8	5	−2	14	−14.3
11 Somerset	16	4	7	5	−3	11	−27.3
12 Warwickshire . . .	20	3	8	9	−5	11	−45.5
13 Leicestershire . . .	21	3	10	8	−7	13	−53.8
14 Essex	18	2	7	9	−5	9	−55.6
15 Derbyshire	21	2	15	4	−13	17	−76.5
16 Gloucestershire .	22	1	13	8	−12	14	−85.7

Essex v Leics, Leyton; Essex v Middlesex, Leyton; Derbys v Notts, Glossop: all abandoned without a ball bowled.

BEST INDIVIDUAL SCORES

276 EG Hayes, Surrey v Hants, Oval
272* RR Relf, Sussex v Worcs, Eastbourne
208 E Humphreys, Kent v Gloucs, Catford
205 JB Hobbs, Surrey v Hants, Oval

BEST INNINGS ANALYSES

9-31 H Dean, Lancs v Somerset, Old Trafford
9-35 H Dean, Lancs v Warwicks, Liverpool
9-42 C Blythe, Kent v Leics, Leicester
9-44 C Blythe, Kent v Northants,
Northampton

BEST MATCH ANALYSES

16-102 C Blythe, Kent v Leics, Leicester
14-75 C Blythe, Kent v Northants,
Northampton
14-77 H Dean, Lancs v Somerset, Old
Trafford

14-123 SG Smith, Northants v Derbys,
Northampton

LEADING BATSMEN

	Inns	NO	Runs	HS	Avge
JR Mason (Kent)	12	2	738	179*	73.80
AP Day (Kent)	19	0	905	177	47.63
CB Fry (Hants)	15	1	658	132	47.00
RH Spooner (Lancs)	10	1	421	113	46.77
JB Hobbs (Surrey)	40	1	1771	205	45.41
KL Hutchings (Kent)	30	1	1251	155	43.13
EG Arnold (Worcs)	34	5	1184	200*	40.62
FB Roberts (Gloucs)	10	0	406	129	40.60
RR Relf (Sussex)	39	3	1451	272*	40.30
E Humphreys (Kent)	34	4	1207	208	40.23

LEADING BOWLERS

	Runs	Wkts	Avge
S Haigh (Yorks)	1407	111	12.69
WC Smith (Surrey)	1057	83	12.73
JS Heap (Lancs)	480	37	12.97
GJ Thompson (Northants)	1629	118	13.80
C Blythe (Kent)	2506	178	14.07
DW Carr (Kent)	725	51	14.21
W Rhodes (Yorks)	1635	107	15.28
H Dean (Lancs)	1582	86	15.59
W Brearley (Lancs)	1821	115	15.83
AE Lewis (Somerset)	1174	73	16.08

LEADING ALL-ROUNDERS

	Runs	(Avge)	Wkts	(Avge)
W Rhodes (Yorks)	1351	(35.55)	107	(15.28)
FA Tarrant (Middx)	1223	(37.06)	105	(17.23)

LEADING WICKET-KEEPERS

	Dismissals		Total
H Strudwick (Surrey)	57ct	9st	66
HR Butt (Sussex)	58ct	5st	63

1910

<table>
<tr><th colspan="6">FINAL TABLE</th></tr>
<tr><th></th><th>P</th><th>W</th><th>L</th><th>D</th><th>%</th></tr>
<tr><td>I Kent . . . .</td><td>25</td><td>19</td><td>3</td><td>3</td><td>76.00</td></tr>
<tr><td>2 Surrey . . . .</td><td>28</td><td>16</td><td>7</td><td>5</td><td>57.14</td></tr>
<tr><td>3 Middlesex . . . . . .</td><td>22</td><td>11</td><td>5</td><td>6</td><td>50.00</td></tr>
<tr><td>4 Lancashire . . . . . .</td><td>29</td><td>14</td><td>5</td><td>10</td><td>48.27</td></tr>
<tr><td>5 Nottinghamshire</td><td>20</td><td>9</td><td>4</td><td>7</td><td>45.00</td></tr>
<tr><td>6 Hampshire . . . . . .</td><td>24</td><td>10</td><td>10</td><td>4</td><td>41.66</td></tr>
<tr><td>7 Sussex . . . .</td><td>25</td><td>10</td><td>9</td><td>6</td><td>40.00</td></tr>
<tr><td>8 Yorkshire . . . .</td><td>27</td><td>10</td><td>7</td><td>10</td><td>37.03</td></tr>
<tr><td>9 Northamptonshire</td><td>19</td><td>7</td><td>8</td><td>4</td><td>36.84</td></tr>
<tr><td>10 Leicestershire . . .</td><td>17</td><td>6</td><td>11</td><td>0</td><td>35.29</td></tr>
<tr><td>11 Essex . . . .</td><td>17</td><td>5</td><td>8</td><td>4</td><td>29.41</td></tr>
<tr><td>12 Gloucestershire . .</td><td>20</td><td>5</td><td>11</td><td>4</td><td>25.00</td></tr>
<tr><td>13 Worcestershire . .</td><td>22</td><td>5</td><td>8</td><td>9</td><td>22.72</td></tr>
<tr><td>14 Warwickshire . . . .</td><td>19</td><td>4</td><td>8</td><td>7</td><td>21.05</td></tr>
<tr><td>15 Derbyshire . . . . . .</td><td>20</td><td>2</td><td>14</td><td>4</td><td>10.00</td></tr>
<tr><td>16 Somerset . . . .</td><td>18</td><td>0</td><td>15</td><td>3</td><td>0.00</td></tr>
</table>

New method of championship ranking: percentage of wins to matches played.
Surrey v Derbys, Oval: abandoned after 2 days due to death of King Edward VII. Surrey v Essex, Oval; Lancs v Kent, Old Trafford; Leics v Yorks, Leicester; Warwicks v Northants, Edgbaston; Sussex v Derbys, Eastbourne: all limited to 2 days on account of the Royal funeral. None of the above matches were counted towards the championship as a result.

BEST INDIVIDUAL SCORES

234 A Hartley, Lancs v Somerset, Old Trafford
216 C Charlesworth, Warwicks v Derbys, Blackwell
204 SG Smith, Northants v Gloucs, Northampton
200* E Humphreys, Kent v Lancs, Tunbridge Wells
200* RH Spooner, Lancs v Yorks, Old Trafford

BEST INNINGS ANALYSES

9-23 GH Hirst, Yorks v Lancs, Headingley
9-77 H Dean, Lancs v Somerset, Bath
9-83 W Shipman, Leics v Surrey, Oval
9-95 AE Relf, Sussex v Warwicks, Hove

BEST MATCH ANALYSES

16-103 H Dean, Lancs v Somerset, Bath
14-29 WC Smith, Surrey v Northants, Oval
14-91 TG Wass, Notts v Surrey, Trent Bridge
14-141 AE Lewis, Somerset v Kent, Tunbridge Wells

LEADING BATSMEN

	Inns	NO	Runs	HS	Avge
JT Tyldesley (Lancs)	42	2	1961	158	49.02
PF Warner (Middx)	32	4	1248	150*	44.57
KL Hutchings (Kent)	31	2	1222	144	42.13
RH Spooner (Lancs)	16	4	479	200*	39.91
J Seymour (Kent)	41	4	1457	193	39.37
FA Tarrant (Middx)	35	2	1295	142	39.24
A Hartley (Lancs)	43	4	1511	234	38.74
E Humphreys (Kent)	41	2	1483	200*	38.02
FH Knott (Kent)	10	1	332	114	36.88
HK Foster (Worcs)	23	0	845	119	36.73

LEADING BOWLERS

	Runs	Wkts	Avge
DW Carr (Kent)	730	60	12.16
JT Hearne (Middx)	1427	116	12.30
WC Smith (Surrey)	2702	215	12.56
FE Woolley (Kent)	1630	124	13.14
C Blythe (Kent)	2042	149	13.70
GH Hirst (Yorks)	2017	134	15.05
H Dean (Lancs)	2024	133	15.21
FA Tarrant (Middx)	1946	123	15.82
GHT Simpson-Hayward (Worcs)	618	36	17.16
J Iremonger (Notts)	1317	76	17.32

LEADING ALL-ROUNDERS

	Runs (Avge)	Wkts (Avge)
GH Hirst (Yorks)	1425 (32.38)	134 (15.05)
CB Llewellyn (Hants)	1110 (29.21)	133 (20.45)
AE Relf (Sussex)	1098 (24.95)	128 (19.99)
FA Tarrant (Middx)	1295 (39.24)	123 (15.82)

LEADING WICKET-KEEPERS

	Dismissals		Total
FH Huish (Kent)	42ct	28st	70
H Strudwick (Surrey)	49ct	11st	60

1911

FINAL TABLE

	P	W	L	D W	D L	Poss Pts	Pts	%
1 Warwickshire ...	20	13	4	3	0	100	74	74.00
2 Kent	26	17	4	3	2	130	96	73.84
3 Middlesex	22	14	5	3	0	110	79	71.81
4 Lancashire	30	15	7	5	3	150	93	62.00
5 Surrey	30	15	7	4	4	150	91	60.66
6 Essex	18	8	5	4	1	90	53	58.88
7 Yorkshire	27	14	8	1	4	135	77	57.03
8 Nottinghamshire	20	9	5	3	3	100	57	57.00
9 Worcestershire ..	24	12	11	0	1	120	61	50.83
10 Northamptonshire	17	8	9	0	0	85	40	47.05
11 Hampshire	24	7	10	4	3	120	50	41.66
12 Gloucestershire..	20	5	12	0	3	100	28	28.00
13 Sussex	24	4	16	2	2	120	28	23.33
14 Derbyshire......	18	2	13	0	3	90	13	14.44
15 Leicestershire ...	22	1	16	2	3	110	14	12.72
16 Somerset	16	1	13	0	2	80	7	8.75

Points system: 5 for a win; 3 for 1st-innings lead in a drawn game (W), 1 point for team behind on 1st-innings (L) in drawn game. Counties ranked by percentage of points to possible points.
Yorks v Northants, Dewsbury: innings not completed on each side, match not counted.

BEST INDIVIDUAL SCORES

268* S Kinneir, Warwicks v Hants, Edgbaston
258* CB Fry, Hants v Gloucs, Southampton
234* JW Hearne, Middx v Somerset, Lord's
224 RH Spooner, Lancs v Surrey, Oval

BEST INNINGS ANALYSES

9-41 GH Hirst, Yorks v Worcs, Worcester
9-67 TG Wass, Notts v Derbys, Blackwell
9-71 A Morton, Derby v Notts, Blackwell
9-82 JW Hearne, Middx v Surrey, Lord's

BEST MATCH ANALYSES

15-189 AR Litteljohn, Middx v Lancs, Lord's
14-84 C Blythe, Kent v Gloucs, Cheltenham
14-115 JA Cuffe, Worcs v Gloucs, Dudley
14-137 TG Wass, Notts v Derbys, Blackwell

LEADING BATSMEN

	Inns	NO	Runs	HS	Avge
CB Fry (Hants)	18	1	1299	258*	76.41
CP Mead (Hants)	34	5	1706	207*	58.82
RH Spooner (Lancs)	30	0	1700	224	56.66
PA Perrin (Essex)	27	2	1281	114	51.24
FA Tarrant (Middx)	35	4	1587	207*	51.19
TW Hayward (Surrey)	44	5	1963	202	50.33
J Hardstaff (Notts)	36	6	1464	145	48.80
JW Hearne (Middx)	32	2	1423	234*	47.43
J Seymour (Kent)	40	5	1619	218*	46.25
CJB Wood (Leics)	40	7	1487	117*	45.06

LEADING BOWLERS

	Runs	Wkts	Avge
W Huddleston (Lancs)	279	23	12.13
GJ Thompson (Northants)	1421	96	14.80
E Humphreys (Kent)	457	30	15.23
AP Day (Kent)	540	33	16.36
W East (Northants)	946	57	16.59
S Haigh (Yorks)	1463	87	16.81
H Dean (Lancs)	3067	175	17.52
DW Carr (Kent)	985	55	17.90
PM Fairclough (Lancs)	414	23	18.00
JT Hearne (Middx)	1954	108	18.09

LEADING ALL-ROUNDERS

	Runs (Avge)	Wkts (Avge)
JA Cuffe (Worcs)	1054 (25.70)	110 (23.56)
FR Foster (Warwicks)	1383 (44.61)	116 (19.51)
GH Hirst (Yorks)	1540 (35.00)	119 (18.61)
AE Relf (Sussex)	1375 (31.97)	116 (20.95)

LEADING WICKET-KEEPERS

	Dismissals		Total
FH Huish (Kent)	54ct	36st	90
H Strudwick (Surrey)	54ct	11st	65

1912

FINAL TABLE

	P	W	L	D W	D L	NR	Poss Pts	Pts	%
1 Yorkshire	28	13	1	7	4	3	125	90	72.00
2 Northamptonshire	18	10	1	2	4	1	85	60	70.58
3 Kent	26	14	5	3	3	1	125	82	65.60
4 Lancashire	22	8	2	4	3	5	85	55	64.70
5 Middlesex	20	7	4	5	2	2	90	52	57.77
6 Hampshire	24	7	3	4	4	6	90	51	56.66
7 Surrey	26	7	5	6	5	3	115	58	50.43
8 Nottinghamshire	18	5	5	5	2	1	85	42	49.41
9 Warwickshire	22	6	5	3	4	4	90	43	47.77
10 Sussex	28	6	10	6	4	2	130	52	40.00
11 Gloucestershire	18	3	8	1	1	5	65	19	29.23
12 Derbyshire	18	2	7	2	3	4	70	19	27.14
13 Leicestershire	22	3	13	2	2	2	100	23	23.00
14 Somerset	16	2	8	1	3	2	70	16	22.85
15 Essex	18	1	8	2	3	4	70	14	20.00
16 Worcestershire	20	1	10	0	6	3	85	11	12.94

Yorks v Surrey, Sheffield; Lancs v Essex, Old Trafford; Lancs v Warwicks, Old Trafford; Gloucs v Notts, Gloucester; Gloucs v Surrey, Cheltenham: all abandoned without a ball bowled, but included in 'Played' total, listed as No Result (NR). No Result games not counted towards possible points total.

BEST INDIVIDUAL SCORES

245 PA Perrin, Essex v Derby, Leyton
221 D Denton, Yorks v Kent, Tunbridge Wells
211 J Sharp, Lancs v Leics, Old Trafford
200 D Denton, Yorks v Warwicks, Edgbaston

BEST INNINGS ANALYSES

9–25 S Haigh, Yorks v Gloucs, Headingley
8–21 J Iremonger, Notts v Gloucs, Trent Bridge
8–22 EG Hayes, Surrey v Gloucs, Oval
8–24 GR Cox, Sussex v Derbys, Derby

BEST MATCH ANALYSES

16–146 EG Dennett, Gloucs v Hants, Bristol
15–45 C Blythe, Kent v Leics, Leicester
15–77 AE Relf, Sussex v Leics, Hove
15–108 H Dean, Lancs v Kent, Old Trafford

LEADING BATSMEN

	Inns	NO	Runs	HS	Avge
AC Johnston (Hants)	18	1	939	175	55.23
D Denton (Yorks)	38	4	1831	221	53.85
KS Ranjitsinhji (Sx)	11	0	554	176	50.36

RH Spooner (Lancs)	14	1	642	127	49.38
CP Mead (Hants)	32	9	1133	135	49.26
J Sharp (Lancs)	23	2	1025	211	48.80
EG Hayes (Surrey)	32	1	1453	143*	46.87
JT Tyldesley (Lancs)	26	1	1111	174	44.44
FE Woolley (Kent)	30	4	1104	117	42.46
EIM Barrett (Hants)	32	8	986	120*	41.08

LEADING BOWLERS

	Runs	Wkts	Avge
DW Carr (Kent)	470	49	9.59
C Blythe (Kent)	1930	170	11.35
S Haigh (Yorks)	1101	96	11.46
SG Smith (Northants)	1021	84	12.15
H Dean (Lancs)	1433	109	13.14
FE Woolley (Kent)	1329	95	13.98

FA Tarrant (Middx)			1325	94	14.09
GJ Thompson (Northants)			1547	106	14.59
JT Hearne (Middx)			1012	67	15.10
GR Cox (Sussex)			1099	71	15.47

LEADING ALL-ROUNDERS

	Runs (Avge)	Wkts (Avge)
FA Tarrant (Middx)	1015 (31.71)	94 (14.09)
FE Woolley (Kent)	1104 (42.46)	95 (13.98)

LEADING WICKET-KEEPERS

	Dismissals		Total
FH Huish (Kent)	32ct	31st	63
H Strudwick (Surrey)	42ct	13st	55

1913

FINAL TABLE

	P	W	L	D W	Poss L	Pts	Poss Pts	%
1 Kent	28	20	3	3	1	135	110	81.48
2 Yorkshire	28	16	4	4	3	135	95	70.37
3 Surrey	26	13	5	4	4	130	81	62.30
4 Northamptonshire	22	12	4	1	5	110	68	61.81
5 Nottinghamshire	20	8	5	3	4	100	53	53.00
6 Middlesex	20	7	6	4	3	100	50	50.00
7 Sussex	28	10	10	4	3	135	65	48.14
8 Lancashire	26	7	11	7	0	125	56	44.80
9 Gloucestershire ..	22	8	11	1	2	110	45	40.90
10 Hampshire	26	7	11	4	4	130	51	39.23
11 Warwickshire ...	24	7	11	3	3	120	47	39.16
12 Worcestershire ..	20	6	9	1	3	95	36	37.89
13 Derbyshire	18	4	10	2	2	90	28	31.11
14 Leicestershire ...	22	4	13	1	4	110	27	24.54
15 Essex	18	2	9	2	4	85	20	23.52
16 Somerset	16	2	11	2	1	80	17	21.25

Kent v Worcs, Tunbridge Wells; Lancs v Essex, Old Trafford; Sussex v Yorks, Hastings: no result on first innings.

BEST INDIVIDUAL SCORES

257* LC Braund, Someset v Worcs, Worcester
230* WH Denton, Northants v Essex, Leyton
210 JT Tyldesley, Lancs v Surrey, Oval
201 FL Bowley, Worcs v Gloucs, Worcester

BEST INNINGS ANALYSES

8–20 FA Tarrant, Middx v Hants, Lord's
8–28 JS Heap, Lancs v Middx, Liverpool
8–48 JW Hitch, Surrey v Kent, Oval
8–59 A Drake, Yorks v Gloucs, Sheffield

BEST MATCH ANALYSES

15–47 FA Tarrant, Middx v Hants, Lord's
14–134 WC Smith, Surrey v Sussex, Hastings
13–71 EG Dennett, Gloucs v Warwicks,
         Cheltenham
13–94 C Blythe, Kent v Leics, Canterbury

LEADING BATSMEN

	Inns	NO	Runs	HS	Avge
JW Hearne (Middx)	32	2	1576	189	52.53
JB Hobbs (Surrey)	46	3	2238	184	52.04
G Gunn (Notts)	36	4	1596	170	49.87
CP Mead (Hants)	50	6	2146	171*	48.77
GN Foster (Worcs)	10	0	473	175	47.30
JR Gunn (Notts)	36	6	1397	126	46.56
HTW Hardinge (Kent)	50	6	1949	168	44.29
LH Tennyson (Hants)	17	1	702	116	43.87
GH Hirst (Yorks)	41	9	1383	166*	43.21
FE Woolley (Kent)	40	5	1507	177	43.05

LEADING BOWLERS

	Runs	Wkts	Avge
C Blythe (Kent)	2254	145	15.54
FA Tarrant (Middx)	1864	113	16.49
SG Smith (Northants)	1652	100	16.52
NJ Holloway (Sussex)	799	48	16.64
WC Smith (Surrey)	1127	65	17.33
A Drake (Yorks)	1771	102	17.36
GJ Thompson (Northants)	2415	138	17.50
AE Relf (Sussex)	2039	116	17.57
FE Woolley (Kent)	1462	83	17.61
DW Carr (Kent)	872	47	18.55

LEADING ALL-ROUNDERS

	Runs	(Avge)	Wkts	(Avge)
MW Booth (Yorks)	1020	(28.33)	158	(19.03)
JW Hearne (Middx)	1576	(52.53)	104	(22.11)
AE Relf (Sussex)	1560	(34.66)	116	(17.57)
SG Smith (Northants)	1292	(34.91)	100	(16.52)
FA Tarrant (Middx)	1279	(41.25)	113	(16.49)

LEADING WICKET-KEEPERS

	Dismissals		Total
FH Huish (Kent)	58ct	26st	84
A Dolphin (Yorks)	54ct	13st	67

Colin ('Charley') Blythe of Kent topped the bowling averages for two consecutive seasons. A sensitive character and an excellent musician, his cricketing exploits had an adverse effect on his nervous health. In the First World War, however, he died a hero at Passchendaele (Hulton Picture Company)

1914

FINAL TABLE

	P	W	L	D W	L	NR	Poss Pts	Pts	%
1 Surrey	26	15	2	5	3	1	125	93	74.40
2 Middlesex	20	11	2	4	3	0	100	70	70.00
3 Kent	28	16	7	1	4	0	140	87	62.14
4 Yorkshire	28	14	4	3	7	0	140	86	61.42
5 Hampshire	28	13	4	3	8	0	140	82	58.57
6 Sussex	27	10	6	4	6	1	130	68	52.30
7 Warwickshire ...	24	9	7	4	4	0	120	61	50.83
8 Essex	24	9	4	4	2	0	120	59	49.16
9 Northamptonshire	21	7	6	4	4	0	105	51	48.57
10 Nottinghamshire	20	5	5	6	3	1	95	46	48.42
11 Lancashire	26	6	9	5	6	0	130	51	39.23
12 Derbyshire......	20	5	12	3	0	0	100	34	34.00
13 Leicestershire ...	23	4	11	5	3	0	115	38	33.04
14 Worcestershire ..	22	2	13	3	3	1	105	22	20.95
15 Somerset	19	3	16	0	0	0	95	15	15.78
16 Gloucestershire..	22	1	17	3	1	0	110	15	13.63

Somerset v Northants, Taunton; Sussex v Surrey, Hove; Surrey v Leics, Oval: abandoned due to outbreak of war.

BEST INDIVIDUAL SCORES

305* FR Foster, Warwicks v Worcs, Dudley
276 FL Bowley, Worcs v Hants, Dudley
253 JT Tyldesley, Lancs v Kent, Canterbury
252* S Coe, Leics v Northants, Leicester

BEST INNINGS ANALYSES

10–35 A Drake, Yorks v Somerset, Weston
9–38 AJ Conway, Worcs v Gloucs, Moreton-in-Marsh
9–46 JC White, Somerset v Gloucs, Bristol
9–97 C Blythe, Kent v Surrey, Lord's

BEST MATCH ANALYSES

16–176 FA Tarrant, Middx v Lancs, Old Trafford
15–50 A Drake, Yorks v Somerset, Weston
15–87 AJ Conway, Worcs v Gloucs, Moreton-in-Marsh
14–54 A Jaques, Hants v Somerset, Bath

LEADING BATSMEN

	Inns	NO	Runs	HS	Avge
JW Hearne (Middx)	31	7	1828	204	76.16
JB Hobbs (Surrey)	42	2	2499	226	62.47
CP Mead (Hants)	45	5	2235	213	55.87
FA Tarrant (Middx)	33	3	1524	250*	50.80
JR Gunn (Notts)	33	5	1291	154*	46.10
FE Woolley (Kent)	44	2	1933	160*	46.02
RR Relf (Sussex)	20	1	829	130	43.63
A Ducat (Surrey)	38	6	1370	118	42.81
JT Tyldesley (Lancs)	45	4	1710	253	41.70
SG Smith (Northants)	31	2	1193	177	41.13

LEADING BOWLERS

	Runs	Wkts	Avge
C Blythe (Kent)	2391	159	15.03
JC White (Somerset)	1278	83	15.39
CH Parkin (Lancs)	535	34	15.73
J Horsley (Derbys)	915	56	16.33
A Drake (Yorks)	2209	135	16.36
SG Smith (Northants)	1647	99	16.63
HC McDonell (Hants)	609	35	17.40
W Rhodes (Yorks)	1965	110	17.86
FR Foster (Warwicks)	2135	117	18.24
A Jaques (Hants)	2046	112	18.26

LEADING ALL-ROUNDERS

	Runs (Avge)		Wkts (Avge)	
JWHT Douglas (Essex)	1151	(39.68)	118	(18.80)
FR Foster (Warks)	1396	(34.90)	117	(18.24)
JW Hearne (Middx)	1828	(76.16)	106	(21.97)
FA Tarrant (Middx)	1524	(50.80)	112	(19.08)
FE Woolley (Kent)	1933	(46.02)	112	(18.91)

LEADING WICKET-KEEPERS

	Dismissals		Total
A Dolphin (Yorks)	52ct	16st	68
GB Street (Sussex)	54ct	14st	68
H Strudwick (Surrey)	57ct	11st	68

1919

FINAL TABLE

	P	W	D	L	%
1 Yorkshire	26	12	11	3	46.15
2 Kent	14	6	7	1	42.85
3 Nottinghamshire	14	5	8	1	35.71
4 Surrey	20	7	10	3	35.00
5 Somerset	12	4	5	3	33.33
Lancashire	24	8	12	4	33.33
7 Hampshire	16	5	7	4	31.25
8 Gloucestershire . .	16	4	5	7	25.00
9 Leicestershire . . .	14	3	7	4	21.42
Derbyshire	14	3	2	9	21.42
11 Sussex	20	4	5	11	20.00
12 Northamptonshire	12	2	6	4	16.66
13 Middlesex	14	2	9	3	14.28
14 Essex	18	2	12	4	11.76
15 Warwickshire	14	1	6	7	7.14

Rankings by percentage of wins to matches played. Somerset v Sussex, Taunton: the tie in this match was counted as a draw, no provision having been made by the Advisory Committee.

BEST INDIVIDUAL SCORES

272 JT Tyldesley, Lancs v Derby, Chesterfield
271 A Ducat, Surrey v Hants, Southampton
218* JW Hearne, Middx v Hants, Lord's
207 CP Mead, Hants v Essex, Leyton

BEST INNINGS ANALYSES

9–29 AC Williams, Yorks v Hants, Dewsbury
8–35 CH Parkin, Lancs v Yorks, Old Trafford
8–35 W Wells, Northants v Yorks, Sheffield
8–36 JC White, Somerset v Worcs, Bath

BEST MATCH ANALYSES

16–83 JC White, Somerset v Worcs, Bath
14–81 JS Heap, Lancs v Gloucs, Bristol
14–104 AE Dipper, Gloucs v Leics, Cheltenham
14–123 CH Parkin, Lancs v Yorks, Old Trafford

LEADING BATSMEN

	Inns	NO	Runs	HS	Avge
G Gunn (Notts)	21	2	1236	185*	65.05
CP Mead (Hants)	27	5	1332	207	60.54
DJ Knight (Surrey)	14	1	760	146	58.46
EH Hendren (Middx)	23	4	1024	201	53.89
HTW Hardinge (Kent)	20	3	888	172*	52.23
JB Hobbs (Surrey)	32	2	1540	106	51.33
JWHT Douglas (Essex)	25	8	866	144	50.94
JH Parsons (Warwicks)	12	1	535	125	48.63
JR Gunn (Notts)	22	4	869	111*	48.27
WRD Payton (Notts)	19	6	621	84*	47.76

LEADING BOWLERS

	Runs	Wkts	Avge
W Rhodes (Yorks)	1764	142	12.42
CH Parkin (Lancs)	417	28	14.89
R Kilner (Yorks)	573	38	15.07
EF Field (Warwicks)	325	21	15.47
JC White (Somerset)	1352	86	15.72
ER Wilson (Yorks)	417	26	16.03
FE Woolley (Kent)	1458	90	16.20
JR Gunn (Notts)	333	20	16.65
JS Heap (Lancs)	1040	62	16.77
A Waddington (Yorks)	1676	95	17.64

LEADING ALL-ROUNDERS

	Runs	(Avge)	Wkts	(Avge)
W Rhodes (Yorks)	891	(34.26)	142	(12.42)
JWHT Douglas (Essex)	866	(50.94)	85	(26.10)

LEADING WICKET-KEEPERS

	Dismissals		Total
A Dolphin (Yorks)	42ct	25st	67
H Strudwick (Surrey)	46ct	5st	51

1920

FINAL TABLE

	P	W	L	D W	L	NR	Poss Pts	Pts	%
1 Middlesex	20	15	2	1	2	0	100	77	77.00
2 Lancashire	28	19	5	1	1	2	130	97	74.61
3 Surrey	24	15	6	2	0	1	115	79	68.69
4 Yorkshire	28	15	6	3	0	4	120	81	67.50
5 Kent	26	16	6	1	2	1	125	82	65.60
6 Sussex	30	18	8	0	2	2	140	90	64.28
7 Nottinghamshire	20	10	6	2	0	2	90	54	60.00
8 Gloucestershire	20	8	9	0	0	3	85	40	47.05
9 Essex	24	9	9	0	4	2	110	45	40.90
10 Somerset	20	7	10	2	1	0	100	39	39.00
11 Hampshire	26	7	14	3	1	1	125	41	32.80
12 Warwickshire . . .	26	7	13	2	2	2	120	39	32.50
13 Leicestershire . . .	24	7	14	0	1	2	110	35	31.81
14 Northamptonshire	20	3	16	0	1	0	100	15	15.00
15 Worcestershire . .	18	1	16	0	0	1	85	5	5.88
16 Derbyshire	18	0	17	0	0	1	85	0	0.00

Derbys v Notts, Chesterfield: no play, counted as No Result.
Points system: 5 for win, 2 for 1st-innings lead in drawn match.
Ranking by percentage of points to possible points. Matches with
no result on 1st innings (NR) not counted.

BEST INDIVIDUAL SCORES

302* P Holmes, Yorks v Hants, Portsmouth
244 E Tyldesley, Lancs v Warwicks, Edgbaston
232* G Brown, Hants v Yorks, Headingley
232 EH Hendren, Middx v Notts, Lord's

BEST INNINGS ANALYSES

9–30 AE Thomas, Northants v Yorks, Bradford
9–33 AS Kennedy, Hants v Lancs, Liverpool
9–35 CWL Parker, Gloucs v Leics, Cheltenham
9–36 E Robinson, Yorks v Lancs, Bradford

BEST MATCH ANALYSES

14–57 CWL Parker, Gloucs v Leics, Cheltenham
14–104 SWA Cadman, Derbys v Northants,
　　　　Northampton
13–48 A Waddington, Yorks v Northants,
　　　　Northampton
13–60 GTS Stevens, Middx v Sussex, Hove

LEADING BATSMEN

	Inns	NO	Runs	HS	Avge
EH Hendren (Middx)	31	4	1826	232	67.62
JW Hearne (Middx)	30	4	1552	215*	59.69
P Holmes (Yorks)	41	4	2029	302*	54.83
JB Hobbs (Surrey)	38	2	1935	169	53.75
FH Gillingham (Essex)	15	2	671	151	51.61
CP Mead (Hants)	40	5	1773	178*	50.65
JR Gunn (Notts)	31	5	1241	131	47.73
HW Lee (Middx)	33	4	1352	221*	46.62
G Brown (Hants)	44	2	1863	232*	44.35
GW Stephens (Warwicks)	5	1	612	111	43.71

LEADING BOWLERS

	Runs	Wkts	Avge
W Rhodes (Yorks)	1846	143	12.90
FE Woolley (Kent)	2203	164	13.43
PT Mills (Gloucs)	748	52	14.38
JC White (Somerset)	1879	130	14.45
CH Parkin (Lancs)	572	39	14.66
L Cook (Lancs)	2245	150	14.96
ER Wilson (Yorks)	604	39	15.48
CWL Parker (Gloucs)	1974	125	15.79
H Dean (Lancs)	2004	124	16.16
JF Bridges (Somerset)	1400	86	16.27

LEADING ALL-ROUNDERS

	Runs (Avge)	Wkts (Avge)
JWHT Douglas (Essex)	1087 (35.06)	114 (19.85)
JW Hearne (Middx)	1552 (59.69)	119 (16.82)
FE Woolley (Kent)	1548 (39.69)	164 (13.43)

LEADING WICKET-KEEPERS

	Dismissals		Total
A Dolphin (Yorks)	28ct	27st	55
EJ Smith (Warwicks)	37ct	13st	50
H Strudwick (Surrey)	39ct	11st	50

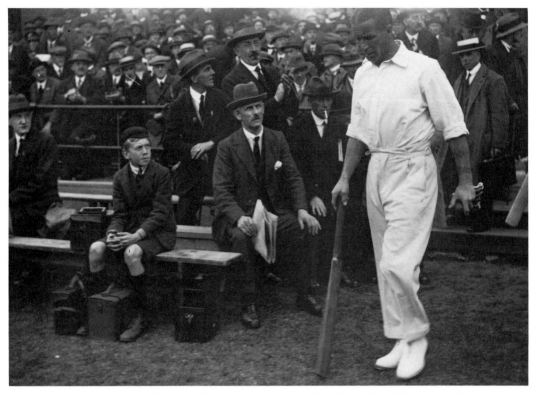

'Johnny-Won't-Hit-Today' Douglas, whose captaincy and outstanding all-round form failed to inspire Essex above mid-table respectability. In 1921, Douglas achieved the fastest ever all-rounder's 'double' (Hulton Picture Company)

1921

FINAL TABLE

	P	W	L	D W	D L	D NR	Poss Pts	Pts	%
1 Middlesex	20	15	2	0	2	1	95	75	78.94
2 Surrey	24	15	2	3	3	1	115	81	70.43
3 Yorkshire	26	16	3	4	2	1	125	88	70.40
4 Kent	26	16	7	2	1	0	130	84	64.61
5 Lancashire	28	15	4	4	3	2	130	83	63.84
6 Hampshire	28	14	9	4	1	0	140	78	55.71
7 Gloucestershire..	24	12	12	0	0	0	120	60	50.00
8 Nottinghamshire	24	10	8	3	2	1	115	56	48.69
9 Sussex	28	13	12	1	2	0	140	67	47.85
10 Somerset	22	8	11	2	1	0	110	44	40.00
11 Leicestershire ...	26	10	14	0	2	0	130	50	38.46
12 Derbyshire	20	5	12	3	0	0	100	31	31.00
13 Northamptonshire	24	5	15	1	2	1	115	27	23.47
14 Worcestershire ..	22	5	15	0	2	0	110	25	22.72
15 Essex	26	5	13	2	6	0	130	29	22.30
16 Warwickshire ...	26	5	18	1	2	0	130	27	20.76
17 Glamorgan	18	2	14	1	0	1	85	12	14.11

BEST INDIVIDUAL SCORES

292* A Sandham, Surrey v Northants, Oval

290* A Ducat, Surrey v Essex, Leyton

286 JR Freeman, Essex v Northants, Northampton

280* CP Mead, Hants v Notts, Southampton

BEST INNINGS ANALYSES

10–40 W Bestwick, Derbys v Glamorgan, Cardiff

10–43 T Rushby, Surrey v Somerset, Taunton

10–76 JC White, Somerset v Worcs, Worcester

10–79 CWL Parker, Gloucs v Somerset, Bristol

BEST INNINGS ANALYSES

15–116 AJ Nash, Glamorgan v Worcs, Swansea

15–175 JC White, Somerset v Worcs, Worcester

14–91 JWHT Douglas, Essex v Hants, Bournemouth

14–110 JC White, Somerset v Glamorgan, Swansea

JWHT Douglas (Essex) 1161 (46.44) 108 (17.99)

AS Kennedy (Hants) 1167 (25.93) 168 (20.70)

JA Newman (Hants) 1012 (31.62) 172 (20.84)

W Rhodes (Yorks) 1184 (43.85) 117 (12.71)

FE Woolley (Kent) 1621 (50.65) 123 (15.77)

LEADING WICKET-KEEPERS

	Dismissals		Total
WH Livsey (Hants)	46ct	30st	76
TE Sidwell (Leics)	56ct	12st	68

LEADING BATSMEN

	Inns	NO	Runs	HS	Avge
CP Mead (Hants)	40	4	2438	280*	67.72
EH Hendren (Middx)	33	5	1613	113	57.60
CAG Russell (Essex)	36	2	1930	273	56.76
A Sandham (Surrey)	37	4	1826	292*	55.33
E Tyldesley (Lancs)	37	6	1697	165	54.74
A Ducat (Surrey)	34	3	1683	290*	54.29
JW Hearne (Middx)	25	1	1259	202	52.45
HTW Hardinge (Kent)	42	5	1919	207	51.86
TF Shepherd (Surrey)	36	4	1658	212	51.81
FE Woolley (Kent)	33	1	1621	174	50.65

LEADING BOWLERS

	Runs	Wkts	Avge
ER Wilson (Yorks)	465	41	11.34
W Rhodes (Yorks)	1488	117	12.71
JC White (Somerset)	2133	137	15.56
FE Woolley (Kent)	1940	123	15.77
GG Macaulay (Yorks)	1528	94	16.25
AE Relf (Sussex)	619	38	16.28
CWL Parker (Gloucs)	2581	156	16.54
H Howell (Warwicks)	1662	100	16.62
W Bestwick (Derbys)	2458	147	16.72
AP Freeman (Kent)	2667	156	17.09
CH Parkin (Lancs)	735	43	17.09

LEADING ALL-ROUNDERS

	Runs	(Avge)	Wkts	(Avge)
WE Astill (Leics)	1348	(27.51)	152	(20.25)

Somerset's Jack White (left) and Bill Bestwick of Derbyshire both enjoyed fine seasons; for Bestwick, at 46, it was his best ever. They are pictured after the Somerset–Derbyshire game at Bath – Bestwick had match figures of 13–150, but White's 10–106 ensured a win for the home side (Hulton Picture Company)

1922

FINAL TABLE

	P	W	L	D W	D L	D NR	Poss Pts	Pts	%
1 Yorkshire	30	19	2	6	2	1	145	107	73.79
2 Nottinghamshire	28	17	5	4	0	2	130	93	71.53
3 Surrey	24	13	1	6	3	1	115	77	66.95
4 Kent	28	16	3	3	5	1	135	86	63.70
5 Lancashire	30	15	7	2	4	2	140	79	56.42
6 Hampshire	28	13	6	3	4	2	130	71	54.61
7 Middlesex	22	10	6	3	3	0	110	56	50.90
8 Essex	26	7	4	6	5	4	110	47	42.72
9 Sussex	30	11	16	1	2	0	150	57	38.00
10 Somerset	24	6	11	6	1	0	120	42	35.00
11 Derbyshire	22	6	10	2	2	2	100	34	34.00
12 Warwickshire . . .	28	8	15	0	2	3	125	40	32.00
13 Gloucestershire . .	28	8	17	1	1	1	135	42	31.11
14 Leicestershire . . .	26	6	11	4	4	1	125	38	30.40
15 Northamptonshire	22	5	14	0	2	1	105	25	23.80
16 Glamorgan	22	1	18	1	1	1	105	7	6.66
17 Worcestershire . .	26	1	16	1	8	0	130	7	5.38

BEST INDIVIDUAL SCORES

277* EH Hendren, Middx v Kent, Lord's
249* HTW Hardinge, Kent v Leics, Leicester
235   CP Mead, Hants v Worcs, Worcester
232   H Sutcliffe, Yorks v Surrey, Oval

BEST INNINGS ANALYSES

10–65 GC Collins, Kent v Notts, Dover
9–11 AP Freeman, Kent v Sussex, Hove
9–21 TL Richmond, Notts v Hants, Trent
    Bridge
9–36 CWL Parker, Gloucs v Yorks, Bristol

BEST MATCH ANALYSES

17–67   AP Freeman, Kent v Sussex, Hove
16–83   GC Collins, Kent v Notts, Dover
15–116 AS Kennedy, Hants v Somerset, Bath
14–61   CWL Parker, Gloucs v Warwicks,
    Cheltenham

LEADING BATSMEN

	Inns	NO	Runs	HS	Avge
EH Hendren (Middx)	31	7	1812	277*	75.50
JB Hobbs (Surrey)	35	4	1968	168	63.48
CP Mead (Hants)	43	10	2270	235	63.05
HTW Hardinge (Kent)	42	6	2068	249*	57.44
FE Woolley (Kent)	38	3	1868	188	53.37
JW Hearne (Middx)	36	5	1636	221*	52.77
CAG Russell (Essex)	42	3	2042	172	52.35
E Tyldesley (Lancs)	46	5	2026	178	49.41
J Seymour (Kent)	41	5	1727	170	47.97
A Sandham (Surrey)	38	5	1550	167	46.96

LEADING BOWLERS

	Runs	Wkts	Avge
W Rhodes (Yorks)	1068	84	12.71
CWL Parker (Gloucs)	2570	195	13.17
GG Macaulay (Yorks)	1598	120	13.31
TL Richmond (Notts)	2279	169	13.48
GM Louden (Essex)	699	49	14.26
R Kilner (Yorks)	1454	101	14.39
AP Freeman (Kent)	2839	194	14.60
JC White (Somerset)	2207	146	15.11
A Waddington (Yorks)	1956	127	15.40
AS Kennedy (Hants)	2861	177	16.16

LEADING ALL-ROUNDERS

	Runs	(Avge)	Wkts	(Avge)
WE Astill (Leics)	1127	(23.97)	136	(18.80)
PGH Fender (Surrey)	1114	(39.78)	143	(19.49)
AS Kennedy (Hants)	1016	(23.09)	177	(16.16)
R Kilner (Yorks)	1085	(30.13)	101	(14.39)
FE Woolley (Kent)	1868	(53.37)	142	(18.00)

LEADING WICKET-KEEPERS

	Dismissals		Total
GB Street (Sussex)	55ct	22st	77
TW Oates (Notts)	42ct	22st	64

1923

FINAL TABLE

	P	W	L	D W	D L	D NR	Poss Pts	Pts	%
1 Yorkshire	32	25	1	4	1	1	155	133	85.80
2 Nottinghamshire	26	15	3	5	2	1	125	85	68.00
3 Lancashire	30	15	2	6	6	1	145	87	60.00
4 Surrey	26	11	2	6	4	3	115	67	58.26
5 Kent..........	28	15	9	0	3	1	135	75	55.55
6 Sussex	30	15	8	2	5	0	150	79	52.66
7 Hampshire	28	10	8	6	3	1	135	62	45.92
8 Middlesex	22	7	7	5	3	0	110	45	40.90
9 Somerset	24	9	11	1	3	0	120	47	39.16
10 Derbyshire......	22	4	7	6	4	1	105	32	30.47
11 Gloucestershire..	28	7	16	3	2	0	140	41	29.29
12 Warwickshire ...	26	6	12	3	4	1	125	36	28.80
13 Essex	26	6	11	3	6	0	130	36	27.69
14 Leicestershire ...	24	5	13	4	2	0	120	33	27.50
15 Worcestershire ..	26	5	16	1	4	0	130	27	20.76
16 Glamorgan......	24	2	17	2	3	0	120	14	11.66
17 Northamptonshire	22	2	16	1	3	0	110	12	10.90

BEST INDIVIDUAL SCORES

270 FE Woolley, Kent v Middx, Canterbury
252* AE Dipper, Gloucs v Glamorgan,
    Cheltenham
236 JL Bryan, Kent v Hants, Canterbury
236 E Tyldesley, Lancs v Surrey, Oval

BEST INNINGS ANALYSES

10–51 H Howell, Warwicks v Yorks, Edgbaston
9–41 WE Astill, Leics v Warwicks, Edgbaston
9–50 FCL Matthews, Notts v Northants,
    Trent Bridge
8–26 R Kilner, Yorks v Glamorgan, Cardiff

BEST MATCH ANALYSES

17–89 FCL Matthews, Notts v Northants,
    Trent Bridge
15–95 CH Parkin, Lancs v Glamorgan,
    Blackpool
14–106 RC Robertson-Glasgow, Somerset v
    Sussex, Eastbourne
14–161 AP Freeman, Kent v Warwicks, Dover

LEADING BATSMEN

	Inns	NO	Runs	HS	Avge
EH Hendren (Middx)	35	9	2263	200*	87.03
CP Mead (Hants)	43	8	2265	222	64.71
JW Hearne (Middx)	23	3	1143	232	57.15
JWH Makepeace (Lancs)	45	6	1976	203	50.66
DR Jardine (Surrey)	11	4	344	127	49.14
WRD Payton (Notts)	37	7	1379	154	45.96
JL Bryan (Kent)	17	1	694	236	43.37
E Tyldesley (Lancs)	40	5	1509	236	43.11
C Hallows (Lancs)	32	7	1067	179*	42.68
FE Woolley (Kent)	44	5	1662	270	42.61

LEADING BOWLERS

	Runs	Wkts	Avge
W Rhodes (Yorks)	1353	120	11.27
R Kilner (Yorks)	1586	139	11.41
MW Tate (Sussex)	2296	174	13.19
GG Macaulay (Yorks)	1989	149	13.34
E Robinson (Yorks)	1343	95	14.13
CH Parkin (Lancs)	2623	176	14.90
AER Gilligan (Sussex)	1937	129	15.01
FCL Matthews (Notts)	1760	115	15.30
RK Tyldesley (Lacs)	1633	106	15.40
JC White (Somerset)	2177	141	15.43

LEADING ALL-ROUNDERS

	Runs	(Avge)	Wkts	(Avge)
WE Astill (Leics)	1023	(26.23)	100	(21.94)
PGH Fender (Surrey)	1106	(32.52)	136	(18.44)
AS Kennedy (Hants)	1146	(26.04)	156	(20.19)
R Kilner (Yorks)	1126	(35.18)	139	(11.41)
FA Pearson (Worcs)	1046	(25.51)	105	(23.48)
W Rhodes (Yorks)	1023	(31.00)	120	(11.27)
MW Tate (Sussex)	1000	(23.25)	174	(13.19)

LEADING WICKET-KEEPERS

	Dismissals		Total
GB Street (Sussex)	60ct	20st	80
A Dolphin (Yorks)	44ct	23st	67

1924

FINAL TABLE

	P	W	L	D W	L	T	NR	Poss Pts	Pts	%
1 Yorkshire	30	16	3	2	2	0	7	115	88	76.52
2 Middlesex	22	11	3	4	2	0	2	100	69	69.00
3 Surrey..........	24	9	1	6	4	0	4	100	67	67.00
4 Lancashire	30	11	2	6	6	0	5	125	79	63.20
5 Kent	28	12	4	5	4	1	2	130	81	62.30
6 Gloucestershire ..	26	9	7	6	1	0	3	115	64	55.65
7 Nottinghamshire .	27	9	3	4	7	0	4	115	64	55.65
8 Somerset	22	9	7	1	2	1	2	100	52	52.00
9 Warwickshire....	25	7	6	2	5	0	5	100	46	46.00
10 Sussex	26	7	12	5	1	0	1	125	51	40.80
11 Leicestershire ...	25	7	12	4	2	0	0	125	49	39.20
12 Hampshire	28	5	9	4	6	0	4	120	43	35.83
13 Glamorgan	21	5	11	3	1	0	1	100	35	35.00
14 Worcestershire ..	24	4	11	3	5	0	1	115	34	29.56
15 Essex	26	2	12	4	5	0	3	115	27	23.47
16 Northamptonshire	22	2	9	0	6	0	5	85	16	18.82
17 Derbyshire	24	0	13	4	4	0	3	105	16	15.23

Points system: 5 for win, 3 for 1st-innings lead in drawn match, 1 for draw after 1st-innings deficit. Matches with no 1st-innings result not counted. Ranking still on percentage of points to points possible.
Warwicks v Notts, Edgbaston; Surrey v Essex, Oval; Leics v Surrey, Leicester; Somerset v Essex, Bath; Glamorgan v Somerset, Cardiff: all abandoned without a ball bowled.

BEST INDIVIDUAL SCORES

255* H Sutcliffe, Yorks v Essex, Southend
219 MD Lyon, Somerset v Derbys, Burton
213 H Sutcliffe, Yorks v Somerset, Dewsbury
203* JB Hobbs, Surrey v Notts, Trent Bridge

BEST INNINGS ANALYSES

9–32 CH Parkin, Lancs v Leics, Ashby-de-la-Zouche
9–35 H Howell, Warwicks v Somerset, Taunton
9–38 RC Robertson-Glasgow, Somerset v Middlesex, Lord's
9–40 CF Root, Worcs v Essex, Worcester

BEST MATCH ANALYSES

15–109 CWL Parker, Gloucs v Derbys, Derby
14–71 H Howell, Warwicks v Somerset, Taunton

14–131 CWL Parker, Gloucs v Middlesex, Bristol
13–61 JC White, Somerset v Essex, Ilford

LEADING BATSMEN

	Inns	NO	Runs	HS	Avge
A Sandham (Surrey)	23	1	1377	169	62.59
JB Hobbs (Surrey)	25	6	1155	203*	60.78
WW Whysall (Notts)	41	4	1786	151	48.27
EH Hendren (Middx)	29	6	1095	106*	47.60
E Tyldesley (Lancs)	40	6	1607	148*	47.26
H Sutcliffe (Yorks)	33	4	1342	255*	46.27
FE Woolley (Kent)	32	1	1418	141	45.74
CP Mead (Hants)	40	5	1543	154	44.08
JCW MacBryan (Som)	33	2	1355	132	43.70
NVH Riches (Glam)	12	0	504	170	42.00

LEADING BOWLERS

	Runs	Wkts	Avge
GG Macaulay (Yorks)	1866	159	11.73
R Kilner (Yorks)	1370	113	12.12
MW Tate (Sussex)	1753	139	12.61
W Wells (Northants)	811	61	13.29
CH Parkin (Lancs)	2260	169	13.37
W Rhodes (Yorks)	1085	81	13.39
CWL Parker (Gloucs)	2486	184	13.51
RK Tyldesley (Lancs)	1890	135	14.00
CS Marriott (Kent)	607	43	14.11
JC White (Somerset)	1936	135	14.34

LEADING ALL-ROUNDERS

	Runs (Avge)		Wkts (Avge)	
MW Tate (Sussex)	1095	(30.41)	139	(12.61)
WE Astill (Leics)	965	(27.57)	86	(20.96)
G Geary (Leics)	781	(22.97)	101	(16.22)

LEADING WICKET-KEEPERS

	Dismissals		Total
H Smith (Gloucs)	34ct	22st	56
HR Murrell (Middx)	32ct	20st	52

1925

FINAL TABLE

	P	W	L	D W	L	NR	Poss Pts	Pts	%
1 Yorkshire	32	21	0	3 3		5	135	117	86.66
2 Surrey	26	14	2	4 2		4	110	84	76.36
3 Lancashire	32	19	4	7 1		1	155	117	75.48
4 Nottinghamshire	26	15	3	1 6		1	125	84	67.20
5 Kent	28	15	7	1 1		4	120	79	65.83
6 Middlesex	24	12	3	2 5		2	110	71	64.54
7 Essex	28	9	7	5 5		2	130	65	50.00
8 Warwickshire	26	8	11	4 2		1	125	54	43.20
9 Hampshire	28	6	11	6 0		5	115	48	41.73
10 Gloucestershire	28	9	13	3 3		0	140	57	40.71
11 Northamptonshire	24	9	12	0 3		0	120	48	40.00
12 Leicestershire	26	7	13	3 2		1	125	46	36.80
13 Sussex	30	9	16	1 3		1	145	51	35.17
14 Derbyshire	24	5	12	2 4		1	115	35	30.43
15 Somerset	26	3	15	4 2		2	120	29	24.16
16 Worcestershire	26	5	18	0 3		0	130	28	21.53
17 Glamorgan	26	1	20	1 2		2	120	10	8.33

BEST INDIVIDUAL SCORES

315* P Holmes, Yorks v Middlesex, Lord's
250* WR Hammond, Gloucs v Lancs, Old Trafford
240 EH Hendren, Middx v Kent, Tonbridge
235 H Sutcliffe, Yorks v Middlesex, Headingley

BEST INNINGS ANALYSES

9–32 H Howell, Warwicks v Hants, Edgbaston
9–44 CWL Parker, Gloucs v Essex, Gloucester
9–55 TL Richmond, Notts v Northants, Trent Bridge
9–118 CWL Parker, Gloucs v Surrey, Gloucester

BEST MATCH ANALYSES

17–56 CWL Parker, Gloucs v Essex, Gloucester
15–52 VWC Jupp, Northants v Glamorgan, Swansea
14–58 MW Tate, Sussex v Glamorgan, Hove
14–83 TL Richmond, Notts v Gloucs, Cheltenham

LEADING BATSMEN

	Inns	NO	Runs	HS	Avge
P Holmes (Yorks)	41	7	2123	315*	62.44
JB Hobbs (Surrey)	37	3	2084	215	61.29
EH Hendren (Middx)	38	6	1922	240	60.06
A Sandham (Surrey)	42	6	2056	181	57.11
FE Woolley (Kent)	40	4	1990	215	55.27
AW Carr (Notts)	38	4	1815	206	53.38
C Hallows (Lancs)	42	5	1938	163	52.37
H Sutcliffe (Yorks)	40	5	1787	235	51.05
E Tyldesley (Lancs)	21	2	961	114	50.57
AC Russell (Essex)	43	3	1942	150	48.55

LEADING BOWLERS

	Runs	Wkts	Avge
MW Tate (Sussex)	2608	194	13.44
FM Sibbles (Lancs)	579	43	13.46
CWL Parker (Gloucs)	2930	200	14.65
W Bestwick (Derbys)	525	35	15.00
GG Macaulay (Yorks)	2678	176	15.21
RK Tyldesley (Lancs)	1835	116	15.81
R Kilner (Yorks)	1891	116	16.30
JC White (Somerset)	2001	121	16.53
FBR Browne (Sussex)	333	20	16.65
G Geary (Leics)	1518	90	16.86

LEADING ALL-ROUNDERS

	Runs (Avge)	Wkts (Avge)
VWC Jupp (Northants)	1143 (27.21)	110 (19.54)
MW Tate (Sussex)	1162 (24.72)	194 (13.44)

LEADING WICKET-KEEPERS

	Dismissals		Total
WL Cornford (Sussex)	45ct	16st	61
JC Hubble (Kent)	43ct	17st	60

1926

FINAL TABLE

	P	W	L	D W	L	NR	Poss Pts	Pts	%
1 Lancashire	32	17	2	6 3	4		140	106	75.51
2 Yorkshire	31	14	0	10 4	3		140	104	74.28
3 Kent	28	15	2	3 8	0		140	92	65.71
4 Nottinghamshire	29	13	7	4 5	0		145	82	56.55
5 Surrey	26	7	4	8 3	4		110	62	56.36
6 Middlesex	24	9	4	0 6	5		95	51	53.68
7 Hampshire	28	10	5	4 8	1		135	70	51.85
8 Glamorgan	24	9	9	1 0	5		95	48	50.52
9 Essex	30	6	9	9 3	2		140	62.5	44.64
10 Sussex	27	6	10	6 5	0		135	53	39.25
11 Derbyshire	23	5	7	4 6	1		110	43	39.09
12 Warwickshire ...	28	2	9	8 5	4		120	39	32.50
13 Leicestershire ...	27	5	12	3 4	3		120	38	31.66
14 Somerset	26	3	9	3 6	4		110	32.5	29.54
15 Gloucestershire	30	5	17	3 4	1		145	38	26.20
16 Northamptonshire	25	3	13	4 5	0		125	32	25.60
17 Worcestershire ..	28	3	13	3 4	5		115	28	24.34

Essex and Somerset totals include 2.5 points for tie. Yorks v Notts, Headingley; Derbys v Leics, Chesterfield; Northants v Sussex, Northampton: all abandoned without a ball bowled.

BEST INDIVIDUAL SCORES

316* JB Hobbs, Surrey v Middlesex, Lord's
235   A Ducat, Surrey v Leics, Oval
226   E Tyldesley, Lancs v Sussex, Old Trafford
225   JT Bell, Glamorgan v Worcs, Dudley

BEST INNINGS ANALYSES

9–33 G Geary, Leics v Lancs, Ashby-de-la-Zouche
9–50 GR Cox, Sussex v Warwicks, Horsham
9–71 MW Tate, Sussex v Middx, Lord's
8–15 RK Tyldesley, Lancs v Northants,
      Kettering

BEST MATCH ANALYSES

17–106 GR Cox, Sussex v Warwicks, Horsham
14–77   W Rhodes, Yorks v Somerset,
        Huddersfield
14–86   G Geary, Leics v Hants, Southampton
14–92   GG Macaulay, Yorks v Gloucs, Bristol

LEADING BATSMEN

	Inns	NO	Runs	HS	Avge
JB Hobbs (Surrey)	21	2	1560	316*	82.10
E Tyldesley (Lancs)	38	4	2365	226	69.55
EH Hendren (Middx)	28	4	1639	213	68.29
CP Mead (Hants)	43	8	2274	177*	64.97
APF Chapman (Kent)	12	1	629	159	57.18
H Sutcliffe (Yorks)	29	4	1424	200	56.96
JW Hearne (Middx)	21	2	1052	151*	55.36
HTW Harding (Kent)	48	5	2174	176	50.55
JWH Makepeace (Lancs)	47	5	2100	180	50.00
P Holmes (Yorks)	37	4	1624	143	49.21

LEADING BOWLERS

	Runs	Wkts	Avge
W Rhodes (Yorks)	1388	100	13.88
CH Parkin (Lancs)	545	36	15.13
RK Tyldesley (Lancs)	1901	125	15.20
J Mercer (Glam)	1852	119	15.56
GG Macaulay (Yorks)	1990	126	15.79
MW Tate (Sussex)	1678	106	15.83
CWL Parker (Gloucs)	3501	198	17.68
G Geary (Leics)	1831	103	17.77
EW Clark (Northants)	2016	111	18.16
H Larwood (Notts)	1755	96	18.28

LEADING ALL-ROUNDERS

	Runs (Avge)	Wkts (Avge)
VWC Jupp (Northants)	1422 (36.46)	101 (18.55)
JA Newman (Hants)	1156 (28.90)	145 (23.82)
W Rhodes (Yorks)	1022 (40.88)	100 (13.88)
MW Tate (Sussex)	1054 (34.00)	106 (15.83)

LEADING WICKET-KEEPERS

	Dismissals		Total
B Lilley (Notts)	51ct	29st	80
JC Hubble (Kent)	43ct	32st	75

1927

FINAL TABLE

	P	W	L	D W	D L	D NR	Poss Pts	Pts	%
1 Lancashire	28	10	1	11	5	1	224	154	68.75
2 Nottinghamshire	28	12	3	8	4	1	224	152	67.85
3 Yorkshire	27	10	3	5	6	3	216	135	62.54
4 Kent	26	12	6	4	3	1*	208	129	62.01
5 Derbyshire	20	8	3	2	3	4	160	99	61.87
6 Surrey	22	8	3	4	5	2*	176	107	60.79
7 Leicestershire . . .	22	7	3	5	5	2*	176	104	59.09
8 Essex	26	8	8	5	3	2	208	106	50.96
9 Middlesex	20	5	5	5	4	1	160	81	50.62
10 Sussex	28	7	9	6	2	4*	224	108	48.92
11 Warwickshire . . .	23	3	4	7	7	2	184	88	47.82
12 Gloucestershire	26	6	7	1	9	3	208	92	44.23
13 Hampshire	23	5	9	5	3	1	184	78	42.39
14 Somerset	23	3	9	4	7	0	184	65	35.32
15 Glamorgan	21	1	8	7	4	1	168	59	35.11
16 Northamptonshire	24	4	12	1	6	1	192	59	30.72
17 Worcestershire . .	27	1	17	2	6	1	216	40	18.51

Includes tie on 1st innings.

Points system: 8 for a win; 5 for 1st-innings lead in drawn game; 3 for draw with 1st-innings deficit. Tie or no result – 4 pts to each side if 6 hours play took place. Less than 6 hours play – not counted.

Yorks v Kent, Bradford; Glamorgan v Northants, Pontypridd; Lancs v Glamorgan, Blackpool; Worcs v Hants, Worcester; Gloucs v Kent, Bristol: all abandoned without a ball bowled.

BEST INDIVIDUAL SCORES

277* TF Shepherd, Surrey v Gloucs, Oval
260 APF Chapman, Kent v Lancs, Maidstone
245* JW Hearne, Middx v Gloucs, Bristol
238* JA Cutmore, Essex v Gloucs, Bristol

BEST INNINGS ANALYSES

9–46 CWL Parker, Gloucs v Northants, Northampton
9–103 CWL Parker, Gloucs v Somerset, Bristol
9–141 SJ Staples, Notts v Kent, Canterbury
8–23 JA Newman, Hants v Somerset, Weston

BEST MATCH ANALYSES

16–88 JA Newman, Hants v Somerset, Weston
16–154 CWL Parker, Gloucs v Somerset, Bristol

15–173 CWL Parker, Gloucs v Northants, Gloucester
14–96   CWL Parker, Gloucs v Northants, Northampton

LEADING BATSMEN

	Inns	NO	Runs	HS	Avge
APF Chapman (Kent)	11	1	867	260	86.70
CP Mead (Hants)	40	9	2331	200*	75.19
EH Hendren (Middx)	30	4	1875	201*	72.11
WR Hammond (Gloucs)	38	3	2522	197	72.05
C Hallows (Lancs)	37	10	1889	233*	69.96
A Sandham (Surrey)	32	4	1721	230	61.46
TF Shepherd (Surrey)	35	6	1681	277*	57.96
EH Bowley (Sussex)	36	3	1882	220	57.03
JB Hobbs (Surrey)	22	0	1163	150	52.86
H Sutcliffe (Yorks)	35	4	1625	176	52.41

LEADING BOWLERS

	Runs	Wkts	Avge
H Larwood (Notts)	1500	91	16.48
H Howell (Warwicks)	505	30	16.83
AP Freeman (Kent)	2718	158	17.20
J Mercer (Glamorgan)	1551	89	17.42
GM Lee (Notts)	1268	72	17.61
CF Root (Worcs)	2597	145	17.91
GG Macaulay (Yorks)	2122	118	17.98
G Geary (Leics)	1287	71	18.12
LF Townsend (Derbys)	1206	66	18.27
CWL Parker (Gloucs)	3460	183	18.90

LEADING ALL-ROUNDERS

	Runs (Avge)		Wkts (Avge)	
JA Newman (Hants)	1281	(32.02)	105	(21.46)
MW Tate (Sussex)	1346	(34.51)	119	(20.09)

LEADING WICKET-KEEPERS

	Dismissals		Total
H Smith (Gloucs)	32ct	26st	58
B Lilley (Notts)	47ct	10st	57

The popular 'Patsy' Hendren topped the averages three times in the early 1920s and won many admirers with his infectious enthusiasm and patent love of the game (Hulton Picture Company)

It was a highly successful decade for Sussex's Maurice Tate; in 1925 he achieved his best ever season as a wicket-taker and completed the 'double' for the third successive season (Hulton Picture Company)

Harold Larwood's express bowling for Nottinghamshire enabled him to top the averages. Here, in an unusual study for him, he prepares to go out to bat. Larwood was to finish top bowler four times in six seasons, showing he was much more than the scourge of the Aussies (Hulton Picture Company)

1928

FINAL TABLE

	P	W	L	D W	D L	NR*	Poss Pts	Pts	%
1 Lancashire	30	15	0	9	3	3	240	186	77.50
2 Kent..........	30	15	5	8	1	1	240	167	69.58
3 Nottinghamshire	31	13	3	9	5	1	248	168	67.96
4 Yorkshire.......	26	8	0	8	7	3	208	137	65.86
5 Gloucestershire..	28	9	6	9	0	4	224	133	59.37
6 Surrey	25	5	3	10	6	1	200	112	56.00
7 Sussex	30	12	8	4	6	0	240	134	55.83
8 Middlesex	24	6	5	7	5	1	192	102	53.17
9 Leicestershire ...	28	6	4	6	11	1	224	115	51.33
10 Derbyshire......	25	6	6	4	7	2	200	97	48.50
11 Warwickshire ...	28	3	6	10	7	2	224	103	45.98
12 Hampshire......	28	5	7	5	11	0	224	98	43.75
13 Northamptonshire	28	7	13	3	5	0	224	86	38.37
14 Somerset	23	4	11	3	5	0	184	62	33.69
15 Glamorgan......	24	2	9	1	10	2	192	59	30.72
16 Essex	28	2	13	5	6	2	224	67	29.91
17 Worcestershire ..	30	0	19	2	8	1	240	38	15.83

*NR – more than 6 hours played, but no result on 1st innings.
Less than 6 hours play: Surrey v Glamorgan, Oval; Surrey v
Essex, Oval; Derbys v Somerset, Chesterfield; Surrey v Sussex,
Oval; Yorks v Sussex, Hull; Essex v Notts, Southend; Yorks v
Glamorgan, Huddersfield.

BEST INDIVIDUAL SCORES

300* FB Watson, Lancs v Surrey, Old Trafford
282* A Sandham, Surrey v Lancs, Old Trafford
275 P Holmes, Yorks v Warwicks, Bradford
263* HTW Hardinge, Kent v Gloucs, Gloucester

BEST INNINGS ANALYSES

9-23 WR Hammond, Gloucs v Worcs,
      Cheltenham
8-24 PGH Fender, Surrey v Warwicks, Oval
8-29 VWC Jupp, Northants v Worcs, Dudley
8-40 FJ Durston, Middx v Essex, Leyton

BEST MATCH ANALYSES

15-128 WR Hammond, Gloucs v Worcs,
        Cheltenham
15-154 EA McDonald, Lancs v Kent, Old
        Trafford
15-224 AP Freeman, Kent v Leics, Tonbridge

14-181 AP Freeman, Kent v Essex, Canterbury

LEADING BATSMEN

	Inns	NO	Runs	HS	Avge
H Sutcliffe (Yorks)	29	4	2137	228	85.48
WR Hammond (Gloucs)	35	5	2474	244	82.46
CP Mead (Hants)	44	9	2843	180	81.22
E Tyldesley (Lancs)	33	6	2130	242	78.88
EH Hendren (Middx)	36	4	2471	209*	77.21
JW Hearne (Middx)	12	3	682	223*	75.77
JB Hobbs (Surrey)	27	4	1728	200*	75.13
M Leyland (Yorks)	25	4	1451	247	69.09
FB Watson (Lancs)	39	4	2403	300*	68.65
C Hallows (Lancs)	38	4	2253	232	66.26

LEADING BOWLERS

	Runs	Wkts	Avge
H Larwood (Notts)	1636	116	14.10
AP Freeman (Kent)	3681	216	17.04
MW Tate (Sussex)	2351	127	18.51
VWC Jupp (Northants)	2321	122	19.02
JC White (Somerset)	2452	128	19.15
CS Marriott (Kent)	958	50	19.16
EA McDonald (Lancs)	3443	178	19.34
W Rhodes (Yorks)	1995	103	19.36
RK Tyldesley (Lancs)	1772	85	20.84
J Mercer (Glamorgan)	1966	90	21.84

LEADING ALL-ROUNDERS

	Runs	(Avge)	Wkts	(Avge)
VWC Jupp (Northants)	1407	(41.38)	122	(19.02)
CF Root (Worcs)	1044	(20.88)	116	(29.07)
MW Tate (Sussex)	1174	(30.10)	127	(18.51)

LEADING WICKET-KEEPERS

	Dismissals		Total
LEG Ames (Kent)	52ct	48st	100
G Duckworth (Lancs)	63ct	28st	91

1929

FINAL TABLE

	P	W	L	D W	D L	D NR	Pts
1 Nottinghamshire	28	14	2	4	6	2	158
2 Lancashire	28	12	3	6	6	1	148
3 Yorkshire	28	10	2	9	5	2	148
4 Gloucestershire ..	28	15	6	1	4	2	145
5 Sussex	28	13	6	7	2	0	145
6 Middlesex	28	12	7	6	3	0	135
7 Derbyshire	28	10	6	8	3	1	133
8 Kent	28	12	8	6	2	0	132
9 Leicestershire ...	28	9	6	9	4	0	129
10 Surrey	28	8	7	5	6	2	115
11 Hampshire	28	8	10	0	8	2	96
12 Essex	28	6	9	3	9	1	94
13 Northamptonshire	28	7	13	2	6	0	84
14 Warwickshire....	28	5	13	4	5	1	79
15 Somerset	28	3	17	5	3	0	58
16 Worcestershire ..	28	2	15	3	6	2	57
17 Glamorgan	28	3	19	3	3	0	48

Fixed schedule of 28 matches each county.
Tie or No Result – 4 pts to each side.

BEST INDIVIDUAL SCORES

285* JW Hearne, Middx v Essex, Leyton
285 P Holmes, Yorks v Notts, Trent Bridge
280* EH Bowley, Sussex v Gloucs, Hove
246 KS Duleepsinhji, Sussex v Kent, Hastings

BEST INNINGS ANALYSES

10–18 G Geary, Leics v Glam, Pontypridd
10–40 GOB Allen, Middx v Lancs, Lord's
10–131 AP Freeman, Kent v Lancs, Maidstone
9–39   W Rhodes, Yorks v Essex, Leyton

BEST MATCH ANALYSES

16–96 G Geary, Leics v Glam, Pontypridd
14–43 W Voce, Notts v Northants, Trent Bridge
14–87 AS Kennedy, Hants v Glam, Swansea
14–131 AP Freeman, Kent v Notts, Canterbury

LEADING BATSMEN

	Inns	NO	Runs	HS	Avge
JB Hobbs (Surrey)	27	4	1750	204	76.08
WR Hammond (Gloucs)	31	5	1730	238*	66.53
A Sandham (Surrey)	38	2	2038	187	56.61
KS Duleepsinhji (Sussex)	36	0	2028	246	56.33
RES Wyatt (Warwicks)	40	5	1940	161*	55.42
WW Whysall (Notts)	40	2	2079	244	54.71
H Sutcliffe (Yorks)	28	3	1361	150	54.44
JWH Makepeace (Lancs)	15	3	628	163*	52.33
J O'Connor (Essex)	41	2	1966	157	50.41
CP Mead (Hants)	33	6	1329	166*	49.22

LEADING BOWLERS

	Runs	Wkts	Avge
JC White (Somerset)	2181	149	14.63
MW Tate (Sussex)	1695	114	14.86
JC Clay (Glamorgan)	569	36	15.80
RK Tyldesley (Lancs)	2164	136	15.91
TWJ Goddard (Gloucs)	2460	154	15.97
W Voce (Notts)	1716	107	16.03
AP Freeman (Kent)	3244	199	16.30
G Geary (Leics)	2297	138	16.64
W Rhodes (Yorks)	1464	85	17.22
CWL Parker (Gloucs)	2253	130	17.33

LEADING ALL-ROUNDERS

	Runs (Avge)	Wkts (Avge)
NE Haig (Middx)	1136 (25.24)	100 (22.52)
JC White (Somerset)	1059 (29.41)	149 (14.63)

LEADING WICKET-KEEPERS

	Dismissals		Total
LEG Ames (Kent)	62ct	40st	102
WH Livsey (Hants)	42ct	29st	71

1930

FINAL TABLE

	P	W	L	D W	L	NR	Pts
I Lancashire	28	10	0	8	5	5	155
2 Gloucestershire ..	28	15	4	2	6	1	152
3 Yorkshire	28	11	2	6	4	5	150
4 Nottinghamshire .	28	9	1	10	5	3	149
5 Kent	28	12	7	5	4	0	133
6 Essex	28	7	5	7	6	3	121
7 Sussex	28	7	5	6	8	2	118
8 Surrey..........	28	3	4	13	5	3	116
9 Derbyshire	28	7	8	4	6	3	106
10 Worcestershire ..	28	5	9	8	5	1	99
11 Glamorgan	28	5	9	6	4	4	98
12 Leicestershire ...	28	4	10	6	5	3	89
13 Hampshire	28	5	8	1	14	0	87
14 Somerset	28	4	11	7	4	2	87
15 Warwickshire....	28	2	9	8	7	2	85
16 Middlesex	28	3	9	3	10	3	81
17 Northamptonshire	28	4	12	3	5	4	78

BEST INDIVIDUAL SCORES

333 KS Duleepsinhji, Sussex v Northants, Hove
278 TE Cook, Sussex v Hants, Hove
262* M Nichol, Worcs v Hants, Bournemouth
256* E Tyldesley, Lancs v Warwicks, Old
  Trafford

BEST INNINGS ANALYSES

10-53 AP Freeman, Kent v Essex, Southend
 9-44 CWL Parker, Gloucs v Warwicks,
  Cheltenham
 9-50 AP Freeman, Kent v Derbys, Ilkeston
 9-60 H Verity, Yorks v Glam, Swansea

BEST MATCH ANALYSES

16-94 AP Freeman, Kent v Essex, Southend
15-91 CWL Parker, Gloucs v Surrey, Cheltenham
14-48 AG Slater, Derbys v Somerset, Chesterfield
14-97 CWL Parker, Gloucs v Warwicks,
  Cheltenham

LEADING BATSMEN

	Inns	NO	Runs	HS	Avge
M Leyland (Yorks)	26	4	1473	211*	66.95
H Sutcliffe (Yorks)	19	3	980	150*	61.25
KS Duleepsinhji (Sussex)	25	2	1375	333	59.78
E Oldroyd (Yorks)	26	7	1112	164*	58.52
E Tyldesley (Lancs)	41	8	1811	256*	54.87
JB Hobbs (Surrey)	22	1	1142	137	54.38
A Mitchell (Yorks)	34	6	1441	176	51.46
A Sandham (Surrey)	40	3	1884	204	50.91
WR Hammond (Gloucs)	27	4	1168	199	50.78
FE Woolley (Kent)	40	4	1823	120	50.63

LEADING BOWLERS

	Runs	Wkts	Avge
IAR Peebles (Middx)	480	44	10.90
H Verity (Yorks)	595	52	11.44
CWL Parker (Gloucs)	1929	162	11.90
H Larwood (Notts)	1125	89	12.64
RK Tyldesley (Lancs)	1783	121	14.73
AP Freeman (Kent)	3850	249	15.46
GOB Allen (Middx)	449	26	17.26
WE Bowes (Yorks)	1317	76	17.32
JC Clay (Glamorgan)	468	27	17.33
JC White (Somerset)	1461	111	17.66

LEADING ALL-ROUNDERS

	Runs (Avge)		Wkts (Avge)	
WE Astill (Leics)	1010	(25.89)	106	(21.59)
Jas Langridge (Sussex)	1094	(29.56)	99	(19.39)
JC White (Somerset)	958	(27.37)	111	(17.66)

LEADING WICKET-KEEPERS

	Dismissals		Total
LEG Ames (Kent)	41ct	41st	82
WL Cornford (Sussex)	42ct	24st	66

1931

FINAL TABLE

	P	W	L	D W	D L	NR	Pts
1 Yorkshire	28	16	1	4	1	6	287
2 Gloucestershire . .	28	11	4	7	5	1	219
3 Kent	28	12	7	3	3	3	216
4 Sussex	28	10	6	8	1	3	205
5 Nottinghamshire .	28	9	3	9	6	1	202
6 Lancashire	28	7	4	7	6	4	174
7 Derbyshire	28	7	6	8	3	4	170
8 Surrey	28	6	4	7	7	4	162
9 Warwickshire	28	6	5	5	7	5*	156
10 Essex	28	7	11	5	4	1	146
11 Middlesex	28	5	8	9	2	4	142
12 Hampshire	28	5	9	4	6	4	129
13 Somerset	28	6	11	2	8	1	128
14 Worcestershire . .	28	5	10	4	7	2	124
15 Glamorgan	28	4	11	1	8	4	105
16 Leicestershire . . .	28	2	7	7	10	2*	103
17 Northamptonshire	28	2	13	3	9	1	76

Including one tie on 1st innings.
Changes to points system: 15 for a win, 7.5 to each side if scores are level in finished match. 1st innings tie in drawn match – 4 pts to each side.

BEST INDIVIDUAL SCORES

250 P Holmes, Yorks v Warwicks, Edgbaston
232 EH Hendren, Middx v Notts, Trent Bridge
230 H Sutcliffe, Yorks v Kent, Folkestone
206 ET Killick, Middx v Warwicks, Lord's

BEST INNINGS ANALYSES

10–36 H Verity, Yorks v Warwicks, Headingley
10–79 AP Freeman, Kent v Lancs, Old Trafford
9–23 CF Root, Worcs v Lancs, Worcester
9–26 AEG Baring, Hants v Essex, Colchester

BEST MATCH ANALYSES

15–94   AP Freeman, Kent v Somerset, Canterbury
15–113 CWL Parker, Gloucs v Notts, Bristol
15–142 AP Freeman, Kent v Essex, Gravesend
15–144 AP Freeman, Kent v Leics, Maidstone

LEADING BATSMEN

	Inns	NO	Runs	HS	Avge
H Sutcliffe (Yorks)	27	6	2049	230	97.57
EH Hendren (Middx)	42	7	2122	232	60.62
KS Duleepsinhji (Sussex)	34	2	1859	162	58.09
JH Parsons (Warwicks)	23	6	957	119*	56.29
DR Jardine (Surrey)	14	6	406	80*	50.75
CB Harris (Notts)	18	9	456	64	50.66
JB Hobbs (Surrey)	40	5	1748	147	49.94
A Sandham (Surrey)	42	7	1624	175	46.40
WR Hammond (Gloucs)	36	6	1389	168*	46.30
FE Woolley (Kent)	41	4	1659	188	44.83

LEADING BOWLERS

	Runs	Wkts	Avge
H Larwood (Notts)	1294	105	12.32
H Verity (Yorks)	1703	138	12.34
CWL Parker (Gloucs)	2962	205	14.44
MW Tate (Sussex)	1638	111	14.75
CS Marriott (Kent)	927	61	15.19
AP Freeman (Kent)	3667	241	15.21
LF Townsend (Derbys)	1098	72	15.25
JC Clay (Glamorgan)	458	30	15.26
WE Bowes (Yorks)	1667	109	15.29
GG Macaulay (Yorks)	1170	76	15.39

LEADING ALL-ROUNDERS

	Runs (Avge)		Wkts (Avge)	
VWC Jupp (Northants)	1329	(30.90)	100	(24.20)
MS Nichols (Essex)	761	(20.02)	89	(18.58)

LEADING WICKET-KEEPERS

	Dismissals		Total
H Elliott (Derbys)	43ct	29st	72
WFF Price (Middx)	44ct	19st	63

THE TYKE ASCENDANCY

The inter-war period undeniably belonged to the North of England; apart from 1920 and 1921 when Middlesex, perhaps to their own surprise, 'pulled out a Plum', the Championship was usually a Lancashire/ Yorkshire carve-up, with the only relief coming also from the North in the form of Notts and Derbyshire, Champions once each.

In the twenties, the Roses counties were roughly on a par. The Red Rose attack of Parkin, Dick Tyldesley and the mighty Tasmanian McDonald just about matched their Yorkshire counterparts in Roy Kilner, the veteran Rhodes, Waddington, Robinson and Macaulay. Yorkshire had a great opening pair, Sutcliffe and Holmes, but perhaps Ernest Tyldesley, Hallows, Watson et al gave Lancashire the edge in batting depth. Duckworth (Lancs) and Dolphin (Yorks) sound as if water-sports should have been their hobby, but they were in fact outstanding wicket-keepers.

The North at this time had things all its own way; for the South, Middlesex faded away from their early triumphs, while Surrey rarely showed. No challenge of any sort emanated from the Midlands.

If Lancashire stayed with them in the twenties, Yorkshire certainly took over in the next decade. To some extent their 1930s dominance was a surprise. Hirst and Rhodes – all-rounders without equal – had gone, and before long they were followed by Holmes and Edgar Oldroyd, both fine batsmen. On the bowling front, the much-loved Roy Kilner had died; paceman Abe Waddington gave up the unequal battle

with injuries; archetypal Yorkshireman Emmott Robinson, as intense a competitor as ever wore the white rose, found age and his feet finally getting the better of him; while George Macaulay, though lasting well into the thirties, saw his best days in the previous decade. Meanwhile wicket-keeper Arthur Dolphin departed when his friend Kilner died, and almost a whole team of established players had been lost.

Luckily the county was able to dip into what then seemed to be a bottomless pit of talent. On the batting front, the established Sutcliffe and Leyland were joined by such doughty warriors as Wilf Barber, 'Ticker' Mitchell and, best of all, the young Leonard Hutton. Skipper Brian Sellers – unique among pre-war Yorkshire skippers in being *nearly* worth a place – wicket-keeper Arthur Booth and all-rounders Frank Smailes and Colin Turner made up a middle-order daunting enough to give high blood-pressure to opposing bowlers, for whom early encouragement from the top batting was rare. Finally the slow left-armer Verity and the pacey Bowes were bowlers in the authentic Yorkshire tradition of meanness and malice, and with Smailes, off-spinner Ellis Robinson and the rarely-needed Leyland and Turner, made up a pretty awesome attack.

Yorkshire would aim for a big score, leaving the best part of two days to roll over the opposition twice. A simple ploy, not always attractive to the uncommitted, but mightily effective nonetheless.

But this Yorkshire team should *not* have been so effective. Player-by-player they were not emphatically superior to some other counties, dressing-room harmony and bonhomie were in short supply, and young newcomers were rarely welcomed or made to feel part of the team. Yet for ten years, all challenges for their top spot were treated with disdain, and at the outbreak of war their position seemed as unassailable as ever.

Bill Bowes contributed much towards Yorkshire's success, though his 'express deliveries' sometimes provoked criticisms, alleging unnecessary intimidation (Hulton Picture Company)

1932

FINAL TABLE

	P	W	L	D W	D L	NR	Pts
1 Yorkshire	28	19	2	3	1	3	315
2 Sussex	28	14	1	4	4	5	262
3 Kent	28	14	3	1	7	3	248
4 Nottinghamshire	28	13	4	6	4	1	241
5 Surrey	28	9	2	10	3	4	210
6 Lancashire	28	8	6	7	4	3	179
7 Somerset	28	8	7	3	7	3	168
8 Hampshire	28	8	10	3	6	1	157
9 Warwickshire	28	5	5	8	8	2	147
10 Derbyshire	28	6	8	5	6	3	145
11 Middlesex	28	6	9	8	5	0	145
12 Leicestershire . . .	28	6	11	7	3	1	138
13 Gloucestershire . .	28	6	12	6	1	3	135
14 Essex	28	4	14	2	6	2	96
15 Glamorgan	28	3	12	2	9	2	90
16 Northamptonshire	28	3	15	3	5	2	83
17 Worcestershire . .	28	1	12	6	5	4	76

No play possible on first 2 days – match played to one-day laws: winning side 10 pts, losing side 3.

BEST INDIVIDUAL SCORES

313 H Sutcliffe, Yorks v Essex, Leyton
270 H Sutcliffe, Yorks v Sussex, Headingley
264 WR Hammond, Gloucs v Lancs, Liverpool
242 WW Keeton, Notts v Glamorgan, Trent
  Bridge

BEST INNINGS ANALYSES

10–10   H Verity, Yorks v Notts, Headingley
10–127 VWC Jupp, Northants v Kent,
       Tunbridge Wells
9–51   JC White, Somerset v Glamorgan, Bath
9–61   AP Freeman, Kent v Warwicks,
       Folkestone

BEST MATCH ANALYSES

17–92   AP Freeman, Kent v Warwicks,
       Folkestone
16–82   AP Freeman, Kent v Northants,
       Tunbridge Wells

15–96   JC White, Somerset v Glamorgan, Bath
14–198 TWJ Goddard, Gloucs v Hants,
       Gloucester

LEADING BATSMEN

	Inns	NO	Runs	HS	Avge
H Sutcliffe (Yorks)	35	5	2624	313	87.46
LEG Ames (Kent)	36	6	1958	180	65.26
WR Hammond (Gloucs)	37	4	2039	264	61.78
M Leyland (Yorks)	29	2	1624	189	60.11
JB Hobbs (Surrey)	30	3	1460	123	54.07
E Tyldesley (Lancs)	44	6	1962	225*	51.63
LG Crawley (Essex)	15	0	744	155	49.60
J O'Connor (Essex)	31	6	1212	119	48.48
EH Hendren (Middx)	34	3	1488	145	48.00
P Holmes (Yorks)	23	3	946	224*	47.30

LEADING BOWLERS

	Runs	Wkts	Avge
H Larwood (Notts)	1639	141	11.62
H Verity (Yorks)	1856	135	13.74
WE Bowes (Yorks)	2364	169	14.77
AP Freeman (Kent)	3205	209	15.33
MW Tate (Sussex)	1932	124	15.58
JC White (Somerset)	1616	102	15.84
FR Brown (Surrey)	1519	95	15.98
J Iddon (Lancs)	1216	76	16.00
Jas Langridge (Sussex)	1498	92	16.28
CS Marriott (Kent)	1040	63	16.50

LEADING ALL-ROUNDERS

	Runs (Avge)	Wkts (Avge)
VWC Jupp (Northants)	1539 (34.20)	106 (21.09)
LF Townsend (Derby)	1350 (30.68)	104 (18.63)

LEADING WICKET-KEEPERS

	Dismissals		Total
LEG Ames (Kent)	32ct	52st	84
JA Smart (Warwicks)	54ct	23st	77

1933

FINAL TABLE

	P	W	L	D W	D L	NR	Poss Pts	Pts	%
1 Yorkshire	30	19	3	3	5	0	450	315	70.00
2 Sussex	32	18	5	7	2	0	480	311	64.79
3 Kent	30	15	8	3	3	1	450	253	56.22
4 Essex	28	13	8	4	3	0	420	224	53.33
5 Lancashire	28	9	1	10	7	1	420	210	50.00
6 Derbyshire......	28	11	11	3	3	0	420	189	45.00
7 Warwickshire ...	28	9	5	5	8	1	420	188	44.76
8 Nottinghamshire	28	7	3	7	8	3	420	176	41.90
9 Surrey	26	6	5	12	3	0	390	159	40.76
10 Gloucestershire..	30	10	13	5	2	0	450	181	40.22
11 Somerset	26	6	10	2	5	3	390	127	32.56
12 Middlesex	26	7	14	2	2	1	390	125	32.05
13 Northamptonshire	24	5	11	5	3	0	360	109	30.27
14 Hampshire......	28	2	9	4	11	2	420	91	21.66
15 Worcestershire ..	30	2	13	7	6	2	450	91	20.22
16 Glamorgan......	24	1	9	5	7	2	360	69	19.16
17 Leicestershire ...	26	3	15	1	7	0	390	71	18.20

Points system unchanged; rankings revert to percentage of points to possible points.

BEST INDIVIDUAL SCORES

301* EH Hendren, Middx v Worcs, Dudley
295　LEG Ames, Kent v Gloucs, Folkestone
283　EH Bowley, Sussex v Middx, Hove
269　TH Barling, Surey v Hants, Southampton

BEST INNINGS ANALYSES

9-33 JL Hopwood, Lancs v Leics, Old
　　　Trafford
9-44 H Verity, Yorks v Essex, Leyton
9-59 H Verity, Yorks v Kent, Dover
8-26 LF Townsend, Derbys v Gloucs,
　　　Chesterfield

BEST MATCH ANALYSES

17-91　H Verity, Yorks v Essex, Leyton
15-122 AP Freeman, Kent v Middx, Lord's
14-90　LF Townsend, Derbys v Gloucs,
　　　　Chesterfield
14-149 AP Freeman, Kent v Sussex, Hastings

LEADING BATSMEN

	Inns	NO	Runs	HS	Avge
CP Mead (Hants)	42	6	2478	227	68.83
WR Hammond (Gloucs)	44	4	2578	239	64.45
EH Hendren (Middx)	46	7	2479	301*	63.56
M Leyland (Yorks)	39	4	1969	210*	56.25
LEG Ames (Kent)	45	4	2150	295	52.43
CF Walters (Worcs)	45	3	2165	226	51.54
RES Wyatt (Warwicks)	37	6	1592	187*	51.35
J Iddon (Lancs)	36	6	1520	204*	50.66
AH Bakewell (Northants)	40	1	1925	257	49.35
A Mitchell (Yorks)	40	8	1547	150*	48.34

LEADING BOWLERS

	Runs	Wkts	Avge
H Verity (Yorks)	1826	153	11.93
AP Freeman (Kent)	3740	252	14.84
GG Macaulay (Yorks)	1761	115	15.31
Jas Langridge (Sussex)	2109	136	15.50
K Farnes (Essex)	1077	67	16.07
LF Townsend (Derbys)	1472	87	16.91
WE Bowes (Yorks)	2139	123	17.39
TWJ Goddard (Gloucs)	3016	170	17.74
EW Clark (Northants)	1264	68	18.58
TB Mitchell (Derbys)	2568	136	18.88

LEADING ALL-ROUNDERS

	Runs (Avge)		Wkts (Avge)	
Jas Langridge (Sussex)	1340	(41.87)	136	(15.50)
MS Nichols (Essex)	1290	(31.46)	114	(21.41)
AW Wellard (Somerset)	1055	(27.76)	103	(25.01)

LEADING WICKET-KEEPERS

	Dismissals		Total
H Elliott (Derbys)	65ct	19st	84
EWJ Brooks (Surrey)	66ct	7st	73

1934

FINAL TABLE

	P	W	L	D W	L	NR	Poss Pts	Pts	%
1 Lancashire	30	13	3	10	4	0	450	257	57.11
2 Sussex	30	12	2	7	8	1	450	243	54.00
3 Derbyshire......	28	12	6	6	3	1	420	223	53.09
4 Warwickshire ...	24	10	4	4	4	2	360	190	52.77
5 Kent..........	30	12	7	6	5	0	450	225	50.00
6 Yorkshire.......	30	12	7	5	4	2	450	225	50.00
7 Gloucestershire..	30	12	10	2	4	2	450	210	46.66
8 Essex	28	9	4	5	9	1	420	191	45.47
9 Nottinghamshire	28	8	7	7	6	0	420	173	41.10
10 Middlesex	28	8	9	7	2	2	420	169	40.23
11 Surrey	26	6	8	9	3	0	390	144	36.92
12 Leicestershire ...	24	6	9	3	6	0	360	123	34.16
13 Glamorgan......	24	3	8	5	5	3	360	97	26.94
14 Hampshire......	28	3	11	8	5	1	420	104	24.76
15 Somerset	24	3	10	0	11	0	360	78	21.66
16 Worcestershire ..	28	3	12	3	9	1	420	91	21.66
17 Northamptonshire	24	2	17	3	2	0	360	51	14.16

BEST INDIVIDUAL SCORES

332 WH Ashdown, Kent v Essex, Brentwood
302* WR Hammond, Gloucs v Glamorgan, Bristol
290 WR Hammond, Gloucs v Kent,
   Tunbridge Wells
265* WR Hammond, Gloucs v Worcs, Dudley

BEST INNINGS ANALYSES

9-34 Jas Langridge, Sussex v Yorks, Sheffield
9-37 TWJ Goddard, Gloucs v Leics, Bristol
9-66 RJ Partridge, Northants v Warwicks,
   Kettering
9-92 JM Sims, Middx v Lancs, Old Trafford

BEST MATCH ANALYSES

14-206 AP Freeman, Kent v Northants, Dover
13-88 TB Mitchell, Derbys v Worcs,
   Stourbridge
13-90 JL Hopwood, Lancs v Derbys, Old
   Trafford
13-113 TB Mitchell, Derbys v Middx, Derby

LEADING BATSMEN

	Inns	NO	Runs	HS	Avge
WR Hammond (Gloucs)	20	4	2020	302*	126.25
CF Walters (Worcs)	22	3	1172	178	61.68
LEG Ames (Kent)	29	4	1512	202*	60.48
J O'Connor (Essex)	44	6	2221	248	58.44
E Tyldesley (Lancs)	47	8	2227	239	57.10
TE Cook (Sussex)	43	6	2072	220	56.00
J Iddon (Lancs)	47	6	2261	200*	55.14
A Mitchell (Yorks)	34	4	1652	181	55.06
HHI Gibbons (Worcs)	51	6	2452	157	54.58
FE Woolley (Kent)	47	1	2447	176	53.19

LEADING BOWLERS

	Runs	Wkts	Avge
H Verity (Yorks)	1210	79	15.31
WE Bowes (Yorks)	1530	97	15.77
K Farnes (Essex)	607	37	16.40
JC Clay (Glamorgan)	1655	100	16.55
G Geary (Leics)	981	59	16.62
GAE Paine (Warwicks)	2521	150	16.80
H Larwood (Notts)	1316	78	16.87
IAR Peebles (Middx)	751	44	17.06
CIJ Smith (Middx)	2407	139	17.31
TB Mitchell (Derbys)	2400	138	17.39

LEADING ALL-ROUNDERS

	Runs (Avge)	Wkts (Avge)
JL Hopwood (Lancs)	1583 (41.65)	110 (17.89)
RA Sinfield (Gloucs)	1152 (32.00)	119 (22.70)

LEADING WICKET-KEEPERS

	Dismissals		Total
G Duckworth (Lancs)	52ct	24st	76
H Elliott (Derbys)	56ct	19st	75
A Wood (Yorks)	63ct	12st	75

1935

FINAL TABLE

	P	W	L	D W	D L	NR	Poss Pts	Pts	%
1 Yorkshire	30	19	1	3	7	0	450	321	71.33
2 Derbyshire	28	16	6	4	2	0	420	266	63.33
3 Middlesex	24	11	5	6	1	1	360	202	56.11
4 Lancashire	28	12	6	8	1	1	420	227	54.04
5 Nottinghamshire	28	10	3	8	5	2	420	213	50.71
6 Leicestershire . . .	24	11	9	2	2	0	360	181	50.27
7 Sussex	32	13	10	3	2	4	480	232	48.33
8 Warwickshire . . .	24	9	6	3	6	0	360	168	46.66
9 Essex	28	11	12	3	2	0	420	186	44.28
10 Kent	30	10	12	5	2	1	450	185	41.11
11 Surrey	26	7	5	5	7	2	390	159	40.76
12 Worcestershire . .	30	9	16	0	4	1	450	151	33.55
13 Glamorgan	26	6	11	5	2	2	390	129	33.07
14 Somerset	26	5	11	4	6	0	390	113	28.97
15 Gloucestershire . .	30	6	16	2	6	0	450	118	26.22
16 Hampshire	30	5	16	1	8	0	450	104	23.11
17 Northamptonshire	24	1	16	3	2	2	360	44	12.22

Sussex v Northants – tie on first innings.

BEST INDIVIDUAL SCORES

305* WH Ashdown, Kent v Derbys, Dover
255 W Barber, Yorks v Surrey, Sheffield
252 WR Hammond, Gloucs v Leics, Leicester
229 FE Woolley, Kent v Surrey, Oval

BEST INNINGS ANALYSES

10–64 TB Mitchell, Derbys v Leics, Leicester
9–45 PF Jackson, Worcs v Somerset, Dudley
9–54 JC Clay, Glamorgan v Northants, Llanelli
8–17 WE Bowes, Yorks v Northants, Kettering

BEST INNINGS ANALYSES

16–35 WE Bowes, Yorks v Northants, Kettering
15–86 JC Clay, Glamorgan v Northants, Llanelli
14–78 H Verity, Yorks v Hants, Hull
14–115 AP Freeman, Kent v Essex, Gravesend

LEADING BATSMEN

	Inns	NO	Runs	HS	Avge
H Sutcliffe (Yorks)	36	3	1966	212	59.57
EH Hendren (Middx)	38	6	1649	195	51.53
W Barber (Yorks)	36	3	1678	255	50.84
ERT Holmes (Surrey)	35	4	1570	206	50.64
RES Wyatt (Warwicks)	34	5	1400	111*	48.27
E Tyldesley (Lancs)	14	1	602	137	46.30
WR Hammond (Gloucs)	42	3	1803	252	46.23
A Melville (Sussex)	38	3	1555	110	44.42
J Iddon (Lancs)	28	2	1155	141	44.42
HW Parks (Sussex)	47	13	1495	119*	43.97

LEADING BOWLERS

	Runs	Wkts	Avge
JC Clay (Glamorgan)	713	56	12.73
WE Bowes (Yorks)	1819	138	13.18
H Verity (Yorks)	2196	161	13.63
G Geary (Leics)	1652	110	15.01
MS Nichols (Essex)	2069	132	15.67
WH Copson (Derbys)	1174	71	16.53
RWV Robins (Middx)	1022	60	17.03
HA Smith (Leics)	2598	143	18.16
Jas Langridge (Sussex)	1653	90	18.36
CIJ Smith (Middx)	1642	89	18.44

LEADING ALL-ROUNDERS

	Runs (Avge)	Wkts (Avge)
MS Nichols (Essex)	1100 (23.91)	132 (15.67)
E Davies (Glam)	1202 (27.31)	93 (20.77)
JL Hopwood (Lancs)	1282 (30.52)	95 (19.58)
Jas Langridge (Sussex)	1122 (32.05)	90 (18.36)
JH Parks (Sussex)	1605 (34.89)	95 (20.06)
AW Wellard (Somerset)	1198 (33.27)	97 (20.75)

LEADING WICKET-KEEPERS

	Dismissals		Total
H Elliott (Derbys)	67ct	21st	88
B Lilley (Notts)	56ct	4st	60
JA Smart (Warwicks)	43ct	17st	60
A Wood (Yorks)	43ct	17st	60

1936

FINAL TABLE

	P	W	L	D W	D L	D NR	Poss Pts	Pts	%
1 Derbyshire	28	13	4	5	5	1	420	239	56.90
2 Middlesex	26	10	4	8	3	1	390	203	52.05
3 Yorkshire	30	10	2	12	4	2	450	230	51.11
4 Gloucestershire	30	10	7	*4	8	1	450	203	45.11
5 Nottinghamshire	28	8	3	9	8	0	420	189	45.00
6 Surrey	30	9	7	6	6	2	450	191	42.44
7 Somerset	26	9	10	2	3	2	390	162	41.53
8 Kent	28	9	9	4	5	1	420	174	41.42
9 Essex	26	8	8	5	5	0	390	160	41.02
10 Hampshire	30	7	5	9	9	0	450	177	39.33
11 Lancashire	30	7	6	7	5	5	450	175	38.88
12 Worcestershire	28	7	9	4	7	1	420	150	35.71
13 Warwickshire	24	4	8	2	7	3	360	103	28.61
14 Sussex	30	4	10	7	6	3	450	125	27.77
15 Leicestershire	24	2	5	8	8	1	360	98	27.22
16 Glamorgan	26	1	12	6	5	2	390	68	17.43
17 Northamptonshire	24	0	9	*5	9	1	360	61	16.94

*Includes 1 point for a win on 1st innings under one-day laws.

BEST INDIVIDUAL SCORES

317 WR Hammond, Gloucs v Notts, Gloucester
280* RJ Duckfield, Glamorgan v Surrey, Oval
263 M Leyland, Yorks v Essex, Hull
257 AE Fagg, Kent v Hants, Southampton

BEST INNINGS ANALYSES

10–51 J Mercer, Glamorgan v Worcs,
  Worcester
9–12 H Verity, Yorks v Kent, Sheffield
9–32 MS Nichols, Essex v Notts, Trent Bridge
9–48 H Verity, Yorks v Essex, Westcliff

BEST MATCH ANALYSES

15–38 H Verity, Yorks v Kent, Sheffield
15–100 H Verity, Yorks v Essex, Westcliff
14–139 HL Hazell, Somerset v Northants,
  Kettering
14–146 AR Gover, Surrey v Warwicks,
  Edgbaston

LEADING BATSMEN

	Inns	NO	Runs	HS	Avge
NS Mitchell-Innes (Somerset)	11	2	499	182	55.44
LB Fishlock (Surrey)	41	9	1656	133*	51.75
GOB Allen (Middx)	14	5	456	137	50.66
CS Dempster (Leics)	32	6	1271	164*	48.88
E Paynter (Lancs)	49	9	1930	177	48.25
EH Hendren (Middx)	42	1	1963	156	47.87
WR Hammond (Gloucs)	33	3	1432	317	47.73
RJO Meyer (Somerset)	11	2	420	202*	46.66
M Leyland (Yorks)	32	4	1291	263	46.10
CJ Barnett (Gloucs)	46	2	1885	204*	42.84

LEADING BOWLERS

	Runs	Wkts	Avge
WE Bowes (Yorks)	1344	109	12.33
H Verity (Yorks)	1942	153	12.69
WH Copson (Derbys)	1792	140	12.80
H Larwood (Notts)	1499	116	12.92
CIJ Smith (Middx)	1575	104	15.14
AR Gover (Surrey)	2638	171	15.42
GOB Allen (Middx)	899	54	16.64
AV Pope (Derbys)	1666	94	17.72
AW Wellard (Somerset)	2436	134	18.17
LC Eastman (Essex)	1187	65	18.26

LEADING ALL-ROUNDERS

	Runs (Avge)	Wkts (Avge)
MS Nichols (Essex)	1224 (29.85)	108 (18.47)
WLC Creese (Hants)	1295 (31.58)	92 (22.57)
LJ Todd (Kent)	1124 (26.76)	91 (21.59)

LEADING WICKET-KEEPERS

	Dismissals		Total
EWJ Brooks (Surrey)	66ct	6st	72
WFF Price (Middx)	53ct	16st	69

1937

FINAL TABLE

	P	W	L	D W	L	NR	Poss Pts	Pts	%
1 Yorkshire	28	18	2	4	4	0	420	302	71.90
2 Middlesex	24	15	4	3	2	0	360	246	68.33
3 Derbyshire	28	14	6	2	4	2	420	240	57.14
4 Gloucestershire . .	30	15	10	2	3	0	450	244	54.22
5 Sussex	32	13	7	8	4	0	480	247	51.45
6 Essex	28	13	11	2	1	1	420	212	50.47
7 Glamorgan	28	11	7	4	6	0	420	203	48.33
8 Surrey	26	8	5	7	4	2	390	175	44.87
9 Lancashire	32	9	5	12	6	0	480	213	44.37
10 Nottinghamshire	28	6	4	8	8	2	420	162	38.57
11 Warwickshire . . .	24	6	8	6	4	0	360	132	36.66
12 Kent	28	8	16	2	2	0	420	136	32.38
13 Somerset	28	7	14	2	5	0	420	130	30.95
14 Hampshire	28	7	16	4	1	0	420	128	30.47
15 Worcestershire . .	30	8	17	0	5	0	450	135	30.00
16 Leicestershire . . .	26	1	11	3	11	0	390	63	16.15
17 Northamptonshire	24	0	16	4	3	1	360	33	9.16

BEST INDIVIDUAL SCORES

322 E Paynter, Lancs v Sussex, Hove
316 RH Moore, Hants v Warwicks,
    Bournemouth
271* L Hutton, Yorks v Derbys, Sheffield
266 J Hardstaff, Notts v Leics, Leicester
266 E Paynter, Lancs v Essex, Old Trafford

BEST INNINGS ANALYSES

10-113 TWJ Goddard, Gloucs v Worcs,
    Cheltenham
9-42 J Iddon, Lancs, v Yorks, Sheffield
9-43 H Verity, Yorks v Warwicks, Headingley
9-59 JC Clay, Glamorgan v Essex, Westcliff

BEST MATCH ANALYSES

17-212 JC Clay, Glamorgan v Worcs, Swansea
16-181 TWJ Goddard, Gloucs v Worcs,
    Cheltenham
15-106 RTD Perks, Worcs v Essex, Worcester
14-92 H Verity, Yorks v Warwicks, Headingley

LEADING BATSMEN

	Inns	NO	Runs	HS	Avge
J Hardstaff (Notts)	29	2	1802	266	66.74
WR Hammond (Gloucs)	40	4	2393	217	66.47
E Paynter (Lancs)	42	2	2356	322	58.90
L Hutton (Yorks)	36	5	1728	271*	55.74
CS Dempster (Leics)	21	2	1042	154*	54.84
RES Wyatt (Warwicks)	36	3	1807	232	54.75
LEG Ames (Kent)	37	2	1909	201*	54.54
LG Berry (Leics)	48	4	2245	184*	51.02
JH Parks (Sussex)	54	3	2578	168	50.54
RJ Gregory (Surrey)	41	3	1889	154	49.71

LEADING BOWLERS

	Runs	Wkts	Avge
ADG Matthews (Glam)	556	41	13.56
H Verity (Yorks)	2270	157	14.45
CIJ Smith (Middx)	1926	118	16.32
TWJ Goddard (Gloucs)	3530	215	16.41
JC Clay (Glamorgan)	2956	170	17.38
MS Nichols (Essex)	2365	129	18.33
TPB Smith (Essex)	2718	146	18.61
WH Copson (Derbys)	1343	72	18.65
AR Gover (Surrey)	2625	139	18.88
JM Sims (Middx)	1728	91	18.98

LEADING ALL-ROUNDERS

	Runs (Avge)		Wkts (Avge)	
WHR Andrews (Somerset)	1044	(20.88)	131	(19.45)
SH Martin (Worcs)	1073	(21.89)	103	(20.43)
MS Nichols (Essex)	1072	(24.93)	129	(18.33)

LEADING WICKET-KEEPERS

	Dismissals		Total
WFF Price (Middx)	55ct	24st	79
WT Luckes (Somerset)	52ct	23st	75

1938

FINAL TABLE

		P	W	L	D	LI	DI	Pts	Avge
I	Yorkshire	28	20	2	6	0	4	256	9.14
2	Middlesex	22	15	5	2	0	I	184	8.36
3	Surrey	25	12	6	7	2	5	172	6.88
4	Lancashire	28	14	6	8	0	6	192	6.85
5	Derbyshire	25	11	8	6	3	4	160	6.40
6	Essex	26	12	11	3	3	2	164	6.30
7	Somerset	25	10	9	6	I	5	144	5.76
8	Sussex	29	11	9	9	3	3	156	5.37
9	Kent	27	8	14	5	2	4	120	4.44
10	Gloucestershire . .	28	8	13	7	2	4	122	4.35
11	Worcestershire . .	30	9	11	10	2	3	128	4.26
12	Nottinghamshire .	25	7	10	8	2	3	106	4.24
13	Warwickshire . . .	22	7	7	8	0	2	92	4.18
14	Hampshire	30	9	16	5	4	0	124	4.13
15	Leicestershire . . .	22	4	9	9	I	7	80	3.63
16	Glamorgan	22	5	9	8	I	3	76	3.45
17	Northamptonshire	24	0	17	7	3	I	16	0.66

LI – Ist-innings lead in match lost. DI – Ist-innings lead in match drawn.

Points system: I2pts for win, 6 to each side if scores are level in finished match; 4 pts for Ist-innings lead (by a side which does not win) and 2 pts for Ist-innings tie. In case of no play or no result on Ist innings, match is not included in 'Played' total. If no play on first two days, one-day laws apply, with 8 points for win. Championship rankings decided by points gained divided by matches played.

BEST INDIVIDUAL SCORES

291 E Paynter, Lancs v Hants, Southampton
271 WR Hammond, Gloucs v Lancs, Bristol
245 WJ Edrich, Middx v Notts, Lord's
244 AE Fagg, Kent v Essex, Colchester

BEST INNINGS ANALYSES

9–37 MS Nichols, Essex v Gloucs, Gloucester
9–57 GS Boyes, Hants v Somerset, Yeovil
8–38 K Farnes, Essex v Glamorgan, Clacton
8–40 HA Smith, Leics v Gloucs, Bristol

BEST MATCH ANALYSES

15–113 K Farnes, Essex v Glamorgan, Clacton
15–165 MS Nichols, Essex v Gloucs, Gloucester
14–85 AR Gover, Surrey v Worcs,
Kidderminster
14–90 AE Watt, Kent v Middx, Maidstone

LEADING BATSMEN

	Inns	NO	Runs	HS	Avge
WR Hammond (Gloucs)	28	2	2180	271	83.84
WJ Edrich (Middx)	29	3	1675	245	64.42
E Paynter (Lancs)	35	4	1873	291	60.41
J Hardstaff (Notts)	25	4	1215	162	57.85
AE Fagg (Kent)	47	5	2297	244	54.69
HT Bartlett (Sussex)	24	3	1072	114	51.04
DCS Compton (Middx)	27	3	1195	180*	49.79
BH Valentine (Kent)	29	1	1363	242	48.67
CS Dempster (Leics)	21	1	970	142	48.50
Jn Langridge (Sussex)	52	4	2302	227	47.95

LEADING BOWLERS

	Runs	Wkts	Avge
H Verity (Yorks)	1523	111	13.72
ADG Matthews (Glam)	356	25	14.24
WE Bowes (Yorks)	1426	100	14.26
K Farnes (Essex)	834	56	14.89
IAR Peebles (Middx)	550	32	17.18
HJ Butler (Notts)	621	36	17.25
JC Clay (Glamorgan)	1577	91	17.32
M Leyland (Yorks)	846	48	17.62
EA Watts (Surrey)	2017	114	17.69
W Wooller (Glamorgan)	365	20	18.25

LEADING ALL-ROUNDERS

	Runs (Avge)		Wkts (Avge)	
MS Nichols (Essex)	1238	(36.41)	143	(19.53)
WHR Andrews (Somerset)	962	(22.37)	122	(21.27)
R Howorth (Worcs)	972	(21.60)	106	(25.21)

LEADING WICKET-KEEPERS

	Dismissals		Total
W Farrimond (Lancs)	64ct	14st	78
TH Wade (Essex)	58ct	16st	74

Les Townsend, who achieved his only 'double' in 1932, was one of a number of accomplished all-rounders who were to help Derbyshire to the top in the 1930s (Hulton Picture Company)

Maurice Nichols achieved an outstanding total of six 'doubles' in the 1930s and his form saw Essex make great progress. He maintained remarkably consistent all-round effectiveness (Hulton Picture Company)

Hugh Bartlett was often able to 'murder' the bowling in his best season, 1938, but the war perhaps robbed the Sussex man of what were potentially his best years (Hulton Picture Company)

Cyril Washbrook would emerge after the war as a top run-getter, with scoring which bore comparison with any in Lancashire's history. He topped the averages in 1948 (Hulton Picture Company)

1939

FINAL TABLE

	P	W	L	D(T)	LI	DI	Pts	Avge
1 Yorkshire	28	20	4	4	2	3	260	9.28
2 Middlesex	22	14	6	2	3	1	180	8.18
3 Gloucestershire . .	26	15	7	4	1	3	196	7.53
4 Essex	24	12	10	2	4	2	170	7.08
5 Kent	26	14	9	3	2	1	180	6.92
6 Lancashire	21	10	6	5	3	2	140	6.66
7 Worcestershire . .	27	11	10	5(1)	2	4	162	6.00
8 Surrey	24	11	7	6	0	2	140	5.83
9 Derbyshire	25	10	8	7	1	5	144	5.76
10 Sussex	29	10	12	7	1	4	140	4.82
11 Warwickshire . . .	22	7	8	7	1	2	98	4.45
12 Nottinghamshire	23	6	8	9	2	5	100	4.34
13 Glamorgan	24	6	8	10	1	5	96	4.00
14 Somerset	27	6	11	9(1)	2	4	102	3.77
15 Hampshire	26	3	17	6	8	4	84	3.23
16 Northamptonshire	22	1	12	9	3	3	36	1.63
17 Leicestershire . . .	20	1	14	5	1	0	16	0.80

Middlesex record includes 2 pts for win in one-day match; Essex and Warwickshire totals include 2 pts each for 1st-innings tie in match lost. Lancs v Surrey; abandoned after 2 days owing to threat of war, not included in table. Middlesex v Kent, Gloucs v Notts, Lancs v Leics; were not started due to 'the European situation'.

BEST INDIVIDUAL SCORES

312* WW Keeton, Notts v Middx, Oval
302 WR Hammond, Gloucs v Glamorgan, Newport
287* E Davies, Glamorgan v Gloucs, Newport
280* L Hutton, Yorks v Hants, Sheffield

BEST INNINGS ANALYSES

10-47 TF Smailes, Yorks v Derbys, Sheffield
10-67 EA Watts, Surrey v Warwicks, Edgbaston
 9-38 TWJ Goddard, Gloucs v Kent, Bristol
 9-40 RTD Perks, Worcs v Glamorgan, Stourbridge

BEST MATCH ANALYSES

17-106 TWJ Goddard, Gloucs v Kent, Bristol
16-80 DVP Wright, Kent v Somerset, Bath
16-99 TWJ Goddard, Gloucs v Worcs, Bristol

14-58 TWJ Goddard, Gloucs v Somerset, Bristol
14-58 TF Smailes, Yorks v Derbys, Sheffield

LEADING BATSMEN

	Inns	NO	Runs	HS	Avge
WR Hammond (Gloucs)	36	5	2121	302	68.41
DCS Compton (Middx)	34	4	1853	214*	61.76
L Hutton (Yorks)	40	4	2167	280*	60.19
J Hardstaff (Notts)	37	4	1818	159	55.09
WW Keeton (Notts)	35	5	1644	312*	54.80
J Iddon (Lancs)	42	11	1682	217*	54.25
WJ Edrich (Middx)	38	1	1948	161	52.64
H Sutcliffe (Yorks)	26	2	1230	234*	51.25
Jas Langridge (Sussex)	42	8	1652	161	48.58
E Paynter (Lancs)	41	3	1776	222	46.73

LEADING BOWLERS

	Runs	Wkts	Avge
H Verity (Yorks)	2095	165	12.69
WE Bowes (Yorks)	1389	96	14.46
TWJ Goddard (Gloucs)	2654	181	14.66
DVP Wright (Kent)	2051	131	15.65
WH Copson (Derbys)	1856	109	17.02
C Lewis (Kent)	959	56	17.12
MS Nichols (Essex)	2027	115	17.62
L Hutton (Yorks)	681	37	18.40
K Farnes (Essex)	613	33	18.57
GH Pope (Derbys)	1474	78	18.89

LEADING ALL-ROUNDERS

	Runs (Avge)		Wkts (Avge)	
SH Martin (Worcs)	1167	(24.31)	105	(24.56)
MS Nichols (Essex)	1514	(37.54)	115	(17.62)

LEADING WICKET-KEEPERS

	Dismissals		Total
WFF Price (Middx)	52ct	21st	73
A Wood (Yorks)	39ct	27st	66

1946

FINAL TABLE

	P	W	L	D	ND	LI	DI	Pts
1 Yorkshire	26	17	1	5	3	0	5	216
2 Middlesex	26	16	5	5	0	1	2	204
3 Lancashire	26	15	4	5	2	1	4	200
4 Somerset	26	12	6	7	1	2	3	166
5 Gloucestershire . .	26	12	6	4	4	1	3	160
6 Glamorgan	26	10	8	6	2	3	3	144
7 Kent	26	11	8	7	0	0	3	144
8 Essex	26	8	9	8	1	2	4	120
9 Worcestershire . .	26	9	12	2	3	3	0	120
10 Hampshire	26	8	15	3	0	2	2	112
11 Leicestershire . . .	26	7	13	4	2	2	2	100
12 Surrey	26	6	11	7	2	3	4	100
13 Nottinghamshire .	26	6	8	11	1	1	5	96
14 Warwickshire . . .	26	7	15	3	1	1	1	92
15 Derbyshire	26	5	12	8	1	3	4	88
16 Northamptonshire	26	2	11	11	2	2	8	64
17 Sussex	26	4	11	10	1	2	1	60

Each team plays 26 matches; team with most points wins the title. All scheduled matches listed as 'Played'; those with no 1st-innings result listed as ND – no points to either side. Yorkshire record includes 8 pts for win on 1st innings in one-day game; Somerset includes 2 pts for tie on 1st innings in match lost.

BEST INDIVIDUAL SCORES

264 P Vaulkhard, Notts v Derbys, Trent Bridge
235 DCS Compton, Middx v Surrey, Lord's
233* TH Barling, Surrey v Notts, Oval
231 H Gimblett, Somerset v Middx, Taunton

BEST INNINGS ANALYSES

10–49 WE Hollies, Warwicks v Notts, Edgbaston
 9–42 RTD Perks, Worcs v Gloucs, Cheltenham
 9–82 TWJ Goddard, Gloucs v Surrey, Cheltenham
 8–25 WHR Andrews, Somerset v Hants, Portsmouth

BEST MATCH ANALYSES

14–96 RTD Perks, Worcs v Gloucs, Cheltenham
14–107 JE Walsh, Leics v Kent, Headingley

14–169 TWJ Goddard, Gloucs v Essex, Brentwood
14–181 JE Walsh, Leics v Sussex, Leicester

LEADING BATSMEN

	Inns	NO	Runs	HS	Avge
WR Hammond (Gloucs)	16	3	1404	214	108.00
C Washbrook (Lancs)	26	6	1475	182	73.75
DCS Compton (Middx)	34	4	1840	235	61.33
D Brookes (Northants)	39	5	1932	200	56.82
WJ Edrich (Middx)	39	7	1749	222*	54.34
DR Wilcox (Essex)	10	2	411	134	51.37
L Hutton (Yorks)	26	4	1112	171	50.54
LB Fishlock (Surrey)	41	2	1963	172	50.33
H Gimblett (Somerset)	39	2	1731	231	46.78
HP Crabtree (Essex)	15	1	650	146	46.42

LEADING BOWLERS

	Runs	Wkts	Avge
A Booth (Yorks)	1000	84	11.90
JC Clay (Glamorgan)	1527	120	12.72
ADG Matthews (Glam)	1126	82	13.73
WE Bowes (Yorks)	778	56	13.89
EP Robinson (Yorks)	1810	129	14.03
WE Hollies (Warwicks)	2653	175	15.16
JF Parker (Surrey)	719	45	15.97
LH Gray (Middx)	1475	91	16.20
JA Young (Middx)	1603	95	16.87
HL Hazell (Somerset)	888	52	17.07

LEADING ALL-ROUNDERS

	Runs (Avge)		Wkts (Avge)	
VE Jackson (Leics)	1025	(25.00)	88	(21.90)
Jas Langridge (Sussex)	1123	(31.19)	89	(19.52)

LEADING WICKET-KEEPERS

	Dismissals		Total
WT Luckes (Somerset)	47ct	23st	70
P Corrall (Leics)	31ct	31st	62

1947

FINAL TABLE

	P	W	L	D(T)	ND	LI	DI	Pts
I Middlesex	26	19	5	2	0	I	I	236
2 Gloucestershire ..	26	17	4	5	0	I	2	216
3 Lancashire	26	13	I	10(1)	I	0	6	186
4 Kent	26	12	8	6	0	2	5	172
5 Derbyshire......	26	II	9	5	I	3	4	160
6 Surrey	26	10	7	8	I	0	5	140
7 Worcestershire ..	26	7	II	8	0	4	5	120
8 Yorkshire.......	26	8	7	10	I	I	5	120
9 Glamorgan......	26	8	8	8	2	3	2	116
10 Sussex	26	9	12	5	0	I	I	116
II Essex	26	6	9	10(1)	0	I	4	100*
12 Nottinghamshire	26	6	6	13	I	I	6	100
13 Somerset	26	8	12	6	0	0	I	100
14 Leicestershire ...	26	6	14	5	I	2	3	92
15 Warwickshire ...	26	6	12	7	I	2	I	84
16 Hampshire......	26	4	II	8(1)	2	0	6	78
17 Northamptonshire	26	2	16	6(1)	I	2	4	54

Notts total includes 2 points for tie on Ist innings in match lost.

BEST INDIVIDUAL SCORES

270* L Hutton, Yorks v Hants, Bournemouth
267* WJ Edrich, Middx v Northants,
    Northampton
264 MM Walford, Somerset v Hants, Weston
257 WJ Edrich, Middx v Leics, Leicester

BEST INNINGS ANALYSES

9–41 TWJ Goddard, Gloucs v Notts, Bristol
9–42 C Cook, Gloucs v Yorks, Bristol
9–77 TPB Smith, Essex v Middx, Colchester
9–119 C Gladwin, Derbys v Lancs, Buxton

BEST MATCH ANALYSES

16–215 TPB Smith, Essex v Middx, Colchester
15–81 TWJ Goddard, Gloucs v Notts, Bristol
15–101 AW Wellard, Somerset v Worcs, Bath
15–134 TWJ Goddard, Gloucs v Leics,
    Gloucester

LEADING BATSMEN

	Inns	NO	Runs	HS	Avge
DCS Compton (Middx)	28	7	2033	178	96.80
C Washbrook (Lancs)	26	5	1639	252*	78.04
WJ Edrich (Middx)	34	5	2257	267*	77.82
EI Lester (Yorks)	11	2	657	142	73.00
LEG Ames (Kent)	37	7	2137	212*	71.23
L Hutton (Yorks)	23	1	1551	270*	70.50
J Hardstaff (Notts)	37	5	2230	221*	69.68
MM Walford (Som)	16	2	942	264	67.28
JDB Robertson (Middx)	37	3	2214	229	65.11
W Place (Lancs)	37	5	2023	171	63.21

LEADING BOWLERS

	Runs	Wkts	Avge
JA Young (Middx)	1929	122	15.81
JC Clay (Glamorgan)	855	54	15.83
TWJ Goddard (Gloucs)	3284	206	15.94
JC Laker (Surrey)	1099	66	16.65
R Howorth (Worcs)	1978	118	16.76
WE Bowes (Yorks)	1036	61	16.98
C Gladwin (Derbys)	1807	102	17.71
CJ Barnett (Gloucs)	804	44	18.27
BL Muncer (Glamorgan)	1867	101	18.48
R Pollard (Lancs)	2427	131	18.52

LEADING ALL-ROUNDERS

	Runs	(Avge)	Wkts	(Avge)
R Howorth (Worcs)	1064	(26.60)	118	(16.76)
R Smith (Essex)	1180	(30.25)	111	(36.95)

LEADING WICKET-KEEPERS

	Dismissals		Total
LH Compton (Middx)	56ct	18st	74
TH Wade (Essex)	37ct	37st	74
H Yarnold (Worcs)	41ct	32st	73

1948

FINAL TABLE

	P	W	L	D	ND	LI	DI	Pts
1 Glamorgan	26	13	5	6	2	1	3	172
2 Surrey	26	13	9	4	0	1	3	168†
3 Middlesex	26	13	4	8	1	0	1	160
4 Yorkshire	26	11	4	10	1	3	3	156
5 Lancashire	26	8	2	15	1	0	14	152
6 Derbyshire	26	11	6	7	2	0	4	148
7 Warwickshire	26	9	7	8	2	1	5	132
8 Gloucestershire	26	9	7	9	1	1	4	128
9 Hampshire	26	9	8	8	1	2	1	120
10 Worcestershire	26	6	8	11	1	1	7	104
11 Leicestershire	26	6	11	8	1	1	5	96
12 Somerset	26	5	14	6	1	4	4	92
13 Essex	26	5	8	11*	2	2	4	90
14 Nottinghamshire	26	5	10	9*	2	1	3	82
15 Kent	26	4	11	10	1	0	7	76
16 Sussex	26	4	11	10	1	1	5	72
17 Northamptonshire	26	3	9	14	0	1	3	52

*Essex and Notts, scores level, 6 points each
†Surrey total includes 8 pts for win on 1st innings in match reduced to one day.

BEST INDIVIDUAL SCORES

310 H Gimblett, Somerset v Sussex, Eastbourne
253 LB Fishlock, Surrey v Leics, Leicester
252* DCS Compton, Middx v Somerset, Lord's
215 E Davies, Glamorgan v Essex, Brentwood

BEST INNINGS ANALYSES

9–35 V Broderick, Northants v Sussex, Horsham
9–62 BL Muncer, Glamorgan v Essex, Brentwood
9–108 TPB Smith, Essex v Kent, Maidstone
9–117 TPB Smith, Essex v Notts, Southend

BEST MATCH ANALYSES

15–100 JE Walsh, Leics v Sussex, Hove
15–161 BL Muncer, Glamorgan v Essex, Brentwood
15–201 BL Muncer, Glam v Sussex, Swansea
14–86 JE Walsh, Leics v Glamorgan, Leicester

LEADING BATSMEN

	Inns	NO	Runs	HS	Avge
C Washbrook (Lancs)	17	2	1391	200	92.73
L Hutton (Yorks)	22	5	1565	176*	92.05
DCS Compton (Middx)	25	5	1236	252*	61.80
WJ Edrich (Middx)	25	3	1331	168*	60.50
JF Crapp (Gloucs)	28	3	1435	127	57.40
AE Fagg (Kent)	45	3	2404	203	57.23
JDB Robertson (Middx)	39	5	1855	147	54.54
HE Dollery (Warwicks)	40	7	1649	167	49.96
TN Pearce (Essex)	36	6	1487	211*	49.56
H Gimblett (Somerset)	37	1	1741	310	48.36

LEADING BOWLERS

	Runs	Wkts	Avge
JC Clay (Glamorgan)	374	27	13.85
JA Young (Middx)	1406	93	15.11
C Gladwin (Derbys)	1953	124	15.75
BL Muncer (Glamorgan)	2278	139	16.38
WMS Trick (Glamorgan)	607	36	16.86
NG Hever (Glamorgan)	1313	77	17.05
GH Pope (Derbys)	1724	100	17.24
TL Pritchard (Warwicks)	2848	163	17.47
JH Wardle (Yorks)	2273	129	17.62
J Bailey (Hants)	1959	109	17.97

LEADING ALL-ROUNDERS

	Runs (Avge)	Wkts (Avge)
J Bailey (Hants)	1310 (32.75)	109 (17.97)
GH Pope (Derbys)	1152 (38.40)	100 (17.24)

LEADING WICKET-KEEPERS

	Dismissals		Total
EA Meads (Notts)	57ct	16st	73
H Yarnold (Worcs)	41ct	25st	66

1949

FINAL TABLE

		P	W	L	D	ND	LI	DI	Pts
I	Middlesex	26	14	3	9	0	I	5	192
	Yorkshire	26	14	2	10	0	0	6	192
3	Worcestershire ..	26	12	7	7	0	2	5	172
4	Warwickshire ...	26	12	5	8	I	0	6	168
5	Surrey	26	II	8	6	I	2	4	156
6	Northamptonshire	26	10	7	9	0	2	3	140
7	Gloucestershire..	26	10	7	7	2	0	3	132
8	Glamorgan	26	7	6	12	I	2	7	120
9	Essex	26	7	9	10	0	0	6	108
	Somerset	26	8	15	3	0	2	I	108
II	Lancashire	26	6	7	13	0	0	7	100
	Nottinghamshire	26	6	5	13	2	0	7	100
13	Kent...........	26	7	15	4	0	I	2	96
	Sussex	26	7	10	7	2	I	2	96
15	Derbyshire......	26	6	13	6	I	2	2	88
16	Hampshire......	26	6	13	6	I	2	I	84
17	Leicestershire ...	26	3	14	8	I	3	2	56

BEST INDIVIDUAL SCORES

331* JDB Robertson, Middx v Worcs, Worcester

269* L Hutton, Yorks v Northants, Wellingborough

257 D Brookes, Northants v Gloucs, Bristol

238 RT Simpson, Notts v Lancs, Old Trafford

BEST INNINGS ANALYSES

10–66 JKR Graveney, Gloucs v Derbys, Chesterfield

10–90 TE Bailey, Essex v Lancs, Clacton

9–51 DVP Wright, Kent v Leics, Maidstone

9–53 JH Cornford, Sussex v Northants, Peterborough

BEST MATCH ANALYSES

15–107 TWJ Goddard, Gloucs v Derbys, Bristol

15–163 DVP Wright, Kent v Leics, Maidstone

15–164 JE Walsh, Leics v Notts, Loughborough

14–103 BL Muncer, Glamorgan v Lancs, Llanelli

LEADING BATSMEN

	Inns	NO	Runs	HS	Avge
J Hardstaff (Notts)	34	7	1872	162*	69.33
RT Simpson (Notts)	32	4	1906	238	68.07
John Langridge (Sx)	41	4	2441	234*	65.97
DJ Insole (Essex)	17	4	850	219*	65.38
L Hutton (Yorks)	38	5	2098	269*	63.57
WW Keeton (Notts)	36	1	1944	210	55.54
MM Walford (Somerset)	16	2	763	120	54.50
DCS Compton (Middx)	39	4	1773	182	50.65
N Oldfield (Northants)	45	3	2114	168	50.33
C Washbrook (Lancs)	22	0	1069	141	48.59

LEADING BOWLERS

	Runs	Wkts	Avge
R Aspinall (Yorks)	156	22	7.09
JA Young (Middx)	2207	125	17.65
JC Laker (Surrey)	1851	104	17.79
R Howorth (Worcs)	1833	101	18.14
TWJ Goddard (Gloucs)	2827	152	18.59
A Coxon (Yorks)	1638	88	18.61
AV Bedser (Surrey)	1535	81	18.95
HL Hazell (Somerset)	1989	104	19.12
RO Jenkins (Worcs)	2784	140	19.88
C Gladwin (Derbys)	2210	110	20.09

LEADING ALL-ROUNDERS

	Runs (Avge)		Wkts (Avge)	
FR Brown (Northants)	993	(27.58)	93	(23.84)
C Gladwin (Derbys)	903	(29.12)	110	(20.09)

LEADING WICKET-KEEPERS

	Dismissals		Total
H Yarnold (Worcs)	53ct	42st	95
HW Stephenson (Somerset)	36ct	43st	79

1950

FINAL TABLE

		P	W	L	D(T)	ND	LI	DI	Pts
1	Lancashire	28	16	2	10	0	1	6	220
	Surrey	28	17	4	6	1	0	4	220
3	Yorkshire	28	14	2	10	2	0	8	200
4	Warwickshire	28	8	6	13	1	1	8	132
5	Derbyshire	28	8	9	9	2	3	4	124
6	Worcestershire	28	7	9	9	3	0	7	114
7	Gloucestershire	28	6	6	16	0	2	9	112
	Somerset	28	8	8	10	2	1	3	112
9	Kent	28	6	12	8(1)	1	3	5	108
10	Northamptonshire	28	6	4	15	3	2	6	104
11	Glamorgan	28	6	4	9	9	0	7	100
12	Hampshire	28	7	9	9(1)	2	0	2	96
13	Sussex	28	5	11	11	1	6	2	92
14	Middlesex	28	5	12	8	3	2	4	84
15	Nottinghamshire	28	3	6	17	2	0	8	68
16	Leicestershire	28	3	13	11	1	2	5	64
17	Essex	28	4	12	11	1	0	3	60

Schedule increased to 28 matches.

BEST INDIVIDUAL SCORES

243* RT Simpson, Notts v Worcs, Trent Bridge
241 John Langridge, Sussex v Somerset, Worthing
239* CB Harris, Notts v Hants, Trent Bridge
230* RT Simpson, Notts v Glamorgan, Swansea

BEST INNINGS ANALYSES

9–56 WE Hollies, Warwicks v Northants, Edgbaston
8–20 TL Pritchard, Warwicks v Worcs, Dudley
8–23 RR Dovey, Kent v Surrey, Blackheath
8–26 JH Wardle, Yorks v Middx, Lord's

BEST MATCH ANALYSES

13–75 RR Dovey, Kent v Surrey, Blackheath
13–87 C Cook, Gloucs v Lancs, Gloucester
13–95 TWJ Goddard, Gloucs v Sussex, Worthing
13–113 TPB Smith, Essex v Surrey, Oval

LEADING BATSMEN

	Inns	NO	Runs	HS	Avge
RT Simpson (Notts)	28	6	1873	243*	85.13
W Watson (Yorks)	11	2	636	132	70.66
JG Dewes (Middlesex)	12	0	739	139	61.58
L Hutton (Yorks)	21	2	1125	156	59.21
C Washbrook (Lancs)	25	3	1294	111*	58.81
DCS Compton (Middx)	16	2	795	144	56.78
J Hardstaff (Notts)	28	4	1343	149	55.95
G Cox (Sussex)	42	6	1813	165*	50.36
FC Gardner (Warwicks)	48	11	1801	215*	48.67
WGA Parkhouse (Glamorgan)	33	2	1486	162	47.93

LEADING BOWLERS

	Runs	Wkts	Avge
R Tattersall (Lancs)	1988	163	12.19
JC Laker (Surrey)	2066	142	14.54
E Davies (Glamorgan)	688	46	14.95
MJ Hilton (Lancs)	1881	125	15.04
JB Statham (Lancs)	569	36	15.80
JH Wardle (Yorks)	2282	144	15.84
P Greenwood (Lancs)	588	34	17.29
J Lawrence (Somerset)	1956	108	18.11
WE Hollies (Warwicks)	2122	117	18.13
C Gladwin (Derbys)	1406	77	18.25

LEADING ALL-ROUNDERS

	Runs (Avge)		Wkts (Avge)	
R Smith (Essex)	1078	(24.50)	97	(34.32)
J Lawrence (Somerset)	881	(20.97)	108	(18.11)
VE Jackson (Leics)	1210	(26.30)	78	(25.71)

LEADING WICKET-KEEPERS

	Dismissals		Total
H Yarnold (Worcs)	52ct	25st	77
HW Stephenson (Somerset)	35ct	38st	73

1951

FINAL TABLE

	P	W	L	D	ND	LI	DI	Pts
1 Warwickshire ...	28	16	2	10	0	0	6	216
2 Yorkshire	28	12	3	11	2	0	10	184
3 Lancashire	28	8	2	14	4	1	9	136
4 Worcestershire ..	28	9	7	10	2	2	4	132
5 Glamorgan	28	8	4	13	3	1	7	128
6 Surrey	28	7	6	13	2	0	9	120
7 Middlesex	28	7	6	13	2	1	7	116
8 Essex	28	6	2	18	2	0	9	110
9 Hampshire	28	5	7	13	3	1	9	100
10 Sussex	28	6	6	15	1	0	5	94
11 Derbyshire	28	5	6	16	1	2	6	92
12 Gloucestershire ..	28	5	9	12	2	1	6	88
13 Northamptonshire	28	4	4	17	3	1	7	80
14 Somerset	28	5	15	6	2	3	1	76
15 Leicestershire ...	28	4	7	16	1	0	4	64
16 Kent	28	4	15	8	1	1	2	60
17 Nottinghamshire .	28	1	11	13	3	0	7	40

Essex and Sussex totals include 2 points each for a tie on 1st innings in a drawn match.

BEST INDIVIDUAL SCORES

258* F Jakeman, Northants v Essex, Northampton

247 J Hardstaff, Notts v Northants, Trent Bridge

232* SM Brown, Middx v Somerset, Lord's

221 AE Fagg, Kent v Notts, Trent Bridge

BEST INNINGS ANALYSES

8-21 E Smith, Derbys v Worcs, Chesterfield

8-26 RW Clarke, Northants v Hants, Portsmouth

8-38 RR Dovey, Kent v Glamorgan, Swansea

8-40 C Gladwin, Derbys v Notts, Ilkeston

BEST MATCH ANALYSES

15-78 EP Robinson, Somerset v Sussex, Weston

14-93 TL Pritchard, Warwicks v Glamorgan, Edgbaston

14-153 JE McConnon, Glamorgan v Derbys, Cardiff

12-43 R Appleyard, Yorks v Essex, Brentwood

LEADING BATSMEN

	Inns	NO	Runs	HS	Avge
PBH May (Surrey)	10	2	614	167	76.75
JDB Robertson (Middx)	43	3	2452	201*	61.30
F Jakeman (Northants)	36	5	1819	258*	58.67
L Hutton (Yorks)	26	5	1222	194*	58.19
DS Sheppard (Sussex)	21	2	1042	183	54.84
DCS Compton (Middx)	24	3	1150	172	54.76
JT Ikin (Lancs)	23	6	927	125*	54.52
TW Graveney (Gloucs)	37	3	1654	146	48.64
RT Simpson (Notts)	31	2	1382	212	47.65
W Place (Lancs)	39	5	1617	163	47.55

LEADING BOWLERS

	Runs	Wkts	Avge
R Appleyard (Yorks)	2355	169	13.93
JB Statham (Lancs)	1319	90	14.65
AV Bedser (Surrey)	1025	63	16.26
JE McConnon (Glam)	2072	123	16.84
R Tattersall (Lancs)	1275	74	17.22
TE Bailey (Essex)	1360	78	17.43
MJ Hilton (Lancs)	1972	112	17.60
WE Hollies (Warwicks)	2566	145	17.69
C Gladwin (Derbys)	2192	123	17.82
R Howorth (Worcs)	2121	118	17.97

LEADING ALL-ROUNDERS

	Runs (Avge)		Wkts (Avge)	
VE Jackson (Leics)	1173	(30.07)	87	(24.35)
RO Jenkins (Worcs)	831	(25.18)	108	(26.03)
R Smith (Essex)	1089	(31.11)	89	(30.33)

LEADING WICKET-KEEPERS

	Dismissals		Total
H Yarnold (Worcs)	57ct	28st	85
RT Spooner (Warwicks)	53ct	20st	73

1952

FINAL TABLE

	P	W	L	D(T)	ND	LI	DI	Pts
1 Surrey	28	20	3	5	0	0	4	256
2 Yorkshire	28	17	2	8	I	0	5	224
3 Lancashire	28	12	3	II(I)	I	I	8	188
4 Derbyshire......	28	II	8	9	0	2	6	164
5 Middlesex	28	II	12	4	I	0	I	136
6 Leicestershire ...	28	9	9	9	I	I	5	132
7 Glamorgan......	28	8	7	13	0	2	6	130
8 Northamptonshire	28	7	8	12	I	3	8	128
9 Gloucestershire	28	7	10	II	0	4	6	124
10 Essex	28	8	4	13(I)	2	I	4	120
Warwickshire ...	28	8	10	8(I)	I	0	4	120
12 Hampshire......	28	7	II	9	I	4	3	112
13 Sussex	28	7	12	6(I)	2	0	2	96
14 Worcestershire ..	28	6	II	10	I	I	3	90
15 Kent	28	5	15	8	0	2	4	84
16 Nottinghamshire	28	3	II	13	I	2	7	72
17 Somerset	28	2	12	13	I	I	4	44

Warwickshire and Lancashire totals include 8 pts for 1st-innings lead (4) in match tied (4). Sussex and Essex 4 pts for tie, no 1st-innings lead. Glamorgan and Worcestershire records include 2 pts for a tie on 1st innings in drawn match.

BEST INDIVIDUAL SCORES

230 JV Wilson, Yorks v Derbys, Sheffield
224 AV Avery, Essex v Northants, Northampton
219 CJ Poole, Notts v Derbys, Ilkeston
216 RT Simpson, Notts v Sussex, Trent Bridge

BEST INNINGS ANALYSES

9–39 CW Grove, Warwicks v Sussex, Edgbaston
9–41 C Gladwin, Derbys v Worcs, Stourbridge
9–60 HL Jackson, Derbys v Lancs, Old Trafford
9–65 RG Thompson, Warwicks v Notts, Edgbaston

BEST MATCH ANALYSES

16–84 C Gladwin, Derbys v Worcs, Stourbridge
15–133 RG Marlar, Sussex v Glamorgan, Swansea
13–46 AV Bedser, Surrey v Notts, Oval
13–76 R Tattersall, Lancs v Kent, Old Trafford

LEADING BATSMEN

	Inns	NO	Runs	HS	Avge
PBH May (Surrey)	14	2	804	197	67.00
L Hutton (Yorks)	26	1	1482	189	59.28
W Watson (Yorks)	32	8	1305	114	54.37
JT Ikin (Lancs)	35	4	1638	154	52.83
EI Lester (Yorks)	33	5	1432	178	51.14
DS Sheppard (Sussex)	10	1	453	140	50.33
RT Simpson (Notts)	36	1	1674	216	47.82
D Brookes (Northants)	48	6	1991	204*	47.40
J Hardstaff (Notts)	38	5	1543	144*	46.75
AV Avery (Essex)	35	4	1396	224	45.03

LEADING BOWLERS

	Runs	Wkts	Avge
FS Trueman (Yorks)	455	32	14.21
RG Marlar (Sussex)	845	55	15.36
AV Bedser (Surrey)	1583	102	15.51
GAR Lock (Surrey)	1918	116	16.53
JC Laker (Surrey)	1451	86	16.87
JH Wardle (Yorks)	2707	158	17.13
R Tattersall (Lancs)	2261	130	17.39
CW Grove (Warwicks)	1977	113	17.49
BL Muncer (Glamorgan)	1693	96	17.63
JB Statham (Lancs)	1799	100	17.99

LEADING ALL-ROUNDERS

	Runs (Avge)		Wkts (Avge)	
DB Close (Yorks)	978	(36.22)	98	(24.04)
BL Muncer (Glam)	1058	(25.19)	96	(17.63)
R Smith (Essex)	937	(25.32)	124	(28.30)
GE Tribe (Northants)	969	(29.36)	116	(25.46)
JE Walsh (Leics)	991	(24.17)	112	(24.43)

LEADING WICKET-KEEPERS

	Dismissals		Total
J Firth (Leics)	57ct	25st	82
PA Gibb (Essex)	62ct	15st	77

1953

FINAL TABLE

	P	W	L	D(T)	ND	LI	DI	Pts
I Surrey	28	13	4	10	I	0	7	184
2 Sussex	28	II	3	13	I	I	8	168
3 Lancashire	28	10	4	10	4	I	8	156
Leicestershire ...	28	10	7	II	0	3	6	156
5 Middlesex	28	10	5	II(I)	I	I	5	150
6 Derbyshire......	28	9	7	9	3	2	5	136
Gloucestershire..	28	9	7	10	2	2	5	136
8 Nottinghamshire	28	9	10	8	I	4	I	128
9 Warwickshire ...	28	6	7	14	I	2	II	124
10 Glamorgan......	28	8	4	14	2	0	6	120
II Northamptonshire	28	6	3	15(I)	3	2	7	114
12 Essex	28	6	7	13	2	I	6	100
Yorkshire.......	28	6	6	13	3	I	6	100
14 Hampshire......	28	6	II	II	0	2	4	96
15 Worcestershire ..	28	5	12	10	I	I	2	72
16 Kent..........	28	4	14	8	2	I	3	64
17 Somerset	28	2	19	6	I	0	3	36

Points-system change: When scores are level, with 2 innings apiece completed, the side batting fourth scores 6 points, no points to the other side other than those they may have gained on 1st innings.

BEST INDIVIDUAL SCORES

269* AE Fagg, Kent v Notts, Trent Bridge
259* FA Lowson, Yorks v Worcs, Worcester
238* D Kenyon, Worcs v Yorks, Worcester
211 WJ Edrich, Middx v Essex, Lord's

BEST INNINGS ANALYSES

10–102 R Berry, Lancs v Worcs, Blackpool
9–28   PJ Loader, Surrey v Kent, Blackheath
9–40   R Tattersall, Lancs v Notts, Old Trafford
9–77   D Shackleton, Hants v Glamorgan, Newport

BEST MATCH ANALYSES

14–73   R Tattersall, Lancs v Notts, Old Trafford
14–115 JA Young, Middx v Kent, Canterbury
14–125 R Berry, Lancs v Worcs, Blackpool

13–69   GAR Lock, Surrey v Hants, Bournemouth

LEADING BATSMEN

	Inns	NO	Runs	HS	Avge
DW Barrick (Northants)	30	7	1407	166*	61.17
L Livingston (Northants)	32	5	1564	140	57.92
L Hutton (Yorks)	21	1	1149	178	57.45
PBH May (Surrey)	34	8	1488	159	57.23
RT Simpson (Notts)	36	4	1815	157	56.71
DS Sheppard (Sussex)	43	7	1982	186*	55.05
R Subba Row (Surrey)	19	4	808	128	53.86
TE Bailey (Essex)	19	6	647	84	49.76
D Kenyon (Worcs)	45	2	2063	238*	47.97
WJ Edrich (Middx)	41	4	1748	211	47.24

LEADING BOWLERS

	Runs	Wkts	Avge
GAR Lock (Surrey)	830	67	12.38
JA Bailey (Essex)	326	25	13.04
CJ Knott (Hants)	521	38	13.71
JB Statham (Lancs)	1302	87	14.96
HL Jackson (Derbys)	1466	90	15.27
B Dooland (Notts)	2442	152	16.06
R Tattersall (Lancs)	2005	122	16.43
JC Laker (Surrey)	1555	93	16.72
PJ Loader (Surrey)	1132	67	16.89
AV Bedser (Surrey)	1427	84	16.98

LEADING ALL-ROUNDERS

	Runs (Avge)		Wkts (Avge)	
GE Tribe (Northants)	1010	(36.07)	83	(23.44)
VE Jackson (Leics)	1328	(28.86)	72	(21.47)
W Wooller (Glamorgan)	1020	(36.42)	72	(23.09)

LEADING WICKET-KEEPERS

	Dismissals		Total
PA Gibb (Essex)	58ct	13st	71
LH Compton (Middx)	54ct	10st	64

The eccentric Paul Gibb, the first Cambridge Blue to turn professional for a county, proved his worth with Essex in 1953, topping the wicket-keepers' list and batting with his customary stubbornness and skill
(Hulton Picture Company)

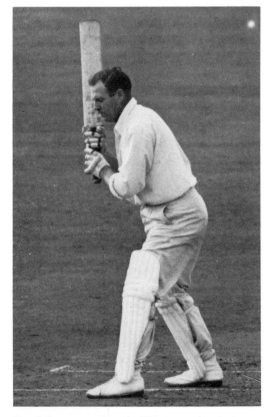

Tom Dollery was another splendid batsman whose best years were probably lost to the war; his peak was reached in 1951 as professional skipper of the County Champions, Warwickshire (Hulton Picture Company)

The versatile Bob Appleyard – medium fast with the new ball, then off-spinners – reached his peak in the mid-1950s, despite continued indifferent health (Hulton Picture Company)

SURREY'S MAGNIFICENT SEVEN

A shared title to start with, then seven outright championships in succession; there can be little argument that Surrey dominated the 1950s as no other side has any decade, either before or since. True, Yorkshire in the thirties, and even in the first decade of the century, finished further ahead on wins over losses, but championships were no longer decided this way, and Surrey took advantage of contemporary regulations. No other side has ever been top seven seasons in succession and it is probably safe to say it will remain a unique achievement. Almost throughout the fifties there were just two kinds of county teams: Surrey and the others. That is a fair measure of their superiority.

Having been a useful side under the gentlemanly Michael Barton, for Surrey the vital gap was bridged when Stuart Surridge took over in 1952. Surridge's captaincy is analysed elsewhere (*see page 175*); suffice to say here that he was captain for five seasons and the title was brought home each time.

The shared 1950 title and sixth place in 1951 – when a group of average Warwickshire players enjoyed its *annus mirabilis* – gave notice of the possibilities for the team, nothing more. In 1950, Surrey's batting was still led by pre-war stars Fishlock and Parker, and they were more than matched by such Lancashire stalwarts as Washbrook and Ikin. Both Lancashire and Surrey also had strong spin attacks; off-spinners Tattersall and Laker virtually cancelled one another out, but the Lancashire left-handers Hilton and Berry were more than a match for Tony Lock. At the faster pace, Lancashire had no-one like Alec Bedser, but given their greater apparent all-round depth, it was slightly surprising that the Red Rose did not clinch the title.

Warwickshire won their first title in 40 years in 1951 under the charismatic leadership of Tom Dollery, but from then on it was all Surrey. It was obviously a help playing half their matches on the 'sporting' Oval pitches – the same for both sides, true, but Surrey were used to them – and in Alec Bedser, Laker, Lock and Loader Surrey had a quartet of bowlers equipped to take full advantage of any assistance in the pitch. During the decade, Lock took 1070 wickets for an average of 14.78, Laker 957 at 16.61, Alec Bedser 855 at 17.57, Loader 595 at 16.93.

Useful support came from the enthusiastic pace of Surridge and the off-spin of Eric Bedser, but little more was ever required. Team after team, seeing demons in the pitch and apprehensive not just of the bowlers' power and ability but also of the consummate support given by the close catching and wicket-keeping, seemed to surrender themselves. Season after season, Surrey steamrollered their way to what seemed the inevitable title.

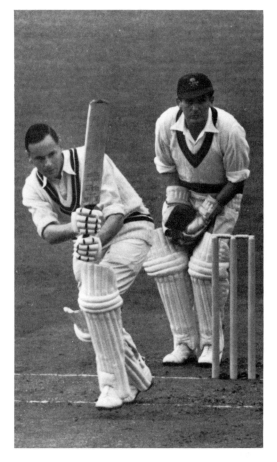

The great Peter May – a phenomenal run-getter for Surrey in their great decade (Hulton Picture Company)

The plan was different from that of 1930s Yorkshire, but as simple in formulation and execution, and mightily effective. Surrey would hope for a 'sporty' wicket, unleash the mighty quartet on already dubious batsmen, and hope to score enough to snatch victory. Fortunately they had Peter May, a batting giant among ordinary mortals; support for him was workaday but just adequate for the needs of the side.

Sadly, all was not sunshine; there were clouds in the form of doubts about the bowling actions of Lock and Loader, and the unbiased opinion of many good judges was that they were fortunate to go through to 1959 with unblemished records. When moves were made to rid the game of doubtful actions, Lock and Loader were among the first to be scrutinised. The former remodelled his action, the latter apparently did not, but neither was ever again the force of old.

Grumbles had also grown in intensity about the Oval wickets; certainly they were 'lively' throughout most of the fifties, and in the long run Surrey's path to success saw the game as the loser. But nothing can take away 8 titles in 9; nor 7 in succession.

1954

FINAL TABLE

		P	W	L	D(T)	ND	LI	DI	Pts
1	Surrey	28	15	3	8	2	1	6	208
2	Yorkshire	28	13	3	8(1)	3	0	5	186
3	Derbyshire......	28	11	6	9	2	3	6	168
4	Glamorgan......	28	11	5	10	2	0	4	148
5	Nottinghamshire	28	10	6	8	4	2	4	144
6	Warwickshire ...	28	10	5	10	3	1	4	140
7	Middlesex	28	10	5	10	3	1	3	136
	Northamptonshire	28	9	9	9	1	3	4	136
9	Sussex	28	8	7	12	1	1	5	120
10	Lancashire	28	6	3	12	7	1	8	108
11	Kent...........	28	5	7	15	1	3	7	100
	Worcestershire ..	28	5	12	9	2	2	7	100
13	Gloucestershire..	28	5	11	10	2	4	5	96
14	Hampshire......	28	4	10	13	1	1	7	80
15	Essex	28	3	11	12	2	2	5	64
16	Leicestershire ...	28	3	9	11(1)	4	0	5	62
17	Somerset	28	2	18	8	0	2	2	40

BEST INDIVIDUAL SCORES

253* D Kenyon, Worcs v Leics, Worcester
222 TW Graveney, Gloucs v Derbys, Chesterfield
211* PBH May, Surrey v Notts, Trent Bridge
210* D Brookes, Northants v Somerset, Northampton

BEST INNINGS ANALYSES

9-25 JH Wardle, Yorks v Lancs, Old Trafford
9-47 DJ Shepherd, Glamorgan v Northants, Cardiff
9-48 JH Wardle, Yorks v Sussex, Hull
9-63 CT Spencer, Leics v Yorks, Huddersfield

BEST MATCH ANALYSES

16-83   B Dooland, Notts v Essex, Trent Bridge
16-112 JH Wardle, Yorks v Sussex, Hull
14-111 PJ Loader, Surrey v Worcs, Worcester
13-112 B Dooland, Notts v Northants, Trent Bridge

LEADING BATSMEN

	Inns	NO	Runs	HS	Avge
TW Graveney (Gloucs)	26	4	1626	222	73.90
L Livingston (Northants)	42	7	1912	207*	54.62
DCS Compton (Middx)	21	2	1029	112	54.15
D Kenyon (Worcs)	46	6	2138	253*	53.45
PE Richardson (Worcs)	17	2	779	185	51.93
DS Sheppard (Sussex)	29	4	1265	120	50.60
PBH May (Surrey)	24	5	947	211*	49.84
DJ Insole (Essex)	43	6	1664	172*	44.97
AVG Wolton (Warwicks)	45	4	1685	165	41.09
WJ Edrich (Middx)	37	3	1381	195	40.61

LEADING BOWLERS

	Runs	Wkts	Avge
JB Statham (Lancs)	896	73	12.27
AV Bedser (Surrey)	1184	89	13.30
GAR Lock (Surrey)	1352	101	13.38
AJ Watkins (Glamorgan)	1398	98	14.26
JC Laker (Surrey)	1620	112	14.46
R Appleyard (Yorks)	1849	127	14.55
B Dooland (Notts)	2611	179	14.58
HL Jackson (Derbys)	1786	120	14.88
FS Trueman (Yorks)	1755	114	15.39
JE McConnon (Glamorgan)	1478	94	15.72

LEADING ALL-ROUNDERS

	Runs (Avge)		Wkts (Avge)	
AJ Watkins (Glamorgan)	1403	(35.07)	98	(14.26)
W Wooller (Glamorgan)	1055	(25.11)	99	(18.83)

LEADING WICKET-KEEPERS

	Dismissals		Total
HW Stephenson (Somerset)	49ct	34st	83
EJ Rowe (Notts)	45ct	18st	63

1955

FINAL TABLE

	P	W	L	D(T)	ND	LI	DI	Pts
1 Surrey	28	23	5	0	0	2	0	284
2 Yorkshire	28	21	5	2	0	2	2	268
3 Hampshire	28	16	5	6(1)	0	0	3	210
4 Sussex	28	13	8	6(1)	0	3	5	196
5 Middlesex	28	14	12	2	0	6	0	192
6 Leicestershire ...	28	11	10	7	0	3	2	154
7 Northamptonshire	28	9	10	9	0	3	7	148
8 Derbyshire	28	9	10	9	0	2	7	146
9 Lancashire	28	10	9	8	1	2	3	140
Warwickshire ...	28	10	9	9	0	2	3	140
11 Nottinghamshire	28	10	11	7	0	1	2	132
12 Gloucestershire..	28	9	13	6	0	2	3	128
13 Kent	28	8	13	7	0	0	2	104
14 Essex	28	6	15	7	0	3	4	100
15 Worcestershire ..	28	5	17	6	0	2	4	84
16 Glamorgan	28	5	14	8	1	2	3	80
17 Somerset	28	4	17	7	0	2	2	64

Derbyshire and Leicestershire totals include 2 points for a tie on 1st innings in drawn match. Sussex includes 2 points for tie on 1st innings in match lost.

BEST INDIVIDUAL SCORES

260* R Subba Row, Northants v Lancs, Northampton
227 A Hamer, Derbys v Notts, Trent Bridge
214* W Watson, Yorks v Worcs, Worcester
205* JM Parks, Sussex v Somerset, Hove

BEST INNINGS ANALYSES

9–30 JA Flavell, Worcs v Kent, Dover
9–35 JD Bannister, Warwicks v Yorks, Sheffield
9–45 GE Tribe, Northants v Yorks, Bradford
9–46 RG Marlar, Sussex v Lancs, Hove

BEST MATCH ANALYSES

15–75 GE Tribe, Northants v Yorks, Bradford
15–95 FJ Titmus, Middx v Somerset, Bath
15–119 RG Marlar, Sussex v Lancs, Hove
14–29 D Shackleton, Hants v Somerset, Weston

LEADING BATSMEN

	Inns	NO	Runs	HS	Avge
W Watson (Yorks)	38	13	1424	214*	56.96
MC Cowdrey (Kent)	16	3	737	139	56.69
PE Richardson (Worcs)	12	3	508	91*	56.44
JG Dewes (Middx)	14	2	644	117	53.66
DJ Insole (Essex)	47	4	1907	142	44.34
TW Graveney (Gloucs)	30	1	1283	128	44.24
L Livingston (Northants)	51	5	1957	172*	42.54
KJ Grieves (Lancs)	32	5	1146	137	42.44
JM Parks (Sussex)	47	7	1686	205*	42.15
PBH May (Surrey)	26	4	921	122*	41.86

LEADING BOWLERS

	Runs	Wkts	Avge
R Appleyard (Yorks)	843	73	11.54
RE Marshall (Hants)	298	25	11.92
GAR Lock (Surrey)	1840	149	12.34
JB Statham (Lancs)	1015	79	12.84
D Shackleton (Hants)	1923	147	13.08
HL Jackson (Derbys)	877	61	14.37
JH Wardle (Yorks)	1977	133	14.86
FJ Titmus (Middx)	2075	137	15.14
C Gladwin (Derbys)	2155	139	15.50
FS Trueman (Yorks)	1823	118	15.44

LEADING ALL-ROUNDERS

	Runs (Avge)	Wkts (Avge)
VE Jackson (Leics)	1451 (30.87)	106 (20.21)
AJ Watkins (Glamorgan)	1026 (24.42)	105 (20.37)

LEADING WICKET-KEEPERS

	Dismissals		Total
HG Davies (Glamorgan)	54ct	20st	74
HW Stephenson (Somerset)	48ct	23st	71

1956

FINAL TABLE

	P	2	L	D	ND	LI	DI	Pts
1 Surrey	28	15	5	6	2	1	4	200
2 Lancashire	28	12	2	12	2	0	9	180
3 Gloucestershire..	28	14	7	5	2	1	1	176
4 Northamptonshire	28	8	5	15	0	2	11	148
5 Middlesex	28	11	9	7	1	1	2	144
6 Hampshire......	28	9	6	10	3	1	7	140
7 Yorkshire.......	28	8	7	10	3	4	6	136
8 Nottinghamshire.	28	7	4	15	2	1	9	128
9 Sussex	28	7	10	9	2	2	5	112
Worcestershire..	28	8	4	14	2	0	4	112
11 Essex	28	6	10	9	3	5	4	110
12 Derbyshire......	28	7	6	11	4	0	4	102
13 Glamorgan......	28	6	9	9	4	2	5	100
14 Warwickshire ...	28	5	11	9	3	3	2	80
15 Somerset	28	4	15	8	1	3	4	76
16 Kent...........	28	4	12	10	2	1	2	60
17 Leicestershire ...	28	3	12	9	4	1	4	56

Nottinghamshire total includes 8 points for 1st innings lead in drawn game restricted to last day.
Derbyshire and Essex records include 2 points for tie on 1st innings in drawn match.

BEST INDIVIDUAL SCORES

259   D Kenyon, Worcs v Yorks, Kidderminster
208* WJ Edrich, Middx v Derbys, Chesterfield
203* D Brookes, Northants v Somerset, Taunton
201   WGA Parkhouse, Glamorgan v Kent, Swansea

BEST INNINGS ANALYSES

10-54 GAR Lock, Surrey v Kent, Blackheath
10-66 K Smales, Notts v Gloucs, Stroud
 9-65 JJ Warr, Middx v Kent, Lord's
 8-20 B Dooland, Notts v Worcs, Trent Bridge

BEST MATCH ANALYSES

16-85   GAR Lock, Surrey v Kent, Blackheath
15-193 B Dooland, Notts v Kent, Gravesend
14-69   AV Bedser, Surrey v Glamorgan, Cardiff
14-90   R Tattersall, Lancs v Yorks, Headingley

LEADING BATSMEN

	Inns	NO	Runs	HS	Avge
TW Graveney (Gloucs)	36	2	1787	200	52.55
TE Bailey (Essex)	24	7	888	141*	52.23
L Livingston (Northants)	44	6	1846	188*	48.57
DJ Insole (Essex)	41	2	1774	162	45.48
W Watson (Yorks)	33	6	1193	149	44.18
D Kenyon (Worcs)	46	3	1802	259	41.20
A Wharton (Lancs)	39	5	1389	116	40.85
JM Parks (Sussex)	46	6	1593	114	39.87
D Brookes (Northants)	49	6	1678	203*	39.02
PE Richardson (Worcs)	26	0	978	147	37.61

LEADING BOWLERS

	Runs	Wkts	Avge
GAR Lock (Surrey)	1224	117	10.46
RK Platt (Yorks)	328	26	12.61
R Tattersall (Lancs)	1310	96	13.64
R Illingworth (Yorks)	1197	85	14.08
MJ Hilton (Lancs)	1814	128	14.17
DJ Shepherd (Glamorgan)	2214	156	14.19
JB Statham (Lancs)	1042	73	14.27
C Cook (Gloucs)	2001	139	14.39
PJ Loader (Surrey)	1544	102	15.13
AE Moss (Middx)	458	29	15.79
D Shackleton (Hants)	1998	126	15.85

LEADING ALL-ROUNDERS

	Runs (Avge)		Wkts (Avge)	
GE Tribe (Northants)	1166	(32.38)	122	(18.82)
FJ Titmus (Middx)	948	(26.33)	84	(20.27)

LEADING WICKET-KEEPERS

	Dismissals		Total
JT Murray (Middx)	61ct	8st	69
B Taylor (Essex)	54ct	9st	63

1957

FINAL TABLE

	P	W	L	D	ND	LI	DI	Bon	Pts
1 Surrey	28	21	3	3	I	3	3	48	312
2 Northamptonshire	28	15	2	10	I	0	8	22	218
3 Yorkshire	28	13	4	II	0	0	5	24	190
4 Derbyshire......	28	10	8	9	I	2	4	30	162
5 Essex	28	II	6	10	I	0	5	16	158
6 Lancashire	28	10	8	8	2	2	4	24	156
7 Middlesex	28	10	12	3	3	2	I	22	148
8 Somerset	28	9	14	5	0	3	2	20	138
9 Glamorgan......	28	10	9	8	I	0	2	12	136
Sussex	28	8	9	9	2	2	6	24	136
II Warwickshire ...	28	9	7	II	I	0	5	16	134
12 Gloucestershire..	28	8	13	6	I	I	5	24	132
13 Hampshire......	28	7	12	8	I	I	5	20	116
14 Kent	28	6	13	9	0	2	3	8	90
15 Nottinghamshire	28	5	13	9	I	3	4	14	88
16 Worcestershire ..	28	4	9	14	I	I	4	8	72
17 Leicestershire ...	28	2	16	9	I	2	5	2	40

Worcestershire total includes 6 points for levelling scores in 4th innings of a match with Sussex.

Points change: For 1st innings lead alone, 2 points. Further 2 points scored by scoring faster, on runs per over. The latter are bonus points, retained in addition to points secured by the results. If there is no play in the first two-thirds of a match, and it is not taken further than 1st innings, the side leading on 1st innings scores 8 points.

BEST INDIVIDUAL SCORES

201* JDB Robertson, Middx v Essex, Lord's
200* D Kenyon, Worcs v Notts, Worcester
181 WB Stott, Yorks v Essex, Sheffield
176 MR Hallam, Leics v Kent, Leicester

BEST INNINGS ANALYSES

9–39 DJ Halfyard, Kent v Glamorgan, Neath
9–42 R Illingworth, Yorks v Worcs, Worcester
8–34 JB Statham, Lancs v Warwicks, Coventry
8–42 B Dooland, Notts v Lancs, Trent Bridge

BEST MATCH ANALYSES

15–89 JB Statham, Lancs v Warwicks, Coventry
14–81 TE Bailey, Essex v Hants, Romford
14–111 D Shackleton, Hants v Lancs, Old Trafford

13–86 C Gladwin, Derbys v Somerset, Bath

LEADING BATSMEN

	Inns	NO	Runs	HS	Avge
PBH May (Surrey)	27	2	1391	125	55.64
TW Graveney (Gloucs)	31	3	1393	134	49.75
TE Bailey (Essex)	28	6	1094	132	49.72
DRW Silk (Somerset)	12	3	409	73	45.44
MC Cowdrey (Kent)	27	5	979	165	44.50
DJ Insole (Essex)	38	4	1501	150*	44.14
DV Smith (Sussex)	38	2	1580	166	43.88
JM Parks (Sussex)	48	5	1861	101	43.27
CA Milton (Gloucs)	27	9	758	89	42.11
W Watson (Yorks)	29	1	1177	162	42.03

LEADING BOWLERS

	Runs	Wkts	Avge
GAR Lock (Surrey)	1773	153	11.58
JC Laker (Surrey)	1055	85	12.41
JB Statham (Lancs)	1257	100	12.57
EA Bedser (Surrey)	804	60	13.40
CS Smith (Lancs)	414	29	14.27
TE Bailey (Essex)	1020	70	14.57
PJ Loader (Surrey)	1488	101	14.73
FS Trueman (Yorks)	1177	76	15.48
AV Bedser (Surrey)	1698	109	15.57
D Shackleton (Hants)	2260	144	15.69

LEADING ALL-ROUNDERS

	Runs	(Avge)	Wkts	(Avge)
B Dooland (Notts)	1374	(27.48)	129	(22.22)
R Illingworth (Yorks)	1066	(33.10)	86	(17.46)
GE Tribe (Northants)	911	(24.62)	124	(16.70)

LEADING WICKET-KEEPERS

	Dismissals		Total
JT Murray (Middx)	62ct	13st	75
R Booth (Worcs)	50ct	18st	68

1958

FINAL TABLE

	P	W	L	D	ND	LI	DI	Bon	Pts
1 Surrey	28	14	5	8	1	0	6	32	212
2 Hampshire......	28	12	6	10	0	3	4	28	186
3 Somerset	28	12	9	7	0	2	3	20	174
4 Northamptonshire	28	11	6	6	5	0	5	18	160
5 Derbyshire......	28	9	9	8	2	4	5	24	151
6 Essex	28	9	7	7	5	4	3	24	146
7 Lancashire	28	9	7	8	4	3	5	18	142
8 Kent...........	28	9	10	7	2	1	4	20	139
9 Worcestershire ..	28	9	7	8	4	1	2	20	134
10 Middlesex	28	7	4	16	1	1	10	18	130
11 Yorkshire	28	7	5	10	6	2	6	14	126
12 Leicestershire ...	28	7	13	6	2	3	1	12	104
13 Sussex	28	6	7	11	4	2	4	18	102
14 Gloucestershire..	28	5	9	11	3	3	4	14	89
15 Glamorgan......	28	5	11	11	1	1	5	10	82
16 Warwickshire ...	28	3	7	14	4	2	6	16	68
17 Nottinghamshire	28	3	15	8	2	1	4	4	50

Yorkshire total includes 16 pts from 2 matches restricted by rain to last third of time allotted; Middlesex 8 pts in similar match, where 1st innings lead was obtained. Derbyshire's record includes 1 point for a tie on 1st innings in match lost; Kent & Gloucestershire 1 point for 1st-innings tie in drawn match.
Points change: 2 bonus points now awarded only if the side attaining 1st innings lead have faster scoring rate at the time of passing the opponent's total.
In the event of a tie on points, the side with most wins are Champions; if still equal, the side with most bonus points prevails.

BEST INDIVIDUAL SCORES

300 R Subba Row, Northants v Surrey, Oval
194 DM Young, Gloucs v Hants, Southampton
186 KG Suttle, Sussex v Essex, Hove
178 KG Suttle, Sussex v Notts, Trent Bridge

BEST INNINGS ANALYSES

9-17 PJ Loader, Surrey v Warwicks, Oval
9-26 BA Langford, Somerset v Lancs, Weston
9-43 GE Tribe, Northants v Worcs, Northampton
9-59 D Shackleton, Hants v Gloucs, Bristol

BEST MATCH ANALYSES

15-31 GE Tribe, Northants v Yorks, Northampton
15-54 BA Langford, Somerset v Lancs, Weston
15-182 GAR Lock, Surrey v Kent, Blackheath
14-99 J Savage, Leics v Northants, Northampton

LEADING BATSMEN

	Inns	NO	Runs	HS	Avge
PBH May (Surrey)	27	4	1274	174	55.39
W Watson (Leics)	38	8	1469	141	48.96
MJK Smith (Warwicks)	33	3	1344	103*	44.80
R Subba Row (Northants)	39	5	1482	300	43.58
G Atkinson (Somerset)	12	1	425	164	38.63
DM Young (Gloucs)	50	4	1755	194	38.15
TW Graveney (Gloucs)	34	5	1106	156	38.13
RE Marshall (Hants)	46	2	1627	138	36.97
MC Cowdrey (Kent)	30	3	986	139	36.51
AH Phebey (Kent)	34	4	1087	157	36.23

LEADING BOWLERS

	Runs	Wkts	Avge
HL Jackson (Derbys)	1311	126	10.40
JB Statham (Lancs)	1277	112	11.40
FS Trueman (Yorks)	739	62	11.91
GAR Lock (Surrey)	1468	114	12.87
JC Laker (Surrey)	1263	93	13.58
A Hurd (Essex)	464	34	13.64
DM Sayer (Kent)	370	27	13.70
M Ryan (Yorks)	330	22	15.00
JH Wardle (Yorks)	1154	76	15.18
D Shackleton (Hants)	2469	161	15.33

LEADING ALL-ROUNDERS

	Runs (Avge)		Wkts (Avge)	
TE Bailey (Essex)	739	(22.39)	102	(16.19)

| GE Tribe (Northants) | 722 (22.56) | 107 | (16.46) |
| AJ Watkins (Glamorgan) | 1164 (29.10) | 75 | (18.06) |

LEADING WICKET-KEEPERS

	Dismissals		Total
KV Andrew (Northants)	46ct	25st	71
JT Murray (Middx)	65ct	6st	71

1959

FINAL TABLE

	P	W	L	D(T)	ND	LI	DI	Bon	Pts
1 Yorkshire	28	14	7	7	0	0	5	26	204
2 Gloucestershire . .	28	12	11	4(1)	0	1	3	28	186
3 Surrey	28	12	5	11	0	0	8	26	186
4 Warwickshire	28	13	10	5	0	2	1	22	184
5 Lancashire	28	12	7	9	0	1	5	28	184
6 Glamorgan	28	12	8	7	1	3	4	20	178
7 Derbyshire	28	12	6	10	0	3	2	20	174
8 Hampshire	28	11	10	7	0	1	4	26	168
9 Essex	28	11	7	9(1)	0	0	4	22	168
10 Middlesex	28	10	9	9	0	3	3	24	157
11 Northamptonshire	28	8	10	10	0	4	9	24	146
12 Somerset	28	8	13	7	0	4	3	20	130
13 Kent	28	8	12	8	0	2	5	18	128
14 Worcestershire . .	28	6	8	13	1	1	7	18	106
15 Sussex	28	6	11	10	1	3	3	18	102
16 Leicestershire . . .	28	5	16	7	0	0	2	8	72
17 Nottinghamshire .	28	4	14	9	1	1	3	6	62

Middlesex total includes 1 pt for tie on 1st innings in match lost.

BEST INDIVIDUAL SCORES

250 MC Cowdrey, Kent v Essex, Blackheath
229 D Kenyon, Worcs v Hants, Portsmouth
222* PB Wight, Somerset v Kent, Taunton
212 MJ Horton, Worcs v Essex, Leyton

BEST INNINGS ANALYSES

9–61 DJ Halfyard, Kent v Worcs, Maidstone
9–81 D Shackleton, Hants v Gloucs, Bristol
8–41 DB Close, Yorks v Kent, Headingley
8–41 CT Spencer, Leics v Essex, Colchester

BEST MATCH ANALYSES

15–117 DJ Halfyard, Kent v Worcs, Maidstone

14–94 CT Spencer, Leics v Essex, Colchester
13–87 JS Manning, Northants v Gloucs, Peterborough
12–99 PJ Loader, Surrey v Yorks, Bradford

LEADING BATSMEN

	Inns	NO	Runs	HS	Avge
MJK Smith (Warwicks)	43	9	2169	200*	63.79
W Watson (Leics)	47	10	2017	173	54.51
PB Wight (Somerset)	36	3	1799	222*	54.51
KF Barrington (Surrey)	32	4	1498	186	53.50
PBH May (Surrey)	10	1	481	143	53.44
JM Parks (Sussex)	49	10	2082	157*	53.38
MC Cowdrey (Kent)	31	3	1487	250	53.10
DJ Insole (Essex)	39	4	1817	180	51.91
DB Carr (Derbys)	49	7	2092	156*	49.80
WGA Parkhouse (Glamorgan)	43	3	1991	154	49.77

LEADING BOWLERS

	Runs	Wkts	Avge
DA Allen (Gloucs)	1091	70	15.58
JJ Warr (Middx)	1735	107	16.21
JB Statham (Lancs)	1600	97	16.49
JE McConnon (Glam)	1866	106	17.60
RG Thompson (Warwicks)	1665	93	17.90
HL Jackson (Derbys)	2114	117	18.06
C Cook (Gloucs)	1635	89	18.37
AE Moss (Middx)	1343	73	18.39
FS Trueman (Yorks)	1712	92	18.60
JB Mortimore (Gloucs)	1586	85	18.65

LEADING ALL-ROUNDERS

	Runs (Avge)	Wkts (Avge)
FJ Titmus (Middx)	1242 (26.42)	102 (24.52)
GE Tribe (Northants)	1001 (27.05)	116 (23.00)

LEADING WICKET-KEEPERS

	Dismissals		Total
JM Parks (Sussex)	79ct	6st	85
L Harrison (Hants)	72ct	5st	77

1960

FINAL TABLE

	P	W	L	D	ND	LI	DI	Bon	Pts	Avge
1 Yorkshire	32	17	6	6	3	2	2	34	246	7.68
2 Lancashire	32	13	8	10	1	3	9	34	214	6.68
3 Middlesex	28	12	4	12	0	0	7	28	186	6.64
4 Sussex	32	12	6	12	2	2	6	28	188	5.87
5 Derbyshire	28	10	7	10	1	1	5	20	152	5.42
6 Essex	28	9	3	14	2	1	7	28	152	5.42
7 Surrey..........	28	9	6	10	3	2	3	20	138	4.92
8 Gloucestershire ..	28	9	7	12	0	0	3	16	130	4.64
9 Northamptonshire	28	8	6	13	1	1	6	16	126	4.50
10 Kent	28	7	7	12	2	1	6	20	118	4.21
11 Glamorgan	32	9	14	7	2	0	4	16	133	4.15
12 Hampshire	32	8	8	14	2	1	6	22	132	4.12
13 Worcestershire ..	32	8	12	10	2	1	6	20	130	4.06
14 Somerset	32	5	11	15	1	2	10	22	106	3.31
15 Warwickshire....	32	4	12	16	0	2	9	26	96	3.00
16 Nottinghamshire .	28	4	16	7	1	4	2	12	72	2.57
17 Leicestershire ...	28	2	13	12	1	0	5	12	46	1.64

Each county could now play either 28 or 32 matches. The Champions were therefore the side with the highest average number of points per match. If two or more sides finished with the same average, the side with the highest wins average would have priority. If still equal, the side with highest bonus points average would prevail.
Glamorgan total includes 1 pt for 1st innings tie in match lost.

BEST INDIVIDUAL SCORES

203* NF Horner, Warwicks v Surrey, Oval
201 D Kenyon, Worcs v Glamorgan, Stourbridge
198 DB Close, Yorks v Surrey, Oval
190 G Atkinson, Somerset v Glamorgan, Bath

BEST INNINGS ANALYSES

9-30 D Shackleton, Hants v Warwicks, Portsmouth
9-43 MJ Cowan, Yorks v Warwicks, Edgbaston
8-37 AE Moss, Middx v Glamorgan, Neath
8-39 F Ridgway, Kent v Lancs, Dartford

BEST MATCH ANALYSES

15-123 R Illingworth, Yorks v Glamorgan, Swansea
14-58 JB Statham, Lancs v Leics, Leicester
14-123 FS Trueman, Yorks v Surrey, Oval
14-125 FS Trueman, Yorks v Northants, Sheffield

LEADING BATSMEN

	Inns	NO	Runs	HS	Avge
R Subba Row (Northants)	19	4	859	147*	57.26
ER Dexter (Sussex)	34	2	1771	157	55.34
MJK Smith (Warwicks)	45	6	1867	169*	47.87
JH Edrich (Surrey)	34	3	1424	154	45.93
JM Parks (Sussex)	36	6	1315	155	43.83
WJ Stewart (Warwicks)	41	3	1652	129	43.47
MJ Stewart (Surrey)	41	5	1533	169*	42.58
H Horton (Hants)	54	8	1943	131	42.23
CJ Poole (Notts)	45	6	1622	133	41.58
RE Marshall (Hants)	55	5	2062	168	41.24

LEADING BOWLERS

	Runs	Wkts	Avge
JB Statham (Lancs)	1059	97	10.91

AE Moss (Middx)	1426	114	12.50
FS Trueman (Yorks)	1689	132	12.79
HL Jackson (Derbys)	1965	146	13.45
JDF Larter (Northants)	750	46	16.30
D Shackleton (Hants)	2146	128	16.76
D Gibson (Surrey)	1407	83	16.95
D Ward (Glamorgan)	489	28	17.46
JJ Warr (Middx)	1176	66	17.81
DJ Shepherd (Glamorgan)	2388	133	17.95

LEADING ALL-ROUNDERS

	Runs (Avge)	Wkts (Avge)
TE Bailey (Essex)	1375 (40.44)	92 (21.52)
FJ Titmus (Middx)	1092 (28.00)	99 (20.77)

LEADING WICKET-KEEPERS

	Dismissals		Total
R Booth (Worcs)	80ct	16st	96
JT Murray (Middx)	87ct	4st	91

1961

FINAL TABLE

	P	W	L	D	ND	LI	DI	Bon	Pts	Avge
1 Hampshire	32	19	7	6	0	1	3	32	268	8.37
2 Yorkshire	32	17	5	10	0	1	5	34	250	7.81
3 Middlesex	28	15	6	6	1	3	1	26	214	7.64
4 Worcestershire	32	16	9	7	0	2	3	24	226	7.06
5 Gloucestershire	28	11	11	5	1	2	2	18	158	5.64
6 Essex	28	10	8	10	0	2	4	26	158	5.64
7 Derbyshire	28	10	9	9	0	3	3	22	154	5.50
8 Sussex	32	11	10	11	0	1	8	20	170	5.31
9 Leicestershire	28	9	13	5	1	2	4	26	146	5.21
10 Somerset	32	10	15	7	0	6	3	24	162	5.06
11 Kent	28	8	8	12	0	1	7	20	132	4.71
12 Warwickshire	32	9	10	13	0	1	7	26	150	4.68
13 Lancashire	32	9	7	15	1	1	7	18	142	4.43
14 Glamorgan	32	9	12	11	0	1	4	10	128	4.00
15 Surrey	28	4	13	11	0	6	8	24	100	3.57
16 Northamptonshire	28	5	13	10	0	1	5	10	82	2.92
17 Nottinghamshire	28	4	20	4	0	6	2	12	76	2.71

The rule whereby a side batting in the fourth innings in a drawn match scores 6 points by levelling the scores changes: no longer applies where an innings has been forfeited, in which event only 2 pts are awarded.

BEST INDIVIDUAL SCORES

229* ASM Oakman, Sussex v Notts, Shireoaks
221* WE Alley, Somerset v Warwicks, Nuneaton
217* W Watson, Leics v Somerset, Taunton
212 RE Marshall, Hants v Somerset, Bournemouth
203* MR Hallam, Leics v Sussex, Worthing
203* K Taylor, Yorks v Warwicks, Edgbaston

BEST INNINGS ANALYSES

8-38 MD Burden, Hants v Somerset, Frome
8-41 BA Langford, Somerset v Northants, Northampton
8-43 JA Flavell, Worcs v Lancs, Old Trafford
8-48 MHJ Allen, Northants v Derbys, Northampton

BEST MATCH ANALYSES

13-98   MHJ Allen, Northants v Derbys, Northampton
13-115 OS Wheatley, Glamorgan v Leics, Leicester
12-58   FS Trueman, Yorks v Leics, Sheffield
12-78   BA Langford, Somerset v Northants, Northampton

LEADING BATSMEN

	Inns	NO	Runs	HS	Avge
KF Barrington (Surrey)	24	5	1348	163	70.94
WE Alley (Somerset)	56	11	2532	221*	56.26
MC Cowdrey (Kent)	20	0	969	156	51.00
G Pullar (Lancs)	41	6	1615	165*	46.14
RAE Tindall (Surrey)	19	4	688	100*	45.86
RE Marshall (Hants)	58	2	2455	212	43.83
W Watson (Leics)	31	3	1222	217*	43.64
B Constable (Surrey)	46	8	1606	179	42.26
MJK Smith (Warwicks)	51	3	2009	145	41.85
MR Hallam (Leics)	54	8	1822	203*	39.60

LEADING BOWLERS

	Runs	Wkts	Avge
R Illingworth (Yorks)	1618	101	16.01
BS Boshier (Leics)	1542	96	16.06
FS Trueman (Yorks)	1781	109	16.33
DA Allen (Gloucs)	1578	96	16.43
AJG Pearson (Somerset)	405	23	17.60
JB Statham (Lancs)	1399	78	17.93
JA Flavell (Worcs)	2501	139	17.99
CT Spencer (Leics)	2065	112	18.43
AE Moss (Middx)	2079	112	18.56
HL Jackson (Derbys)	1481	78	18.98

LEADING ALL-ROUNDERS

	Runs	(Avge)	Wkts	(Avge)
TE Bailey (Essex)	1096	(28.84)	114	(20.10)
KE Palmer (Somerset)	1017	(26.76)	113	(19.68)
FJ Titmus (Middx)	1501	(36.60)	123	(21.58)

LEADING WICKET-KEEPERS

	Dismissals		Total
R Booth (Worcs)	74ct	14st	88
DG Ufton (Kent)	73ct	12st	85

1962

FINAL TABLE

	P	W	L	D	ND	LI	DI	Bon	Pts	Avge
1 Yorkshire	32	14	4	14	0	1	9	36	224	7.00
2 Worcestershire	32	14	3	14	1	1	8	34	220	6.87
3 Warwickshire	32	12	5	15	0	2	11	32	202	6.31
4 Gloucestershire	28	11	11	6	0	5	4	24	174	6.21
5 Surrey	28	10	3	14	1	2	9	32	174	6.21
6 Somerset	32	12	7	13	0	1	7	30	190	5.93
7 Derbyshire	28	8	6	13	1	2	8	28	144	5.14
8 Northamptonshire	28	7	5	16	0	1	10	22	128	4.57
9 Essex	28	8	6	13	1	2	7	12	126	4.50
10 Hampshire	32	7	5	19	1	2	11	30	140	4.37
11 Kent	28	7	9	10	2	2	3	16	110	3.92
12 Sussex	32	7	12	13	0	4	6	18	122	3.81
13 Middlesex	28	6	8	13	1	2	4	18	102	3.64
14 Glamorgan	32	6	13	13	0	1	4	14	96	3.00
15 Nottinghamshire	28	4	12	11	1	0	1	4	54	1.92
16 Lancashire	32	2	16	14	0	6	5	14	60	1.87
17 Leicestershire	28	2	12	13	1	2	5	12	50	1.78

BEST INDIVIDUAL SCORES

233 MJ Horton, Worcs v Somerset, Worcester
216 JH Edrich, Surrey v Notts, Trent Bridge
215 PB Wight, Somerset v Yorks, Taunton
213* JR Gray, Hants v Derbys, Portsmouth

BEST INNINGS ANALYSES

8-36 D Shackleton, Hants v Glamorgan, Cardiff
8-39 TW Cartwright, Warwicks v Somerset, Weston
8-55 AE Moss, Middx v Gloucs, Lord's
8-65 WE Alley, Somerset v Surrey, Oval

BEST MATCH ANALYSES

13-73 HL Jackson, Derbys v Leics, Derby
13-140 PD Watts, Northants v Hants, Bournemouth
13-159 JC Laker, Essex v Kent, Dover
12-85 KC Preston, Essex v Lancs, Leyton

LEADING BATSMEN

	Inns	NO	Runs	HS	Avge
RT Simpson (Notts)	18	4	791	105	56.50
PBH May (Surrey)	27	5	1180	135	53.63
JH Edrich (Surrey)	38	4	1676	216	49.23
MC Cowdrey (Kent)	32	3	1412	155	48.68
KF Barrington (Surrey)	34	7	1310	130*	48.51
TW Graveney (Worcs)	38	6	1539	164*	48.09
ER Dexter (Sussex)	31	5	1243	167	47.80
DC Morgan (Derbys)	44	12	1468	124	45.87
MJK Smith (Warwicks)	54	9	1988	163	44.17
PJ Watts (Northants)	48	9	1718	145	44.05

LEADING BOWLERS

	Runs	Wkts	Avge
DAD Sydenham (Surrey)	1750	107	16.35
C Cook (Gloucs)	954	56	17.03
FS Trueman (Yorks)	1889	106	17.82
LJ Coldwell (Worcs)	2400	132	18.18
R Illingworth (Yorks)	1871	102	18.34
OS Wheatley (Glamorgan)	2358	126	18.71
JC Laker (Essex)	962	51	18.86
JDF Larter (Northants)	1590	84	18.92
LA Flavell (Worcs)	1495	78	19.16
PJ Loader (Surrey)	2089	107	19.52

LEADING ALL-ROUNDERS

	Runs (Avge)	Wkts (Avge)
WE Alley (Somerset)	1783 (36.38)	107 (20.91)
TE Bailey (Essex)	1346 (36.37)	105 (20.93)
TW Cartwright (Warwicks)	1082 (31.82)	101 (20.31)
R Illingworth (Yorks)	1468 (35.80)	102 (18.34)

LEADING WICKET-KEEPERS

	Dismissals		Total
R Booth (Worcs)	81ct	14st	95
KV Andrew (Northants)	81ct	6st	87

1963

FINAL TABLE

	P	W	L	D	ND	LI	DI	Pts
1 Yorkshire	28	13	3	11	1	1	6	144
2 Glamorgan	28	11	8	8	1	1	6	124
3 Somerset	28	10	6	11	1	2	7	118
4 Sussex	28	10	6	12	0	1	7	116
Warwickshire	28	10	3	14	1	1	7	116
6 Middlesex	28	9	5	11	3	1	7	106
7 Northamptonshire	28	9	8	11	0	1	5	105
8 Gloucestershire	28	9	7	11	1	2	3	100
9 Nottinghamshire	28	6	8	13	1	4	7	82
10 Hampshire	28	7	8	10	3	1	4	80
11 Surrey	28	5	6	17	0	1	11	74
12 Essex	28	6	4	17	1	0	5	70
13 Kent	28	5	6	17	0	1	8	68
14 Worcestershire	28	4	8	13	3	2	8	60
15 Lancashire	28	4	10	13	1	2	7	58
16 Leicestershire	28	3	13	10	2	2	3	40
17 Derbyshire	28	2	14	9	3	1	3	28

New points-system: 10 for a win, 5 pts each side in a tie.
When scores are equal in drawn match, the side batting second score 5 pts, the opponents no points other than any gained in 1st innings. Northants total includes 5 pts in drawn match by levelling the scores batting last.
For 1st innings lead in match lost or drawn, 2 pts; if 1st innings scores are equal, the losers score 1 point. If drawn, both teams score 2 points. If no play in first two-thirds of match, and match decided on 1st innings, winning side scores 6 pts. If the scores are equal in such a match, the side batting second scores 3 pts. Rankings: if points are equal, number of wins decides placings.

BEST INDIVIDUAL SCORES

211 D Nicholls, Kent v Derbys, Folkestone
202* JB Bolus, Notts v Glamorgan, Trent Bridge
191* LJ Lenham, Sussex v Warwicks, Edgbaston
187* A Jones, Glamorgan v Somerset, Glastonbury

BEST INNINGS ANALYSES

9–57 KE Palmer, Somerset v Notts, Trent Bridge
8–40 OS Wheatley, Glamorgan v Worcs, Swansea
8–41 JDF Larter, Northants v Sussex, Worthing
8–45 TW Cartwright, Warwicks v Hants, Coventry
8–45 FS Trueman, Yorks v Gloucs, Bradford

BEST MATCH ANALYSES

13–96   AS Brown, Gloucs v Derbys, Derby
13–104 FE Rumsey, Somerset v Notts, Taunton
12–59   FE Rumsey, Somerset v Glamorgan, Neath
12–101 TW Cartwright, Warwicks v Hants, Coventry

LEADING BATSMEN

	Inns	NO	Runs	HS	Avge
KF Barrington (Surrey)	29	6	1090	100*	47.39
G Boycott (Yorks)	38	7	1446	165*	46.64
MJK Smith (Warwicks)	32	4	1288	144*	46.00
JB Bolus (Notts)	42	4	1728	202*	45.47
PE Richardson (Kent)	45	2	1798	172	41.81
JH Edrich (Surrey)	39	6	1330	125*	40.30
SE Leary (Kent)	36	5	1234	158	39.80
CC Inman (Leics)	48	9	1482	83	38.00
RE Marshall (Hants)	48	3	1696	161*	37.68
G Atkinson (Somerset)	39	2	1363	177	36.83

LEADING BOWLERS

	Runs	Wkts	Avge
FS Trueman (Yorks)	976	76	12.84
D Shackleton (Hants)	1721	116	14.83
JB Statham (Lancs)	1522	101	15.06
DAD Sydenham (Surrey)	1528	101	15.12
AE Moss (Middx)	1258	79	15.92
KE Palmer (Somerset)	1936	121	16.00
JDF Larter (Northants)	1765	110	16.04
AG Nicholson (Yorks)	1056	65	16.24
R Illingworth (Yorks)	786	48	16.37
ASM Oakman (Sussex)	868	51	17.01

LEADING ALL-ROUNDERS

	Runs (Avge)	Wkts (Avge)
BR Knight (Essex)	1317 (30.62)	116 (21.27)
JB Mortimore (Gloucs)	1339 (29.10)	93 (20.17)
JS Pressdee (Glamorgan)	1228 (31.48)	94 (20.12)

LEADING WICKET-KEEPERS

	Dismissals		Total
DL Evans (Glamorgan)	70ct	10st	80
JG Binks (Yorks)	73ct	7st	80

1964

FINAL TABLE

	P	W	L	D	ND	LI	DI	Pts
1 Worcestershire ..	28	18	3	6	1	0	5	191
2 Warwickshire ...	28	14	5	9	0	0	5	150
3 Northamptonshire	28	12	4	11	1	0	5	130
4 Surrey	28	11	3	13	1	0	9	129
5 Yorkshire	28	11	3	14	0	0	8	126
6 Middlesex	28	9	6	12	1	2	9	112
7 Kent	28	9	6	12	1	3	6	108
8 Somerset	28	8	8	8	4	4	4	96
9 Sussex	28	8	9	10	1	1	3	88
10 Essex	28	7	11	8	2	5	3	86
11 Glamorgan	28	7	7	12	2	1	6	84
12 Derbyshire	28	5	9	12	2	4	5	68
Hampshire	28	5	8	14	1	1	5	68
14 Lancashire	28	4	10	13	1	4	8	64
15 Nottinghamshire .	28	4	13	11	0	3	4	54
16 Leicestershire ...	28	3	18	5	2	7	0	44
17 Gloucestershire ..	28	3	15	10	0	2	4	43

Surrey and Worcestershire, 1 point each for 1st innings tie in drawn match. Gloucs and Hants totals include 1 point for 1st innings tie in match lost. Hants also scored 5 points in drawn match when scores finished level and they were batting.

BEST INDIVIDUAL SCORES

227* MJ Stewart, Surrey v Middlesex, Oval
207 KF Barrington, Surrey v Notts, Oval
200* PH Parfitt, Middx v Notts, Trent Bridge
193 WE Russell, Middx v Hants, Bournemouth

BEST INNINGS ANALYSES

10-49 NI Thomson, Sussex v Warwicks, Worthing
9-28 DL Underwood, Kent v Sussex, Hastings
9-56 JA Flavell, Worcs v Middx, Kidderminster
9-57 FJ Titmus, Middx v Lancs, Lord's

BEST MATCH ANALYSES

15-75 NI Thomson, Sussex v Warwicks, Worthing
15-108 JB Statham, Lancs v Leics, Leicester
14-101 R Illingworth, Yorks v Kent, Dover
13-94 ME Scott, Northants v Sussex, Hastings

LEADING BATSMEN

	Inns	NO	Runs	HS	Avge
KF Barrington (Surrey)	25	4	1263	207	60.14
G Boycott (Yorks)	28	4	1427	177	59.45
MC Cowdrey (Kent)	27	3	1330	117	55.41
TW Graveney (Worcs)	48	7	2271	164	55.39
MJ Stewart (Surrey)	40	5	1792	227*	51.20
RC Wilson (Kent)	47	5	1979	156	47.11
MD Willett (Surrey)	45	11	1584	126	46.58
WE Russell (Middx)	51	4	2050	193	43.61
JM Parks (Sussex)	34	7	1162	103*	43.03
JH Edrich (Surrey)	35	3	1328	124	41.50

LEADING BOWLERS

	Runs	Wkts	Avge
TW Cartwright (Warwicks)	1765	128	13.78
AG Nicholson (Yorks)	976	70	13.94
JA Standen (Worcs)	750	52	14.42
LJ Coldwell (Worcs)	1124	77	14.59
JA Flavell (Worcs)	1524	101	15.08
NI Thomson (Sussex)	1740	109	15.96
FJ Titmus (Middx)	1623	101	16.06
N Gifford (Worcs)	1688	98	17.22
R Illingworth (Yorks)	1798	104	17.28
C Forbes (Notts)	950	53	17.92

LEADING ALL-ROUNDERS

	Runs (Avge)	Wkts (Avge)
R Illingworth (Yorks)	1055 (36.37)	104 (17.28)
JS Pressdee (Glamorgan)	1428 (38.59)	82 (19.00)

LEADING WICKET-KEEPERS

	Dismissals		Total
R Booth (Worcs)	88ct	7st	95
BSV Timms (Hants)	57ct	18st	75

1965

FINAL TABLE

	P	W	L	D	ND	LI	DI	Pts
1 Worcestershire ..	28	13	4	10	1	1	6	144
2 Northamptonshire	28	13	4	9	2	0	5	140
3 Glamorgan	28	12	6	8	2	2	4	132
4 Yorkshire	28	9	4	14	1	1	11	114
5 Kent	28	8	5	14	1	0	8	96
6 Middlesex	28	8	7	12	1	0	7	94
7 Somerset	28	8	11	8	1	2	4	92
8 Surrey	28	7	4	15	2	1	8	92
9 Derbyshire......	28	7	9	11	1	2	6	86
10 Gloucestershire..	28	7	8	11	2	1	5	82
11 Warwickshire ...	28	5	5	18	0	1	9	70
12 Hampshire......	28	5	4	17	2	0	8	66
13 Lancashire	28	5	13	9	1	0	5	60
14 Leicestershire ...	28	5	11	11	1	2	2	58
15 Essex	28	4	7	16	1	0	7	54
16 Sussex	28	4	10	14	0	2	4	52
17 Nottinghamshire .	28	3	11	13	1	3	6	48

Surrey total includes 6 points for 1st innings lead in match restricted to last third of allotted time.

BEST INDIVIDUAL SCORES

205* JH Edrich, Surrey v Gloucs, Bristol
196* MC Cowdrey, Kent v Notts, Trent Bridge
188 JH Edrich, Surrey v Northants, Northampton
180* JH Edrich, Surrey v Sussex, Hove

BEST INNINGS ANALYSES

9-25 RMH Cottam, Hants v Lancs, Old Trafford
9-43 JS Pressdee, Glamorgan v Yorks, Swansea
9-48 DJ Shepherd, Glamorgan v Yorks, Swansea
8-11 IJ Jones, Glamorgan v Leics, Leicester

BEST MATCH ANALYSES

14-99 D Shackleton, Hants v Warwicks, Bournemouth

13–77 FS Trueman, Yorks v Sussex, Hove

13–96 JA Flavell, Worcs v Somerset, Kiddermisnter

12–56 JDF Larter, Northants v Somerset, Northampton

LEADING BATSMEN

	Inns	NO	Runs	HS	Avge
MC Cowdrey (Kent)	24	5	1230	196*	64.73
TW Graveney (Worcs)	44	9	1684	126	48.11
PH Parfitt (Middx)	32	6	1242	128	47.76
JH Edrich (Surrey)	34	2	1513	205*	47.28
BL D'Oliveira (Worcs)	41	6	1523	163	43.51
WE Russell (Middx)	48	4	1724	156	39.18
WJ Stewart (Warwicks)	38	8	1175	102	39.16
A Jones (Glamorgan)	49	6	1665	142	38.72
ER Dexter (Sussex)	14	1	468	98	36.00
G Boycott (Yorks)	28	1	942	95	34.88

LEADING BOWLERS

	Runs	Wkts	Avge
HJ Rhodes (Derbys)	1276	115	11.09
FS Trueman (Yorks)	1307	115	11.36
AB Jackson (Derbys)	1424	115	12.37
JB Statham (Lancs)	1540	124	12.41
TW Cartwright (Warwicks)	1265	94	13.45
JDF Larter (Northants)	960	71	13.52
FE Rumsey (Somerset)	1367	94	14.54
JA Flavell (Worcs)	1979	132	14.99
DJ Shepherd (Glamorgan)	1615	107	15.09
IJ Jones (Glamorgan)	1147	75	15.29

LEADING ALL-ROUNDERS

	Runs (Avge)		Wkts (Avge)	
BR Knight (Essex)	966	(22.46)	111	(18.45)
BS Crump (Northants)	784	(27.03)	112	(18.88)

LEADING WICKET-KEEPERS

	Dismissals		Total
G Clayton (Somerset)	71ct	14st	85
RW Taylor (Derby)	76ct	6st	82

FINAL TABLE

	P	W	L	D	ND	FIL	Pts
1 Yorkshire	28	15	5	8	0	17	184
2 Worcestershire	28	13	5	9	1	18	166
3 Somerset	28	13	7	7	1	13	156
4 Kent	28	11	8	8	1	17	144
5 Northamptonshire	28	10	9	9	0	15	130
6 Warwickshire	28	8	8	10	2	16	113
7 Surrey	28	8	3	16	1	15	110
8 Leicestershire	28	8	7	12	1	14	108
9 Derbyshire	28	8	12	7	1	8	96
10 Sussex	28	6	11	11	0	16	92
11 Hampshire	28	5	4	18	1	16	87
12 Lancashire	28	6	11	8	3	13	86
13 Middlesex	28	6	5	14	3	13	86
14 Glamorgan	28	6	8	13	1	10	85
15 Gloucestershire	28	6	12	9	1	7	75
16 Essex	28	4	10	11	3	10	60
17 Nottinghamshire	28	3	11	12	2	8	46

Points for first innings lead (FIL) now retained whatever the result. The 1st innings in the opening 102 matches (out of 238) was restricted to 65 overs.

Warwicks and Hants totals include 1 points each for a 1st-innings tie. Hants and Glamorgan each include 5 points, batting in drawn match when scores finished level.

1966

BEST INDIVIDUAL SCORES

223 AR Lewis, Glamorgan v Kent, Gravesend

203 C Milburn, Northants v Essex, Clacton

183 BW Luckhurst, Kent v Surrey, Blackheath

172* KG Suttle, Sussex v Middlesex, Hove

BEST INNINGS ANALYSES

9–37 DL Underwood, Kent v Essex, Westcliff

9–44 DW White, Hants v Leics, Portsmouth

8–18 AB Jackson, Derbys v Warwicks, Coventry

8–23 A Buss, Sussex v Notts, Hove

BEST MATCH ANALYSES

13–57 DL Underwood, Kent v Essex, Westcliff

13–97 TW Cartwright, Warwicks v Northants,
       Edgbaston
13–119 E Smith, Derbys v Hants, Chesterfield
13–164 RNS Hobbs, Essex v Glamorgan,
       Swansea

1967

LEADING BATSMEN

	Inns	NO	Runs	HS	Avge
TW Graveney (Worcs)	32	5	1277	166	47.29
JH Edrich (Surrey)	44	3	1913	137	46.65
C Milburn (Northants)	33	3	1398	203	46.60
MJK Smith (Warwicks)	44	8	1607	117	44.63
PH Parfitt (Middx)	50	8	1860	114*	44.28
AR Lewis (Glamorgan)	51	4	1960	223	41.70
KF Barrington (Surrey)	29	6	928	117*	40.34
G Boycott (Yorks)	31	3	1097	164	39.17
RM Prideaux (Northants)	51	5	1670	153*	36.30
BL D'Oliveira (Worcs)	33	5	1004	126	35.85

LEADING BOWLERS

	Runs	Wkts	Avge
DL Underwood (Kent)	1745	143	12.20
JA Flavell (Worcs)	1891	135	14.00
JB Statham (Lancs)	1424	100	14.24
R Illingworth (Yorks)	1234	85	14.51
AG Nicholson (Yorks)	1581	105	15.05
N Gifford (Worcs)	1429	90	15.87
OS Wheatley (Glamorgan)	1607	100	16.07
D Wilson (Yorks)	1443	87	16.58
DJ Shepherd (Glamorgan)	1844	111	16.61
DR Smith (Gloucs)	947	57	16.61

LEADING ALL-ROUNDERS

	Runs	(Avge)	Wkts	(Avge)
SJ Storey (Surrey)	1013	(24.70)	103	(18.39)
PT Marner (Leics)	1063	(24.72)	74	(25.74)
DC Morgan (Derbys)	962	(23.46)	84	(20.17)
KE Palmer (Somerset)	851	(21.82)	98	(18.75)

LEADING WICKET-KEEPERS

	Dismissals		Total
G Clayton (Somerset)	73ct	10st	83
APE Knott (Kent)	68ct	8st	76

FINAL TABLE

	P	W	L	D(T)	ND	FIL	Pts
1 Yorkshire	28	12	5	9	2	18	186
2 Kent	28	11	3	12	2	16	176
3 Leicestershire ...	28	10	3	12	3	18	176
4 Surrey	28	8	4	12	4	15	148
5 Worcestershire ..	28	6	6	16	0	13	132
6 Derbyshire	28	5	5	17	1	14	130
7 Middlesex	28	5	4	14(1)	4	14	128
8 Somerset	28	5	7	14	2	13	120
9 Northamptonshire	28	7	8	11	2	10	118
10 Warwickshire ...	28	5	4	15	4	11	118
11 Lancashire	28	4	3	17	4	12	116
12 Hampshire	28	5	6	13(1)	3	10	114
13 Sussex	28	5	9	12	2	10	104
14 Glamorgan	28	4	7	15	2	9	100
15 Essex	28	3	9	14	2	9	88
16 Nottinghamshire .	28	0	4	22	2	11	88
17 Gloucestershire ..	28	3	11	9	5	11	86

Points-system: 8 for win, 4 each for tie; 2 each for draw, provided a 1st innings result has been achieved. All the above in addition to 1st innings points, which are 4 for lead, 2 each for tie. If the innings of the side batting second is not completed, only that side scores 4 pts. Where scores are equal in a drawn game, 4 pts go to the side batting, plus any for 1st innings. Warwickshire and Hants totals include 4 pts from drawn matches where scores finished level and they were batting. Lancs, Warwicks, Hants and Glamorgan include 2 points for tie on 1st innings.

BEST INDIVIDUAL SCORES

226* JH Edrich, Surrey v Middx, Oval
220* G Boycott, Yorks v Northants, Sheffield
181   MJ Smith, Middx v Lancs, Old Trafford
176* DL Amiss, Warwicks v Notts, Coventry

BEST INNINGS ANALYSES

9–62 AG Nicholson, Yorks v Sussex,
      Eastbourne
8–25 AW Greig, Sussex v Gloucs, Hove
8–41 GG Arnold, Surrey v Gloucs, Oval
8–50 TW Cartwright, Warwicks v Glamorgan,
      Swansea

BEST MATCH ANALYSES

15–89   TW Cartwright, Warwicks v
        Glamorgan, Swansea
14–82   DL Underwood, Kent v Sussex,
        Hastings
13–52   D Wilson, Yorks v Warwicks,
        Middlesbrough
13–116 GAR Lock, Leics v Glamorgan,
        Leicester

LEADING BATSMEN

	Inns	NO	Runs	HS	Avge
KF Barrington	22	6	1058	158*	66.12
(Surrey)					
DL Amiss (Warwicks)	28	5	1260	176*	54.78
JH Edrich (Surrey)	36	5	1658	226*	53.48
G Boycott (Yorks)	28	2	1260	220*	48.46
CA Milton (Gloucs)	46	4	1971	145	46.92
MJ Stewart (Surrey)	28	3	1133	112	45.32
RM Prideaux	35	5	1285	115	42.83
(Northants)					
PH Parfitt (Middx)	45	9	1520	162*	42.22
WE Russell (Middx)	42	5	1498	125	40.48
C Milburn (Northants)	38	4	1369	141*	40.23

LEADING BOWLERS

	Runs	Wkts	Avge
DL Underwood (Kent)	1344	111	12.10
GA Cope (Yorks)	409	32	12.78
JN Graham (Kent)	1446	104	13.90
HJ Rhodes (Derby)	1484	94	15.78
TW Cartwright	2092	132	15.84
(Warwicks)			
K Higgs (Lancs)	1187	74	16.04
D Shackleton (Hants)	1836	112	16.39
JB Statham (Lancs)	1459	89	16.39
DR Cook (Warwicks)	330	20	16.50
AB Jackson (Derbys)	1057	63	16.77

LEADING ALL-ROUNDERS

	Runs (Avge)	Wkts (Avge)
DC Morgan (Derbys)	1062 (31.23)	76 (19.35)
J Birkenshaw (Leics)	809 (25.28)	97 (22.26)
KE Palmer	852 (24.34)	81 (19.44)
(Somerset)		

FJ Titmus (Middx)   871 (33.50) 90   (19.76)

LEADING WICKET-KEEPERS

	Dismissals		Total
APE Knott (Kent)	81ct	8st	89
G Clayton (Somerset)	58ct	9st	67

1968

FINAL TABLE

	P	W	L	D	Ab	Bt	Bl	Pts
1 Yorkshire	28	11	4	13	0	46	114	270
2 Kent	28	12	5	11	0	41	95	256
3 Glamorgan	28	11	6	9	2	42	85	237
4 Nottinghamshire	28	7	3	17	1	53	99	222
5 Hampshire	28	8	5	15	0	43	92	215
6 Lancashire	28	8	6	14	0	24	105	209
7 Worcestershire	28	8	7	13	0	26	97	203
8 Derbyshire	28	6	5	16	1	47	92	199
9 Leicestershire	28	6	10	12	0	52	85	197
10 Middlesex	28	8	6	14	0	21	91	192
11 Warwickshire	28	7	8	12	1	38	82	190
12 Somerset	28	5	11	11	1	36	86	172
13 Northamptonshire	28	5	6	17	0	34	86	170
14 Essex	28	5	6	16	1	31	88	169
15 Surrey	28	4	7	17	0	25	92	157
16 Gloucestershire	28	2	8	17	1	40	93	153
17 Sussex	28	2	12	14	0	43	77	140

*Changes to points system: 10 plus bonus pts for win. 5 each
plus bonus pts for tie. Scores equal in drawn match – side
batting scores 5 plus bonus pts.*
*First innings bonus points awarded over first 85 overs: 1 point
(Bt) for every 25 runs above 150 runs, 1 (Bl) for every 2
wickets taken.*
*In match starting with less than 8 hours' play left, no bonus
points can be scored.*

BEST INDIVIDUAL SCORES

253   R Kanhai, Warwicks v Notts, Trent
      Bridge
233   DM Green, Gloucs v Sussex, Hove
228* KWR Fletcher, Essex v Sussex, Hastings
206   BA Richards, Hants v Notts, Portsmouth

BEST INNINGS ANALYSES

9-60 OS Wheatley, Glamorgan v Sussex,
      Ebbw Vale
8-16 R Harman, Surrey v Derbys, Ilkeston
8-22 AG Nicholson, Yorks v Kent, Canterbury
8-25 AA Jones, Sussex v Lancs, Eastbourne

BEST MATCH ANALYSES

15-115 RE East, Essex v Warwicks, Leyton
14-113 RD Harman, Surrey v Derbys, Ilkeston
13-133 RNS Hobbs, Essex v Worcs,
        Chelmsford
12-69   N Gifford, Worcs v Yorks, Sheffield

LEADING BATSMEN

	Inns	NO	Runs	HS	Avge
G Boycott (Yorks)	15	5	774	180*	77.40
BA Richards (Hants)	47	5	2039	206	48.54
MC Cowdrey (Kent)	20	2	841	129	46.72
RM Prideaux	42	5	1679	108*	45.37
(Northants)					
RB Kanhai (Warwicks)	38	3	1584	253	45.25
GS Sobers (Notts)	42	7	1570	105*	44.85
KWR Fletcher (Essex)	41	6	1515	228*	43.28
DC Morgan (Derbys)	34	10	955	103*	39.79
DM Green (Gloucs)	49	1	1875	233	39.06
JB Bolus (Notts)	46	5	1580	140	38.53

LEADING BOWLERS

	Runs	Wkts	Avge
GA Cope (Yorks)	211	20	10.55
A Ward (Derbys)	308	26	11.84
D Wilson (Yorks)	1275	102	12.50
OS Wheatley (Glam)	1062	82	12.95
DL Underwood (Kent)	1236	91	13.58
R Illingworth (Yorks)	1178	86	13.69
K Higgs (Lancs)	1481	105	14.10
TW Cartwright (Warwicks)	1032	68	15.17
JCJ Dye (Kent)	489	32	15.28
BL D'Oliveira (Worcs)	913	58	15.74

LEADING ALL-ROUNDERS

	Runs (Avge)	Wkts (Avge)
GS Sobers (Notts)	1570 (44.85)	83 (22.67)
FJ Titmus (Middx)	846 (25.63)	100 (20.65)

LEADING WICKET-KEEPERS

	Dismissals		Total
DL Murray (Notts)	65ct	7st	72
EW Jones (Glamorgan)	61ct	4st	65

Glamorgan, County Champions in 1969, were the first side to remain unbeaten since 1930
(Hulton Picture Company)

1969

FINAL TABLE

	P	W	L	D	Bt	Bl	Pts
1 Glamorgan	24	11	0	13	67	73	250
2 Gloucestershire . .	24	10	6	8	26	93	219
3 Surrey	24	7	1	16	64	76	210
4 Warwickshire	24	7	3	14	41	89	205
5 Hampshire	24	6	7	11	56	87	203
6 Essex	24	6	6	12	44	85	189
7 Sussex	24	5	8	11	46	89	185
8 Nottinghamshire .	24	6	2	16	49	75	184
9 Northamptonshire	24	5	7	12	47	66	163
10 Kent	24	4	6	14	35	76	151
11 Middlesex	24	3	7	14	40	76	146
12 Worcestershire . .	24	5	7	12*	30	62	142
13 Yorkshire	24	3	6	15	30	77	142
14 Leicestershire . . .	24	4	7	13	26	64	130
15 Lancashire	24	2	1	21	39	67	126
16 Derbyshire	24	3	5	16*	22	67	119
17 Somerset	24	1	9	14	17	69	96

*Includes one match abandoned without a ball bowled.
Warwicks and Yorks totals both include 5 pts from drawn
matches, where the scores finished level and they were batting.
Schedule reduced from 28 matches to 24.

BEST INDIVIDUAL SCORES

223* RMC Gilliat, Hants v Warwicks, Southampton
181* DR Turner, Hants v Surrey, Oval
181 JH Edrich, Surrey v Warwicks, Edgbaston
173 RB Kanhai, Warwicks v Northants, Peterborough

BEST INNINGS ANALYSES

9-49 AE Cordle, Glamorgan v Leics, Colwyn Bay
8-20 JN Graham, Kent v Essex, Brentwood
8-34 DA Allen, Gloucs v Sussex, Lydney
8-65 TJP Eyre, Derbys v Somerset, Chesterfield

BEST MATCH ANALYSES

13-110 AE Cordle, Glamorgan v Leics, Colwyn Bay

12-55 TW Cartwright, Warwicks v Yorks, Bradford
11-46 CM Old, Yorks v Gloucs, Middlesbrough
11-67 Mushtaq Mohammed, Northants v Yorks, Hull

LEADING BATSMEN

	Inns	NO	Runs	HS	Avge
JH Edrich (Surrey)	24	5	1416	181	74.52
GS Sobers (Notts)	11	0	591	104	53.72
Mushtaq Mohammed (Northants)	36	8	1487	156*	53.10
EJO Hemsley (Worcs)	13	3	514	88	51.40
BA Richards (Hants)	28	5	1102	155	47.91
KWR Fletcher (Essex)	25	4	928	134*	44.19
Younis Ahmed (Surrey)	40	7	1449	127*	43.90
G Boycott (Yorks)	22	4	785	105*	43.61
A Jones (Glamorgan)	37	3	1441	122*	42.38
BW Luckhurst (Kent)	40	2	1593	169	41.92

LEADING BOWLERS

	Runs	Wkts	Avge
A Ward (Derbys)	724	56	12.92
MJ Procter (Gloucs)	1561	103	15.15
R Illingworth (Leics)	585	38	15.39
TW Cartwright (Warwicks)	1527	95	16.07
JA Snow (Sussex)	1069	66	16.19
CM Old (Yorks)	941	55	17.10
DL Underwood (Kent)	978	57	17.15
D Wilson (Yorks)	1528	85	17.97
JN Graham (Kent)	1400	77	18.18
HJ Rhodes (Derbys)	1088	59	18.44

LEADING ALL-ROUNDERS

	Runs	(Avge)	Wkts	(Avge)
Mushtaq Mohammed (Northants)	1487	(53.10)	68	(22.75)
KD Boyce (Essex)	840	(27.09)	70	(22.75)

LEADING WICKET-KEEPERS

	Dismissals		Total
EW Jones (Glamorgan)	61ct	6st	67
GR Stephenson (Surrey)	55ct	3st	58

1970

FINAL TABLE

		P	W	L	D	Bt	Bl	Pts
I	Kent	24	9	5	10	70	77	237
2	Glamorgan	24	9	6	9	48	82	220
3	Lancashire	24	6	2	16	78	78	216
4	Yorkshire	24	8	5	II	49	86	215
5	Surrey..........	24	6	4	14	60	83	203
6	Worcestershire ..	24	7	I	16	46	84	200
7	Derbyshire	24	7	7	10	51	78	199
8	Warwickshire....	24	7	6	II	53	71	199
9	Sussex	24	5	7	12	62	87	199
10	Hampshire	24	4	6	14	69	88	197
II	Nottinghamshire .	24	4	8	12	71	73	184
12	Essex	24	4	6	14	64	76	180
13	Somerset	24	5	10	9	40	86	176
14	Northamptonshire	24	4	6	14	60	74	174
15	Leicestershire ...	24	5	6	13	46	77	173
16	Middlesex	24	5	5	14	47	69	166
17	Gloucestershire ..	24	3	8	13	56	80	166

BEST INDIVIDUAL SCORES

260* G Boycott, Yorks v Essex, Colchester
208 HM Ackerman, Northants v Leics, Leicester
189* RE Marshall, Hants v Middlesex, Lord's
187* RB Kanhai, Warwicks v Derbys, Coventry

BEST INNINGS ANALYSES

8–37 LR Gibbs, Warwicks v Glamorgan, Edgbaston
8–39 D Breakwell, Northants v Kent, Dover
8–56 JSE Price, Middlesex v Kent, Lord's
8–74 Intikhab Alam, Surrey v Middx, Oval

BEST MATCH ANALYSES

14–89 JSE Price, Middx v Kent, Lord's
14–213 DL Underwood, Kent v Warwicks, Gravesend

12–89 DJ Shepherd, Glamorgan v Warwicks, Edgbaston
12–94 TW Cartwright, Somerset v Essex, Leyton

LEADING BATSMEN

	Inns	NO	Runs	HS	Avge
GS Sobers (Notts)	23	8	1154	160	76.93
RB Kanhai (Warwicks)	25	3	1500	187*	68.18
TW Graveney (Worcs)	33	13	1243	114	62.15
GM Turner (Worcs)	45	7	2346	154*	61.73
BA Richards (Hants)	25	1	1410	153	58.75
JB Bolus (Notts)	47	8	2033	147*	52.12
G Boycott (Yorks)	31	3	1425	260*	50.89
DW White (Hants)	12	9	150	57	50.00
MC Cowdrey (Kent)	27	6	1013	126	48.23
JH Edrich (Surrey)	32	3	1388	143	47.86

LEADING BOWLERS

	Runs	Wkts	Avge
DJ Shepherd (Glamorgan)	1891	101	18.72
CM Old (Yorks)	1136	60	18.93
B Wood (Lancs)	567	29	19.55
GD McKenzie (Leics)	1522	76	20.02
J Sullivan (Lancs)	449	22	20.40
N Gifford (Worcs)	1986	96	20.68
MJ Procter (Gloucs)	1039	50	20.78
VA Holder (Worcs)	1696	81	20.93
RNS Hobbs (Essex)	1820	86	21.16
K Shuttleworth (Lancs)	1544	72	21.44

LEADING ALL-ROUNDERS

	Runs	(Avge)	Wkts	(Avge)
RA Hutton (Yorks)	755	(26.96)	67	(22.43)
TW Cartwright (Somerset)	766	(21.88)	86	(21.98)

LEADING WICKET-KEEPERS

	Dismissals		Total
FM Engineer (Lancs)	77ct	3st	80
EW Jones (Glamorgan)	71ct	8st	79

1971

FINAL TABLE

	P	W	L	D	Bt	Bl	Pts
1 Surrey..........	24	11	3	10	63	82	255
2 Warwickshire....	24	9	9	6	73	92	255
3 Lancashire	24	9	4	11	76	75	241
4 Kent...........	24	7	6	11	82	82	234
5 Leicestershire ...	24	6	2	16	76	74	215
6 Middlesex	24	7	6	11	61	81	212
7 Somerset	24	7	4	13	50	89	209
8 Gloucestershire..	24	7	3	13	50	81	201
9 Hampshire	24	4	6	14	70	82	192
10 Essex	24	6	5	13	43	84	187
11 Sussex	24	5	9	10	55	77	182
12 Nottinghamshire .	24	3	7	14	58	83	171
13 Yorkshire.......	24	4	8	12	47	75	162
14 Northamptonshire	24	4	8	12	36	83	159
15 Worcestershire ..	24	3	7	14	46	76	152
16 Glamorgan	24	3	5	15	55	63	148
17 Derbyshire......	24	1	4	19	51	81	142

*Leics total includes 5 pts from drawn match v Surrey when
scores finished level and they were batting.
Gloucs v Glamorgan: abandoned without ball bowled.*

BEST INDIVIDUAL SCORES

233 G Boycott, Yorks v Essex, Colchester
217* CH Lloyd, Lancs v Warks, Old Trafford
195* JH Edrich, Surrey v Somerset, Taunton
195 JF Steele, Leics v Derbys, Leicester

BEST INNINGS ANALYSES

8-42 AW Greig, Sussex v Kent, Tunbridge
Wells
8-76 PJ Sainsbury, Hants v Gloucs,
Portsmouth
7-8 GD McKenzie, Leics v Glamorgan,
Leicester
7-23 LR Gibbs, Warwicks v Essex, Edgbaston

BEST MATCH ANALYSES

12-79 KJ O'Keeffe, Somerset v Sussex,
Taunton
12-125 GI Burgess, Somerset v Gloucs, Bath
12-127 PJ Sainsbury, Hants v Gloucs,
Portsmouth
12-157 KJ O'Keeffe, Somerset v Worcs,
Taunton

LEADING BATSMEN

	Inns	NO	Runs	HS	Avge
G Boycott (Yorks)	24	4	2197	233	109.85
JH Edrich (Surrey)	30	1	1718	195*	59.24
MJ Harris (Notts)	40	1	1977	177	50.69
MJK Smith (Warwicks)	41	7	1689	122	49.67
Asif Iqbal (Kent)	14	2	585	120	48.75
RB Kanhai (Warwicks)	38	8	1452	135*	48.40
RC Fredericks (Glam)	29	3	1253	145*	48.19
BW Luckhurst (Kent)	24	1	1103	155*	47.95
MJ Procter (Gloucs)	41	4	1762	167	47.62
AR Lewis (Glamorgan)	32	6	1211	111	46.57

LEADING BOWLERS

	Runs	Wkts	Avge
GG Arnold (Surrey)	1221	75	16.28
DL Underwood (Kent)	1630	97	16.80
TW Cartwright (Somerset)	1731	96	18.03
PJ Sainsbury (Hants)	1834	101	18.15
RA Hutton (Yorks)	1038	57	18.21
GD McKenzie (Leics)	1514	81	18.69
R Illingworth (Leics)	789	42	18.78
LR Gibbs (Warwicks)	2318	123	18.84
MJ Procter (Gloucs)	1187	62	19.14
D Wilson (Yorks)	979	49	19.97

LEADING ALL-ROUNDERS

	Runs (Avge)		Wkts (Avge)	
PJ Sainsbury (Hants)	947	(33.82)	101	(18.15)
AW Greig (Sussex)	1138	(27.09)	71	(28.18)
MJ Procter (Gloucs)	1762	(47.62)	62	(19.14)
RA White (Notts)	772	(28.59)	72	(28.72)

LEADING WICKET-KEEPERS

	Dismissals		Total
DL Bairstow (Yorks)	58ct	6st	64
DJS Taylor (Somerset)	55ct	7st	62

1972

FINAL TABLE

		P	W	L	D	Bt	Bl	Pts
1	Warwickshire	20	9	0	11	68	69	227
2	Kent	20	7	4	9	69	52	191
3	Gloucestershire ..	20	7	4	9	38	77	185
4	Northamptonshire	20	7	3	10	34	77	181
5	Essex	20	6	4	10	50	63	173
6	Leicestershire ...	20	6	2	12	43	68	171
7	Worcestershire ..	20	4	4	12	59	68	167
8	Middlesex	20	5	5	10	48	61	159
9	Hampshire	20	4	6	10	50	64	154
10	Yorkshire	20	4	5	11	39	73	152
11	Somerset	20	4	2	14	34	71	145
12	Surrey..........	20	3	5	12	49	61	140
13	Glamorgan	20	1	7	12	55	61	126
14	Nottinghamshire .	20	1	6	13	38	73	121
15	Lancashire	19	2	3	14	42	56	118
16	Sussex	20	2	8	10	46	49	115
17	Derbyshire	19	1	5	13	27	60	97

Derby v Lancashire at Buxton: abandoned without a ball bowled, and not included.
Schedule reduced to 20 matches.

BEST INDIVIDUAL SCORES

228* RC Fredericks, Glamorgan v Northants, Swansea
204* G Boycott, Yorks v Leics, Leicester
204 Majid Khan, Glamorgan v Surrey, Oval
203 RE Marshall, Hants v Derby, Derby

BEST INNINGS ANALYSES

9-51 AA Jones, Somerset v Sussex, Hove
8-42 RS Herman, Hants v Warwicks, Portsmouth
8-44 B Stead, Notts v Somerset, Trent Bridge
8-44 RGD Willis, Warwicks v Derbys, Edgbaston

BEST MATCH ANALYSES

13-108 TW Cartwright, Somerset v Derbys, Chesterfield
13-128 JW Holder, Hants v Gloucs, Gloucester

13-135 RA Woolmer, Kent v Sussex, Canterbury
12-78 Intikhab Alam, Surrey v Yorks, Oval

LEADING BATSMEN

	Inns	NO	Runs	HS	Avge
G Boycott (Yorks)	17	5	1156	204*	96.33
BW Luckhurst (Kent)	23	4	1345	184*	70.78
KWR Fletcher (Essex)	30	6	1644	181*	68.50
Majid Khan (Glamorgan)	22	2	1332	204	66.60
DL Amiss (Warwicks)	24	7	1129	192	66.41
Mushtaq Mohammed (Northants)	35	6	1743	137*	60.10
RB Kanhai (Warwicks)	28	4	1437	199	59.87
AW Greig (Sussex)	14	3	640	112	58.18
APE Knott (Kent)	13	4	478	127*	53.11
H Pilling (Lancs)	24	4	1031	118	51.55

LEADING BOWLERS

	Runs	Wkts	Avge
R Illingworth (Leics)	394	24	16.41
MJ Procter (Gloucs)	954	58	16.44
CM Old (Yorks)	931	54	17.24
JA Snow (Sussex)	453	26	17.42
JCJ Dye (Northants)	1360	75	18.13
TW Cartwright (Somerset)	1735	93	18.65
AG Nicholson (Yorks)	1149	60	19.15
KD Boyce (Essex)	1542	80	19.27
AS Brown (Gloucs)	947	48	19.72
RA Woolmer (Kent)	853	43	19.83

LEADING ALL-ROUNDERS

	Runs	(Avge)	Wkts	(Avge)
MJ Procter (Gloucs)	1215	(41.89)	58	(16.44)
KD Boyce (Essex)	925	(30.83)	80	(19.27)

LEADING WICKET-KEEPERS

	Dismissals		Total
GR Stephenson (Hants)	41ct	9st	50
RW Tolchard (Leics)	42ct	6st	48
R Swetman (Gloucs)	42ct	6st	48

1973

FINAL TABLE

		P	W	L	D(T)	Bt	Bl	Pts
1	Hampshire	20	10	0	10	84	81	265
2	Surrey	20	9	3	8	71	73	234
3	Northamptonshire	20	8	4	8	53	75	208
4	Kent	20	4	3	13	98	59	197
5	Gloucestershire	19	6	4	9	63	70	193
6	Worcestershire	20	6	4	10	56	75	191
7	Warwickshire	20	5	5	10	74	62	186
8	Essex	20	6	5	9	46	72	178
9	Leicestershire	19	4	3	12	66	60	166
10	Somerset	20	7	2	11	29	60	159
11	Glamorgan	20	4	8	8	44	68	152
12	Lancashire	20	4	6	10	44	67	151
13	Middlesex	20	4	5	10(1)	49	54	148
14	Yorkshire	20	3	5	11(1)	28	69	132
15	Sussex	20	2	10	8	42	67	129
16	Derbyshire	20	2	10	8	15	67	102
17	Nottinghamshire	20	1	8	11	28	63	101

Gloucs v Leics, Bristol: abandoned without a ball bowled.
First innings points changed as follows: 1 point for 75 runs in first 25 overs; 1 for scoring 150 runs in first 50 overs. 1 point for each 25 runs above 150. 1 point for every 2 wickets taken. All bonus points awarded in first 85 overs only, as before.

BEST INDIVIDUAL SCORES

240   BA Richards, Hants v Warwicks, Coventry
230*   RB Kanhai, Warwicks v Somerset, Edgbaston
215   BW Luckhurst, Kent v Derbys, Derby
204*   JA Ormrod, Worcs v Kent, Dartford

BEST INNINGS ANALYSES

8–9   DL Underwood, Kent v Sussex, Hastings
8–80   PG Lee, Lancs v Notts, Old Trafford
7–36   DL Acfield, Essex v Sussex, Ilford
7–36   RD Jackman, Surrey v Yorks, Oval

BEST MATCH ANALYSES

13–52   DL Underwood, Kent v Sussex, Hastings
13–89   TW Cartwright, Somerset v Derby, Weston
12–130   RE East, Essex v Derby, Chelmsford

11–41   DR O'Sullivan, Hants v Notts, Bournemouth

LEADING BATSMEN

	Inns	NO	Runs	HS	Avge
APE Knott (Kent)	13	6	554	87	79.14
GM Turner (Worcs)	16	2	1036	140	74.00
MJ Procter (Gloucs)	25	4	1351	152	64.33
FC Hayes (Lancs)	16	3	709	154*	54.53
Younis Ahmed (Surrey)	32	6	1389	155*	53.42
GRJ Roope (Surrey)	20	5	791	93*	52.73
CG Greenidge (Hants)	35	4	1620	196*	52.25
BF Davison (Leics)	26	3	1181	105	51.34
MJ Smith (Middlesex)	35	4	1549	116	49.96
MC Cowdrey (Kent)	26	7	948	123*	49.89

LEADING BOWLERS

	Runs	Wkts	Avge
TW Cartwright (Somerset)	1350	88	15.34
PJ Sainsbury (Hants)	869	49	17.73
CM Old (Yorks)	568	32	17.75
PH Edmonds (Middx)	535	30	17.83
JSE Price (Middx)	466	26	17.92
BS Bedi (Northants)	1558	86	18.11
AG Nicholson (Yorks)	1145	63	18.17
BM Brain (Worcs)	1528	84	18.19
RMH Cottam (Northants)	1262	69	18.28
A Hodgson (Northants)	522	28	18.64

LEADING ALL-ROUNDERS

	Runs	(Avge)	Wkts	(Avge)
JN Shepherd (Kent)	684	(27.36)	78	(22.69)
Intikhab Alam (Surrey)	600	(28.57)	72	(26.27)

LEADING WICKET-KEEPERS

	Dismissals		Total
GR Stephenson (Hants)	58ct	5st	63
DL Bairstow (Yorks)	54ct	5st	59

1974

FINAL TABLE

		P	W	L	D(T)	Bt	Bl	Pts
1	Worcestershire ..	20	11	3	6	45	72	227
2	Hampshire	19	10	3	6	55	70	225
3	Northamptonshire	20	9	2	9	46	67	203
4	Leicestershire ...	20	7	7	6	47	69	186
5	Somerset	20	6	4	10	49	72	181
6	Middlesex	20	7	5	8	45	56	171
7	Surrey	20	6	4	10	42	69	171
8	Lancashire	20	5	0	15	47	66	163
9	Warwickshire ...	20	5	5	10	44	65	159
10	Kent	20	5	8	7	33	63	146
11	Yorkshire	19	4	7	8	37	69	146
12	Essex	20	4	3	12(1)	44	52	141
13	Sussex	20	4	9	6(1)	29	63	137
14	Gloucestershire..	19	4	9	6	29	55	124
15	Nottinghamshire .	20	1	9	10	42	66	118
16	Glamorgan	19	2	7	10	28	56	104
17	Derbyshire	20	1	6	13	23	62	95

Hants v Yorks, Bournemouth: Gloucs v Glamorgan, Bristol: abandoned without a ball bowled.
A maximum of 4 batting and 4 bowling bonus points now available on 1st innings. See page 16 for details.

BEST INDIVIDUAL SCORES

240* JA Jameson, Warwicks v Gloucs, Edgbaston
227 BL D'Oliveira, Worcs v Yorks, Hull
225* BA Richards, Hants v Notts, Trent Bridge
213* RB Kanhai, Warwicks v Gloucs, Edgbaston

BEST INNINGS ANALYSES

8–47 AME Roberts, Hants v Glamorgan, Cardiff
8–85 DA Graveney, Gloucs v Notts, Cheltenham
7–15 N Gifford, Worcs v Essex, Chelmsford
7–18 R Illingworth, Leics v Notts, Leicester

BEST MATCH ANALYSES

14–114 FJ Titmus, Middx v Yorks, Middlesbrough
12–80 DL Underwood, Kent v Gloucs, Dover
12–101 RA White, Notts v Someset, Trent Bridge
12–137 FJ Titmus, Middx v Derbys, Lord's

LEADING BATSMEN

	Inns	NO	Runs	HS	Avge
CH Lloyd (Lancs)	30	8	1403	178*	63.77
RT Virgin (Northants)	36	5	1845	144*	59.51
G Boycott (Yorks)	26	5	1220	149*	58.09
BA Richards (Hants)	23	4	1059	225*	55.73
JH Hampshire (Yorks)	22	6	879	158	54.93
GM Turner (Worcs)	28	8	1098	181	54.90
GS Sobers (Notts)	27	4	1110	132*	48.26
DL Amiss (Warwicks)	15	2	620	195	47.69
BF Davison (Leics)	32	2	1392	142	46.40
MJ Harris (Notts)	35	3	1431	133	44.71

LEADING BOWLERS

	Runs	Wkts	Avge
GG Arnold (Surrey)	515	51	10.09
AME Roberts (Hants)	1493	111	13.45
VA Holder (Worcs)	1358	87	15.60
DL Underwood (Kent)	645	40	16.12
MJ Procter (Gloucs)	670	39	17.17
CM Old (Yorks)	567	33	17.18
RS Herman (Hants)	1218	70	17.40
BL D'Oliveira (Worcs)	697	40	17.42
MNS Taylor (Hants)	1101	63	17.47
S Turner (Essex)	1228	68	18.05

LEADING ALL-ROUNDERS

	Runs	(Avge)	Wkts	(Avge)
S Turner (Essex)	851	(32.73)	68	(18.05)
RA Woolmer (Kent)	713	(27.42)	54	(18.16)

LEADING WICKET-KEEPERS

	Dismissals		Total
GR Stephenson (Hants)	56ct		56
DL Bairstow (Yorks)	41ct	9st	50

1975

FINAL TABLE

		P	W	L	D	Bt	Bl	Pts
1	Leicestershire ...	20	12	1	7	61	59	240
2	Yorkshire	20	10	1	9	56	68	224
3	Hampshire	20	10	6	4	51	72	223
4	Lancashire	20	9	3	8	57	72	219
5	Kent	20	8	4	8	59	70	209
6	Surrey..........	20	8	3	9	55	67	202
7	Essex	20	7	6	7	61	67	198
8	Northamptonshire	20	7	9	4	40	72	182
9	Glamorgan	20	7	8	5	45	66	181
10	Worcestershire ..	20	5	6	9	55	63	168
11	Middlesex	20	6	7	7	45	59	164
12	Somerset	20	4	8	8	51	65	156
13	Nottinghamshire .	20	3	9	8	59	67	156
14	Warwickshire....	20	4	10	6	48	65	153
15	Derbyshire	20	5	7	8	33	69	152
16	Gloucestershire ..	20	4	10	6	43	62	145
17	Sussex	20	2	13	5	37	62	119

LEADING BATSMEN

	Inns	NO	Runs	HS	Avge
RB Kanhai (Warwicks)	21	9	1053	178*	87.75
G Boycott (Yorks)	33	7	1891	201*	72.73
CH Lloyd (Lancs)	26	4	1390	167*	63.18
BA Richards (Hants)	30	4	1456	135*	56.00
JM Brearley (Middx)	39	8	1656	150	53.41
GM Turner (Worcs)	26	4	1093	154*	49.68
Asif Iqbal (Kent)	30	4	1262	140	48.53
BF Davison (Leics)	33	6	1309	184	48.48
Zaheer Abbas (Gloucs)	31	1	1426	111	47.53
DL Amiss (Warwicks)	32	2	1422	158*	47.40

LEADING BOWLERS

	Runs	Wkts	Avge
AME Roberts (Hants)	826	57	14.49
DL Underwood (Kent)	839	57	14.71
P Lever (Lancs)	889	54	16.46
M Hendrick (Derbys)	906	55	16.47
BD Julien (Kent)	585	35	16.71
KD Boyce (Essex)	1270	72	17.63
PG Lee (Lancs)	1991	107	18.60
TE Jesty (Hants)	937	49	19.12
JW Solanky (Glamorgan)	1093	57	19.17
Sarfraz Nawaz (Northants)	1882	94	19.38

BEST INDIVIDUAL SCORES

259 CG Greenidge, Hants v Sussex,
     Southampton
226 AW Greig, Sussex v Warwicks, Hastings
217* IVA Richards, Somerset v Yorks, Harrogate
201* G Boycott, Yorks v Middx, Lord's

BEST INNINGS ANALYSES

9–20 FW Swarbrook, Derby v Sussex, Hove
9–56 MA Nash, Glamorgan v Hants,
     Basingstoke
8–55 BM Brain, Worcs v Essex, Worcester
8–56 MA Nash, Glamorgan v Hants, Swansea

BEST MATCH ANALYSES

15–147 JN Shepherd, Kent v Sussex, Maidstone
14–137 MA Nash, Glamorgan v Hants,
       Basingstoke
13–62 FW Swarbrook, Derby v Sussex, Hove
12–62 PG Lee, Lancs v Warwicks, Edgbaston

LEADING ALL-ROUNDERS

	Runs	(Avge)	Wkts	(Avge)
FW Swarbrook (Derbys)	615	(21.96)	61	(25.21)
CEB Rice (Notts)	1128	(33.17)	53	(25.73)
JN Shepherd (Kent)	695	(33.09)	50	(27.54)

LEADING WICKET-KEEPERS

	Dismissals		Total
FM Engineer (Lancs)	68ct	2st	70
GR Stephenson (Hants)	57ct	9st	66

1976

FINAL TABLE

		P	W	L	D	Bt	Bl	Pts
I	Middlesex	20	11	5	4	57	67	234
2	Northamptonshire	20	9	3	8	54	74	218
3	Gloucestershire	19	9	5	5	54	66	210
4	Leicestershire	20	9	3	8	51	68	209
5	Warwickshire	20	6	7	7	65	70	195
6	Essex	20	7	4	9	57	62	189
7	Somerset	20	7	8	5	47	63	180
8	Yorkshire	20	6	6	8	49	67	176
9	Surrey	20	6	4	10	54	61	175
10	Sussex	20	5	8	7	49	71	170
11	Worcestershire	19	6	3	10	50	59	169
12	Hampshire	20	4	10	6	52	67	159
13	Nottinghamshire	20	4	7	9	58	60	158
14	Kent	20	5	7	8	48	57	155
15	Derbyshire	20	4	7	9	39	70	149
16	Lancashire	20	3	7	10	43	75	148
17	Glamorgan	20	3	10	7	37	60	127

Gloucs v Worcs, Bristol: abandoned without a ball bowled.

BEST INDIVIDUAL SCORES

246 CEB Rice, Notts v Sussex, Hove
230* Zaheer Abbas, Gloucs v Kent, Canterbury
227 P Willey, Northants v Somerset, Northampton
217 EJ Barlow, Derby v Surrey, Ilkeston

BEST INNINGS ANALYSES

8–38 R Illingworth, Leics v Glamorgan, Swansea
8–63 AW Allin, Glamorgan v Sussex, Cardiff
8–79 RD Jackman, Surrey v Notts, Oval
8–114 PJ Sainsbury, Hants v Gloucs, Southampton

BEST MATCH ANALYSES

13–99 Imran Khan, Worcs v Lancs, Worcester
13–104 RMH Cottam, Northants v Lancs, Old Trafford
13–237 EE Hemmings, Warwicks v Hants, Bournemouth
12–135 FJ Titmus, Middx v Derbys, Lord's

LEADING BATSMEN

	Inns	NO	Runs	HS	Avge
Zaheer Abbas (Gloucs)	36	5	2431	230*	78.41
DL Amiss (Warks)	29	5	1523	178*	63.45
KWR Fletcher (Essex)	33	7	1479	128*	56.88
BF Davison (Leics)	38	8	1669	132	55.63
G Boycott (Yorks)	22	3	1040	161*	54.73
H Pilling (Lancs)	34	5	1547	149*	53.34
RA Woolmer (Kent)	24	1	1222	143	53.13
Mustaq Mohammed (Northants)	34	4	1574	204*	52.46
GM Turner (Worcs)	35	2	1719	169	52.09
B Wood (Lancs)	21	6	749	198	49.93

LEADING BOWLERS

	Runs	Wkts	Avge
NG Featherstone (Middx)	472	32	14.75
RMH Cottam (Northants)	527	29	18.17
JC Balderstone (Leics)	465	25	18.60
PJ Sainsbury (Hants)	1236	66	18.72
EJ Barlow (Derby)	750	40	18.75
R Illingworth (Leics)	695	36	19.30
K Higgs (Leics)	999	50	19.98
AW Allin (Glamorgan)	833	41	20.31
G Miller (Derby)	1208	59	20.47
P Willey (Northants)	533	25	21.32

LEADING ALL-ROUNDERS

	Runs	(Avge)	Wkts	(Avge)
IT Botham (Somerset)	944	(33.71)	60	(27.41)
Imran Khan (Worcs)	1059	(40.73)	61	(23.90)
MJ Procter (Gloucs)	1005	(31.40)	63	(27.53)
Sarfraz Nawaz (Northants)	666	(27.75)	82	(22.76)

LEADING WICKET-KEEPERS

	Dismissals		Total
G Sharp (Northants)	63ct	8st	71
A Long (Sussex)	55ct	8st	63

1977

FINAL TABLE

		P	W	L	D	Bt	Bl	Pts
1	Middlesex	22	9	5	8	43	76	227
	Kent	21	9	2	10	54	65	227
3	Gloucestershire ..	20	9	5	6	44	70	222
4	Somerset	21	6	4	11	58	64	194
5	Leicestershire ...	22	6	4	12	44	73	189
6	Essex	21	7	5	9	38	65	187
7	Derbyshire	21	7	3	11	38	64	186
8	Sussex	22	6	5	11	52	60	184
9	Northamptonshire	20	6	6	8	43	68	183
10	Warwickshire....	22	4	8	10	61	72	181
11	Hampshire	22	6	5	11	53	54	179
12	Yorkshire	21	6	5	10	36	63	171
13	Worcestershire ..	22	5	10	7	29	55	144
14	Glamorgan	21	3	7	11	36	60	132
	Surrey..........	21	3	6	12	42	54	132
16	Lancashire	21	2	4	15	36	57	117
17	Nottinghamshire .	22	1	11	10	34	52	98

12 points now awarded for a win.
Gloucs v Northants, Gloucester; Somerset v Derbys, Taunton;
Northants v Glam, Northampton; Essex v Kent, Colchester;
Gloucs v Yorks, Bristol; Lancs v Surrey, Old Trafford: all
abandoned without a ball bowled.

BEST INDIVIDUAL SCORES

241* IVA Richards, Somerset v Gloucs, Bristol
230 JA Hopkins, Glamorgan v Worcs, Worcester
218 KS McEwan, Essex v Sussex, Chelmsford
208 CG Greenidge, Hants v Yorks, Headingley

BEST INNINGS ANALYSES

8–30 RE East, Essex v Notts, Ilford
8–31 J Garner, Somerset v Glamorgan, Cardiff
8–57 RE East, Essex v Derbys, Leyton
8–58 JD Inchmore, Worcs v Yorks, Worcester

BEST MATCH ANALYSES

14–150 PH Edmonds, Middx v Gloucs, Lord's
13–73   MJ Procter, Gloucs v Worcs, Cheltenham
12–101 RE East, Essex v Notts, Ilford
12–113 RE East, Essex v Glamorgan, Leyton

LEADING BATSMEN

	Inns	NO	Runs	HS	Avge
RP Baker (Surrey)	10	8	204	77*	102.00
JM Brearley (Middx)	14	2	820	152	68.33
IVA Richards (Somerset)	33	2	2090	241*	67.41
DL Amiss (Warwicks)	26	4	1431	162*	65.04
CG Greenidge (Hants)	32	3	1771	208	61.06
FC Hayes (Lancs)	23	3	1146	157*	57.30
Zaheer Abbas (Gloucs)	34	6	1579	205*	56.39
GRJ Roope (Surrey)	28	4	1252	115	52.16
B Wood (Lancs)	30	6	1219	155*	50.79
JH Edrich (Surrey)	23	4	945	140	49.73

LEADING BOWLERS

	Runs	Wkts	Avge
M Hendrick (Derbys)	615	39	15.76
RW Hills (Kent)	467	29	16.10
DL Underwood (Kent)	534	33	16.18
G Miller (Derbys)	1315	78	16.85
WW Daniel (Middx)	1206	71	16.98
Sarfraz Nawaz (Northants)	1246	73	17.06
MJ Procter (Gloucs)	1926	108	17.83
JD Inchmore (Worcs)	550	30	18.33
J Garner (Somerset)	402	21	19.14
RE East (Essex)	1399	73	19.16

LEADING ALL-ROUNDERS

	Runs	(Avge)	Wkts	(Avge)
G Miller (Derbys)	638	(31.90)	78	(16.85)
MJ Procter (Gloucs)	842	(29.03)	108	(17.83)

LEADING WICKET-KEEPERS

	Dismissals		Total
GW Humpage (Warwicks)	59ct	2st	61
DJS Taylor (Somerset)	50ct	4st	54

1978

FINAL TABLE

	P	W	L	D	Bt	Bl	Pts
1 Kent	22	13	3	6	56	80	292
2 Essex	22	12	1	9	55	74	273
3 Middlesex	21	11	5	5	48	75	255
4 Yorkshire	22	10	3	9	58	55	233
5 Somerset	22	9	4	9	44	76	228
6 Leicestershire . . .	22	4	5	13	57	68	173
7 Nottinghamshire .	22	3	7	12	63	67	166
8 Hampshire	21	4	6	11	53	60	161
9 Sussex	22	4	7	11	39	64	151*
10 Gloucestershire . .	21	4	8	9	42	55	145
11 Warwickshire	22	4	5	13	39	56	143
12 Lancashire	21	4	8	9	28	59	135*
13 Glamorgan	22	3	8	11	43	54	133
14 Derbyshire	22	3	7	12	33	63	132
15 Worcestershire . .	22	2	5	15	56	51	131
16 Surrey	22	3	7	12	36	58	130
17 Northamptonshire	20	2	6	12	41	56	121

Six points deducted for breach of rules.

Gloucs v Northants, Bristol; Middx v Hants, Lord's; Lancs v Northants, Old Trafford: all abandoned without a ball bowled.

BEST INDIVIDUAL SCORES

213* CEB Rice, Notts v Lancs, Trent Bridge
213 CEB Rice, Notts v Glamorgan, Swansea
213 Zaheer Abbas, Gloucs v Sussex, Hove
211 CG Greenidge, Hants v Sussex, Hove

BEST INNINGS ANALYSES

9–32 DL Underwood, Kent v Surrey, Oval
8–34 JH Childs, Gloucs v Hants, Basingstoke
8–41 RE East, Essex v Northants,
      Northampton
8–65 GB Stevenson, Yorks v Lancs, Headingley

BEST MATCH ANALYSES

13–49   DL Underwood, Kent v Surrey, Oval
13–145 JK Lever, Essex v Northants, Ilford
12–58   JH Childs, Gloucs v Hants,
        Basingstoke
12–111 SP Perryman, Warwicks v Lancs, Old
        Trafford

LEADING BATSMEN

	Inns	NO	Runs	HS	Avge
CEB Rice (Notts)	35	7	1727	213*	61.67
Javed Miandad (Sussex)	12	2	586	127	58.60
DL Amiss (Warwicks)	39	3	2001	162	55.58
CG Greenidge (Hants)	32	1	1711	211	55.19
GM Turner (Worcs)	38	7	1711	202*	55.19
JH Hampshire (Yorks)	33	6	1463	132	54.18
BF Davison (Leics)	34	3	1628	180*	52.51
G Boycott (Yorks)	19	0	968	129	50.94
MJ Procter (Gloucs)	35	3	1625	203	50.78
Asif Iqbal (Kent)	25	6	934	171	49.15

LEADING BOWLERS

	Runs	Wkts	Avge
RJ Hadlee (Notts)	521	36	14.47
DL Underwood (Kent)	1594	110	14.49
WW Daniel (Middx)	1088	75	14.50
RA Woolmer (Kent)	292	20	14.60
M Hendrick (Derbys)	704	47	14.97
MW Gatting (Middx)	316	21	15.04
JK Lever (Essex)	1518	97	15.69
PH Edmonds (Middx)	619	39	15.87
J Garner (Somerset)	351	22	15.95
RE East (Essex)	1506	92	16.36

LEADING ALL-ROUNDERS

	Runs	(Avge)	Wkts	(Avge)
MJ Procter (Gloucs)	1625	(50.78)	69	(23.89)
NE Phillip (Essex)	645	(26.87)	65	(23.96)

LEADING WICKET-KEEPERS

	Dismissals		Total
DL Bairstow (Yorks)	57ct	8st	65
DJS Taylor (Somerset)	53ct	9st	62

1979

FINAL TABLE

	P	W	L	D	Bt	Bl	Pts
1 Essex	21	13	4	4	56	69	281
2 Worcestershire ..	21	7	4	10	58	62	204
3 Surrey..........	21	6	3	12	50	70	192
4 Sussex	20	6	4	10	47	65	184
5 Kent	22	6	3	13	49	60	181
6 Leicestershire ...	21	4	5	12	60	68	176
7 Yorkshire	21	5	3	13	52	63	175
8 Somerset	21	5	1	15	56	53	171
9 Nottinghamshire .	19	6	4	9	43	54	169
10 Gloucestershire ..	20	5	4	11	53	54	167
11 Northamptonshire	21	3	6	12	59	58	153
12 Hampshire	21	3	9	9	39	66	141
13 Lancashire	22	4	4	14	37	55	140
Middlesex	20	3	3	14	44	60	140
15 Warwickshire....	21	3	7	11	46	51	133
16 Derbyshire	21	1	6	14	46	60	118
17 Glamorgan	21	0	10	11	35	58	93

Sussex v Gloucs, Hove; Derbys v Notts, Derby; Gloucs v Somerset, Bristol; Middx v Sussex, Lord's; Northants v Glam, Northampton; Surrey v Essex, Oval; Warwicks v Worcs, Edgbaston; Yorks v Notts, Sheffield; Leics v Hants, Leicester; Middx v Notts, Lord's: all abandoned without a ball bowled.

BEST INDIVIDUAL SCORES

232* DL Amiss, Warwicks v Gloucs, Bristol
221* Younis Ahmed, Worcs v Notts, Trent Bridge
209 DW Randall, Notts v Middx, Trent Bridge
208* KS McEwan, Essex v Warwicks, Edgbaston

BEST INNINGS ANALYSES

9-57 PI Pocock, Surrey v Glamorgan, Cardiff
8-28 DL Underwood, Kent v Hants, Bournemouth
8-30 MJ Procter, Gloucs v Worcs, Worcester
8-49 JK Lever, Essex v Warwicks, Edgbaston

BEST MATCH ANALYSES

13-71 DL Underwood, Kent v Notts, Folkestone
13-87 JK Lever, Essex v Warwicks, Edgbaston
13-102 DL Underwood, Kent v Glamorgan, Cardiff
13-117 JK Lever, Essex v Leics, Chelmsford

LEADING BATSMEN

	Inns	NO	Runs	HS	Avge
G Boycott (Yorks)	15	5	1160	175*	116.00
Younis Ahmed (Worcs)	29	7	1508	221*	68.54
AJ Lamb (Northants)	32	6	1614	178	62.07
Sadiq Mohammed (Gloucs)	27	2	1504	171	60.16
GM Turner (Worcs)	31	2	1669	150*	57.55
PH Edmonds (Middx)	12	5	398	141*	56.85
KC Wessels (Sussex)	31	2	1619	187	55.82
AI Kallicharran (Warwicks)	25	5	1080	170*	54.00
DW Randall (Notts)	20	1	980	209	51.57
DL Amiss (Warwicks)	35	3	1613	232*	50.40

LEADING BOWLERS

	Runs	Wkts	Avge
J Garner (Somerset)	761	55	13.83
DL Underwood (Kent)	1521	104	14.62
JK Lever (Essex)	1460	99	14.74
Imran Khan (Sussex)	1091	73	14.94
RJ Hadlee (Notts)	625	37	16.89
RD Jackman (Surrey)	1515	87	17.41
GG Arnold (Sussex)	900	50	18.00
ST Clarke (Surrey)	684	38	18.00
K Higgs (Leics)	865	46	18.80
MJ Procter (Gloucs)	1491	74	20.14

LEADING ALL-ROUNDERS

	Runs	(Avge)	Wkts	(Avge)
MJ Procter (Gloucs)	1200	(38.70)	74	(20.14)
Imran Khan (Sussex)	700	(35.00)	73	(14.94)

LEADING WICKET-KEEPERS

	Dismissals		Total
DJ Humphries (Worcs)	48ct	8st	56
CJ Richards (Surrey)	48ct	7st	55

Nottinghamshire faces from both ends of the 1970s:
Richard Hadlee (above) promised much and did not
disappoint, performing the first all-rounder's double for 18
years in 1984, a feat barely approached since the reduction in
the fixture list in 1969 (Allsport/Adrian Murrell)

For Brian Bolus (right), 1970 was one of the best seasons of a
three county career – also including spells for Yorkshire and
Derbyshire – notable for some class batting, but also for its
vicissitudes (Hulton Picture Company)

1980

FINAL TABLE

	P	W	L	D	Bt	Bl	Pts
1 Middlesex	22	10	2	10	58	80	258
2 Surrey..........	22	10	4	8	51	74	245
3 Nottinghamshire .	22	6	5	11	42	64	178
4 Sussex	22	4	3	15	60	60	168
5 Somerset	21	3	5	13	56	70	168
6 Yorkshire	22	4	3	15	51	64	163
7 Gloucestershire ..	21	4	5	12	39	74	161
8 Essex	22	4	3	15	48	64	160
9 Derbyshire	20	4	3	13	47	62	157
Leicestershire ...	22	4	2	16	45	58	157
11 Worcestershire ..	21	3	7	11	54	61	151
12 Northamptonshire	22	5	4	13	41	47	148
13 Glamorgan	21	4	4	13	43	57	148
14 Warwickshire....	22	3	4	15	55	54	145
15 Lancashire	20	4	3	13	26	58	132
16 Kent	22	2	8	12	36	59	119
17 Hampshire	22	1	10	11	34	56	102

Leicestershire v Somerset totals each include 6 points for levelling the scores in drawn match.

Glam v Worcs, Swansea; Gloucs v Derbys, Bristol; Somerset v Lancs, Bath; Derbys v Lancs, Buxton: all abandoned without a ball bowled.

New regulations introduced this season whereby a 1st innings may be forfeited, subject to provisions of Rule 14.2.

BEST INDIVIDUAL SCORES

254 KC Wessels, Sussex v Middlesex, Hove
228* GM Turner, Worcs v Gloucs, Worcester
228 IT Botham, Somerset v Gloucs, Taunton
213* PN Kirsten, Derbys v Glamorgan, Derby

BEST INNINGS ANALYSES

8-57 GB Stevenson, Yorks v Northants, Headingley
8-58 RD Jackman, Surrey v Lancs, Old Trafford
7-16 MJ Procter, Gloucs v Worcs, Cheltenham
7-19 M Hendrick, Derbys v Hants, Chesterfield

BEST MATCH ANALYSES

14-76 MJ Procter, Gloucs v Worcs, Cheltenham

12-99 DL Underwood, Kent v Essex, Folkestone
12-107 JE Emburey, Middx v Notts, Lord's
11-64 A Sidebottom, Yorks v Kent, Sheffield

LEADING BATSMEN

	Inns	NO	Runs	HS	Avge
J Whitehouse (Warwicks)	17	8	718	197	79.77
AJ Lamb (Northants)	37	12	1720	152	68.80
PN Kirsten (Derbys)	34	6	1891	213*	67.53
KC Wessels (Sussex)	29	5	1562	254	65.08
IT Botham (Somerset)	14	0	875	228	62.50
GM Turner (Worcs)	33	4	1755	228*	60.31
JH Hampshire (Yorks)	24	8	954	124	59.62
Javed Miandad (Glam)	31	5	1442	181	55.46
BC Rose (Somerset)	17	2	793	150*	52.86
CEB Rice (Notts)	35	9	1358	131*	52.23

LEADING BOWLERS

	Runs	Wkts	Avge
M Hendrick (Derby)	660	47	14.04
VAP van der Bijl (Middx)	1252	85	14.72
RJ Hadlee (Notts)	342	23	14.86
RD Jackman (Surrey)	1713	114	15.02
Imran Khan (Sussex)	917	52	17.63
MJ Procter (Gloucs)	857	48	17.85
JF Steele (Leics)	650	36	18.05
PJW Allott (Lancs)	452	23	19.65
JE Emburey (Middx)	1202	61	19.70
PJ Hacker (Notts)	964	48	20.08

LEADING ALL-ROUNDERS

	Runs	(Avge)	Wkts	(Avge)
GB Stevenson (Yorks)	620	(31.00)	67	(24.10)
G Miller (Derbys)	641	(32.05)	54	(25.66)
DS Steele (Derbys)	660	(30.00)	54	(22.61)

LEADING WICKET-KEEPERS

	Dismissals		Total
CJ Richards (Surrey)	58ct	2st	60
AJ Brassington (Gloucs)	38ct	13st	51

1981

FINAL TABLE

		P	W	L	D	Bt	Bl	Pts
1	Nottinghamshire .	21	11	4	6	56	72	304
2	Sussex	20	11	3	6	58	68	302
3	Somerset	22	10	2	10	54	65	279
4	Middlesex	21	9	3	9	49	64	257
5	Essex	21	8	4	9	62	64	254
6	Surrey.........	21	7	5	9	52	72	236
7	Hampshire	21	6	7	8	45	65	206
8	Leicestershire ...	21	6	6	9	45	58	199
9	Kent	22	5	7	10	51	58	189
10	Yorkshire	22	5	9	8	41	66	187
11	Worcestershire ..	22	5	9	8	44	52	172
12	Derbyshire......	21	4	7	10	51	57	172
13	Gloucestershire ..	19	4	3	12	51	55	170
14	Glamorgan......	21	3	10	8	50	69	167
15	Northamptonshire	21	3	6	12	51	67	166
16	Lancashire	22	4	7	11	47	57	164
17	Warwickshire....	22	2	11	9	56	47	135

New points-scoring: 16 pts for a win; 8 pts for a tie; 8 points for side batting when scores level in drawn match.
Lancashire and Worcestershire totals include 12 pts for win in one-innings match.
Glam v Gloucs, Cardiff; Derbys v Notts, Derby; Essex v Gloucs, Chelmsford; Middx v Sussex, Lord's; Northants v Leics, Northampton; Surrey v Hants, Oval; Gloucs v Sussex, Bristol: all abandoned without a ball bowled.

BEST INDIVIDUAL SCORES

248* WN Slack, Middx v Worcs, Lord's
228 PN Kirsten, Derbys v Somerset, Taunton
215* Zaheer Abbas, Gloucs v Somerset, Bath
204* PN Kirsten, Derbys v Lancs, Blackpool

BEST INNINGS ANALYSES

9–56 JH Childs, Gloucs v Somerset, Bristol
8–43 HL Alleyne, Worcs v Middx, Lord's
8–48 PJW Allott, Lancs v Northants, Northampton
8–49 JK Lever, Essex v Yorks, Headingley

BEST MATCH ANALYSES

13–129 EE Hemmings, Notts v Derbys, Trent Bridge

12–123 RE East, Essex v Kent, Chelmsford
12–147 KBS Jarvis, Kent v Surrey, Oval
12–154 DL Underwood, Kent v Essex, Canterbury

LEADING BATSMEN

	Inns	NO	Runs	HS	Avge
Zaheer Abbas (Gloucs)	34	8	2230	215*	85.76
Javed Miandad (Glam)	36	7	2060	200*	71.03
AJ Lamb (Northants)	38	8	1962	162	65.40
MW Gatting (Middx)	15	3	782	186*	65.16
GA Gooch (Essex)	17	0	1091	164	64.17
PN Kirsten (Derbys)	33	6	1563	228	57.88
IVA Richards (Somerset)	33	3	1718	196	57.26
GM Turner (Worcs)	40	4	2043	168	56.75
CEB Rice (Notts)	30	4	1462	172	56.23
DI Gower (Leics)	21	3	1009	156*	56.05

LEADING BOWLERS

	Runs	Wkts	Avge
RJ Hadlee (Notts)	1564	105	14.89
J Garner (Somerset)	1312	87	15.08
ST Clarke (Surrey)	679	44	15.43
MA Holding (Lancs)	715	40	17.87
A Sidebottom (Yorks)	867	46	18.84
CEB Rice (Notts)	1248	65	19.20
MD Marshall (Hants)	1321	68	19.42
GS Le Roux (Sussex)	1582	81	19.53
TE Jesty (Hants)	1019	51	19.98
EA Moseley (Glamorgan)	880	44	20.00

LEADING ALL-ROUNDERS

	Runs	(Avge)	Wkts	(Avge)
RJ Hadlee (Notts)	745	(32.39)	105	(14.89)
CEB Rice (Notts)	1462	(56.23)	65	(19.20)
Imran Khan (Sussex)	857	(40.80)	66	(22.18)
IA Greig (Sussex)	789	(30.34)	60	(21.06)

LEADING WICKET-KEEPERS

	Dismissals		Total
IJ Gould (Middx)	57ct	4st	61
DJS Taylor (Somerset)	53ct	6st	59

1982

FINAL TABLE

	P	W	L	D	Bt	Bl	Pts
1 Middlesex	22	12	2	8	59	74	325
2 Leicestershire ...	22	10	4	8	57	69	286
3 Hampshire	22	8	6	8	48	74	250
4 Nottinghamshire .	21	7	7	7	44	65	221
5 Surrey	22	6	6	10	56	62	214
6 Somerset	22	6	6	10	51	66	213
7 Essex	22	5	5	12	57	75	212
8 Sussex	22	6	7	9	43	68	207
9 Northamptonshire	22	5	3	14	61	54	195
10 Yorkshire	21	5	1	15	48	51	179
11 Derbyshire	22	4	3	15	45	64	173
12 Lancashire	22	4	3	15	48	55	167
13 Kent	22	3	4	15	55	63	166
14 Worcestershire ..	22	3	5	14	43	54	141
15 Gloucestershire ..	22	2	9	11	46	55	133
16 Glamorgan	22	1	8	13	43	60	119
17 Warwickshire	22	0	8	14	58	53	111

Worcestershire total includes 12 points for a win in a one-innings match. Yorks v Notts, Harrogate: no play.

BEST INDIVIDUAL SCORES

311* GM Turner, Worcs v Warwicks, Worcester
254 GW Humpage, Warwicks v Lancs, Southport
235 AI Kallicharran, Warwicks v Worcs, Worcester
230* AI Kallicharran, Warwicks v Lancs, Southport

BEST INNINGS ANALYSES

9–61 WW Daniel, Middx v Glamorgan, Swansea
8–56 AME Roberts, Leics v Glamorgan, Leicester
8–70 G Miller, Derbys v Leics, Coalville
8–71 MD Marshall, Hants v Worcs, Southampton

BEST MATCH ANALYSES

14–94 AME Roberts, Leics v Glamorgan, Leicester
12–130 NGB Cook, Leics v Essex, Colchester
12–138 G Miller, Derbys v Leics, Coalville

11–80 J Garner, Somerset v Hants, Bath

LEADING BATSMEN

	Inns	NO	Runs	HS	Avge
GM Turner (Worcs)	15	2	932	311*	71.69
AI Kallicharran (Warwicks)	36	5	2118	235	68.32
MW Gatting (Middx)	21	2	1273	192	67.00
PN Kirsten (Derbys)	37	7	1941	164*	64.70
G Boycott (Yorks)	37	6	1913	159	61.70
Zaheer Abbas (Gloucs)	12	1	667	162*	60.63
BF Davison (Leics)	35	4	1789	172	57.70
JG Wright (Derbys)	39	6	1830	190	55.45
AJ Lamb (Northants)	17	1	882	140	55.12
J Simmons (Lancs)	21	12	487	79*	54.11
DM Smith (Surrey)	23	4	1000	160	52.63

LEADING BOWLERS

	Runs	Wkts	Avge
RJ Hadlee (Notts)	836	59	14.16
M Hendrick (Notts)	401	26	15.42
MD Marshall (Hants)	2108	134	15.73
Imran Khan (Sussex)	458	29	15.79
WW Daniel (Middx)	1245	71	17.53
J Garner (Somerset)	583	33	17.66
IT Botham (Somerset)	719	39	18.43
GS Le Roux (Sussex)	1210	65	18.61
PH Edmonds (Middx)	1348	71	18.98
AME Roberts (Leics)	1027	54	19.01

LEADING ALL-ROUNDERS

	Runs	(Avge)	Wkts	(Avge)
MD Marshall (Hants)	633	(22.60)	134	(15.73)
JE Emburey (Middx)	734	(33.36)	74	(22.01)
RJ Hadlee (Notts)	807	(31.03)	59	(14.16)
GS Le Roux (Sussex)	734	(32.04)	65	(18.61)
N Phillip (Essex)	684	(25.33)	68	(24.97)
DS Steele (Northants)	775	(36.90)	67	(24.22)

LEADING WICKET-KEEPERS

	Dismissals		Total
RJ Parks (Hants)	70ct	6st	76
DE East (Essex)	65ct	9st	74

1983

FINAL TABLE

	P	W	L	D	Bt	Bl	Pts
1 Essex	24	11	5	8	69	79	324
2 Middlesex	23	11	4	8	60	72	308
3 Hampshire	24	10	2	12	62	71	289
4 Leicestershire ...	24	9	3	12	52	81	277
5 Warwickshire....	24	10	3	11	52	64	276
6 Northamptonshire	24	7	4	13	63	77	252
7 Kent	24	7	4	13	68	70	250
8 Surrey.........	24	7	4	13	65	70	247
9 Derbyshire......	24	7	5	12	46	65	219
10 Somerset	24	3	7	14	57	75	180
11 Sussex	23	3	10	10	50	72	170
12 Gloucestershire ..	23	3	8	12	56	61	165
Lancashire	24	3	4	17	56	61	165
14 Nottinghamshire .	24	3	10	11	39	62	149
15 Glamorgan......	24	2	10	12	45	64	141
16 Worcestershire ..	24	2	11	11	43	54	129
17 Yorkshire	23	1	5	17	45	64	125

Hampshire and Derbyshire totals include 12 points for a win in one-innings matches. Gloucs v Sussex, Gloucester; Middlesex v Yorks, Lord's: both abandoned without a ball bowled.

BEST INDIVIDUAL SCORES
252 W Larkins, Northants v Glamorgan, Cardiff
243* AI Kallicharran, Warwicks v Glamorgan, Edgbaston
236 W Larkins, Northants v Derbys, Derby
216 IVA Richards, Somerset v Leics, Leicester

BEST INNINGS ANALYSES
8-42 SR Barwick, Glamorgan v Worcs, Worcester
8-46 ST Jefferies, Lancs v Notts, Trent Bridge
7-23 EE Hemmings, Notts v Lancs, Trent Bridge
7-29 MD Marshall, Hants v Somerset, Bournemouth

BEST MATCH ANALYSES
14-158 DL Underwood, Kent v Worcs, Canterbury
13-161 DL Underwood, Kent v Notts, Trent

Bridge
12-89 P Carrick, Yorks v Derbys, Sheffield
12-95 JK Lever, Essex v Sussex, Hove

LEADING BATSMEN
	Inns	NO	Runs	HS	Avge
IVA Richards (Somerset)	20	4	1204	216	75.25
KS McEwan (Essex)	35	5	2051	189*	68.36
CG Greenidge (Hants)	27	5	1438	154	65.36
JA Carse (Northants)	10	8	129	36*	64.50
MW Gatting (Middx)	23	5	1157	160	64.27
CL Smith (Hants)	33	3	1831	193	61.03
Imran Khan (Sussex)	25	3	1260	124*	57.27
G Boycott (Yorks)	40	5	1941	214*	55.45
CS Cowdrey (Kent)	32	9	1256	123	54.60
AI Kallicharran (Warwicks)	32	4	1637	243*	54.56

LEADING BOWLERS
	Runs	Wkts	Avge
MD Marshall (Hants)	1327	80	16.58
JK Lever (Essex)	1647	98	16.80
M Hendrick (Notts)	1122	66	17.00
JE Emburey (Middx)	1677	96	17.46
DL Underwood (Kent)	2024	105	19.27
LB Taylor (Leics)	1338	69	19.39
J Garner (Somerset)	659	34	19.38
N Phillip (Essex)	1338	68	19.67
PH Edmonds (Middx)	1491	72	20.70
PB Clift (Leics)	1481	71	20.85

LEADING ALL-ROUNDERS
	Runs (Avge)		Wkts (Avge)	
JN Shepherd (Gloucs)	1025	(36.60)	67	(30.55)
P Carrick (Yorks)	697	(29.04)	62	(28.22)
PB Clift (Leics)	795	(22.12)	71	(20.85)
JE Emburey (Mddx)	772	(27.57)	96	(17.46)

LEADING WICKET-KEEPERS
	Dismissals		Total
DE East (Essex)	60ct	5st	65
RC Russell (Gloucs)	45ct	17st	62

1984

FINAL TABLE

	P	W	L	D(T)	Bt	Bl	Pts
1 Essex	24	13	3	8	64	83	355
2 Nottinghamshire .	24	12	3	0	68	81	341
3 Middlesex	24	8	7	9	63	78	269
4 Leicestershire ...	24	8	2	14	60	78	266
5 Kent	24	8	3	11(2)	45	65	254
6 Sussex	24	7	6	10(1)	54	79	249
7 Somerset	24	6	7	11	60	78	234
8 Surrey	24	6	6	12	62	72	230
9 Warwickshire ...	24	6	7	11	71	60	227
10 Worcestershire ..	24	5	5	14	66	74	220
11 Northamptonshire	24	5	9	9(1)	58	56	202
12 Derbyshire......	24	4	6	14	72	66	202
13 Glamorgan......	24	4	2	18	65	71	200
14 Yorkshire.......	24	5	4	15	59	55	194
15 Hampshire......	24	3	13	8	58	62	168
16 Lancashire	24	1	9	14	49	72	137
17 Gloucestershire..	24	1	10	13	56	61	133

Sussex total includes 12 points for a win in a one-innings match.

BEST INDIVIDUAL SCORES

258 MW Gatting, Middx v Somerset, Bath
227 GA Gooch, Essex v Derbys, Chesterfield
226 G Fowler, Lancs v Kent, Maidstone
220 GA Gooch, Essex v Hants, Southampton

BEST INNINGS ANALYSES

8-26 PB Clift, Leics v Warwicks, Edgbaston
8-37 JK Lever, Essex v Gloucs, Bristol
8-44 KE Cooper, Notts v Middx, Lord's
8-53 PH Edmonds, Middx v Hants, Bournemouth

BEST MATCH ANALYSES

12-120 PH Edmonds, Middx v Hants, Bournemouth
12-121 DL Underwood, Kent v Hants, Bournemouth
12-123 EE Hemmings, Notts v Glamorgan, Trent Bridge
11-76 RJ Hadlee, Notts v Gloucs, Trent Bridge

LEADING BATSMEN

	Inns	NO	Runs	HS	Avge
GA Gooch (Essex)	40	7	2281	227	69.12
Javed Miandad (Glam)	13	1	800	212*	66.66
MW Gatting (Middx)	37	7	1998	258	66.60
G Boycott (Yorks)	35	10	1567	153*	62.68
JG Wright (Derbys)	21	1	1201	177	60.05
DL Amiss (Warwicks)	47	10	2137	122	57.75
DI Gower (Leics)	13	1	660	117*	55.00
VJ Marks (Somerset)	31	9	1197	134	54.40
MD Crowe (Somerset)	38	5	1769	190	53.60
RJ Hadlee (Notts)	31	8	1179	210*	51.26

LEADING BOWLERS

	Runs	Wkts	Avge
RJ Hadlee (Notts)	1645	117	14.05
PJW Allott (Lancs)	1014	59	17.18
DL Underwood (Kent)	1511	77	19.62
NG Cowans (Middx)	1300	65	20.00
A Sidebottom (Yorks)	1265	63	20.07
IT Botham (Somerset)	691	33	20.93
TM Tremlett (Hants)	1403	67	20.94
RM Ellison (Kent)	1111	53	20.96
GA Gooch (Essex)	756	36	21.00
GS Le Roux (Sussex)	1612	76	21.21

LEADING ALL-ROUNDERS

	Runs (Avge)	Wkts (Avge)
RJ Hadlee (Notts)	1179 (51.26)	117 (14.05)
AM Ferreira (Warwicks)	766 (31.91)	75 (28.13)
VJ Marks (Somerset)	1197 (54.40)	78 (26.44)
G Miller (Derbys)	817 (34.04)	84 (24.26)
RC Ontong (Glamorgan)	1182 (34.76)	65 (29.86)
JF Steele (Glamorgan)	796 (30.61)	65 (27.38)

LEADING WICKET-KEEPERS

	Dismissals		Total
DE East (Essex)	73ct	1st	74
BN French (Notts)	66ct	7st	73

1985

FINAL TABLE

	P	W	L	D	Bt	Bl	Pts
1 Middlesex	24	8	4	12	61	85	274
2 Hampshire	24	7	2	15	66	78	256
3 Gloucestershire ..	23	7	3	13	51	78	241
4 Essex	23	7	2	14	42	70	224
5 Worcestershire ..	24	5	6	13	65	68	221
6 Surrey..........	24	5	5	14	62	76	218
7 Sussex	23	6	1	16	52	57	205
8 Nottinghamshire .	24	4	2	18	66	69	199
9 Kent	24	4	5	15	51	71	186
10 Northamptonshire	24	5	4	15	52	51	183
11 Yorkshire	23	3	4	16	58	59	165
12 Glamorgan	24	4	4	16	41	50	163
13 Derbyshire	24	3	9	12	46	69	163
14 Lancashire	24	3	7	14	44	67	159
15 Warwickshire....	24	2	8	14	47	74	153
16 Leicestershire ...	24	2	3	19	48	65	145
17 Somerset	24	1	7	16	70	45	131

Worcestershire v Glamorgan totals include 8 points for levelling the scores in drawn matches.
Sides level on points are separated by the number of wins.
Yorks v Essex, Sheffield; Gloucs v Sussex, Bristol: both abandoned without a ball bowled.

BEST INDIVIDUAL SCORES

322 IVA Richards, Somerset v Warwicks, Taunton
204 CG Greenidge, Hants v Warwicks, Edgbaston
202 GA Gooch, Essex v Notts, Trent Bridge
200 CT Radley, Middx v Northants, Uxbridge

BEST INNINGS ANALYSES

9–70 JP Agnew, Leics v Kent, Leicester
8–17 VJ Marks, Somerset v Lancs, Bath
8–40 AH Gray, Surrey v Yorks, Sheffield
8–41 RJ Hadlee, Notts v Lancs, Trent Bridge

BEST MATCH ANALYSES

13–106 RC Ontong, Glamorgan v Notts, Trent Bridge
13–128 CA Walsh, Gloucs v Warwicks, Cheltenham

11–73 VJ Marks, Somerset v Lancs, Bath
11–118 JP Agnew, Leics v Kent, Leicester

LEADING BATSMEN

	Inns	NO	Runs	HS	Avge
IT Botham (Somerset)	17	5	1211	152	100.91
GA Gooch (Essex)	17	2	1368	202	91.20
G Boycott (Yorks)	31	11	1545	184	77.25
IVA Richards (Somerset)	24	0	1836	322	76.50
Imran Khan (Sussex)	19	7	846	117*	70.50
RT Robinson (Notts)	21	3	1107	130*	61.50
P Bainbridge (Gloucs)	33	8	1456	151*	58.24
JG Wright (Derbys)	16	2	797	177*	56.92
Younis Ahmed (Glam)	28	7	1190	177	56.66
MA Lynch (Surrey)	37	7	1672	145	55.73

LEADING BOWLERS

	Runs	Wkts	Avge
RJ Hadlee (Notts)	1026	59	17.38
MD Marshall (Hants)	1680	95	17.68
GE Sainsbury (Gloucs)	380	21	18.09
PJW Allott (Lancs)	927	49	18.91
RM Ellison (Kent)	863	44	19.61
Imran Khan (Sussex)	952	48	19.83
CA Walsh (Gloucs)	1636	82	19.95
NG Cowans (Middx)	1268	60	21.13
LB Taylor (Leics)	1102	52	21.19
TM Tremlett (Hants)	1620	75	21.60

LEADING ALL-ROUNDERS

	Runs (Avge)	Wkts (Avge)
RC Ontong (Glam)	1105 (50.22)	62 (27.83)
MD Marshall (Hants)	768 (24.77)	95 (17.68)

LEADING WICKET-KEEPERS

	Dismissals		Total
GW Humpage (Warwicks)	70ct	3st	73
BN French (Notts)	61ct	7st	68

1986

FINAL TABLE

	P	W	L	D	Bt	Bl	Pts
1 Essex	24	10	6	8	51	76	287
2 Gloucestershire ..	24	9	3	12	50	65	259
3 Surrey..........	24	8	6	10	54	66	248
4 Nottinghamshire .	24	7	2	15	55	80	247
5 Worcestershire ..	24	7	5	12	58	72	242
6 Hampshire	23	7	4	12	54	69	235
7 Leicestershire ...	24	5	7	12	55	67	202
8 Kent	24	5	7	12	42	75	197
9 Northamptonshire	24	5	3	16	53	60	193
10 Yorkshire	24	4	5	15	62	59	193
11 Derbyshire	24	5	5	14	42	70	188
12 Middlesex	24	4	9	11	47	65	176
Warwickshire....	24	4	5	15	61	51	176
14 Sussex	23	4	7	12	46	56	166
15 Lancashire	23	4	5	14	41	51	156
16 Somerset	23	3	7	13	52	52	152
17 Glamorgan	24	2	7	15	39	47	118

Derbyshire total includes 12 points for a win in a one-innings match; Yorkshire includes 8 pts for levelling the scores in a drawn match. Sussex v Somerset, Horsham; Hants v Lancs, Southampton: both abandoned without a ball bowled.

BEST INDIVIDUAL SCORES

234 RA Harper, Northants v Gloucs, Northampton
227* GA Hick, Worcs v Notts, Worcester
224* RJ Bailey, Northants v Glamorgan, Swansea
222 CG Greenidge, Hants v Northants, Northampton

BEST INNINGS ANALYSES

9–70 NV Radford, Worcs v Somerset, Worcester
9–72 CA Walsh, Gloucs v Somerset, Bristol
8–34 Imran Khan, Sussex v Middx, Lord's
8–46 TM Alderman, Kent v Derbys, Derby

BEST MATCH ANALYSES

14–144 TM Alderman, Kent v Leics, Canterbury
14–212 VJ Marks, Somerset v Glamorgan, Cardiff

13–127 RC Ontong, Glamorgan v Notts, Cardiff
12–124 CA Walsh, Gloucs v Hants, Cheltenham

LEADING BATSMEN

	Inns	NO	Runs	HS	Avge
AJ Lamb (Northants)	20	4	1261	160*	78.81
JJ Whitaker (Leics)	28	8	1382	200*	69.10
CG Greenidge (Hants)	32	4	1916	222	68.42
GA Hick (Worcs)	36	6	1934	227*	64.46
BM McMillan (Warwicks)	19	4	895	136	59.66
CL Smith (Hants)	25	8	964	114*	56.70
RJ Hadlee (Notts)	18	5	720	129*	55.38
RJ Bailey (Northants)	36	7	1562	224*	53.86
RT Robinson (Notts)	30	5	1319	150*	52.76
PM Roebuck (Somerset)	32	8	1261	221*	52.54

LEADING BOWLERS

	Runs	Wkts	Avge
RJ Hadlee (Notts)	825	57	14.47
JH Childs (Essex)	1278	85	15.03
MD Marshall (Hants)	1508	100	15.08
ST Clarke (Surrey)	806	48	16.79
CA Walsh (Gloucs)	2145	118	18.17
AH Gray (Surrey)	966	51	18.94
TM Alderman (Kent)	1882	98	19.20
MA Holding (Derbys)	1045	52	20.09
TD Topley (Essex)	651	31	21.00
JE Emburey (Middx)	505	24	21.04

LEADING ALL-ROUNDERS

	Runs	(Avge)	Wkts	(Avge)
PAJ DeFreitas (Leics)	630	(24.23)	89	(22.21)
RA Harper (Northants)	921	(36.84)	62	(26.93)

LEADING WICKET-KEEPERS

	Dismissals		Total
DE East (Essex)	61ct	19st	80
RJ Parks (Hants)	68ct	6st	74

1987

FINAL TABLE

	P	W	L	D(T)	Bt	Bl	Pts
1 Nottinghamshire .	23	9	1	13	68	80	292
2 Lancashire	24	10	4	10	55	73	288
3 Leicestershire ...	24	8	3	13	57	75	260
4 Surrey	24	7	4	13	65	73	250
5 Hampshire......	24	7	3	14	59	73	244
6 Derbyshire......	24	6	5	12(1)	51	70	225
7 Northamptonshire	24	7	4	13	48	68	224
8 Yorkshire.......	23	7	3	13	52	58	222
9 Worcestershire ..	24	5	4	15	58	68	206
10 Gloucestershire..	24	5	8	10(1)	62	50	200
11 Somerset	24	2	3	19	61	70	163
12 Essex	24	2	4	18	45	77	162
13 Glamorgan......	24	3	9	12	40	70	158
14 Kent	24	2	7	15	53	66	151
15 Warwickshire ...	24	2	7	15	48	67	147
16 Middlesex	23	2	8	13	47	60	139
17 Sussex	23	1	8	14	47	56	119

Northants total includes 12 points for a win in a one-innings match; Essex 8 pts for levelling the scores in a drawn match. Middlesex v Notts, Lord's; Sussex v Yorks, Hastings: both abandoned without a ball bowled.

BEST INDIVIDUAL SCORES

217 CL Smith, Hants v Warwicks, Edgbaston
209* RA Smith, Hants v Essex, Southend
206* MD Crowe, Somerset v Warwicks, Edgbaston
204* RJ Blakey, Yorks v Gloucs, Headingley

BEST INNINGS ANALYSES

8-55 NV Radford, Worcs v Notts, Kidderminster
8-62 ST Clarke, Surrey v Northants, Oval
8-76 EAE Baptiste, Kent v Warwicks, Edgbaston
7-15 I Folley, Lancs v Warwicks, Southport

BEST MATCH ANALYSES

13-115 TA Merrick, Warwicks v Lancs, Edgbaston
12-57 I Folley, Lancs v Warwicks, Southport
12-83 RJ Hadlee, Notts v Somerset, Trent Bridge
12-105 ST Clarke, Surrey v Northants, Oval

LEADING BATSMEN

	Inns	NO	Runs	HS	Avge
MD Crowe (Somerset)	29	5	1627	206*	67.79
DI Gower (Leics)	19	4	840	125	56.00
RK Illingworth (Worcs)	19	11	448	120*	56.00
RJ Hadlee (Notts)	27	7	1075	133*	53.75
GA Hick (Worcs)	37	2	1868	173	53.37
MW Gatting (Middx)	18	1	892	196	52.47
KD James (Hants)	15	5	517	142*	51.70
RA Smith (Hants)	24	7	852	209*	50.11
PM Roebuck (Som)	29	5	1199	165*	49.95
DR Turner (Hants)	33	8	1240	184*	49.60

LEADING BOWLERS

	Runs	Wkts	Avge
RJ Hadlee (Notts)	1154	97	11.89
AH Gray (Surrey)	667	44	15.15
ST Clarke (Surrey)	1123	66	17.01
NG Cowans (Middx)	781	44	17.75
GR Dilley (Worcs)	387	21	18.42
TM Tremlett (Hants)	1251	66	18.95
OH Mortensen (Derbys)	1084	55	19.70
MD Marshall (Hants)	1445	72	20.06
NV Radford (Worcs)	2269	109	20.81
PJW Allott (Lancs)	1188	56	21.21

LEADING ALL-ROUNDERS

	Runs (Avge)	Wkts (Avge)
RJ Hadlee (Notts)	1075 (53.75)	97 (11.89)
MD Marshall (Hants)	610 (35.88)	72 (20.06)

LEADING WICKET-KEEPERS

	Dismissals		Total
BJM Maher (Derbys)	70ct	4st	74
P Whitticase (Leics)	65ct	1st	66

THE WORCESTER REVIVAL

To bracket late-1980s Worcestershire with the great county sides of the past after their barren 1990 season may seem surprising; but fourth place after two successive Championships suggests a place among the strongest sides, and arguably top billing.

The recent rise of Worcestershire dates from the early 1980s, when several patchy but largely mediocre seasons had followed their Championship win in 1974. There remained some players of class; a fading Basil D'Oliveira had remained a force to be reckoned with (when the mood took him) in the late 1970s, while Glenn Turner had added versatility to prolificacy at the top of the county's batting. Alan Ormrod's classic touch seemed to mark him down as successor to the great Tom Graveney, and Norman Gifford remained a fine left-arm spinner. Yet the top prizes seemed far away. Come the eighties, a fresh start was made and an early move was the appointment of Phil Neale as captain.

It was a decision which was not universally popular, especially as it coincided with the last season of the long-serving ex-skipper Norman Gifford, who departed to see out his career with neighbours and rivals Warwickshire. Not for nothing was Neale a graduate in Russian, however; he exhibited a quiet determination while building a new spirit in the team, and the club as a whole began a wholesale strengthening campaign.

Among the first notable arrivals in the Neale era were Damien D'Oliveira, Richard Illingworth and Phil Newport in 1982. They joined a small but promising nucleus which included Tim Curtis, an opening bat of patience and ability, and local all-rounder Martin Weston. Further outstanding acquisitions made their bow in 1985: Neil Radford and Steven Rhodes joined the county after less-than-happy spells elsewhere, but both quickly established their international credentials. Then with an eye to spectator and sponsor interest Ian Botham and Graham Dilley arrived in 1987. If the on-field contributions of the last-named signings have been less prolific than expected, their joint effect on membership and spectator interest, not to mention sponsorship, cannot be overstated.

Perhaps the most important and far-reaching event of the 1980s, however, was the arrival of Graeme Hick. An abortive trial with Warwickshire – 'just another overseas player, they are two-a-penny' was the 'expert' verdict from Edgbaston – must have demoralised the 17-year-old in a strange land, but at Worcester he found more perceptiveness and imagination and was quickly taken on.

The rest, as they say, is history. Hick's championship record at the start of 1991 – when he is an 'English' cricketer at last – stands at 10 859 runs, 38 centuries and an average of 65.41. Such a record at 24 years of age, and at such a stage in a career, is unprecedented.

An addition to the staff in 1991 is the gigantic Australian batsman Tom Moody, fresh from an incredible season with Warwickshire, which saw 866 runs, an average of 86.60 and centuries in his first three county matches. His acquisition suggests a batting strength of awesome possibilities.

Age, injury and uncertain recent form, however, suggest that wickets may become a more difficult commodity for the county and could prevent a return to the top. But with batting potential as great as any county for some forty years or more, perhaps only average bowling will be needed to send Worcestershire back to top spot.

Phil Neale proved himself an outstanding skipper for Worcestershire in the late 1980s, as well as making a consistent contribution with the bat (Allsport/Adrian Murrell)

1988

FINAL TABLE

	P	W	L	D	Bt	Bl	Pts
1 Worcestershire ..	22	10	3	9	55	75	290
2 Kent	22	10	5	7	57	72	289
3 Essex	22	9	5	8	61	69	282
4 Surrey..........	22	7	5	10	57	72	241
5 Nottinghamshire .	22	8	8	6	34	71	229
6 Warwickshire....	22	6	8	8	48	74	218
7 Middlesex	22	7	3	12	49	54	215
8 Leicestershire ...	22	6	3	13	56	63	215
9 Lancashire	22	6	7	9	41	67	212
10 Gloucestershire ..	21	6	7	8	52	59	207
11 Somerset	22	5	6	11	48	65	201
12 Northamptonshire	22	5	7	10	48	71	199
13 Yorkshire	22	4	6	12	48	65	177
14 Derbyshire......	22	4	3	15	53	54	171
15 Hampshire	22	4	6	12	33	69	166
16 Sussex	22	3	11	8	37	65	150
17 Glamorgan	21	1	8	12	42	53	111

Notts total includes 12 points for a win in a one-innings match; Essex, Lancashire and Somerset totals include 8 pts for levelling the scores in a drawn match.
Glamorgan v Gloucs, Swansea: abandoned without a ball bowled.

BEST INDIVIDUAL SCORES

405* GA Hick, Worcs v Somerset, Taunton
275 GA Gooch, Essex v Kent, Chelmsford
239* KJ Barnett, Derbys v Leics, Leicester
237 DW Randall, Notts v Derbys, Trent Bridge

BEST INNINGS ANALYSES

8–29 PG Newman, Derbys v Yorks, Headingley
8–52 KT Medlycott, Surrey v Sussex, Hove
8–52 PJ Newport, Worcs v Middx, Lord's
8–58 SD Fletcher, Yorks v Essex, Sheffield

BEST MATCH ANALYSES

14–165 DA Graveney, Gloucs v Worcs, Bristol
12–105 KT Medlycott, Surrey v Sussex, Hove
12–179 TD Topley, Essex v Derbys, Chesterfield
11–90 RJ Shastri, Glamorgan v Lancs, Swansea

LEADING BATSMEN

	Inns	NO	Runs	HS	Avge
SR Waugh (Somerset)	22	6	1286	161	80.37
GA Hick (Worcs)	34	2	2443	405*	76.34
CWJ Athey (Gloucs)	20	6	1037	168*	74.07
GA Gooch (Essex)	23	0	1631	275	59.17
N Hussain (Essex)	11	3	469	165*	58.62
MR Ramprakash (Middx)	11	4	401	68*	57.28
KJ Barnett (Derbys)	27	2	1406	239*	56.24
AJ Lamb (Northants)	15	2	731	155	56.23
MW Gatting (Middx)	29	2	1431	210	53.00
CJ Richards (Surrey)	21	4	861	102*	50.64

LEADING BOWLERS

	Runs	Wkts	Avge
OH Mortensen (Derbys)	464	34	13.64
PW Jarvis (Yorks)	434	31	14.00
ST Clarke (Surrey)	913	63	14.49
NF Williams (Middx)	511	30	17.03
FD Stephenson (Notts)	2161	121	17.85
NG Cowans (Middx)	1290	71	18.16
GC Small (Warwicks)	1380	75	18.40
ARC Fraser (Middx)	1484	77	19.27
PJ Newport (Worcs)	1640	85	19.29
AA Donald (Warwicks)	507	26	19.50

LEADING ALL-ROUNDERS

	Runs (Avge)		Wkts (Avge)	
KM Curran (Gloucs)	1005	(37.22)	65	(21.30)
FD Stephenson (Notts)	962	(28.29)	121	(17.85)

LEADING WICKET-KEEPERS

	Dismissals		Total
SJ Rhodes (Worcs)	69ct	8st	77
D Ripley (Northants)	66ct	6st	72

Kim Barnett, the Derbyshire skipper, always showed outstanding form as an opening bat of the belligerent school (Allsport/Adrian Murrell)

(Above): *Somerset's Jim Cook enjoyed the most successful first Championship season ever, in 1989. The South African carried his form into 1990, and was rewarded with an extended contract* (Allsport/Adrian Murrell)

(Insert): *Warwickshire's Geoff Humpage, an under-rated wicket-keeper who topped the lists in 1985, was also – though the picture suggests otherwise! – nearly Test class as a batsman, yet representative honours were minimal* (Allsport/ Simon Bruty)

1989

FINAL TABLE

		P	W	L	D	Bt	Bl	Pts
1	Worcestershire ..	22	12	3	7	44	83	319
2	Essex	22	13	2	7	59	71	313
3	Middlesex	22	9	2	11	50	72	266
4	Lancashire	22	8	5	9	57	65	250
5	Northamptonshire	22	7	8	7	47	63	222
6	Derbyshire	22	6	6	10	45	75	216
	Hampshire	22	6	8	8	55	65	216
8	Warwickshire	22	5	4	13	44	75	207
9	Gloucestershire ..	22	6	11	5	38	70	204
10	Sussex	22	4	4	14	60	68	192
11	Nottinghamshire .	22	6	6	10	54	65	190
12	Surrey..........	22	4	7	11	50	69	183
13	Leicestershire ...	22	4	8	10	43	74	181
14	Somerset	22	4	6	12	50	54	168
15	Kent	22	3	8	11	53	53	154
16	Yorkshire	22	3	9	10	41	60	149
17	Glamorgan	22	3	6	13	38	59	145

Essex and Notts each had 25 points deducted for sub-standard pitches. Warwickshire's total includes 8 pts for levelling the scores in a drawn match.

BEST INDIVIDUAL SCORES

228 DI Gower, Leics v Glamorgan, Leicester
206* DL Haynes, Middx v Kent, Uxbridge
206* AJ Stewart, Surrey v Essex, Oval
199* AJ Stewart, Surrey v Sussex, Oval

BEST INNINGS ANALYSES

8–41 RJ Maru, Hants v Kent, Southampton
8–47 FD Stephenson, Notts v Essex, Trent Bridge
7–18 DR Pringle, Essex v Glamorgan, Swansea
7–19 CA Walsh, Gloucs v Somerset, Bath

BEST MATCH ANALYSES

15–106 FD Stephenson, Notts v Essex, Trent Bridge
13–75 FD Stephenson, Notts v Yorks, Headingley
13–159 SL Watkin, Glamorgan v Lancs, Old Trafford
12–66 JE Emburey, Middx v Gloucs, Cheltenham

LEADING BATSMEN

	Inns	NO	Runs	HS	Avge
SJ Cook (Somerset)	39	4	2173	156	62.08
RA Smith (Hants)	17	1	959	182	59.93
RF Pienaar (Kent)	25	4	1239	134*	59.00
MW Gatting (Middx)	29	6	1337	158*	58.13
MR Benson (Kent)	27	5	1190	157	54.09
KR Brown (Middx)	11	3	431	90	53.87
GA Hick (Worcs)	35	5	1595	150	53.16
AP Wells (Sussex)	38	7	1629	153	52.54
GA Gooch (Essex)	20	1	994	158	52.31
N Hussain (Essex)	22	3	945	141	49.73

LEADING BOWLERS

	Runs	Wkts	Avge
DR Pringle (Essex)	1447	89	16.25
AA Donald (Warwicks)	1398	86	16.25
MD Marshall (Hants)	1067	64	16.67
SR Lampitt (Worcs)	526	31	16.96
ARC Fraser (Middx)	1343	78	17.21
NGB Cook (Northants)	909	49	18.55
FD Stephenson (Notts)	1699	91	18.67
WKM Benjamin (Leics)	1177	62	18.98
SM McEwan (Worcs)	999	52	19.21
RM Ellcock (Middx)	615	32	19.21

LEADING ALL-ROUNDERS

	Runs	(Avge)	Wkts	(Avge)
KT Medlycott (Surrey)	861	(28.70)	62	(31.83)
DJ Capel (Northants)	1260	(38.18)	51	(30.56)
AIC Dodemaide (Sussex)	683	(32.52)	65	(30.32)

LEADING WICKET-KEEPERS

	Dismissals		Total
WK Hegg (Lancs)	74ct	2st	76
RJ Parks (Hants)	65ct	4st	69

1990

FINAL TABLE

	P	W	L	D	Bt	Bl	Pts
1 Middlesex	22	10	1	11	73	55	288
2 Essex	22	8	2	12	73	56	257
3 Hampshire	22	8	4	10	67	48	243
4 Worcestershire ..	22	7	1	14	70	58	240
5 Warwickshire....	22	7	7	8	55	64	231
6 Lancashire	22	6	3	13	65	56	217
7 Leicestershire ...	22	6	7	9	61	53	210
8 Glamorgan	22	5	6	11	64	48	192
9 Surrey..........	22	4	3	15	54	64	190
10 Yorkshire	22	5	9	8	52	55	187
11 Northamptonshire	22	4	9	9	61	60	185
12 Derbyshire	22	6	7	9	58	52	181
13 Gloucestershire ..	22	4	7	11	51	58	173
Nottinghamshire .	22	4	8	10	51	58	173
15 Somerset	22	3	4	15	73	45	166
16 Kent	22	3	6	13	69	35	152
17 Sussex	22	3	9	10	51	44	143

BEST INDIVIDUAL SCORES

366   NH Fairbrother, Lancs v Surrey, Oval
313*   SJ Cook, Somerset v Glamorgan, Cardiff
291   IA Greig, Surrey v Leics, Oval
263   DM Ward, Surrey v Kent, Canterbury

BEST INNINGS ANALYSES

8-58   CA Walsh, Gloucs v Northants, Cheltenham
7-47   MD Marshall, Hants v Derbys, Portsmouth
7-61   NF Williams, Middx v Kent, Lord's
7-73   Waqar Younis, Surrey v Warwicks, Oval

BEST MATCH ANALYSES

12-155   CEL Ambrose, Northants v Leics, Leicester
11-76   NA Foster, Essex v Surrey, Chelmsford
11-92   MD Marshall, Hants v Glamorgan, Pontypridd
11-99   CA Walsh, Gloucs v Northants, Cheltenham

LEADING BATSMEN

	Inns	NO	Runs	HS	Avge
GA Gooch (Essex)	18	2	1586	215	99.13
GA Hick (Worcs)	33	8	2273	252*	90.92
TM Moody (Warwicks)	12	2	866	168	86.60
NH Fairbrother (Lancs)	24	6	1544	366	85.78
AJ Lamb (Northants)	16	3	1040	235	80.00
ME Waugh (Essex)	32	6	2009	207*	77.27
DM Ward (Surrey)	31	7	1843	263	76.79
SJ Cook (Somerset)	38	6	2432	313*	76.00
MA Atherton (Lancs)	18	4	1053	191	75.21
DJ Bicknell (Surrey)	20	4	1199	186	74.94

LEADING BOWLERS

	Runs	Wkts	Avge
IR Bishop (Derbys)	1087	59	18.42
MD Marshall (Hants)	1381	72	19.18
DJ Millns (Leics)	568	25	22.72
Mohammed Younis (Surrey)	1357	57	23.80
OH Mortensen (Derbys)	764	32	23.87
PA Smith (Warwicks)	497	20	24.85
ARC Fraser (Middx)	1073	41	26.17
MA Atherton (Lancs)	1111	42	26.45
GJ Parsons (Leics)	821	31	26.48
NA Foster (Essex)	2502	94	26.61

LEADING ALL-ROUNDERS

	Runs (Avge)	Wkts	(Avge)
KM Curran (Gloucs)	1261 (52.54)	60	(30.65)
MD Marshall (Hants)	962 (45.81)	72	(19.18)
GD Rose (Somerset)	897 (52.76)	51	(35.43)

LEADING WICKET-KEEPERS

	Dismissals		Total
SJ Rhodes (Worcs)	57ct	8st	65
KM Krikken (Derbys)	58ct	3st	61
BN French (Notts)	47ct	10st	57

4

THE CHAMPIONSHIP RECORDS

*Jack Hobbs, known as 'The Master', played with
effortless ease for Surrey until the age of 51.
He was subsequently knighted for services
to cricket* (Mary Evans Picture Library)

TEAM TOTALS

HIGHEST IN ONE INNINGS
887 Yorks v Warwicks, Edgbaston 1896
863–9 dec Lancs v Surrey, Oval 1990

HIGHEST MATCH AGGREGATE (BOTH SIDES)
Runs–Wkts
1650–19 Surrey v Lancs, Oval 1990
1641–16 Glamorgan v Worcs, Swansea 1990
(Highest in match with definite result)

LOWEST IN ONE INNINGS
12 Northants v Gloucs, Northampton 1907
13 Notts v Yorks, Trent Bridge 1901

LOWEST MATCH AGGREGATE (BOTH SIDES)
Runs–Wkts
158–22 Surrey v Worcs, Oval 1954
165–30 Middlesex v Somerset, Lord's 1899
See also individual county records.

APPEARANCES

MOST IN COUNTY CHAMPIONSHIP
763 W Rhodes (Yorkshire)
707 FE Woolley (Kent)
665 CP Mead (Hants)

Yorkshire's continued high Championship placings owed much to the batting of Herbert Sutcliffe, who played regularly in every inter-war season and only once missed scoring 1000 runs (Allsport)

MOST CONSECUTIVE IN COUNTY CHAMPIONSHIP
423 KG Suttle (Sussex) 1954–69
412 JG Binks (Yorkshire) 1955–69
399 J Vine (Sussex) 1899–1914
344 EH Killick (Sussex) 1898–1912
326 CN Woolley (Northants) 1913–31
305 AH Dyson (Glamorgan) 1930–47
300 B Taylor (Essex) 1961–72

INDIVIDUAL BATTING

BATSMEN WITH OVER 20 000 CHAMPIONSHIP RUNS

	Inns	NO	Runs	HS	Avge	100s
CP Mead (Hants) 1906–36	1115	157	46268	280*	48.29	132
FE Woolley (Kent) 1906–38	1121	62	43703	270	41.26	112
JB Hobbs (Surrey) 1905–34	860	69	38707	316*	48.93	130
EH Hendren (Middx) 1907–37	859	110	37475	301*	50.03	113
H Sutcliffe (Yorks) 1919–39	721	74	32814	313	50.71	96
Ernest Tyldesley (Lancs) 1909–36	782	87	31903	256*	34.90	85
DL Amiss (Warwicks) 1960–87	854	86	31617	232*	41.16	70
WG Quaife (Warwicks) 1895–1928	1018	162	31476	255*	36.77	68
D Kenyon (Worcs) 1946–61	969	48	31375	259	34.06	64
WR Hammond (Gloucs) 1920–51	619	66	31344	317	56.67	107
TW Hayward (Surrey) 1893–1914	804	64	30971	315*	41.85	78
JT Tyldesley (Lancs) 1895–1923	774	50	30865	295*	42.63	73
HTW Hardinge (Kent) 1902–33	923	89	30776	243*	36.90	70
John Langridge (Sussex) 1928–55	866	57	30340	250*	37.50	67
Alan Jones (Glam) 1957–83	995	72	30266	204*	32.79	48
George Gunn (Notts) 1902–32	874	73	29522	220	36.85	52
G Boycott (Yorks) 1962–86	607	101	29485	260*	58.27	94
TW Graveney (Gloucs, Worcs) 1948–70	775	103	29417	222	43.77	68
JM Parks (Somerset, Sussex) 1949–76	945	132	28996	205*	35.66	38
A Sandham (Surrey) 1911–37	738	65	28961	292*	43.03	68
D Denton (Yorks) 1895–1920	890	50	28291	221	33.67	50
LG Berry (Leics) 1924–51	969	46	27942	232	30.27	41
PA Perrin (Essex) 1891–1928	846	82	27703	343*	36.26	61
CA Milton (Gloucs) 1948–74	931	102	27528	170	33.20	48
GH Hirst (Yorks) 1891–1921	869	106	27314	341	35.79	50
KWR Fletcher (Essex) 1962–88	851	107	27123	228*	36.45	41
RE Marshall (Hants) 1955–72	821	42	27095	212	34.78	49
W Rhodes (Yorks) 1898–1930	1020	136	26859	267*	30.38	38
D Brookes (Northants) 1934–59	820	63	26627	257	35.17	60
KG Suttle (Sussex) 1949–71	953	79	26588	204*	30.42	43
LEG Ames (Kent) 1926–51	667	62	26508	295	43.81	70
AE Dipper (Gloucs) 1908–32	817	59	25922	252*	34.20	49
James Langridge (Sussex) 1924–53	861	125	25893	167	35.18	35
J O'Connor (Essex) 1921–39	802	70	25893	248	35.37	67
JW Hearne (Middx) 1909–36	683	68	25819	285*	41.98	70
JH Edrich (Surrey) 1958–78	637	71	25740	226*	45.47	67
MJK Smith (Leics, Warwicks) 1951–75	717	88	25561	200*	40.63	41
DB Close (Somerset, Yorks) 1949–77	899	119	25380	198	32.53	36
AE Fagg (Kent) 1932–57	738	44	25126	269*	36.20	48
J Seymour (Kent) 1902–26	803	56	24962	218*	33.41	52
RES Wyatt (Warwicks, Worcs) 1923–51	729	112	24927	232	40.40	56
JDB Robertson (Middx) 1938–59	675	36	24890	331*	38.95	54
Emrys Davies (Glam) 1926–54	944	77	24831	287*	28.64	31
C Washbrook (Lancs) 1933–59	669	86	24177	251*	41.46	48
WJ Edrich (Middx) 1937–58	605	55	23643	267*	42.98	56
JWH Makepeace (Lancs) 1906–30	702	60	23599	203	36.75	40
EH Bowley (Sussex) 1912–34	703	35	22921	283	34.31	40
WW Keeton (Notts) 1926–52	598	39	22729	242	40.66	53
P Holmes (Yorks) 1913–33	591	60	22680	315*	42.71	55
HE Dollery (Warwicks) 1934–55	638	60	22617	212	39.12	49
J Hardstaff Jnr (Notts) 1930–55	592	63	22585	266	42.69	59

AC Russell (Essex) 1908–30	597	50	22326	273	40.81	59
G Brown (Hants) 1909–33	859	44	22113	232*	27.13	37
JH Hampshire (Derbys, Yorks) 1961–84	738	95	22002	183*	34.21	33
EG Hayes (Leics, Surrey) 1896–1926	700	38	21960	276	33.17	41
MR Hallam (Leics) 1950–70	827	52	21922	210*	28.28	27
CB Fry (Hants, Sussex) 1894–1921	414	28	21916	258*	56.77	75
M Leyland (Yorks) 1920–46	600	73	21871	263	41.50	51
CT Radley (Middx) 1964–87	747	124	21828	200	35.03	36
RT Simpson (Notts) 1946–63	594	42	21708	243*	39.32	45
JR Gunn (Notts) 1896–1925	718	87	21588	294	34.21	37
J Vine (Sussex) 1896–1922	762	60	21399	202	30.48	31
JH King (Leics) 1895–1925	834	61	21343	227*	27.61	30
Younis Ahmed (Glam, Surrey, Worcs) 1967–86	616	96	21290	221*	40.94	35
MC Cowdrey (Kent) 1950–76	594	76	21270	250	41.06	49
RB Nicholls (Gloucs) 1951–75	871	45	21096	137	25.53	14
J Sharp (Lancs) 1899–1925	735	67	21080	211	31.55	35
WGA Parkhouse (Glam) 1948–64	693	44	21006	201	32.36	30
WH Ashdown (Kent) 1920–37	754	72	20997	332	30.78	36
DM Young (Gloucs, Worcs) 1946–64	737	39	20996	194	30.08	33
JA Ormrod (Lancs, Worcs) 1962–85	772	81	20914	204*	30.26	29
WE Russell (Middx) 1956–72	658	46	20913	193	34.17	34
MJ Stewart (Surrey) 1954–72	727	76	20905	227*	32.11	40
FB Watson (Lancs) 1920–37	601	46	20889	300*	37.63	45
JB Bolus (Derbys, Notts, Yorks) 1956–75	695	65	20746	202*	32.93	31
GM Turner (Worcs) 1968–82	464	59	20736	311*	51.20	67
JR Gray (Hants) 1948–66	747	72	20527	213*	30.41	28
J Iddon (Lancs) 1924–39	615	80	20517	217*	38.34	45
WRD Payton (Notts) 1905–31	708	113	20500	169	34.45	37
GM Emmett (Gloucs) 1938–59	694	41	20469	188	31.34	30
CJB Wood (Leics) 1896–1922	699	47	20344	225	31.20	33
JF Crapp (Gloucs) 1936–56	653	67	20261	140	34.57	32
DCS Compton (Middx) 1936–58	455	45	20254	252*	49.40	62
VWC Jupp (Northants, Sussex) 1909–38	733	66	20121	217*	30.16	29
G Barker (Essex) 1955–71	737	42	20069	181*	28.87	27
J Arnold (Hants) 1930–50	661	43	20032	227	32.41	31

HIGHEST INDIVIDUAL SCORES

424 AC MacLaren, Lancs v Somerset, Taunton 1895
405* GA Hick, Worcs v Somerset, Taunton 1988
366 NH Fairbrother, Lancs v Surey, Oval 1990
357* R Abel, Surrey v Somerset, Oval 1899
343* PA Perrin, Essex v Derbys, Chesterfield 1904
341 GH Hirst, Yorks v Leics, Leicester 1905
PA Perrin's 343* is highest for a losing side

MOST (AGGREGATE) RUNS IN A MATCH

446 (244 & 202*) AE Fagg, Kent v Essex, Colchester 1938
424 AC MacLaren, Lancs v Somerset, Taunton 1895
405 GA Hick, Worcs v Somerset, Taunton 1988

MOST RUNS BEFORE DISMISSAL

645 GA Hick (171* 69* 252* 100* 53) 1990
558 F Jakeman (80* 258* 176* 44) 1951

CARRYING BAT THROUGH BOTH COMPLETED INNINGS OF A MATCH

SP Kinneir   70*(239) and   69*(166) Warwicks v Leics, Leicester 1907
CJB Wood   107*(309) and 117*(296) Leics v Yorks, Bradford 1911
SJ Cook   120*(186) and 131*(218) Somerset v Notts, Trent Bridge 1989

The great Walter Hammond, shown here in typically pensive mood (Hulton Picture Company)

1000 RUNS IN A SEASON MOST TIMES

26 CP Mead
25 FE Woolley
23 JB Hobbs
21 A Jones
20 DL Amiss, EH Hendren, H Sutcliffe
19 George Gunn, D Kenyon, WG Quaife
18 TW Hayward, A Sandham, JT Tyldesley
CP Mead's total was in consecutive seasons

MOST CENTURIES IN A SEASON

13 WR Hammond, 1937
12 TW Hayward, 1906
     CP Mead, 1928
     H Sutcliffe, 1932
11 G Boycott, 1971
     DCS Compton, 1947
     EH Hendren, 1928
     JB Hobbs, 1925
     JDB Robertson, 1947
     H Sutcliffe, 1928
10 R Abel, 1900
     C Hallows, 1928
     WR Hammond, 1927, 1933
     John Langridge, 1937, 1949
     JH Parks, 1937
     GM Turner, 1979
     FE Woolley, 1934

HAMPSHIRE'S RUN-STEALER

Phil Mead on film – the only way this writer could ever have seen him – is a most unprepossessing batsman, continually shuffling and fidgeting, nudging runs here and there and certainly lacking the aesthetic qualities of a Hobbs, a Graveney or even a Gower.

Yet in 27 seasons for Hampshire, his adopted county (his native Surrey turned him down), Mead scraped, nudged and scratched his way to 46 268 runs, with 132 centuries; both totals more than any other batsman for any county before or since.

On nine occasions Mead exceeded 2000 runs in a season; no-one else managed this more than five times. A simple 1000 runs was achieved no fewer than 26 times and again he tops the list, though only one ahead of Frank Woolley and three more than Jack Hobbs. His 26 seasons *in succession*, however, place him seven ahead of Woolley with the rest, as they say, nowhere.

Mead's big season was in 1928, when he set one record and equalled another. His 12 centuries in the season matched Tom Hayward's total for Surrey in 1906, but Hayward's record of 2814 runs in a season, also set in 1906, was overtaken by Mead during his last possible innings of the season – 103 not out against Worcestershire at Worcester in early September.

It really was a marvellous performance by Mead which never received the praise and attention it deserved. It represented a season's batting of amazing consistency as the innings-by-innings analysis confirms.

Phil Mead – the highest scoring batsman in County Championship history (Allsport)

1st inns	2nd inns	Match
50	97	v Surrey, Oval
157	—	v Middx, Lord's
129	—	v Worcs, Southampton
50*	110	v Gloucs, Southampton
0	4	v Somerset, Bournemouth
118	18*	v Yorks, Southampton
28	21	v Yorks, Bradford
89*	41*	v Notts, Trent Bridge
28	75	v Sussex, Horsham
8	—	v Middx, Portsmouth
40	30	v Kent, Dover
130	60	v Surrey, Southampton
156	—	v Essex, Leyton
4	63	v Lancs, Southampton
11	130	v Kent, Southampton
180	20*	v Warwicks, Bath
59*	138	v Notts, Bournemouth
79	—	v Essex, Portsmouth
14	117*	v Gloucs, Bristol
76	—	v Northants, Southampton
11	—	v Somerset, Weston
6	148	v Leics, Leicester
48	49*	v Warwicks, Edgbaston
8	—	v Northants, Northampton
56	62	v Sussex, Portsmouth
22	103*	v Worcs, Worcester

Mead's 1000 runs were reached on 19 June against Sussex at Horsham, and the 2000 mark was passed on 27 July. His scoring reached its peak during July, when he averaged over 100 for 821 runs, but he retained his form throughout the season.

Selectorial eccentricity saw to it that he failed to gain Test recognition during his record-breaking season, but his form did win him selection for the 1928/29 Australian tour under Percy Chapman. One wonders how different – if at all – would be the response to a similar season of scoring in the 1990s.

Archie MacLaren's quadruple century, aged 23, was not matched in the County Championship for 93 years. A fine batsman for Lancashire and England, but an over-rated skipper whose post-cricket career was chequered (Hulton Picture Company)

MOST RUNS IN A DAY
333 KS Duleepsinhji, Sussex v Northants, Hove 1930
331* JDB Robertson, Middlesex v Worcs, Worcester 1949
322 E Paynter, Lancs v Sussex, Hove 1937
322 IVA Richards, Somerset v Warwicks, Taunton 1985
316 RH Moore, Hants v Warwicks, Bournemouth 1937

FAST FIFTIES
8 mins CC Inman (57) Leics v Notts, Trent Bridge 1965
11 mins CIJ Smith (66) Middlesex v Gloucs, Bristol 1938

FAST CENTURIES
26 mins TM Moody (103*) Warwicks v Glamorgan, Swansea 1990
35 mins PGH Fender (113*) Surrey v Northants, Northampton 1920
35 mins SJ O'Shaughnessy (105) Lancs v Leics, Old Trafford 1983
37 mins CM Old (107) Yorks v Warwicks, Edgbaston 1977
40 mins GL Jessop (101) Gloucs v Yorks, Harrogate 1897

FAST DOUBLE CENTURIES
120 mins GL Jessop (286) Gloucs v Sussex, Hove 1903
130 mins GL Jessop (234) Gloucs v Somerset, Bristol 1905
135 mins SMJ Woods (215) Somerset v Sussex, Hove 1895

MOST RUNS BEFORE LUNCH
180 KS Ranjitsinhji (234*) Sussex v Surrey, Hastings 1902
173 FR Santall (201*) Warwicks v Northants, Northampton 1933
167 A Ducat (271) Surrey v Hants, Southampton 1919
164 GL Jessop (234) Gloucs v Somerset, Bristol 1905

PRE-LUNCH CENTURIES
IN BOTH INNINGS OF A MATCH
GL Jessop (104 and 139) Gloucs v Yorks, Bradford 1900
Both innings started and finished before lunch

MOST RUNS IN AN OVER
(FROM SIX LEGITIMATE BALLS)
36 GS Sobers, Notts v Glamorgan, Swansea 1968
The bowler was MA Nash, the non-striking batsman JM Parkin
34 FC Hayes, Lancs v Glamorgan, Swansea 1977
The bowler was MA Nash, the non-striker B Wood

Gilbert Jessop gained undying fame for consistent fast scoring, the highlight being his two centuries in one match, both scored before lunch. A middle-order batsman for Gloucs, he somehow managed 12 pre-lunch hundreds, as well as seven centuries in an hour or less and the fastest ever double century in the Championship (Mary Evans Picture Library)

100 RUNS BEFORE LUNCH BY TWO BATSMEN IN SAME INNINGS

LCH Palairet (173) & LC Braund (107) Somerset v Yorks, Headingley 1901
JA Dixon (104*) & JR Gunn (294) Notts v Leics, Trent Bridge 1903
AC MacLaren (108) & RH Spooner (102*) Lancs v Sussex, Old Trafford 1904
CJB Wood (225) & VFS Crawford (102*) Leics v Worcs, Worcester 1906 †
J Seymour (204) & KL Hutchings (101) Kent v Hants, Tonbridge 1907
JB Hobbs (117) & EG Hayes (123) Surrey v Lancs, Oval 1911
FA Tarrant (250*) & JW Hearne (106*) Middlesex v Essex, Leyton 1914
JW Hearne (218*) & EH Hendren (201) Middlesex v Hants, Lord's 1919
A Ducat (167) & EG Hayes (129) Surrey v Hants, Southampton 1919
JF Parker (108*) & ERT Holmes (122*) Surrey v Notts, Trent Bridge 1947
DJ Insole (114) & TE Bailey (114*) Essex v Notts, Southend 1955
GM Turner (107) & PA Neale (101*) Worcs v Warwicks, Worcester 1979
† H Whitehead scored 97* before lunch in the same innings!

MOST SIXES IN ONE INNINGS

13 CG Greenidge (259) Hants v Sussex, Southampton 1975
13 GW Humpage (254) Warwicks v Lancs, Southport 1982
12 IT Botham (138*) Somerset v Warwicks, Edgbaston 1985
12 RA Harper (234) Northants v Gloucs, Northampton 1986
11 CJ Barnett (194) Gloucs v Somerset, Bath 1934
11 GA Hick (405*) Worcs v Somerset, Taunton 1988

MOST SIXES IN ONE MATCH

17 (10+7) WJ Stewart (155 & 125) Warwicks v Lancs, Blackpool 1959

SLOW SCORING

When scoring **102** for Northants v Derbyshire at Derby in 1914, **WH Denton** reached his century in **7 hours**; this is thought to be the slowest century in the Championship.

BR Hardie (4) batted for 142 minutes, Essex v Hants at Chelmsford, 1974.

Norman Gifford scored a complete innings of **1 not out** in **98 minutes** for Worcs v Sussex at Worcester in 1979.

During his innings of 56, **G Fowler** was stuck on the same score for **90 minutes**, Lancs v Warwicks at Edgbaston, 1989.

AV Avery (84*) failed to hit a boundary, Essex v Derbys at Southend, 1939.

AW Shipman (102) hit only one boundary, Leics v Essex at Leyton, 1925.

J Vine (57) took 75 minutes to open his score, Sussex v Notts at Hove, 1901.

INDIVIDUAL BOWLING

BOWLERS WITH OVER 1000 CHAMPIONSHIP WICKETS

'Old Jack' Hearne, a Middlesex stalwart in early years of the Championship. He still holds the record for the lowest season's average when taking more than 100 wickets (Hulton Picture Company)

	Runs	Wkts	Avge
AP Freeman (Kent) 1914–36	54543	3151	17.30
W Rhodes (Yorks) 1898–1930	48911	3112	15.71
CWL Parker (Gloucs) 1905–35	58336	3022	19.30
TWJ Goddard (Gloucs) 1922–52	52102	2678	19.45
D Shackleton (Hants) 1948–69	46070	2542	18.12
AS Kennedy (Hants) 1907–36	51393	2418	21.25
FJ Titmus (Middx, Surrey) 1949–82	46966	2171	21.63
WE Hollies (Warwicks) 1932–57	42826	2105	20.34
GH Hirst (Yorks) 1891–1921	37917	2095	18.09
JC White (Somerset) 1909–37	37184	2082	17.85

C Blythe (Kent) 1899–1914	33180	2032	16.37
JT Hearne (Middx) 1890–1914	36999	2032	18.20
WE Astill (Leics) 1906–39	46369	2029	22.85
MW Tate (Sussex) 1912–37	35415	2019	17.54
DJ Shepherd (Glam) 1950–72	41998	2012	20.87
RTD Perks (Worcs) 1930–55	47931	2009	23.55
EG Dennett (Gloucs) 1903–26	39365	1979	19.89
DL Underwood (Kent) 1963–87	35493	1873	18.94
J Newman (Hants) 1906–30	46101	1861	24.77
N Gifford (Warwicks, Worcs) 1960–88	42420	1813	23.39
GAR Lock (Leics, Surrey) 1946–67	30071	1712	17.56
JB Statham (Lancs) 1950–68	25537	1683	15.17
G Geary (Leics) 1912–38	32536	1669	19.49
GR Cox (Sussex) 1898–1928	37294	1658	22.49
DVP Wright (Kent) 1932–56	37093	1647	22.52
C Cook (Gloucs) 1946–64	32549	1609	20.22
HL Jackson (Derbys) 1947–63	27144	1578	17.29
FE Woolley (Kent) 1906–38	29427	1578	18.64
R Illingworth (Leics, Yorks) 1951–83	29078	1555	18.69
GG Macaulay (Yorks) 1920–35	26295	1551	16.95
T Richardson (Surrey) 1892–1904	27371	1531	17.87
JB Mortimore (Gloucs) 1950–75	35307	1522	23.19
MS Nichols (Essex) 1924–39	32131	1518	21.16
TG Wass (Notts) 1897–1920	30790	1517	20.29
PGH Fender (Surrey, Sussex) 1911–35	36037	1512	23.83
TPB Smith (Essex) 1929–51	39151	1512	25.89
C Gladwin (Derbys) 1939–58	26256	1490	17.62
FS Trueman (Yorks) 1949–68	25341	1488	17.03
TE Bailey (Essex) 1946–67	31823	1449	21.96
NI Thomson (Sussex) 1952–72	29091	1431	20.32
AE Relf (Sussex) 1900–21	30015	1428	21.01
CF Root (Derbys, Worcs) 1910–32	29515	1415	20.85
AW Wellard (Somerset) 1929–50	34614	1415	24.46
TW Cartwright (Glam, Somerset, Warwicks) 1952–77	26183	1397	18.74
JA Flavell (Worcs) 1949–67	29736	1397	21.28
JK Lever (Essex) 1967–89	32796	1380	23.76
JHWT Douglas (Essex) 1901–28	31821	1376	23.12
GS Boyes (Hants) 1921–39	32123	1373	23.39
W Bestwick (Derbys) 1898–1925	28752	1367	21.03
J Mercer (Glam, Northants, Sussex) 1919–47	32252	1361	23.69
JW Hearne (Middx) 1909–36	31012	1356	22.87

The off-spinning of Raymond Illingworth brought him over 1500 Championship wickets (Hulton Picture Company)

Brian ('George') Statham, the Lancashire and England opening bowler, achieved an impressive career average in the Championship (Hulton Picture Company)

TB Mitchell (Derbys) 1928–39	27101	1349	20.08
VWC Jupp (Northants, Sussex) 1909–38	30309	1349	22.46
BA Langford (Somerset) 1953–74	32633	1346	24.24
W Mead (Essex) 1895–1913	25817	1343	19.22
JC Laker (Essex, Surrey) 1947–64	22847	1312	17.41
K Higgs (Lancs, Leics) 1958–69	30376	1307	23.24
H Verity (Yorks) 1930–39	17216	1304	13.20
AW Mold (Lancs) 1890–1901	19945	1300	15.34
RK Tyldesley (Lancs) 1919–31	21902	1297	16.88
PI Pocock (Surrey) 1964–86	33752	1297	26.02
AR Gover (Surrey) 1928–47	30091	1291	23.30
JH Wardle (Yorks) 1946–58	22797	1280	17.81
James Langridge (Sussex) 1924–53	27750	1257	22.07
CT Spencer (Leics) 1952–74	33149	1244	26.64
AV Bedser (Surrey) 1946–60	23753	1241	19.14
WE Bowes (Yorks) 1929–47	18850	1240	15.20
W Voce (Notts) 1927–52	27087	1218	22.23
Ray Smith (Essex) 1934–56	36759	1213	30.39
PJ Sainsbury (Hants) 1953–76	28333	1199	23.63
JC Clay (Glam) 1921–49	23126	1197	19.31
SJ Staples (Notts) 1920–34	26820	1184	22.65
R Howorth (Worcs) 1934–51	24888	1170	21.27
H Dean (Lancs) 1906–21	21723	1169	18.58
JM Sims (Middx) 1929–52	28995	1168	24.82
H Larwood (Notts) 1924–38	18855	1157	16.29
DC Morgan (Derbys) 1950–69	28804	1154	24.96
AS Brown (Gloucs) 1953–76	29124	1150	25.32
WS Lees (Surrey) 1896–1911	24510	1149	21.33
S Santall (Warwicks) 1895–1914	26754	1125	23.78
RD Jackman (Surrey) 1966–82	25349	1124	22.55
JA Young (Middx) 1933–56	20928	1120	18.68
F Barratt (Notts) 1914–31	25218	1119	22.53

JH Mayer (Warwicks) 1926–39	24727	1108	22.31
EE Hemmings (Notts, Warwicks) 1968–90	32667	1107	29.50
JW Hitch (Surrey) 1907–25	23686	1096	21.61
TL Richmond (Notts) 1912–28	22262	1094	20.34
E Smith (Derbys) 1951–71	28728	1091	26.33
JD Bannister (Warwicks) 1950–68	24304	1085	22.40
FJ Durston (Middx) 1919–33	23631	1076	21.96
RA Sinfield (Gloucs) 1925–39	26182	1074	24.37
DR Smith (Gloucs) 1956–70	25572	1071	23.87
J Briggs (Lancs) 1890–1900	17529	1070	16.38
FW Tate (Sussex) 1891–1905	22157	1062	20.86
JR Gunn (Notts) 1896–1925	25643	1061	24.26
PF Jackson (Worcs) 1929–50	28022	1061	26.41
JE Walsh (Leics) 1938–56	25326	1057	23.96
R Tattersall (Lancs) 1948–60	17774	1056	16.83
KC Preston (Essex) 1948–64	27736	1054	26.31
AE Moss (Middx) 1950–63	20522	1053	19.48
EW Clark (Northants) 1922–47	22463	1048	21.43
E Robson (Somerset) 1891–1923	28057	1039	27.00
A Fielder (Kent) 1900–14	21730	1036	20.97
GJ Thompson (Northants) 1905–22	19157	1029	18.61
DW White (Glam, Hants) 1958–72	23780	1016	23.40
A Jepson (Notts) 1938–59	29248	1016	28.78
JH King (Leics) 1895–1925	25498	1008	25.29
RO Jenkins (Worcs) 1938–58	23930	1005	23.81
HA Smith (Leics) 1925–39	25682	1004	25.57
WH Lockwood (Surrey) 1890–1904	18395	1001	18.37

10–4–11–9	AP Freeman, Kent v Sussex, Hove 1922
6.3–3–12–9	H Verity, Yorks v Kent, Sheffield 1936
11.1–7–4–8	D Shackleton, Hants v Somerset, Weston-super-Mare 1955
14–12–7–8	CH Palmer, Leics v Surrey, Leicester 1955
7–4–6–7	A Waddington, Yorks v Sussex, Hull 1922
12.4–6–6–7	RV Webster, Warwicks v Yorks, Edgbaston 1964
13–9–6–7	R Illingworth, Yorks v Gloucs, Harrogate 1967
14–12–6–7	RK Tyldesley, Lancs v Northants, Liverpool 1924
8.4–7–2–6	EF Field, Warwicks v Worcs, Dudley 1914
7–4–3–6	GG Macaulay, Yorks v Derbys, Hull 1921
6–6–0–5	GR Cox, Sussex v Somerset, Weston-super-Mare 1921
5–5–0–5	RK Tyldesley, Lancs v Leics, Old Trafford 1924
6.4–6–0–5	PT Mills, Gloucs v Somerset, Bristol 1928
5–5–0–4	A Hearne, Kent v Somerset, Taunton 1893
2.1–2–0–4	LC Eastman, Essex v Somerset, Weston-super-Mare 1934

George Geary; the Leics player not only confirmed his high ability as a bowler but was also a batsman good enough to achieve 'all-rounder' status (Hulton Picture Company)

OUTSTANDING INNINGS ANALYSES

Overs–Mdns–Runs–Wkts
19.4–16–10–10 H Verity, Yorks v Notts, Headingley 1932
16.2–8–18–10 G Geary, Leics v Glamorgan, Pontypridd 1929

OUTSTANDING MATCH ANALYSES

17–48 (10–30, 7–18)	C Blythe, Kent v Northants, Northampton 1907
17–56 (9–44, 8–12)	CWL Parker, Gloucs v Essex, Gloucester 1925
16–35 (8–18, 8–17)	WE Bowes, Yorks v Northants, Kettering 1935
16–69 (8–25, 8–44)	TG Wass, Notts v Lancs, Liverpool 1906
15–21 (8–9, 7–12)	EG Dennett, Gloucs v Northants, Gloucester 1907
15–31 (7–22, 8–9)	GE Tribe, Northants v Yorks, Northampton 1958
14–29 (6–16, 8–13)	WC Smith, Surrey v Northants, Oval 1910
14–29 (8–4, 6–25)	D Shackleton, Hants v Somerset, Weston-super-Mare 1955
13–38 (6–18, 7–20)	E Wainwright, Yorks v Sussex, Dewsbury 1894
13–40 (8–17, 5–23)	TG Wass, Notts v Derbys, Trent Bridge 1901
13–40 (6–27, 7–13)	S Haigh, Yorks v Warwicks, Sheffield 1907
12–19 (6–12, 6–7)	GH Hirst, Yorks v Northants, Northampton 1908
12–20 (5–6, 7–14)	T Richardson, Surrey v Leics, Leicester 1897

THE ULTIMATE WICKET-TAKERS

Given that 1000 championship wickets have come to be regarded as the ultimate ambition, granted to few, it seems almost beyond belief that two bowlers actually took more than 3100 wickets apiece in the Championship – and both missed four seasons through the First World War!

That 'Tich' Freeman of Kent, top bowler with 3151 wickets, bowled slow leg-breaks and googlies with his right arm, and that Yorkshire's Wilfred Rhodes spent his 33-year career taking 3112 wickets with seductive left-arm spinners, would also test the powers of credence of many modern cricket followers. In the unlikely event of similar bowlers ever playing contemporary county cricket under modern conditions, neither would expect to be brought on other than to give the pacemen a rest between new balls. To preclude the possibility of a few 'easy runs' they would naturally be 'firing it in', and should they happen to get a wicket or two they would be immediately whipped off again and the new batsmen be confronted with the ultimate in entertaining and positive bowling, 'seam'.

The fact remains that the two most prolific bowlers in county championship history bowled slowly; but that was about all they possessed in common.

Alfred Percy Freeman was born in Lewisham, which could then still be regarded as 'Kent'. Twenty-six before getting a chance for his county, the First World War further delayed his career and he was 31 before he could regard himself as a full member of the county side. He certainly made up for lost time.

He took 100 wickets for the first time in 1920 (102 at 16.88) and repeated the feat in each of the following 16 seasons. He stretched his total past 200 for the first time in the 'batsmen's summer' of 1928, and two sea-

sons later actually totalled 249, beating the record of 238 established by Tom Richardson in 1897. He passed 200 again in the two following seasons, and then in 1933, aged 45, he became the first – and last – bowler to exceed 250 wickets in a championship season. As cricket records go, this seems so far beyond any challenge for the possibility to be discounted.

Freeman set another record which seems unbeatable that season; the astounding little man, who celebrated his 45th birthday on the opening day of the third match and took 8–110 in 44.1 overs, altogether bowled 1777 six-ball overs (10 662 balls!) during the season. He never seemed to tire; in the last game he destroyed Middlesex in 2 days with match figures of 15–122 in 70 overs! In that match, only Middlesex's Hendren used his feet, and his two centuries should have served as a salutary lesson to his crease-bound colleagues.

In 1936 Freeman took 103 comparatively costly wickets and thus ended, at 48, a career as remarkable as any in championship history, with 3151 wickets in 19 seasons. All but 26 were taken after his 30th birthday, and 1853 actually came in his forties. Amazing figures, yet this bald, beaky, chain-smoking, hen-pecked little man is now all but forgotten.

Not so Wilfred Rhodes; second as a wicket-taker only to Freeman, and second as an all-rounder to the great George Hirst, his name still figures large and often in talk of cricket's greats. In almost every way, he and Freeman were different. Freeman bowled right arm, Rhodes left; Rhodes had a long Test career, Freeman didn't; Freeman was 30 before establishing himself, Rhodes took his 500th wicket aged 23 and had passed 1000 by 26, the age at which Freeman started. Rhodes also carried on until the age of 52, four years after Freeman called it a day.

To some extent Freeman's was the more conventional caeer, since cricket lore contends that spinners mature with the years after slow starts, and certainly Freeman 'proved the rule', reaching his peak when over 40. In fact the 'ageist theory' in spin bowling is no more valid than numerous other unproven ideas. It does not stand close examination, and in the case of Rhodes, of course, it collapses most dramatically.

The Yorkshireman was at his most incisive and effective from 1900 to 1903 inclusive, from age 22 to 25. During this period he took 685 wickets for 9049 runs, an average of 13.21. He did, of course, continue to take wickets in large quantities for a further 27 years, and enjoyed a little resurgence in his early forties when for a while he approached his early form; but all the figures suggest that he was never more formidable than in his cricketing youth.

Perhaps Rhodes has an excuse for not maintaining his early form with the ball, since from his late twenties until his eyes began to fail, in his mid-forties, he was a good enough batsman to be worth a place on that alone.

Rhodes took 100 wickets in a season 17 times – a record which is surely unbeatable. In no fewer than nine separate seasons he topped the championship averages, the first time in his debut season, the last 28 years later!

Some record – what would he have done had he fulfilled his promise!

Yorkshire's Wilfred Rhodes (left) and 'Tich' Freeman of Kent – the two most prolific wicket-takers in County Championship history (Rhodes – Mary Evans Picture Library; Freeman – Hulton Picture Company)

MOST WICKETS IN A DAY

17–48 C Blythe, Kent v Northants, Northampton 1907
17–91 H Verity, Yorks v Essex, Leyton 1933
17–106 TWJ Goddard, Gloucestershire v Kent, Bristol 1939
16–69 TG Wass, Nottinghamshire v Lancs, Liverpool 1906
16–83 JC White, Somerset v Worcs, Bath 1919
16–103 TG Wass, Nottinghamshire v Essex, Trent Bridge 1908

100 WICKETS IN A SEASON MOST TIMES

18 D Shackleton	AS Kennedy
17 AP Freeman	RTD Perks
W Rhodes	11 MW Tate
16 TWJ Goddard	NI Thomson
CWL Parker	10 JT Hearne
12 WE Hollies	TB Mitchell

INDIVIDUAL ALL-ROUND

PLAYERS WITH BOTH 10000 CHAMPIONSHIP RUNS AND 800 WICKETS

	Runs (Avge)	Wkts (Avge)
WE Astill (Leics) 1906–39	18683 (22.32)	2029 (22.85)
TE Bailey (Essex) 1946–67	19484 (34.18)	1449 (21.96)
J Birkenshaw (Leics, Worcs, Yorks) 1958–81	10452 (22.62)	859 (27.06)
AS Brown (Gloucs) 1953–76	11881 (18.27)	1150 (25.32)
DB Close (Somerset, Yorks) 1949–77	25380 (32.53)	886 (24.78)
GR Cox (Sussex) 1898–1928	12588 (18.34)	1658 (22.49)
TW Cartwright (Glam, Som, Warwicks) 1952–77	11840 (20.55)	1397 (18.74)
Emrys Davies (Glam) 1924–54	24831 (28.64)	810 (29.72)
JHWT Douglas (Essex) 1901–28	16926 (27.97)	1376 (23.12)
LC Eastman (Essex) 1920–39	11890 (20.42)	892 (26.57)
PGH Fender (Surrey, Sussex) 1911–35	14132 (26.91)	1512 (23.83)
G Geary (Leics) 1912–38	10941 (19.53)	1669 (19.49)
JR Gunn (Notts) 1896–1925	21588 (34.21)	1061 (24.16)
NE Haig (Middx) 1912–34	11517 (21.24)	881 (25.57)
JW Hearne (Middx) 1909–36	25819 (41.98)	1356 (22.87)
GH Hirst (Yorks) 1891–1921	27314 (35.79)	2095 (18.09)
VE Jackson (Leics) 1946–56	13479 (29.04)	875 (23.71)
VWC Jupp (Northants, Sussex) 1909–38	20121 (30.16)	1349 (22.46)
R Illingworth (Yorks, Leics) 1951–83	16900 (27.93)	1555 (18.69)
AS Kennedy (Hants) 1907–36	14357 (18.66)	2418 (21.25)
JH King (Leics) 1895–25	21343 (27.61)	1008 (25.29)
James Langridge (Sussex) 1924–53	25893 (35.18)	1257 (22.07)
DC Morgan (Derbys) 1950–69	16810 (25.05)	1154 (24.96)
JB Mortimore (Gloucs) 1950–75	13339 (17.85)	1522 (23.19)
A Morton (Derbys) 1903–26	10348 (19.59)	914 (23.01)
J Newman (Hants) 1906–30	13099 (20.72)	1861 (24.77)
MS Nichols (Essex) 1924–39	14618 (26.19)	1518 (21.16)
WG Quaife (Warwicks) 1895–1928	31476 (36.77)	842 (27.21)
AE Relf (Sussex) 1900–21	16557 (28.11)	1428 (21.01)
W Rhodes (Yorks) 1898–1930	26859 (30.38)	3112 (15.71)
E Robson (Somerset) 1891–1923	11491 (17.81)	1039 (27.07)
PJ Sainsbury (Hants) 1953–76	17942 (26.38)	1199 (23.63)
JN Shepherd (Gloucs, Kent) 1967–85	11065 (26.72)	974 (27.60)
Ray Smith (Essex) 1934–56	10465 (20.12)	1213 (30.30)
FA Tarrant (Middx) 1905–14	11679 (38.80)	952 (17.50)
MW Tate (Sussex) 1912–37	15298 (23.82)	2019 (17.54)
FJ Titmus (Middx, Surrey) 1949–82	15836 (22.27)	2171 (21.63)
LF Townsend (Derbys) 1922–39	17118 (27.52)	919 (21.01)
AW Wellard (Somerset) 1929–50	10863 (19.60)	1415 (24.46)
JC White (Somerset) 1909–37	10878 (18.91)	2082 (17.85)
W Wooller (Glam) 1938–62	11540 (22.89)	826 (26.14)
FE Woolley (Kent) 1906–38	43703 (41.26)	1578 (18.64)

Trevor Bailey, Essex all-rounder and county captain (Hulton Picture Company)

YORKSHIRE'S ALL-ROUND MATCH WINNER

George Hirst – the ideal county all-rounder (Hulton Picture Company)

The genuine all-rounder – the player who consistently, over a long period, produces batting and bowling performances either of which would guarantee a place as a specialist – was always a rare bird (and now seems virtually extinct) on the county scene.

The list of players who have scored 10 000 runs and taken 800 wickets in the Championship is sufficiently short to confirm this rarity value, and in fact a fair number of these entries did not produce the goods in both departments with consistency. Three players, however, stand out: Frank Woolley of Kent (34 703 runs, 1578 wickets) and the Yorkshire pair Wilfred Rhodes and George Hirst, with 26 859 runs, 3112 wickets and 27 314 runs, 2095 wickets respectively. All of them bowled left-armed, Woolley and Rhodes slow, Hirst quick-medium swerve, but Rhodes and Hirst batted right-handed.

Closer examination of the remarkable figures achieved by these three reveals that Hirst managed the season 'double' of 1000 runs and 100 wickets a record eight times. Rhodes did it seven times, Woolley four. Furthermore, Woolley ceased to be a serious bowler long before his retirement, while Rhodes' batting was a long time developing and deteriorated towards the end. Hirst, on the other hand, was regarded as an all-rounder for almost the whole of his career.

What a record Hirst had! Apart from his eight 'doubles', in five other seasons he added more than 80 wickets to over 1000 runs, a milestone he passed on 17 occasions, beaten among *specialist* Yorkshire batsmen by Herbert Sutcliffe alone; while only Rhodes exceeded Hirst's nine 100-wicket seasons. Furthermore Hirst was Yorkshire's fourth most prolific scorer, and its second best wicket-taker overall.

Of Hirst's many outstanding seasons, the best was unarguably 1906; indeed it is statistically the best ever all-round season by a player in the County Championship. His figures, from 28 matches, were:

Batting: 46 inns, 5 NO, 1771 runs, 5 centuries, 122 HS, 43.14 average.

Bowling: 1083 overs, 2701 runs, 182 wickets, 14.84 average.

Thirteen times he took 5 wickets or more in an innings, twice 10 wickets in a match were taken. His best innings analysis was 7–18 against Leicestershire at Leicester, while 14–97 against Notts at Dewsbury were his best match bowling figures; in the same game he completed 100 wickets.

His most impressive all-round match performance occurred in the last game of the season, against Somerset at Bath. Hirst achieved the 'perfect double' in this game, a feat unique in first-class cricket. Batting at number five he scored 111 out of 368 in the first innings, and an unbeaten 117 in 75 minutes when batting first wicket down in the second innings (adding 202 for the 2nd wicket with Rhodes). With the ball, Hirst gained figures of 6–70 in 26 overs in Somerset's first innings of 125, and 5–45 in 15 overs in their second innings 134 all out.

The 'double' for the season was completed in his 17th match, against Derbyshire at Chesterfield on 17 July, by far the earliest date for a 'double'. Furthermore, only JWHT Douglas has completed a 'double' in fewer matches, 15 in 1921.

George Hirst's time with Yorkshire was a tremendously successful spell for the county. The percentage of wins in finished matches during Hirst's 601 championship games was a remarkable 81.04, while 54.07 per cent of all matches were won. Hirst scored runs and took wickets; and was a mighty effective match-winner. Here surely is the county all-rounder to beat them all.

100 RUNS & 10 WICKETS IN A MATCH

	Batting	Bowling	
EG Arnold	200*	3–70, 7–44	Worcs v Warwicks, Edgbaston 1909
J Bailey	62, 88	6–51, 5–19	Hants v Leics, Southampton 1948
TE Bailey	59, 71*	6–32, 8–49	Essex v Hants, Romford 1957
TE Bailey	60*, 46	7–40, 5–61	Essex v Yorks, Headingley 1960
CJ Barnett	168	5–63, 6–40	Gloucs v Lancs, Old Trafford 1938
EA Bedser	71, 30	7–142, 3–89	Surrey v Gloucs, Oval 1951
RHB Bettington	28, 95	4–87, 6–78	Middlesex v Sussex, Lord's 1928
BJT Bosanquet	71, 41*	6–109, 4–61	Middlesex v Kent, Tunbridge Wells 1903
BJT Bosanquet	141	5–112, 5–136	Middlesex v Yorks, Sheffield 1904
BJT Bosanquet	103, 100*	3–75, 8–53	Middlesex v Sussex, Lord's 1905
KD Boyce	113	6–25, 6–48	Essex v Leics, Chelmsford 1975
J Briggs	129*	5–25, 5–16	Lancs v Sussex, Old Trafford 1890
J Briggs	115	8–113, 5–96	Lancs v Yorks, Old Trafford 1892
J Briggs	112	5–51, 6–64	Lancs v Surrey, Oval 1893
DCS Compton	137*	6–94, 6–80	Middlesex v Surrey, Oval 1947
JN Crawford	148	7–85, 4–63	Surrey v Gloucs, Bristol 1906
ER Dexter	113	6–63, 4–46	Sussex v Kent, Tunbridge Wells 1962
ER Dexter	27, 94	7–38, 3–58	Sussex v Surrey, Oval 1962
B Dooland	115*, 11	4–54, 6–48	Notts v Sussex, Worthing 1957
JWHT Douglas	8, 123*	7–91, 7–65	Essex v Worcs, Leyton 1921
JWHT Douglas	210*	9–47, 2–0	Essex v Derbys, Leyton 1921
PGH Fender	104	3–48, 7–76	Surrey v Essex, Leyton 1926
W Flowers	107	6–44, 5–84	Notts v Lancs, Old Trafford 1893
FR Foster	105, 18	9–118, 3–84	Warwicks v Yorks, Edgbaston 1911
CB Fry	89, 65	5–81, 5–66	Sussex v Notts, Trent Bridge 1896
F Geeson	104*	6–128, 6–111	Leics v Derbys, Glossop 1901
RJ Gregory	171	5–36, 5–66	Surrey v Middlesex, Lord's 1930
IA Greig	118*	6–75, 4–57	Sussex v Hants, Hove 1981
JR Gunn	95, 39*	7–77, 4–66	Notts v Gloucs, Gloucester 1904
JR Gunn	148, 6*	8–80, 2–31	Notts v Lancs, Trent Bridge 1921
RJ Hadlee	101, 23*	6–42, 6–41	Notts v Somerset, Trent Bridge 1987
JW Hearne	54, 88	7–83, 4–104	Middlesex v Worcs, Worcester 1913
JW Hearne	106*	7–54, 7–92	Middlesex v Essex, Leyton 1914
JW Hearne	88, 37*	5–78, 5–91	Middlesex v Essex, Lord's 1914
JW Hearne	79, 28	6–74, 4–73	Middlesex v Notts, Lord's 1922
JW Hearne	140, 57*	6–83, 6–45	Middlesex v Sussex, Lord's 1923
JW Hearne	14, 93	5–38, 6–36	Middlesex v Gloucs, Lord's 1924
GH Hirst	101, 4	4–46, 7–33	Yorks v Kent, Catford 1906
GH Hirst	111, 117*	6–70, 5–45	Yorks v Somerset, Bath 1906
GH Hirst	100	9–41, 2–89	Yorks v Worcs, Worcester 1911
JL Hopwood	110, 45	1–20, 9–33	Lancs v Leics, Old Trafford 1933
JT Ikin	67, 85*	5–98, 6–21	Lancs v Notts, Old Trafford 1947
R Illingworth	135	7–49, 7–52	Yorks v kent, Dover 1964
Imran Khan	111*	7–53, 6–46	Worcs v Lancs, Worcester 1976
VE Jackson	108, 13	6–46, 4–53	Leics v Kent, Gillingham 1954
VWC Jupp	102, 33*	6–61, 6–78	Sussex v Essex, Colchester 1921
VWC Jupp	56, 70	5–34, 7–71	Northants v Essex, Colchester 1925
VWC Jupp	113	7–42, 5–79	Northants v Essex, Leyton 1928
James Langridge	13, 103	7–58, 4–66	Sussex v Glamorgan, Swansea 1929
GM Lee	100*	5–65, 7–78	Derbys v Northants, Northampton 1927
HW Lee	119	5–21, 6–47	Middlesex v Sussex, Lord's 1920
AE Lewis	93, 20	6–43, 4–15	Somerset v Hants, Bath 1911
CB Llewellyn	153	5–115, 5–68	Hants v Somerset, Taunton 1901
WH Lockwood	63, 37	6–48, 6–48	Surrey v Lancs, Oval 1902
CP McGahey	66, 91	6–86, 6–71	Essex v Gloucs, Clifton 1901
CP McGahey	89, 14	7–27, 3–37	Essex v Notts, Leyton 1906
JR Mason	72, 46*	4–23, 6–34	Kent v Middlesex, Tonbridge 1900
JR Mason	145	4–26, 8–29	Kent v Somerset, Taunton 1901
JR Mason	126	7–120, 3–60	Kent v Somerset, Beckenham 1904
JR Mason	1, 100	6–71, 4–60	Kent v Somerset, Taunton 1904
JR Mason	133	5–102, 5–120	Kent v Somerset, Taunton 1905
BL Muncer	107*	5–34, 5–23	Glamorgan v Derbys, Chesterfield 1951

JA Newman	66, 42	8-61, 6-87	Hants v Gloucs, Bournemouth 1926
MS Nichols	73, 33	5-67, 5-37	Essex v Sussex, Horsham 1933
MS Nichols	146	4-17, 7-37	Essex v Yorks, Huddersfield 1935
MS Nichols	159	9-37, 6-126	Essex v Gloucs, Gloucester 1938
RC Ontong	130	5-39, 8-67	Glamorgan v Notts, Trent Bridge 1985
MJ Procter	108	7-35, 6-38	Gloucs v Worcs, Cheltenham 1977
MJ Procter	73, 35	7-16, 7-60	Gloucs v Worcs, Cheltenham 1980
WG Quaife	104*	5-51, 7-76	Warwicks v Worcs, Edgbaston 1901
AE Relf	103*	8-41, 7-36	Sussex v Leics, Hove 1912
E Robinson	108	7-25, 4-60	Yorks v Hants, Bradford 1930
SG Smith	5, 136	2-3, 8-39	Northants v Somerset, Bath 1912
SG Smith	82, 20	6-82, 4-25	Northants v Derbys, Northampton 1913
TPB Smith	1, 101	2-69, 8-99	Essex v Middlesex, Chelmsford 1938
GS Sobers	17, 105*	7-69, 4-87	Notts v Kent, Dover 1968
DS Steele	130	6-36, 5-39	Northants v Derbys, Northampton 1978
FD Stephenson	111, 117	4-105, 7-117	Notts v Yorks, Trent Bridge 1988
FA Tarrant	152, 11	7-93, 5-56	Middlesex v Gloucs, Bristol 1908
FA Tarrant	14, 101*	9-105, 7-71	Middlesex v Lancs, Old Trafford 1914
MW Tate	101	6-52, 4-43	Sussex v Hants, Portsmouth 1927
GJ Thompson	5, 131*	6-72, 4-71	Northants v Somerset, Bath 1913
CL Townsend	139	5-121, 5-83	Gloucs v Warwicks, Edgbaston 1898
LF Townsend	106*	6-66, 5-64	Derbys v Somerset, Weston-super-Mare 1934
AE Trott	123, 35*	6-132, 6-68	Middlesex v Sussex, Lord's 1899
AE Trott	112	8-54, 3-84	Middlesex v Essex, Lord's 1901
E Wainwright	10, 104	7-66, 4-57	Yorks v Sussex, Sheffield 1892
AW Wellard	75, 55	6-82, 5-93	Somerset v Gloucs, Taunton 1929
AW Wellard	77, 60	7-43, 3-66	Somerset v Hants, Portsmouth 1933
FE Woolley	77, 111*	7-66, 5-56	Kent v Gloucs, Gloucester 1914
FE Woolley	20, 139*	6-52, 4-80	Kent v Sussex, Horsham 1920
FE Woolley	174	8-22, 3-44	Kent v Gloucs, Maidstone 1921
FE Woolley	15, 109	7-40, 3-76	Kent v Notts, Trent Bridge 1921
FE Woolley	156	4-26, 6-52	Kent v Warwicks, Tunbridge Wells 1928
A Young	63, 70	3-47, 8-30	Somerset v Derbys, Taunton 1930

Frank Tarrant achieved five 'doubles' in 10 seasons in a career curtailed by the First World War. An Anglo-Australian, Test cricket's loss was Middlesex's gain (Hulton Picture Company)

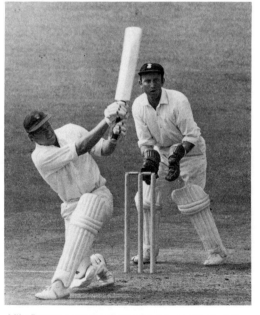

Mike Procter, a genuine all-rounder and one of the best of the several top-class South Africans unable to take his place in Test cricket history (Hulton Picture Company)

CENTURY AND HAT-TRICK IN SAME MATCH

WB Burns (102*) Worcs v Gloucs, Worcester 1913
VWC Jupp (102) Sussex v Essex, Colchester 1921
Emrys Davies (139) Glamorgan v Leics, Leicester 1937
MJ Procter (102) Gloucs v Essex, Westcliff 1972
MJ Procter (122) Gloucs v Leics, Bristol 1979

CATCHES

MOST IN THE FIELD IN AN INNINGS

7 AS Brown, Gloucs v Notts, Trent Bridge 1966
  MJ Stewart, Surrey v Northants, Northampton 1957
6 M Bissex, Gloucs v Sussex, Hove 1968
  RG Broadbent, Worcs v Glamorgan, Stourbridge 1960
  JD Clay, Notts v Derbys, Trent Bridge 1957
  KJ Grieves, Lancs v Sussex, Old Trafford 1951
  WR Hammond, Gloucs v Surrey, Cheltenham 1928
  WR Hammond, Gloucs v Notts, Bristol 1933
  EP Robinson, Yorks v Leics, Bradford 1938
  MJK Smith, Warwicks v Leics, Hinckley 1962
  FA Tarrant, Middlesex v Essex, Leyton 1906
  RK Tyldesley, Lancs v Hants, Liverpool 1921

MOST IN THE FIELD IN A MATCH

10 WR Hammond, Gloucs v Surrey, Cheltenham 1928
 8 AH Bakewell, Northants v Essex, Leyton 1928
  WB Burns, Worcs v Yorks, Bradford 1907
  KJ Grieves, Lancs v Sussex, Old Trafford 1951
  WR Hammond, Gloucs v Worcs, Cheltenham 1932
  GAR Lock, Surrey v Warwicks, Oval 1957
  CA Milton, Gloucs v Sussex, Hove 1952
  JM Prodger, Kent v Gloucs, Cheltenham 1961
  PM Walker, Glamorgan v Derbys, Swansea 1970

MOST IN THE FIELD IN A SEASON

66 John Langridge (Sussex) 1955
65 PM Walker (Glamorgan) 1961
  PJ Sharpe (Yorks) 1962
62 J Tunnicliffe (Yorks) 1901
  MJ Stewart (Surrey) 1957

John Langridge (left), a prolific catcher in the field throughout his long career, pictured here with brother James, a fine all-rounder (Hulton Picture Company)

MOST IN THE FIELD IN CAREER

710 FE Woolley (Kent) 1906–38
705 John Langridge (Sussex) 1928–55
632 CA Milton (Gloucs) 1948–74

WICKET-KEEPING

Herbert Strudwick's 1132 career dismissals for Surrey remain a county record, and third overall (Hulton Picture Company)

MOST DISMISSALS IN AN INNINGS

8	(8ct)	DE East, Essex v Somerset, Taunton 1985
7	(7ct)	KV Andrew, Northants v Lancs, Old Trafford 1962
	(7ct)	DL Bairstow, Yorkshire v Derbys, Scarborough 1982
	(6ct) 1st)	W Farrimond, Lancs v Kent, Old Trafford 1930
	(7ct)	WK Hegg, Lancs v Derbys, Chesterfield 1989
	(7ct)	A Long, Surrey v Sussex, Hove 1964
	(7ct)	WFF Price, Middlesex v Yorkshire, Lord's 1937
	(4ct) 3st)	EJ Smith, Warwicks v Derbys, Edgbaston 1926
	(7ct)	RW Taylor, Derbys v Glamorgan, Derby 1966
	(7ct)	RW Taylor, Derbys v Yorkshire, Chesterfield 1975

David East, the Essex keeper, who tops the list for the most dimissals in one innings
(Allsport)

Jim Parks (left) enjoyed a fine career as wicket-keeper batsman for Sussex, and his son Bobby (right) is the Hampshire 'keeper. Jim senior (centre) was an accomplished Sussex all-rounder in the 1930s (Allsport)

MOST DISMISSALS IN A MATCH

11	(11ct)	WK Hegg, Lancs v Derbys, Chesterfield 1989
	(11ct)	DL Bairstow, Yorkshire v Derbys, Scarborough 1982
	(11ct)	A Long, Surrey v Sussex, Hove 1964
	(11ct)	AJ Stewart, Surrey v Leics, Leicester 1989

MOST DISMISSALS IN A SEASON

102	(62ct 40st) LEG Ames, Kent 1929
100	(52ct 48st) LEG Ames, Kent 1928

96	(88ct 8st) JG Binks, Yorkshire 1960
96	(80ct 16st) R Booth, Worcs 1960
95	(53ct 42st) H Yarnold, Worcs 1949
95	(81ct 14st) R Booth, Worcs 1962
95	(88ct 7st) R Booth, Worcs 1964

MOST DISMISSALS IN A CAREER

1215	(1080ct 135st) RW Taylor, Derbys 1962–83
1144	(824ct 320st) FH Huish, Kent 1895–1914
1132	(963ct 169st) H Strudwick, Surrey 1902–27
1125	(955ct 170st) JT Murray, Middlesex 1952–75
1100	(941ct 159st) B Taylor, Essex 1949–73

THE
COUNTY
RECORDS

Bobbie Peel (right), with a colleague. A reputation for insobriety could not diminish his renown as an incisive left-arm bowler; while with the bat, he contributed a somewhat monolithic 210 to Yorkshire's championship record 887 against Warwickshire in 1896
(Hulton Picture Company)

DERBYSHIRE
Formed: 4 November 1870
Entered official Championship: 1895
Winners: 1936

INNINGS TOTALS

HIGHEST BY THE COUNTY
645 v Hampshire, Derby 1898
577 v Lancashire, Old Trafford 1896
570 v Nottinghamshire, Trent Bridge 1897
561 v Warwickshire, Derby 1902
552 v Essex, Chelmsford 1928

HIGHEST AGAINST THE COUNTY
662 by Yorkshire, Chesterfield 1898
661 by Nottinghamshire, Derby 1901
635 by Warwickshire, Edgbaston 1900
615 by Kent, Derby 1908
611–9 dec by Surrey, Derby 1904

LOWEST BY THE COUNTY
20 v Yorkshire, Sheffield 1939
23 v Yorkshire, Hull 1923
30 v Nottinghamshire, Chesterfield 1913
31 v Essex, Derby 1914
32 v Nottinghamshire, Chesterfield 1904

LOWEST AGAINST THE COUNTY
23 by Hampshire, Burton-on-Trent 1958
28 by Warwickshire, Derby 1937
29 by Middlesex, Chesterfield 1957
35 by Somerset, Derby 1935
36 by Lancashire, Buxton 1954

PARTNERSHIPS

COUNTY BEST FOR EACH WICKET
1st
322 H Storer & J Bowden v Essex, Derby 1929
283 JG Wright & B Wood v Worcs, Chesterfield 1981
2nd
359 CS Elliott & JD Eggar v Notts, Trent Bridge 1947
321* JG Wright & PN Kirsten v Lancs, Old Trafford 1980
3rd
291 PN Kirsten & DS Steele v Somerset, Taunton 1981
246 JM Kelly & DB Carr v Leics, Chesterfield 1957
4th
328 P Vaulkhard & D Smith v Notts, Trent Bridge 1946
308 GA Davidson & W Storer v Lancs, Old Trafford 1896
5th
203 CP Wilkins & IR Buxton v Lancs, Old Trafford 1971
191 AG Slater & A Morton v Hants, Basingstoke 1914
6th
212 GM Lee & TS Worthington v Essex, Chesterfield 1932
210 H Cartwright & FW Swarbrook v Warwicks,
     Chesterfield 1977
7th
241* GH Pope & AEG Rhodes v Hants, Portsmouth 1948
191 JM Kelly & GO Dawkes v Hants, Burton-on-Trent 1954
8th
182 W Carter & AHM Jackson v Leics, Leicester 1922
157 A Hamer & E Smith v Notts, Trent Bridge 1955
9th
283 J Chapman & AR Warren v Warwicks, Blackwell 1910
151 R Sharma & OH Mortensen v Yorks, Chesterfield 1987
10th
132 A Hill & M Jean-Jacques v Yorks, Sheffield 1986
107 G Miller & SJ Base v Yorks, Chesterfield 1990

INDIVIDUAL BATTING

OVER 8000 CHAMPIONSHIP RUNS IN COUNTY CAREER

		Inns	NO	Runs	HS	Avge	100s
D Smith	1927–52	682	57	19575	225	31.32	30
LF Townsend	1922–39	680	58	17118	233	27.52	22
DC Morgan	1950–69	808	137	16810	147	25.05	8
TS Worthington	1924–47	617	51	16174	238*	28.57	25
A Hamer	1950–60	479	18	14469	227	31.38	19
DB Carr	1946–63	528	47	13812	162*	28.71	18
SWA Cadman	1900–26	661	33	13665	126	21.75	8
KJ Barnett	1979–90	388	33	13481	239*	37.97	31
HL Johnson	1949–66	560	59	13158	154	26.26	15
H Storer	1920–36	497	29	13056	232	27.89	18
LG Wright	1895–1909	486	10	12997	195	27.30	19
AC Revill	1946–57	506	38	12415	156*	26.52	13
AE Alderman	1928–48	505	49	11816	175	25.91	10
C Lee	1954–64	435	15	11308	150	26.92	7
CS Elliott	1932–53	446	29	11303	215	27.10	8
A Hill	1972–86	412	40	11167	172*	30.01	16
IR Buxton	1959–73	535	75	10986	118*	23.88	4
MH Page	1964–75	419	41	10661	162	28.20	9
IW Hall	1959–72	448	29	10549	136	25.17	7
A Morton	1903–26	582	54	10348	131	19.59	6
JG Wright	1977–88	253	23	10065	190	43.76	25
GR Jackson	1919–35	419	20	9422	140	23.61	9
RW Taylor	1961–84	682	130	9223	100	16.70	1
GM Lee	1925–33	370	25	9218	191	26.71	16
GO Dawkes	1947–61	567	81	9196	143	18.92	1
JE Morris	1983–90	249	20	8998	191	39.29	23
JM Kelly	1950–60	397	23	8966	131	23.97	9
W Storer	1895–1905	289	22	8225	216*	30.91	13

Alan Ward's searing pace was a great asset to the county. His career was unhappily curtailed by fitness and temperament problems (Hulton Picture Company)

MOST RUNS IN A SEASON

Runs	(Avge)		Season
2092	(49.80)	DB Carr	1959
1954	(44.40)	LF Townsend	1933
1941	(64.70)	PN Kirsten	1982
1891	(67.53)	PN Kirsten	1980
1842	(36.84)	A Hamer	1959
1830	(55.45)	JG Wright	1982

Les Jackson, one of the best of the long line of Derbyshire's coal-miner pacemen; his 1958 average (10.40) was the lowest with more than 100 wickets for 67 years and was not matched thereafter (Hulton Picture Company)

DOUBLE CENTURIES

274 GA Davidson v Lancashire, Old Trafford 1896
264 P Vaulkhard v Nottinghamshire, Trent Bridge 1946
239* KJ Barnett v Leicestershire, Leicester 1988
238* TS Worthington v Sussex, Derby 1937
233 LF Townsend v Leicestershire, Loughborough 1933
232 H Storer v Essex, Derby 1933
229 CA Ollivierre v Essex, Chesterfield 1904
228 PN Kirsten v Somerset, Taunton 1981
227 A Hamer v Nottinghamshire, Trent Bridge 1955
225 D Smith v Hampshire, Chesterfield 1935
219 JD Eggar v Yorkshire, Bradford 1949
217 EJ Barlow v Surrey, Ilkeston 1976
216* W Storer v Leicestershire, Chesterfield 1899
215 CS Elliott v Nottinghamshire, Trent Bridge 1947
213* PN Kirsten v Glamorgan, Derby 1980
210 PD Bowler v Kent, Chesterfield 1990
209 H Storer v Essex, Derby 1929
209* PN Kirsten v Northamptonshire, Derby 1980
207* GH Pope v Hampshire, Portsmouth 1948
206* PN Kirsten v Glamorgan, Chesterfield 1978
204* PN Kirsten v Lancashire, Blackpool 1981
202* PN Kirsten v Essex, Chesterfield 1980
202* D Smith v Nottinghamshire, Trent Bridge 1937
200* TS Worthington v Worcestershire, Chesterfield 1933

INDIVIDUAL BOWLING

OVER 400 CHAMPIONSHIP WICKETS IN COUNTY CAREER

		Runs	Wkts	Avge
HL Jackson	1947–63	27144	1578	17.20
C Gladwin	1939–58	26256	1490	17.62
W Bestwick	1898–1925	28752	1367	20.37
TB Mitchell	1928–39	27101	1349	20.08
DC Morgan	1950–69	28804	1154	24.96
E Smith	1951–71	28728	1091	26.33
WH Copson	1932–50	18587	985	18.87
HJ Rhodes	1955–69	17520	925	18.94
LF Townsend	1922–39	19312	919	21.01
A Morton	1903–26	21036	914	23.01
AR Warren	1897–1920	21132	851	24.83
SWA Cadman	1900–26	19557	769	25.43
TS Worthington	1924–47	17054	606	28.14
AEG Rhodes	1937–54	17111	605	28.28
G Miller	1973–90	16535	598	27.65
GH Pope	1933–48	10694	542	19.73
AV Pope	1930–39	11530	522	22.08
AG Slater	1911–31	9951	470	21.17
M Hendrick	1969–81	9684	452	20.31
IR Buxton	1959–73	11824	441	26.81
AB Jackson	1963–68	7989	421	18.97

MOST WICKETS IN A SEASON

Wkts	(Avge)		Season
160	(19.11)	TB Mitchell	1935
151	(18.55)	C Gladwin	1952
147	(16.72)	W Bestwick	1921
146	(13.45)	HL Jackson	1960
140	(12.80)	WH Copson	1936
139	(15.50)	C Gladwin	1955
138	(17.39)	TB Mitchell	1934
136	(18.88)	TB Mitchell	1933
134	(18.24)	TB Mitchell	1930
131	(16.60)	C Gladwin	1954
130	(19.42)	TB Mitchell	1938
129	(16.06)	HL Jackson	1957
126	(10.40)	HL Jackson	1958
124	(15.75)	C Gladwin	1948
123	(17.82)	C Gladwin	1951
121	(18.28)	C Gladwin	1953
120	(14.88)	HL Jackson	1954

NINE OR MORE WICKETS IN AN INNINGS

10–40 W Bestwick v Glamorgan, Cardiff 1921
10–64 TB Mitchell v Leics, Leicester 1935
9–20 FW Swarbrook v Sussex, Hove 1975
9–39 GA Davidson v Warwicks, Derby 1895
9–41 C Gladwin v Worcs, Stourbridge 1952
9–60 HL Jackson v Lancs, Old Trafford 1952
9–65 W Bestwick v Warwicks, Edgbaston 1921
9–68 GG Walker v Leics, Leicester 1895
9–71 A Morton v Notts, Blackwell 1911
9–119 C Gladwin v Lancs, Buxton 1947

FIFTEEN OR MORE WICKETS IN A MATCH

16–84 C Gladwin v Worcs, Stourbridge 1952
15–84 AR Warren v Notts, Welbeck 1904
15–116 GA Davison v Essex, Leyton 1898

WICKET KEEPING

MOST DISMISSALS IN AN INNINGS

7 (7ct) RW Taylor v Glamorgan, Derby 1966
7 (7ct) RW Taylor v Yorks, Chesterfield 1975

MOST DISMISSALS IN A MATCH

10 (10ct)   RW Taylor v Hants, Chesterfield 1963
10 (8ct 2st) H Elliott v Lancs, Old Trafford 1935

MOST DISMISSALS IN A SEASON

88 (67ct 21st) H Elliott, 1935
84 (65ct 19st) H Elliott, 1933

MOST CAREER DISMISSALS

1215 (1080ct 135st) RW Taylor, 1961–83

ESSEX
Formed: 14 January 1876
Entered official Championship: 1895
Winners: 1979, 1983, 1984, 1986

INNINGS TOTALS

HIGHEST BY THE COUNTY
761–6 dec v Leicestershire, Chelmsford 1990
692 v Somerset, Taunton 1895
673 v Leicestershire, Leicester 1899
616–5 dec v Surrey, Oval 1904
616 v Kent, Chelmsford 1988

HIGHEST AGAINST THE COUNTY
803–4 dec by Kent, Brentwood 1934
662–8 dec by Nottinghamshire, Trent Bridge 1947
636–6 dec by Northamptonshire, Chelmsford 1990
634–7 dec by Middlesex, Chelmsford 1983
621–6 dec by Kent, Tonbridge 1922

LOWEST BY THE COUNTY
30 v Yorkshire, Leyton 1901
34 v Kent, Brentwood 1969
37 v Surrey, Leyton 1899
41 v Yorkshire, Leyton 1901
44 v Nottinghamshire, Trent Bridge 1910
44 v Northamptonshire, Colchester 1986

LOWEST AGAINST THE COUNTY
14 by Surrey, Chelmsford 1983
31 by Derbyshire, Derby 1914
31 by Yorkshire, Huddersfield 1935
43 by Kent, Southend 1925
43 by Glamorgan, Neath 1935

PARTNERSHIPS

COUNTY BEST FOR EACH WICKET
1st
270 AV Avery & TC Dodds v Surrey, Oval 1946
254 GA Gooch & JP Stephenson v Leics, Chelmsford 1990
2nd
403 GA Gooch & PJ Prichard v Derbys, Chesterfield 1989
321 GA Gooch & KS McEwan v Northants, Ilford 1978
3rd
343 PA Gibb & R Horsfall v Kent, Blackheath 1951
333 RM Taylor & J O'Connor v Northants, Colchester 1937
4th
298 AV Avery & R Horsfall v Worcs, Clacton 1948
271 J O'Connor & TN Pearce v Lancs, Clacton 1931
5th
287 J O'Connor & CT Ashton v Surrey, Brentwood 1934
216 DJ Insole & TE Bailey v Hants, Bournemouth 1959
6th
206 JWHT Douglas & J O'Connor v Gloucs, Cheltenham 1923
206 BR Knight & RAG Luckin v Middlesex, Brentwood 1962
7th
261 JWHT Douglas & JR Freeman v Lancs, Leyton 1914
171 TE Bailey & BR Knight v Worcs, Leyton 1959
8th
263 DR Wilcox & RM Taylor v Warwicks, Southend 1946
206 KR Pont & N Smith v Somerset, Leyton 1976
9th
251 JWHT Douglas & SN Hare v Derbys, Leyton 1921
184 AC Russell & LC Eastman v Middlesex, Lord's 1920
10th
218 FH Vigar & TPB Smith v Derbys, Chesterfield 1947
157 AC Russell & AB Hipkin v Somerset, Taunton 1926

Jack O'Connor, a county stalwart with over 25 000 Championship runs and two double centuries (Hulton Picture Company)

INDIVIDUAL BATTING

OVER 8000 CHAMPIONSHIP RUNS IN COUNTY CAREER

		Inns	NO	Runs	HS	Avge	100s
PA Perrin	1896–1928	846	82	27703	343*	36.26	61
KWR Fletcher	1962–88	851	107	27123	228*	36.45	41
J O'Connor	1921–39	802	70	25893	248	35.37	67
AC Russell	1908–30	597	50	22326	273	40.81	59
G Barker	1955–71	737	42	20069	181*	28.87	27
TE Bailey	1946–67	707	137	19484	205	34.18	19
GA Gooch	1973–90	440	40	19172	275	47.93	55
DJ Insole	1947–63	528	50	18873	219*	39.48	45
CP McGahey	1895–1921	637	58	18032	277	31.14	29
JWHT Douglas	1901–28	706	101	16926	210*	27.97	17
TC Dodds	1946–59	604	15	16777	157	28.48	15
B Taylor	1950–73	835	60	16641	135	21.47	8
KS McEwan	1974–85	419	38	16388	218	43.01	47
BR Hardie	1973–90	543	64	15792	162	32.96	20
MS Nichols	1924–39	622	64	14618	205	26.19	20
JA Cutmore	1924–36	549	33	14599	238*	28.29	14
JR Freeman	1905–28	547	52	13818	286	27.91	24
AV Avery	1935–54	420	34	13209	224	34.22	24
HA Carpenter	1895–1920	429	22	12462	199	30.61	22
FL Fane	1895–1921	481	28	11891	217	26.24	17
LC Eastman	1920–39	629	47	11890	161	20.42	7
BEA Edmeades	1961–76	511	60	11715	163	25.97	13
MJ Bear	1954–68	506	41	11317	137	24.33	9
R Smith	1934–56	597	77	10465	132	20.12	5
TN Pearce	1929–50	350	45	10419	211*	34.16	19
TPB Smith	1929–51	598	107	8906	163	18.13	7
FH Gillingham	1903–28	292	21	8790	201	32.43	19
R Horsfall	1947–55	318	21	8747	206	29.45	16
S Turner	1965–86	472	95	8729	121	23.15	4
FH Vigar	1938–54	364	55	8031	144	25.99	10

MOST RUNS IN A SEASON

Runs	(Avge)		Season
2281	(69.12)	GA Gooch	1984
2221	(58.44)	J O'Connor	1934
2051	(68.36)	KS McEwan	1983
2042	(52.35)	AC Russell	1922

2009	(77.27)	ME Waugh		1990
1996	(46.41)	J O'Connor		1933
1966	(50.41)	J O'Connor		1929
1942	(48.55)	AC Russell		1925
1930	(56.76)	AC Russell		1921
1915	(63.83)	AC Russell		1928
1912	(43.68)	J O'Connor		1928
1907	(44.34)	DJ Insole		1955
1877	(48.12)	AV Avery		1948
1861	(48.97)	AC Russell		1926
1818	(41.31)	J O'Connor		1938
1817	(51.91)	DJ Insole		1959
1804	(39.21)	JR Freeman		1926

*The cheerful left-arm
seamer John Lever*
(Allsport/Adrian
Murrell)

DOUBLE CENTURIES
343* PA Perrin v Derbyshire, Chesterfield 1904
286 JR Freeman v Northamptonshire, Northampton 1921
277 CP McGahey v Derbyshire, Leyton 1905
275 GA Gooch v Kent, Chelmsford 1988
273 CAG Russell v Northamptonshire, Leyton 1921
248 J O'Connor v Surrey, Brentwood 1934
245 PA Perrin v Derbyshire, Leyton 1912
243 PJ Prichard v Leicestershire, Chelmsford 1990
238* JA Cutmore v Gloucestershire, Bristol 1927
237 J O'Connor v Somerset, Leyton 1933
230 CP McGahey v Northamptonshire, Northampton 1908
228* KWR Fletcher v Sussex, Hastings 1968
227 GA Gooch v Derbyshire, Chesterfield 1984
225 CP McGahey v Nottinghamshire, Leyton 1904
224 AV Avery v Northamptonshire, Northampton 1952
222 LG Crawley v Glamorgan, Swansea 1928
220 GA Gooch v Hampshire, Southampton 1984
219* DJ Insole v Yorkshire, Colchester 1949
218 KS McEwan v Sussex, Chelmsford 1977
217 FL Fane v Surrey, Oval 1911
215 GA Gooch v Leicestershire, Chelmsford 1990
214* AV Avery v Worcestershire, Clacton 1948
211* TN Pearce v Leicestershire, Westcliff 1948
210* JWHT Douglas v Derbyshire, Leyton 1921
210 AV Avery v Surrey, Oval 1946
208* AV Avery v Glamorgan, Westcliff 1953
208* KS McEwan v Warwickshire, Edgbaston 1979
207 FL Fane v Leicestershire, Leicester 1899
206 R Horsfall v Kent, Blackheath 1951
205 PA Perrin v Kent, Leyton 1900
205 MS Nichols v Hampshire, Southend 1936
205 TE Bailey v Sussex, Eastbourne 1947
204 ME Waugh v Gloucestershire, Ilford 1990
202* JP Stephenson v Somerset, Bath 1990
202 GA Gooch v Nottinghamshire, Trent Bridge 1985
201 FH Gillingham v Middlesex, Lord's 1904

INDIVIDUAL BOWLING

OVER 400 CHAMPIONSHIP WICKETS IN
COUNTY CAREER

		Runs	Wkts	Avge
MS Nichols	1924–39	32131	1518	21.16
TPB Smith	1929–51	39151	1512	25.89

TE Bailey	1946–67	31823	1449	21.96
JK Lever	1967–89	32796	1380	23.76
JWHT Douglas	1901–28	31821	1376	23.12
W Mead	1895–1913	25817	1343	19.22
R Smith	1934–56	36759	1213	30.30
KC Preston	1948–64	27736	1054	26.31
RE East	1966–84	23899	932	25.64
LC Eastman	1920–39	23704	892	26.57
CP Buckenham	1899–1914	23490	886	26.51
DL Acfield	1966–86	21426	785	27.29
S Turner	1965–86	19478	754	25.83
BR Knight	1955–66	15444	707	21.84
RNS Hobbs	1961–75	17874	681	26.24
WT Greensmith	1947–63	18054	624	28.93
KD Boyce	1967–77	14802	615	24.06
NA Foster	1980–90	13273	581	22.84
W Reeves	1897–1921	15238	553	27.55
AB Hipkin	1923–31	12309	485	25.37
J O'Connor	1921–39	15879	480	33.08
DR Pringle	1978–90	10435	429	24.32
LHR Ralph	1953–61	10291	420	24.50
B Tremlin	1900–19	11093	419	26.67

MOST WICKETS IN A SEASON
Wkts	(Avge)		Season
153	(27.54)	TPB Smith	1947
146	(24.19)	TPB Smith	1937
143	(19.53)	MS Nichols	1938
132	(15.67)	MS Nichols	1935
129	(18.33)	MS Nichols	1937
126	(21.95)	JWHT Douglas	1923
124	(28.30)	Ray Smith	1952
122	(15.45)	W Mead	1900
121	(24.19)	TPB Smith	1938
120	(16.00)	W Mead	1907
120	(26.30)	TPB Smith	1950

NINE OR MORE WICKETS IN AN INNINGS
10–32 H Pickett v Leics, Leyton 1895
10–90 TE Bailey v Lancs, Clacton 1949
9–32   MS Nichols v Lancs, Clacton 1949
9–37   MS Nichols v Gloucs, Gloucester 1938
9–40   W Mead v Hants, Southampton 1900
9–47   JWHT Douglas v Derbys, Leyton 1921
9–52   W Mead v Hants, Southampton 1895
9–59   MS Nichols v Hants, Chelmsford 1927
9–75   W Mead v Leics, Leyton 1896
9–77   TPB Smith v Middlesex, Colchester 1947
9–93   FG Bull v Surrey, Oval 1897
9–108 TPB Smith v Kent, Maidstone 1948
9–116 MS Nichols v Middlesex, Leyton 1930
9–117 TPB Smith v Notts, Southend 1948
9–126 B Tremlin v Derbys, Leyton 1905

FIFTEEN OR MORE WICKETS IN A MATCH
17–119 W Mead v Hants, Southampton 1895
16–215 TPB Smith v Middlesex, Colchester 1947
15–113 K Farnes v Glamorgan, Clacton 1938
15–115 W Mead v Leics, Leyton 1903
15–115 RE East v Warwicks, Leyton 1968
15–154 HI Young v Warwicks, Edgbaston 1899
15–165 MS Nichols v Gloucs, Gloucester 1938

WICKET-KEEPING

MOST DISMISSALS IN AN INNINGS
8 (8ct) DE East v Somerset, Taunton 1985

MOST DISMISSALS IN A MATCH
9 (7ct 2st) KL Gibson v Derbys, Leyton 1911
9 (9ct)   DE East v Sussex, Hove 1983

MOST DISMISSALS IN A SEASON
85 (76ct 9st) B Taylor, 1962
80 (61ct 19st) DE East, 1986

MOST CAREER DISMISSALS
1100 (941ct 159st) B Taylor, 1949–73

GLAMORGAN

Formed: 6 July 1888
Entered official Championship: 1921
Winners: 1948, 1969

INNINGS TOTALS

HIGHEST BY THE COUNTY
587–8 dec v Derbyshire, Cardiff Arms Park 1951
587–5 dec v Essex, Brentwood 1948
577–4 v Gloucestershire, Newport 1939
574–7 v Somerset, Newport 1939
550–6 dec v Surrey, Oval 1936

HIGHEST AGAINST THE COUNTY
653–6 dec by Gloucestershire, Bristol 1928
603–6 dec by Gloucestershire, Bristol 1934
579–6 dec by Yorkshire, Huddesfield 1925
564–6 dec by Nottinghamshire, Trent Bridge 1926
564–9 dec by Lancashire, Old Trafford 1938

LOWEST BY THE COUNTY
22 v Lancashire, Liverpool 1924
24 v Leicestershire, Leicester 1970
26 v Lancashire, Cardiff Arms Park 1958
31 v Surrey, Oval 1957
35 v Surrey, Cardiff Arms Park 1923

LOWEST AGAINST THE COUNTY
33 by Lancashire, Ebbw Vale 1965
35 by Sussex, Horsham 1946
40 by Somerset, Cowbridge 1932
40 by Derbyshire, Cardiff Arms Park 1946
40 by Leicestershire, Leicester 1965
40 by Somerset, Swansea 1968

PARTNERSHIPS

COUNTY BEST FOR EACH WICKET
1st
330 RC Fredericks & A Jones v Northants, Swansea 1972
274 AH Dyson & Emrys Davies v Leics, Leicester 1937
2nd
238 A Jones & AR Lewis v Sussex, Hastings 1962
219 WGA Parkhouse & B Hedges v Warwicks, Llanelli 1954
3rd
313 Emrys Davies & WE Jones v Essex, Brentwood 1948
272 AL Jones & Javed Miandad v Hants, Cardiff 1984
4th
263 G Lavis & CC Smart v Worcs, Cardiff 1934
224 MJ Khan & AR Lewis v Somerset, Swansea 1972
5th
264 M Robinson & SW Montgomery v Hants, Bournemouth
1949
206 B Hedges & JS Pressdee v Northants, Northampton
1961
6th
230 WE Jones & BL Muncer v Worcs, Worcester 1953
217 Dai Davies & CC Smart v Lancs, Cardiff 1936
7th
195* W Woooler & WE Jones v Lancs, Liverpool 1947
171 MJ Llewellyn & MA Nash v Surrey, Oval 1976
8th
202 Dai Davies & JJ Hills v Sussex, Eastbourne 1928
174 WE Jones & G Lavis v Essex, Cardiff 1947
9th
203* JJ Hills & JC Clay v Worcs, Swansea 1929
105 RC Ontong & MA Nash v Essex, Cardiff 1978
10th
143 T Davies & SAB Daniels v Gloucs, Swansea 1982
123 RJ Duckfield & JC Clay v Leics, Cardiff 1933

INDIVIDUAL BATTING

OVER 8000 CHAMPIONSHIP RUNS IN COUNTY CAREER

		Inns	NO	Runs	HS	Avge	100s
Alan Jones	1957–83	995	72	30266	204*	32.79	48
Emrys Davies	1924–54	944	77	24831	287*	28.64	31
WGA Parkhouse	1948–64	693	44	21006	201	32.36	30
BE Hedges	1950–67	689	37	16602	141	25.46	19
AH Dyson	1927–48	637	36	16365	208	27.22	20
AJ Watkins	1939–61	602	72	16133	170*	30.43	28
PM Walker	1956–72	679	97	15266	152*	26.23	12
Dai Davies	1923–39	634	59	14190	216	24.67	16
AR Lewis	1955–74	494	42	13283	223	29.38	15
MJL Turnbull	1924–39	458	24	13235	233	30.49	22
JA Hopkins	1970–88	477	32	12263	230	27.55	17
WE Jones	1937–58	497	58	11968	212*	27.26	10
WE Bates	1921–31	470	15	11907	200*	26.16	10
JS Pressdee	1949–65	500	74	11892	133*	27.91	8
W Wooller	1938–62	570	66	11540	128	22.89	4
RC Ontong	1977–89	382	56	10255	204*	31.45	17
Majid J Khan	1968–76	245	14	8889	204	37.61	19

Alan Jones, the most prolific of all Glamorgan batsmen
(Allsport/Adrian Murrell)

MOST RUNS IN A SEASON

Runs	(Avge)		Season
2060	(71.03)	Javed Miandad	1981
2044	(60.12)	AR Butcher	1990
1991	(49.77)	WGA Parkhouse	1959
1960	(41.70)	AR Lewis	1966
1927	(33.80)	B Hedges	1961
1914	(51.73)	H Morris	1990

DOUBLE CENTURIES

287* Emrys Davies v Gloucestershire, Newport 1939
280* RJ Duckfield v Surrey, Oval 1936
233 MJL Turnbull v Worcestershire, Swansea 1937
230 JA Hopkins v Worcestershire, Worcester 1977
228* RC Fredericks v Northamptonshire, Swansea 1972
225 JT Bell v Worcestershire, Dudley 1926
223 AR Lewis v Kent, Gravesend 1966
216 Dai Davies v Somerset, Newport 1939
215 Emrys Davies v Essex, Brentwood 1948
212* WE Jones v Essex, Brentwood 1948
212* Javed Miandad v Leicestershire, Swansea 1984
208 AH Dyson v Surrey, Oval 1932
207 WE Jones v Kent, Gravesend 1948
205 MJL Turnbull v Nottinghamshire, Cardiff Arms Park 1932
204* A Jones v Hampshire, Basingstoke 1980
204 Majid Khan v Surrey, Oval 1972
204* RC Ontong v Middlesex, Swansea 1984
201 WGA Parkhouse v Kent, Swansea 1956
200* WE Bates v Worcestershire, Kidderminster 1927
200* MJL Turnbull v Northamptonshire, Swansea 1933
200* Javed Miandad v Essex, Colchester 1981
200* Javed Miandad v Somerset, Taunton 1981

INDIVIDUAL BOWLING

OVER 400 CHAMPIONSHIP WICKETS IN COUNTY CAREER

		Runs	Wkts	Avge
DJ Shepherd	1950–72	41998	2012	20.87
J Mercer	1923–39	31515	1341	23.50
JC Clay	1921–49	23126	1197	19.31
MA Nash	1967–83	23408	903	25.92
FB Ryan	1923–31	17974	867	20.73
W Wooller	1938–62	21595	826	26.14
Emrys Davies	1924–54	24081	810	29.72
AJ Watkins	1939–61	16586	736	22.53
JE McConnon	1950–60	13782	706	19.52
OS Wheatley	1961–69	12413	680	18.25
PM Walker	1956–72	19302	678	28.46
BL Muncer	1947–54	13288	661	20.10
AE Cordle	1964–76	17210	608	28.30
RC Ontong	1977–89	15925	491	32.43

MOST WICKETS IN A SEASON

Wkts	(Avge)		Season
170	(17.38)	JC Clay	1937
156	(14.19)	DJ Shepherd	1956
139	(16.38)	BL Muncer	1948
133	(17.95)	DJ Shepherd	1960
127	(17.81)	FB Ryan	1925
123	(16.84)	JE McConnon	1951
122	(21.54)	DJ Shepherd	1961
121	(21.42)	FB Ryan	1930
120	(12.72)	JC Clay	1946
120	(14.40)	FB Ryan	1924

NINE OR MORE WICKETS IN AN INNINGS

10-51 J Mercer v Worcs, Worcester 1936
9-43 JS Pressdee v Yorks, Swansea 1965
9-47 DJ Shepherd v Northants, Cardiff Arms Park 1954
9-48 DJ Shepherd v Yorkshire, Swansea 1965
9-49 AE Cordle v Leics, Colwyn Bay 1969
9-54 JC Clay v Northants, Llanelli 1935
9-56 MA Nash v Hants, Basingstoke 1975
9-59 JC Clay v Essex, Westcliff 1937
9-60 OS Wheatley v Sussex, Ebbw Vale 1968
9-62 BL Muncer v Essex, Brentwood 1948
9-66 JC Clay v Worcs, Swansea 1937
9-93 AJ Nash v Sussex, Swansea 1922
9-97 BL Muncer v Surrey, Cardiff Arms Park 1947

FIFTEEN OR MORE WICKETS IN A MATCH

17-212 JC Clay v Worcs, Swansea 1937
15-86 JC Clay v Northants, Llanelli 1935
15-116 AJ Nash v Worcs, Swansea 1921
15-161 BL Muncer v Essex, Brentwood 1948
15-201 BL Muncer v Sussex, Swansea 1948

Emrys Davies did valiant all-round work for Glamorgan, playing until he was 50 before becoming a Test umpire
(Hulton Picture Company)

WICKET-KEEPING

MOST DISMISSALS IN AN INNINGS

6 (5ct 1st) HG Davies v Leics, Leicester 1939
6 (6ct) DLG Evans v Yorks, Swansea 1967
6 (6ct) EW Jones v Essex, Cardiff 1982
6 (6ct) CP Metson v Leics, Neath 1988
6 (6ct) CP Metson v Hants, Southampton 1990
6 (6ct) CP Metson v Warwicks, Edgbaston 1990

MOST DISMISSALS IN A MATCH

8 (8ct) EW Jones v Warwicks, Edgbaston 1970

MOST DISMISSALS IN A SEASON

80 (70ct 10st) DLG Evans, 1963
79 (71ct 8st) EW Jones, 1970

MOST CAREER DISMISSALS

835 (755ct 80st) EW Jones, 1961-83

GLOUCESTERSHIRE

Formed: April 1871
Entered official Championship: 1890
Highest placing: 2nd in 1930, 1931, 1947,
1959, 1969, 1986

INNINGS TOTALS

HIGHEST BY THE COUNTY
653–3 dec v Glamorgan, Bristol 1928
643–5 dec v Nottinghamshire, Bristol 1946
636 v Nottinghamshire, Trent Bridge 1904
634 v Nottinghamshire, Bristol 1898
625–6 dec v Worcestershire, Dudley 1934

HIGHEST AGAINST THE COUNTY
607–6 dec by Kent, Cheltenham 1910
607 by Nottinghamshire, Bristol 1899
594–6 dec by Hampshire, Southampton 1911
579 by Surrey, Bristol 1901
578–6 dec by Essex, Bristol 1927

LOWEST BY THE COUNTY
22 v Somerset, Bristol 1920
25 v Somerset, Cheltenham 1891
31 v Kent, Tonbridge 1903
31 v Middlesex, Bristol 1924
33 v Middlesex, Bristol 1909

LOWEST AGAINST THE COUNTY
12 by Northamptonshire, Gloucester 1907
25 by Somerset, Bristol 1947
31 by Somerset, Bristol 1931
35 by Worcestershire, Cheltenham 1928
35 by Yorkshire, Bristol 1959

PARTNERSHIPS

COUNTY BEST FOR EACH WICKET
1st
315 DM Young & CA Milton v Sussex, Hove 1968
261 Sadiq Mohammed & AW Stovold v Hants,
     Southampton 1979
2nd
256 CTM Pugh & TW Graveney v Derbys, Chesterfield
     1960
251 CJ Barnett & WR Hammond v Sussex, Cheltenham
     1934
3rd
336 WR Hammond & BH Lyon v Leics, Leicester 1933
330 AE Dipper & WR Hammond v Lancs, Old Trafford
     1925
4th
321 WR Hammond & WL Neale v Leics, Gloucester 1937
208 WR Hammond & WL Neale v Glamorgan, Gloucester
     1933
5th
245 JF Crapp & AE Wilson v Worcs, Dudley 1953
242 WR Hammond & BO Allen v Worcs, Dudley 1953
6th
320 JH Board & GL Jessop v Sussex, Hove 1903
285 WR Hammond & BH Lyon v Surrey, Oval 1928
7th
248 WG Grace & EL Thomas v Sussex, Hove 1896
229 KM Curran & RC Russell v Somerset, Bristol 1990
8th
239 WR Hammond & AE Wilson v Lancs, Bristol 1938
192 WL Neale & AE Wilson v Middlesex, Lord's 1938
9th
193 WG Grace & SAP Kitcat v Sussex, Bristol 1896
156 H Wrathall & WAS Brown v Warwicks, Edgbaston
     1898
10th
131 WR Gouldsworthy & J Bessant v Somerset, Bristol
     1923
112 AE Dipper & EG Dennett v Sussex, Gloucester 1908

INDIVIDUAL BATTING

OVER 8000 CHAMPIONSHIP RUNS IN COUNTY CAREER

		Inns	NO	Runs	HS	Avge	100s
WR Hammond	1920–51	619	66	31344	317	56.67	107
CA Milton	1948–74	931	102	27528	170	33.20	48
AE Dipper	1908–32	817	59	25922	252*	34.20	49
RB Nicholls	1951–75	871	45	21096	137	25.53	14
GM Emmett	1938–59	694	41	20469	188	31.34	30
DM Young	1950–75	697	32	20369	194	30.63	33
JF Crapp	1936–56	653	67	20261	140	34.57	32
CJ Barnett	1928–48	641	33	19495	232	32.06	37
GL Jessop	1894–1914	574	23	18275	286	33.16	34
TW Graveney	1948–60	452	44	17525	222	42.95	44
AW Stovold	1973–90	578	30	16356	212*	29.84	20
Zaheer Abbas	1972–84	334	31	14816	230*	48.89	45
RA Sinfield	1925–39	635	77	14163	209*	25.38	12
MJ Procter	1968–81	411	34	13603	203	36.08	32
WL Neale	1923–48	650	72	13403	145*	23.18	11
JB Mortimore	1950–75	853	106	13339	149	17.85	2
H Smith	1912–35	614	52	12870	149	22.90	10
JH Board	1891–1914	723	74	12578	214	19.38	8
BO Allen	1932–51	434	19	12308	220	29.65	13
AS Brown	1953–76	745	95	11881	116	18.27	3
Sadiq Mohammed	1972–82	325	17	11024	176	35.79	22
P Bainbridge	1977–90	390	54	10972	169	32.65	18
T Langdon	1900–14	485	13	9934	156	21.04	6
DR Shepherd	1965–79	444	35	9791	153	23.93	9
AE Wilson	1938–55	445	67	9692	188	25.64	5
H Wrathall	1894–1907	438	17	9536	176	22.56	7
BH Lyon	1921–46	371	17	9000	189	25.42	15
WG Grace	1890–99	255	18	8669	301	36.57	15
CWJ Athey	1984–90	215	29	8368	171*	44.98	20

*The talented Arthur Milton. A batsman of great composure
and natural style, he was also an excellent close fielder and
occasional seam bowler (Hulton Picture Company)*

MOST RUNS IN A SEASON

Runs	(Avge)		Season
2578	(64.45)	WR Hammond	1933
2522	(72.05)	WR Hammond	1927
2474	(82.46)	WR Hammond	1928
2431	(78.41)	Zaheer Abbas	1976
2393	(66.47)	WR Hammond	1937
2180	(83.84)	WR Hammond	1938
2138	(45.48)	CJ Barnett	1934
2121	(68.41)	WR Hammond	1939
2079	(46.20)	AE Dipper	1929
2039	(61.78)	WR Hammond	1932
2020	(126.25)	WR Hammond	1934
2008	(37.18)	AE Dipper	1926
1972	(48.09)	AE Dipper	1927
1971	(46.92)	CA Milton	1967
1970	(42.82)	DM Young	1959
1951	(46.45)	CJ Barnett	1937
1945	(49.87)	AE Dipper	1928
1918	(39.14)	AE Dipper	1923
1911	(47.75)	JF Crapp	1949
1885	(42.84)	CJ Barnett	1936
1881	(44.78)	CA Milton	1952
1875	(39.06)	DM Green	1968
1852	(37.04)	AE Dipper	1925
1825	(44.51)	GM Emmett	1951
1803	(46.23)	WR Hammond	1935

DOUBLE CENTURIES

317 WR Hammond v Nottinghamshire, Gloucester 1936
302* WR Hammond v Glamorgan, Bristol 1934
302 WR Hammond v Glamorgan, Newport 1939
301 WG Grace v Sussex, Bristol 1896
290 WR Hammond v Kent, Tunbridge Wells 1934
288 WG Grace v Sussex, Bristol 1895
286 GL Jessop v Sussex, Bristol 1903
271 WR Hammond v Lancashire, Bristol 1938
265* WR Hammond v Worcestershire, Dudley 1934
264 WR Hammond v Lancashire, Liverpool 1932
257 WG Grace v Kent, Gravesend 1895
256 MW Alleyne v Northamptonshire, Northampton 1990

252* AE Dipper v Glamorgan, Cheltenham 1923
252 WR Hammond v Leicestershire, Leicester 1935
250* WR Hammond v Lancashire, Old Trafford 1925
244 WR Hammond v Essex, Chelmsford 1928
243* WG Grace v Sussex, Hove 1896
240 GL Jessop v Sussex, Bristol 1907
239 WR Hammond v Glamorgan, Gloucester 1933
238* WR Hammond v Warwickshire, Edgbaston 1929
237 WR Hammond v Derbyshire, Bristol 1938
234 GL Jessop v Soemrset, Bristol 1905
233 DM Green v Sussex, Hove 1968
232 CJ Barnett v Lancashire, Gloucester 1937
231 WR Hammond v Derbyshire,.Cheltenham 1933
230* Zaheer Abbas v Kent, Canterbury 1976
228* CJ Barnett v Leicestershire, Gloucester 1947
224* CL Townsend v Essex, Clifton 1899
223 CCR Dacre v Worcestershire, Worcester 1930
222 TW Graveney v Derbyshire, Chesterfield 1954
220 BO Allen v Hampshire, Bournemouth 1947
218* WR Hammond v Glamorgan, Bristol 1928
217 WR Hammond v Nottinghamshire, Bristol 1934
217 WR Hammond v Leicestershire, Gloucester 1937
216* Zaheer Abbas v Surrey, Oval 1976
215* Zaheer Abbas v Somerset, Bath 1981
214 JH Board v Somerset, Bristol 1900
214 CL Townsend v Worcestershire, Cheltenham 1906
214 WR Hammond v Somerset, Bristol 1946
213 Zaheer Abbas v Sussex, Hove 1978
212* AW Stovold v Northamptonshire, Northampton 1982
212 AE Dipper v Worcestershire, Bristol 1927
211* WR Hammond v Nottinghamshire, Bristol 1946
211 TW Graveney v Kent, Gillingham 1953
210 GW Parker v Kent, Dover 1937
209* RA Sinfield v Glamorgan, Cardiff 1935
207 WR Hammond v Essex, Westcliff 1939
206 GL Jessop v Nottinghamshire, Trent Bridge 1904
206 WR Hammond v Leicestershire, Leicester 1933
205* WR Hammond v Surrey, Oval 1928
205* Zaheer Abbas v Sussex, Cheltenham 1977
204* CJ Barnett v Leicestershire, Leicester 1936
203 MJ Procter v Essex, Gloucester 1978
201 TW Graveney v Sussex, Worthing 1950
200 TW Graveney v Glamorgan, Newport 1956

*AE Dipper's consistent run-making for the county includes the third highest undefeated total, against
Glamorgan in 1923* (Hulton Picture Company)

INDIVIDUAL BOWLING

OVER 400 CHAMPIONSHIP WICKETS IN COUNTY CAREER

		Runs	Wkts	Avge
CWL Parker	1905–35	58336	3022	19.30
TWJ Goddard	1922–52	52102	2678	19.45
EG Dennett	1903–26	39365	1979	19.89
C Cook	1946–64	32549	1609	20.22
JB Mortimore	1950–75	35307	1522	23.19
AS Brown	1953–76	29124	1150	25.32
RA Sinfield	1925–39	26182	1074	24.37
DR Smith	1956–70	25572	1071	23.87
GEE Lambert	1938–56	23867	838	28.48
DA Allen	1953–72	17991	798	22.54
MJ Procter	1968–81	15474	790	19.58
FG Roberts	1890–1905	17210	790	21.78
PT MIlls	1902–29	19644	784	24.74
DA Graveney	1972–90	21936	732	29.96
CL Townsend	1893–1922	13690	631	21.69
GL Jessop	1894–1914	13130	589	22.29
HJ Huggins	1901–21	15937	557	28.61
BD Wells	1951–59	10351	484	21.38
CJ Scott	1938–54	15032	478	31.33
WR Hammond	1920–51	13808	475	29.06
CA Walsh	1984–90	9472	428	22.13

MOST WICKETS IN A SEASON

Wkts	(Avge)		Season
215	(16.41)	TW Goddard	1937
206	(15.93)	TW Goddard	1947
205	(14.44)	CWL Parker	1931
200	(14.65)	CWL Parker	1925
198	(17.68)	CWL Parker	1926
195	(13.17)	CWL Parker	1922
189	(20.10)	TW Goddard	1935
184	(13.51)	CWL Parker	1924
184	(15.65)	EG Dennett	1907
183	(18.90)	CWL Parker	1927
181	(14.66)	TW Goddard	1939
170	(17.74)	TW Goddard	1933
167	(18.55)	CWL Parker	1923
162	(11.90)	CWL Parker	1930
160	(17.97)	EG Dennett	1906
159	(19.22)	TW Goddard	1932
156	(16.54)	CWL Parker	1921
154	(15.97)	TW Goddard	1929
153	(20.51)	EG Dennett	1913
152	(18.59)	TW Goddard	1949
150	(17.22)	TW Goddard	1946
149	(20.46)	EG Dennett	1908
146	(19.15)	RA Sinfield	1936
143	(20.37)	TW Goddard	1936
143	(22.60)	CWL Parker	1928
139	(14.39)	C Cook	1956
135	(19.11)	EG Dennett	1909
131	(18.92)	TW Goddard	1930
131	(19.87)	TW Goddard	1950
131	(19.48)	EG Dennett	1905
130	(17.33)	CWL Parker	1929
130	(19.96)	CL Townsend	1898
128	(20.09)	C Cook	1950
128	(21.43)	CWL Parker	1932
127	(20.85)	DM Smith	1960
125	(15.79)	CWL Parker	1920
125	(18.93)	A Paish	1899
124	(12.58)	CL Townsend	1895
123	(19.35)	EG Dennett	1904
122	(18.22)	TW Goddard	1931
122	(19.60)	TW Goddard	1948
122	(22.62)	RA Sinfield	1937
120	(19.24)	EG Dennett	1910
120	(19.90)	C Cook	1947

NINE OR MORE WICKETS IN AN INNINGS

10–40   EG Dennett v Essex, Bristol 1906
10–66   JKR Graveney v Derbys, Chesterfield 1949
10–79   CWL Parker v Somerset, Bristol 1921
10–113 TWJ Goddard v Worcs, Cheltenham 1937
9–23   WR Hammond v Worcs, Cheltenham 1928
9–34   HJ Huggins v Sussex, Bristol 1904
9–35   CWL Parker v Leics, Cheltenham 1920
9–36   CWL Parker v Yorks, Bristol 1922
9–37   TWJ Goddard v Leics, Bristol 1934
9–38   TWJ Goddard v Kent, Bristol 1939
9–41   TWJ Goddard v Notts, Bristol 1947
9–42   C Cook v Yorks, Bristol 1947
9–44   CWL Parker v Essex, Gloucester 1925
9–44   CWL Parker v Warwicks, Cheltenham 1930
9–44   TWJ Goddard v Somerset, Bristol 1939
9–46   CWL Parker v Northants, Northampton 1927
9–48   CL Townsend v Middlesex, Lord's 1898
9–55   TWJ Goddard v Worcs, Bristol 1939
9–56   JH Childs v Somerset, Bristol 1981
9–61   TWJ Goddard v Derbys, Bristol 1949
9–63   EG Dennett v Surrey, Bristol 1913
9–72   CA Walsh v Somerset, Bristol 1986
9–82   TWJ Goddard v Surrey, Cheltenham 1946
9–87   CWL Parker v Derbys, Gloucester 1922
9–103   CWL Parker v Somerset, Bristol 1927
9–111   RA Sinfield v Middlesex, Lord's 1936
9–118   CWL Parker v Surrey, Gloucester 1925
9–128   CL Townsend v Warwicks, Cheltenham 1898

FIFTEEN OR MORE WICKETS IN A MATCH

17–56   CWL Parker v Essex, Gloucester 1925
17–106   TWJ Goddard v Kent, Bristol 1939
16–99   TWJ Goddard v Worcs, Bristol 1939
16–109   CWL Parker v Middlesex, Cheltenham 1930
16–122   CL Townsend v Notts, Trent Bridge 1895
16–146   EG Dennett v Hants, Bristol 1912
16–154   CWL Parker v Somerset, Bristol 1927
16–181   TWJ Goddard v Worcs, Cheltenham 1937
15–21   EG Dennett v Northants, Gloucester 1907
15–81   TWJ Goddard v Notts, Bristol 1947
15–88   EG Dennett v Essex, Bristol 1906
15–91   CWL Parker v Surrey, Cheltenham 1930
15–96   EG Dennett v Middlesex, Bristol 1904
15–97   EG Dennett v Northants, Northampton 1907
15–107   TWJ Goddard v Derbys, Bristol 1949
15–109   CWL Parker v Derbys, Derby 1924
15–113   CWL Parker v Notts, Bristol 1931
15–123   FG Roberts v Kent, Maidstone 1897
15–128   WR Hammond v Worcs, Cheltenham 1928
15–134   TWJ Goddard v Leics, Gloucester 1947
15–134   CL Townsend v Middlesex, Lord's 1898
15–140   EG Dennett v Worcs, Cheltenham 1906
15–141   CL Townsend v Essex, Clifton 1906
15–156   TWJ Goddard v Middlesex, Cheltenham 1947
15–173   CWL Parker v Northants, Gloucester 1927
15–184   CL Townsend v Yorks, Cheltenham 1895
15–195   EG Dennett v Surrey, Bristol 1913
15–205   CL Townsend v Warwicks, Cheltenham 1898

WICKET-KEEPING

MOST DISMISSALS IN AN INNINGS
6 (3ct 3st) H Smith v Sussex, Bristol 1923
6 (6ct)   AE Wilson v Hants, Portsmouth 1953
6 (6ct)   BJ Meyer v Somerset, Taunton 1962

MOST DISMISSALS IN A MATCH
10 (10ct) AE Wilson v Hants, Portsmouth 1953

MOST DISMISSALS IN A SEASON
75 (52ct 23st) JH Board, 1895
70 (55ct 15st) BJ Meyer, 1964

MOST CAREER DISMISSALS
982 (678ct 304st) JH Board, 1891–1914

(Facing page): Charlie Townsend was a cricketing prodigy who found fame as a brilliant schoolboy spin bowler and became a Test-class batsman. A genius rich in gifts but short on cricket ambition, a promising legal career inspired early retirement (Allsport)

HAMPSHIRE

Formed: 12 August 1863
Entered official Championship: 1895
Winners: 1961, 1973

INNINGS TOTALS

HIGHEST BY THE COUNTY
672–7 dec v Somerset, Taunton 1899
642–9 dec v Somerset, Taunton 1901
616–7 dec v Warwickshire, Portsmouth 1920
600–8 dec v Sussex, Southampton 1990
599 v Kent, Southampton 1912

HIGHEST AGAINST THE COUNTY
742 by Surrey, Oval 1909
676–6 dec by Lancashire, Old Trafford 1911
675–9 dec by Somerset, Bath 1924
657–6 dec by Warwickshire, Edgbaston 1899
645 by Derbyshire, Derby 1898

LOWEST BY THE COUNTY
15 v Warwickshire, Edgbaston 1922
23 v Derbyshire, Burton-on-Trent 1958
30 v Worcestershire, Worcester 1903
30 v Nottinghamshire, Southampton 1932
31 v Worcestershire, Bournemouth 1965
31 v Kent, Maidstone 1967

LOWEST AGAINST THE COUNTY
23 by Yorkshire, Middlesbrough 1965
32 by Kent, Southampton 1952
34 by Gloucestershire, Bristol 1914
36 by Glamorgan, Swansea 1922
36 by Warwickshire, Portsmouth 1927

PARTNERSHIPS

COUNTY BEST FOR EACH WICKET
1st
347   VP Terry & CL Smith v Warwicks, Edgbaston 1987
250   CG Greenidge & VP Terry v Northants, Northampton 1986
2nd
321   G Brown & EIM Barrett v Gloucs, Southampton 1920
280   G Brown & EIM Barrett v Warwicks, Portsmouth 1920
3rd
344   G Brown & CP Mead v Yorks, Portsmouth 1927
321   CL Smith & TE Jesty v Derbys, Derby 1983
4th
263   RE Marshall & DA Livingstone v Middlesex, Lord's 1970
259   CP Mead & LH Tennyson v Leics, Portsmouth 1921
259   MCJ Nicholas & RA Smith v Leics, Bournemouth 1985
5th
235   G Hill & DF Walker v Sussex, Portsmouth 1937
231   CB Llewellyn & EIM Barrett v Derbys, Southampton 1903
6th
411   RM Poore & EG Wynyard v Somerset, Taunton 1899
251   CP Mead & JA Newman v Warwicks, Bournemouth 1928
7th
325   G Brown & CH Abercrombie v Essex, Leyton 1913
270   CP Mead & JP Parker v Kent, Canterbury 1926
8th
227   KD James & TM Tremlett v Somerset, Taunton 1985
178   CP Mead & CP Brutton v Worcs, Bournemouth 1925
9th
230   DA Livingstone & AT Castell v Surrey, Southampton 1962

197   CP Mead & WR de la C Shirley v Warwicks, Edgbaston 1923
10th
192   HAW Bowell & WH Livsey v Worcs, Bournemouth 1921
147   EM Sprot & AE Fielder v Gloucs, Bristol 1911

INDIVIDUAL BATTING

OVER 8000 CHAMPIONSHIP RUNS IN COUNTY CAREER

		Inns	NO	Runs	HS	Avge	100s
CP Mead	1906–36	1115	157	46268	280*	48.29	132
RE Marshall	1955–72	821	42	27095	212	34.78	49
G Brown	1909–33	859	44	22113	232*	27.13	37
JR Gray	1948–66	747	72	20527	213*	30.41	28
J Arnold	1930–50	661	43	20032	227	32.41	31
H Horton	1953–67	664	74	19691	148*	33.37	30
CG Greenidge	1970–87	449	35	18910	259	45.67	46
PJ Sainsbury	1953–76	853	173	17942	125*	26.38	6
HAW Bowell	1902–27	765	43	17480	204	24.21	23
DR Turner	1966–89	629	65	16933	184*	30.02	23
NT McCorkell	1932–51	642	62	15016	203	25.88	17
AS Kennedy	1907–36	875	106	14357	163*	18.66	10
NH Rogers	1946–55	469	21	14230	186	31.76	20
BA Richards	1968–78	320	30	14011	240	48.31	34
JA Newman	1906–30	751	119	13099	166*	20.72	8
TE Jesty	1966–84	503	62	12891	187	29.23	22
CL Smith	1980–90	328	37	12456	217	42.80	30
Lord Tennyson	1913–35	534	18	12021	184	23.29	14
DA Livingstone	1960–72	470	56	11430	200	27.60	13
EM Sprot	1899–1914	400	26	10745	147	28.72	13
MCJ Nicholas	1978–90	396	46	10660	147	30.43	23
ACD Ingleby-McKenzie	1951–65	471	52	9882	132*	23.58	7
WLC Creese	1928–39	434	39	9677	241	24.49	6
EDR Eagar	1946–57	473	27	9181	128	20.58	7
AE Pothecary	1927–46	429	38	9037	118	23.11	8
J Bailey	1927–52	388	32	8952	133	25.14	5
VP Terry	1978–90	300	29	8837	180	32.60	14
RMC Gilliat	1966–78	331	39	8779	223*	30.06	16
JA Stone	1901–14	439	53	8689	174	22.51	4
D Shackleton	1948–69	738	68	8190	87*	14.36	—
G Hill	1932–54	557	86	8177	161	17.36	4
L Harrison	1939–66	555	91	8086	153	17.42	6

MOST RUNS IN A SEASON

Runs	(Avge)		Season
2843	(81.22)	CP Mead	1928
2478	(68.83)	CP Mead	1933
2455	(43.83)	RE Marshall	1961
2438	(67.72)	CP Mead	1921
2331	(75.19)	CP Mead	1927
2274	(64.97)	CP Mead	1926
2270	(63.05)	CP Mead	1922
2265	(64.71)	CP Mead	1923
2235	(55.87)	CP Mead	1914
2196	(40.66)	JR Gray	1962
2146	(48.77)	CP Mead	1913
2114	(48.04)	H Horton	1959
2067	(35.63)	H Horton	1961
2062	(41.24)	RE Marshall	1960
2039	(48.54)	BA Richards	1968
2014	(41.95)	NH Rogers	1952
2008	(43.65)	JR Gray	1959
2000	(39.21)	J Arnold	1934
1970	(37.88)	RE Marshall	1959
1950	(33.05)	JR Gray	1961

1943	(42.23)	H Horton	....	1960
1919	(34.26)	H Horton	....	1962
1916	(68.42)	CG Greenidge	....	1986
1872	(52.00)	CP Mead	....	1934
1863	(44.35)	G Brown	....	1920
1854	(46.35)	CP Mead	....	1925
1831	(61.03)	CL Smith	....	1983
1806	(39.26)	RE Marshall	....	1962

Barry Richards, signed as an overseas player, enjoyed an outstanding career with Hampshire. One of the world's finest batsmen, his county career ended prematurely in sad circumstances (Allsport)

DOUBLE CENTURIES

316 RH Moore v Warwickshire, Bournemouth 1937
304 RM Poore v Somerset, Taunton 1899
280* CP Mead v Nottinghamshire, Southampton 1921
268 EG Wynyard v Yorkshire, Southampton 1896
259 CG Greenidge v Sussex, Southampton 1975
258* CB Fry v Gloucestershire, Southampton 1911
249* JG Greig v Lancashire, Liverpool 1901
241 WLC Creese v Northamptonshire, Northampton 1939
240 BA Richards v Warwickshire, Coventry (C) 1973
235 CP Mead v Worcestershire, Worcester 1922
232* G Brown v Yorkshire, Headingley 1920
230 G Brown v Essex, Bournemouth 1962
227 CP Mead v Derbyshire, Ilkeston 1933
227 J Arnold v Glamorgan, Cardiff Arms Park 1932
225* BA Richards v Nottinghamshire, Trent Bridge 1974
225 EG Wynyard v Somerset, Taunton 1899
224 CP Mead v Sussex, Horsham 1921
223* RMC Gilliat v Warwickshire, Southampton 1969
222 CP Mead v Warwickshire, Edgbaston 1923
222 CG Greenidge v Northamptonshire, Northampton 1986
217 CL Smith v Warwickshire, Edgbaston 1987
215 EIM Barrett v Gloucestershire, Southampton 1920
213* CP Mead v Worcestershire, Bournemouth 1925
213* JR Gray v Derbyshire, Portsmouth 1962
213 CP Mead v Yorkshire, Southampton 1914
212 RE Marshall v Somerset, Bournemouth 1961
211* CP Mead v Warwickshire, Southampton 1922
211 CG Greenidge v Sussex, Hove 1978
209* RA Smith v Essex, Southend 1987
208 CG Greenidge v Yorkshire, Headingley 1977
207* CP Mead v Warwickshire, Southampton 1911
207 CP Mead v Essex, Leyton 1919
206 BA Richards v Nottinghamshire, Portsmouth 1968
205 VA Barton v Sussex, Hove 1900
204 HAW Bowell v Lancashire, Bournemouth 1914
204 G Brown v Yorkshire, Portsmouth 1927
204 CG Greenidge v Warwickshire, Edgbaston 1985
203 NT McCorkell v Gloucestershire, Gloucester 1951
203 RE Marshall v Derbyshire, Derby 1972
200* CP Mead v Essex, Southampton 1927
200* CG Greenidge v Surrey, Guildford 1977
200 DA Livingstone v Surrey, Southampton 1962

INDIVIDUAL BOWLING

OVER 400 CHAMPIONSHIP WICKETS IN COUNTY CAREER

		Runs	Wkts	Avge
D Shackleton	1948–69	46070	2542	18.12
AS Kennedy	1907–36	51393	2418	21.25
JA Newman	1906–30	46101	1861	24.77
GS Boyes	1921–39	32123	1373	23.39
PJ Sainsbury	1953–76	28333	1199	23.63
DW White	1958–71	23748	1015	23.39
OW Herman	1929–48	26893	994	27.05
VHD Cannings	1950–59	16696	766	21.79
MD Marshall	1979–90	13100	748	17.51
CB Llewellyn	1901–10	16545	672	24.62
RHM Cottam	1963–71	13635	661	20.62
CJ Knott	1938–54	14187	604	23.48
G Brown	1909–33	17005	584	29.11
G Hill	1932–54	17221	577	29.84
H Baldwin	1895–1905	13681	546	25.05
M Heath	1954–62	11957	483	24.75
TE Jesty	1966–84	12708	451	28.17
J Bailey	1927–52	11992	440	27.25
MD Burden	1953–63	10735	424	25.31

MOST WICKETS IN A SEASON

Wkts	(Avge)		Season
177	(16.16)	AS Kennedy	1922
172	(20.84)	JA Newman	1921
168	(20.76)	AS Kennedy	1921
164	(17.62)	AS Kennedy	1920
161	(15.33)	D Shackleton....................	1953
161	(19.96)	D Shackleton....................	1962
156	(18.45)	JA Newman	1910
156	(20.19)	AS Kennedy	1923
153	(19.13)	D Shackleton....................	1961
148	(20.09)	AS Kennedy	1914
147	(13.08)	D Shackleton....................	1955
145	(23.82)	JA Newman	1926
144	(15.69)	D Shackleton....................	1957
140	(18.45)	AS Kennedy	1929
139	(25.37)	JA Newman	1923
138	(19.98)	D Shackleton....................	1964
134	(18.45)	AS Kennedy	1932
133	(16.31)	D Shackleton....................	1965
133	(20.45)	CB Llewellyn....................	1910
133	(20.70)	D Shackleton....................	1953
133	(21.58)	OW Herman	1947
132	(17.16)	AS Kennedy	1925
128	(16.76)	D Shackleton....................	1960
126	(15.85)	D Shackleton....................	1956
126	(22.43)	D Shackleton....................	1959
122	(16.36)	RHM Cottam	1968
121	(23.14)	JA Newman	1922

Supposedly of dubious fitness, Malcolm Marshall has recently enjoyed some fine bowling seasons for the county, as well as showing batting prowess previously only suspected (Allsport/Gary Mortimore)

NINE OR MORE WICKETS IN AN INNINGS
9-25 RMH Cottam v Lancs, Old Trafford 1965
9-26 AEG Baring v Essex, Colchester 1931
9-30 D Shackleton v Warwicks, Portsmouth 1960
9-33 AS Kennedy v Lancs, Liverpool 1920
9-44 DW White v Leics, Portsmouth 1966
9-46 AS Kennedy v Derbys, Portsmouth 1929
9-57 GS Boyes v Somerset, Yeovil 1938
9-59 D Shackleton v Gloucs, Bristol 1958
9-77 D Shackleton v Glamorgan, Newport 1953
9-81 D Shackleton v Gloucs, Bristol 1959
9-131 JA Newman v Essex, Bournemouth 1921

FIFTEEN OR MORE WICKETS IN A MATCH
16-88 JA Newman v Somerset, Weston-super-Mare 1927
16-116 AS Kennedy v Somerset, Bath 1922
15-142 H Baldwin v Sussex, Hove 1898

WICKET-KEEPING

MOST DISMISSALS IN AN INNINGS
6 (4ct 2st) BSV Timms v Leics, Portsmouth 1964
6 (5ct 1st) GR Stephenson v Middlesex, Lord's 1976
6 (6ct)   RJ Parks v Derbys, Portsmouth 1981
6 (6ct)   RJ Parks v Essex, Colchester 1984
6 (5ct 1st) RJ Parks v Notts, Southampton 1986

MOST DISMISSALS IN A MATCH
10 (10ct) RJ Parks v Derbys, Portsmouth 1981
 9 (4ct 5st) WH Livsey v Warwicks, Portsmouth 1914

MOST DISMISSALS IN A SEASON
77 (72ct 5st) L Harrison, 1959
76 (46ct 30st) WH Livsey, 1921
76 (70ct 6st) RJ Parks, 1982

MOST CAREER DISMISSALS
666 (497ct 169st) NT McCorkell, 1932-51

KENT
Formed: 1 March 1859
Entered official Championship: 1890
Winners: 1906, 1909, 1910, 1913, 1970,
1977 (joint), 1978

INNINGS TOTALS

HIGHEST BY THE COUNTY
803-4 dec v Essex, Brentwood 1934
621-6 dec v Essex, Tonbridge 1922
615 v Derbyshire, Derby 1908
610 v Hampshire, Bournemouth 1906
607-6 dec v Gloucestershire, Cheltenham 1910

HIGHEST AGAINST THE COUNTY
648 by Surrey, Canterbury 1990
627-9 dec by Worcestershire, Worcester 1905
617 by Surrey, Oval 1897
616 by Essex, Chelmsford 1988
602 by Nottinghamshire, Trent Bridge 1904

LOWEST BY THE COUNTY
32 v Hampshire, Southampton 1952
35 v Sussex, Catford 1894
39 v Yorkshire, Sheffield* 1936
42 v Warwickshire, Edgbaston 1925
43 v Middlesex, Lord's 1953
43 v Middlesex, Dover 1957
* Bramall Lane

LOWEST AGAINST THE COUNTY
16 by Warwickshire, Tonbridge 1913
25 by Leicestershire, Leicester 1912
25 by Worcestershire, Tunbridge Wells 1960
26 by Leicestershire, Leicester 1911
31 by Gloucestershire, Tonbridge 1903
31 by Hampshire, Maidstone 1967

PARTNERSHIPS

COUNTY BEST FOR EACH WICKET
1st
283 AE Fagg & PR Sunnucks v Essex, Colchester 1938
256 BW Luckhurst & GW Johnson v Derbys, Derby 1973
2nd
366 SG Hinks & NR Taylor v Middlesex, Canterbury 1990
352 WH Ashdown & FE Woolley v Essex, Brentwood 1934
3rd
321* A Hearne & JR Mason v Notts, Trent Bridge 1899

304 AH Phebey & RC Wilson v Glamorgan, Blackheath 1960
4th
297 HTW Hardinge & APF Chapman v Hants Southampton 1926
296 KL Hutchings & FE Woolley v Northants, Gravesend 1908
5th
254 E Humphreys & AP Day v Lancs, Tunbridge Wells 1910
241* FE Woolley & DW Jennings v Somerset, Tunbridge Wells 1911
6th
284 APF Chapman & GB Legge v Lancs, Maidstone 1927
256* CJ Tavare & APE Knott v Essex, Chelmsford 1982
7th
248 AP Day & E Humphreys v Somerset, Taunton 1908
222 GR Cowdrey & SA Marsh v Essex, Chelmsford 1988
8th
157 AC Wright & AL Hilder v Essex, Gravesend 1924
143 EG Witherden & W Murray-Wood v Surrey, Blackheath 1953
9th
161 BR Edrich & F Ridgway v Sussex, Tunbridge Wells 1949
158 F Marchant & EB Shine v Warwicks, Tonbridge 1897
10th
235 FE Woolley & A Fielder v Worcs, Stourbridge 1909
141 JR Mason & C Blythe v Surrey, Oval 1909

INDIVIDUAL BATTING

OVER 8000 CHAMPIONSHIP RUNS IN COUNTY CAREER

		Inns	NO	Runs	HS	Avge	100s
FE Woolley	1906-38	1121	62	43703	270	41.26	112
HTW Hardinge	1902-33	923	89	30776	243*	36.90	70
LEG Ames	1926-51	667	62	26508	295	43.81	70
AE Fagg	1932-57	738	44	25126	269*	36.20	53
J Seymour	1902-26	803	56	24962	218*	33.41	52
MC Cowdrey	1950-76	594	76	21270	250	41.06	49
WH Ashdown	1920-37	754	72	20997	332	30.78	36
LJ Todd	1927-50	673	88	18632	174	31.84	35
RC Wilson	1952-67	606	36	18513	159*	32.47	29
BW Luckhurst	1958-76	514	53	17023	215	36.92	31

MH Denness	1962–76	525	40	15575	178	32.11	19
SE Leary	1950–71	575	85	14730	158	30.06	16
JR Mason	1893–1914	441	29	14271	183	34.63	29
E Humphreys	1899–1920	527	40	13903	208	28.54	19
BH Valentine	1927–48	459	23	13378	242	30.68	24
CJ Tavare	1974–88	406	48	13189	168*	36.84	25
AH Phebey	1946–61	550	30	13175	157	25.33	11
Asif Iqbal	1968–82	387	39	12702	171	36.50	23
MR Benson	1980–90	335	25	12190	162	39.32	29
GW Johnson	1965–85	538	68	11511	168	24.49	10
RA Woolmer	1968–84	390	58	11301	203	34.03	24
A Hearne	1890–1906	494	32	11236	162*	24.32	10
NR Taylor	1980–90	354	46	11119	204	36.10	24
CS Cowdrey	1977–90	398	56	10627	159	31.07	15
APE Knott	1964–85	471	87	10597	144	27.59	9
AGE Ealham	1966–81	428	58	9792	153	26.46	6
JC Hubble	1904–29	463	56	9565	189	23.50	5
TG Evans	1939–67	429	15	8949	144	21.61	4
PE Richardson	1960–65	264	11	8877	172	35.08	15
AL Dixon	1950–70	541	66	8818	105*	18.56	2
EW Dillon	1900–23	319	21	8786	137	29.48	11
JN Shepherd	1967–81	399	69	8663	170	26.25	8
CJ Burnup	1896–1907	244	16	8643	200	37.90	19

MOST RUNS IN A SEASON

Runs	(Avge)		Season
2582	(58.68)	FE Woolley	1928
2447	(53.19)	FE Woolley	1934
2404	(57.23)	AE Fagg	1948
2297	(54.69)	AE Fagg	1938
2201	(56.43)	HTW Hardinge	1928
2187	(41.26)	FE Woolley	1935
2174	(50.55)	HTW Hardinge	1926
2150	(52.43)	LEG Ames	1933
2141	(45.55)	WH Ashdown	1928
2137	(71.23)	LEG Ames	1947
2068	(57.44)	HTW Hardinge	1922
2046	(42.62)	AE Fagg	1951
2019	(41.20)	AE Fagg	1950
2000	(45.45)	LJ Todd	1947
1997	(38.40)	PE Richardson	1962
1990	(55.27)	FE Woolley	1925
1979	(47.11)	RC Wilson	1964
1958	(65.26)	LEG Ames	1932
1949	(44.29)	HTW Hardinge	1913
1947	(43.26)	AE Fagg	1947
1933	(46.02)	FE Woolley	1914
1926	(46.97)	LEG Ames	1948
1919	(51.86)	HTW Hardinge	1921
1919	(36.62)	PE Richardson	1961
1909	(54.54)	LEG Ames	1937
1868	(53.37)	FE Woolley	1922
1864	(44.38)	LJ Todd	1946
1862	(43.30)	LEG Ames	1949
1854	(37.83)	RC Wilson	1961
1846	(46.15)	LEG Ames	1939
1823	(50.63)	FE Woolley	1930
1812	(42.13)	AE Fagg	1939
1804	(42.95)	J Seymour	1913

DOUBLE CENTURIES
332 WH Ashdown v Essex, Brentwood 1934
305* WH Ashdown v Derbyshire, Dover 1935
295 LEG Ames v Gloucestershire, Folkestone 1933
270 FE Woolley v Middlesex, Canterbury 1923
269* AE Fagg v Nottinghamshire, Trent Bridge 1953
263* HTW Hardinge v Gloucestershire, Gloucester 1928
260 APF Chapman v Lancashire, Maidstone 1927
257 AE Fagg v Hampshire, Southampton 1936
250 MC Cowdrey v Essex, Blackheath 1959
249* HTW Hardinge v Leicestershire, Leicester 1922
244 AE Fagg v Essex, Colchester 1938
242 BH Valentine v Leicestershire, Oakham 1938
236 JL Bryan v Hampshire, Canterbury 1923
234 SG Hinks v Middlesex, Canterbury 1990
229 FE Woolley v Surrey, Oval 1935
221 AE Fagg v Nottinghamshire, Trent Bridge 1951
218* J Seymour v Essex, Leyton 1911
217 FE Woolley v Northamptonshire, Northampton 1926
215 FE Woolley v Somerset, Gravesend 1925
215 BW Luckhurst v Derbyshire, Derby 1973
214 J Seymour v Essex, Tunbridge Wells 1914

212* LEG Ames v Nottinghamshire, Gravesend 1947
212 LEG Ames v Gloucestershire, Dover 1948
211 D Nicholls v Derbyshire, Folkestone 1963
210 LEG Ames v Warwickshire, Tonbridge 1933
208 E Humphreys v Gloucestershire, Catford 1909
207 HTW Hardinge v Surrey, Blackheath 1921
205 HTW Hardinge v Warwickshire, Tunbridge Wells 1928
204 J Seymour v Hampshire, Tonbridge 1907
204 NR Taylor v Surrey, Canterbury 1990
203 AE Fagg v Middlesex, Dover 1948
203 RA Woolmer v Sussex, Tunbridge Wells 1982
202* AE Fagg v Essex, Colchester 1938
202 LEG Ames v Essex, Brentwood 1934
201* LEG Ames v Worcestershire, Gillingham 1937
201 LEG Ames v Worcestershire, Worcester 1939
201 BH Valentine v Nottinghamshire, Trent Bridge 1939
200* E Humphreys v Lancashire, Tunbridge Wells 1910
200 CJ Burnup v Lancashire, Old Trafford 1900
200 LEG Ames v Surrey, Blackheath 1928

Arthur Fagg, whose two double centuries for Kent v Essex at Colchester in 1938 constitute a unique feat (Hulton Picture Company)

INDIVIDUAL BOWLING

OVER 400 CHAMPIONSHIP WICKETS IN COUNTY CAREER

		Runs	Wkts	Avge
AP Freeman	1914–36	54543	3151	17.30
C Blythe	1899–1914	33180	2032	16.37
DL Underwood	1963–87	35493	1873	18.94
DVP Wright	1932–56	37093	1647	22.52
FE Woolley	1906–38	29427	1578	18.64
A Fielder	1900–14	21730	1036	20.97
F Ridgway	1946–61	21576	918	23.50
AL Dixon	1950–70	21814	867	25.16
JN Shepherd	1967–81	20681	775	26.68
WJ Fairservice	1902–21	17177	749	22.93
DJ Halfyard	1956–64	18089	741	24.41
RR Dovey	1938–54	19688	725	27.15
JR Mason	1893–1914	15494	709	21.85
A Hearne	1890–1906	14577	692	21.06
A Brown	1957–70	15790	665	23.74
F Martin	1890–99	12609	645	19.54
KBS Jarvis	1975–87	17588	594	29.60
AE Watt	1929–39	16306	573	28.45
WH Ashdown	1920–37	17857	561	31.83

JN Graham	1964–77	12403	559	22.18
AC Wright	1921–31	13335	554	24.07
LJ Todd	1927–50	14282	519	27.51
GW Johnson	1965–85	15875	512	31.00
WM Bradley	1895–1903	11085	486	22.80
CJT Page	1950–63	13870	478	29.01
W Wright	1890–99	10214	452	22.59
CS Marriott	1924–37	8831	432	20.44
DM Sayer	1955–76	9855	418	23.57

MOST WICKETS IN A SEASON

Wkts	(Avge)		Season
252	(14.84)	AP Freeman	1933
249	(15.46)	AP Freeman	1930
241	(15.21)	AP Freeman	1931
216	(17.04)	AP Freeman	1928
209	(15.33)	AP Freeman	1932
201	(21.81)	AP Freeman	1935
199	(16.30)	AP Freeman	1929
194	(14.63)	AP Freeman	1922
187	(21.87)	AP Freeman	1934
178	(14.07)	C Blythe	1909
170	(11.35)	C Blythe	1912
167	(16.48)	C Blythe	1908
164	(13.43)	FE Woolley	1920
163	(20.29)	AP Freeman	1926
159	(15.03)	C Blythe	1914
158	(19.74)	A Fielder	1906
158	(17.20)	AP Freeman	1927
156	(17.09)	AP Freeman	1921
151	(16.87)	A Fielder	1907
149	(13.70)	C Blythe	1910
148	(17.14)	AP Freeman	1923
146	(15.36)	AP Freeman	1924
146	(17.42)	AP Freeman	1925
145	(15.54)	C Blythe	1913
143	(12.20)	DL Underwood	1966
142	(18.00)	FE Woolley	1920
141	(16.63)	C Blythe	1907
141	(19.58)	DVP Wright	1950
137	(13.05)	C Blythe	1903
136	(18.58)	DVP Wright	1947
131	(15.65)	DVP Wright	1939
130	(19.94)	C Blythe	1905
127	(16.88)	DVP Wright	1955
126	(20.62)	DJ Halfyard	1958
125	(19.46)	C Blythe	1911
124	(13.14)	FE Woolley	1910
123	(15.77)	FE Woolley	1921
123	(22.11)	DJ Halfyard	1960
121	(19.38)	C Blythe	1904
121	(22.85)	AL Dixon	1964
121	(25.22)	DJ Halfyard	1959

NINE OR MORE WICKETS IN AN INNINGS
10–30 C Blythe v Northants, Northampton 1907
10–53 AP Freeman v Essex, Southend 1930
10–65 GC Collins v Notts, Dover 1922
10–79 AP Freeman v Lancs, Old Trafford 1931
10–131 AP Freeman v Lancs, Maidstone 1929
9–11 AP Freeman v Sussex, Hove 1922
9–28 DL Underwood v Sussex, Hastings 1964
9–30 C Blythe v Hants, Tonbridge 1904
9–32 DL Underwood v Surrey, Oval 1978
9–37 DL Underwood v Essex, Westcliff 1966
9–39 DJ Halfyard v Glamorgan, Neath 1957
9–42 C Blythe v Leics, Leicester 1909
9–44 C Blythe v Northants, Northampton 1909
9–47 DVP Wright v Gloucs, Bristol 1939
9–50 AP Freeman v Derbys, Ilkeston 1930
9–51 DVP Wright v Leics, Maidstone 1949
9–61 AP Freeman v Warwicks, Folkestone 1932
9–61 DJ Halfyard v Worcs, Maidstone 1959
9–67 C Blythe v Essex, Canterbury 1903
9–87 WM Bradley v Hants, Tonbridge 1901
9–87 AP Freeman v Sussex, Hastings 1921
9–97 C Blythe v Surrey, Lord's 1914
9–108 A Fielder v Lancs, Canterbury 1907

FIFTEEN OR MORE WICKETS IN A MATCH
17–48 C Blythe v Northants, Northampton 1907

17–67 AP Freeman v Sussex, Hove 1922
17–92 AP Freeman v Warwicks, Folkestone 1932
16–80 DVP Wright v Somerset, Bath 1939
16–82 AP Freeman v Northants, Tunbridge Wells 1932
16–83 GC Collins v Notts, Dover 1922
16–94 AP Freeman v Essex, Southend 1930
16–102 C Blythe v Leics, Leicester 1909
15–45 C Blythe v Leics, Leicester 1912
15–76 C Blythe v Hants, Tonbridge 1904
15–94 AP Freeman v Somerset, Canterbury 1931
15–114 W Hearne v Lancs, Old Trafford 1893
15–117 DJ Halfyard v Worcs, Maidstone 1959
15–122 AP Freeman v Middlesex, Lord's 1933
15–142 AP Freeman v Essex, Gravesend 1931
15–144 AP Freeman v Leics, Maidstone 1931
15–147 JN Shepherd v Sussex, Maidstone 1975
15–163 DVP Wright v Leics, Maidstone 1949
15–173 DVP Wright v Sussex, Hastings 1947
15–224 AP Freeman v Leics, Tonbridge 1928

WICKET-KEEPING

MOST DISMISSALS IN AN INNINGS
6 (1ct 5st) FH Huish v Surrey, Oval 1911
6 (5ct 1st) JC Hubble v Gloucs, Cheltenham 1923
6 (4ct 2st) LEG Ames v Sussex, Folkestone 1930
6 (4ct 2st) WHV Levett v Northants, Northampton 1934
6 (5ct 1st) WHV Levett v Glamorgan, Neath 1939
6 '4ct 2st) APE Knott v Middlesex, Gravesend 1966
6 (5ct 1st) APE Knott v Northants, Maidstone 1966
6 (6ct)   APE Knott v Lancs, Folkestone 1967
6 (6ct)   APE Knott v Worcs, Dartford 1973
6 (6ct)   D Nicholls v Notts, Trent Bridge 1974
6 (6ct)   APE Knott v Hants, Southampton 1975
6 (6ct)   APE Knott v Hants, Maidstone 1982

MOST DISMISSALS IN A MATCH
10 (1ct 9st) FH Huish v Surrey, Oval 1911
10 (9ct 1st) JC Hubble v Gloucs, Cheltenham 1923

MOST DISMISSALS IN A SEASON
102 (62ct 40st) LEG Ames, 1929
100 (52ct 48st) LEG Ames, 1928

MOST CAREER DISMISSALS
1144 (824ct 320st) FH Huish, 1895–1914

Leslie Ames, the first wicket-keeper to achieve 100 dismissals in a season, also invented a new sort of 'double' – 100 dismissals and 1000 runs – which he achieved in 1928 and 1929. It remains a feat unique to him (Hulton Picture Company)

LANCASHIRE

Formed: 12 January 1864
Entered official Championship: 1890
Winners: 1897, 1904, 1926, 1927, 1928, 1930, 1934, 1950 (joint)

INNINGS TOTALS

HIGHEST BY THE COUNTY
863-9 dec v Surrey, Oval 1990
801 v Somerset, Taunton 1895
676-7 dec v Hampshire, Old Trafford 1911
640-8 dec v Sussex, Hove 1937
627 v Nottinghamshire, Trent Bridge 1905

HIGHEST AGAINST THE COUNTY
707-9 dec by Surrey, Oval 1990
634 by Surrey, Oval 1898
577 by Derbyshire, Old Trafford 1896
567 by Surrey, Old Trafford 1928
561 by Somerset, Bath 1901
561 by Gloucestershire, Bristol 1938

LOWEST BY THE COUNTY
27 v Surrey, Old Trafford 1958
33 v Northamptonshire, Northampton 1977
36 v Derbyshire, Buxton 1954
37 v Nottinghamshire, Liverpool 1907
49 v Glamorgan, Liverpool 1924

LOWEST AGAINST THE COUNTY
22 by Glamorgan, Liverpool 1924
24 by Sussex, Old Trafford 1890
26 by Glamorgan, Cardiff 1958
29 by Sussex, Liverpool 1907
31 by Somerset, Old Trafford 1894

PARTNERSHIPS

COUNTY BEST FOR EACH WICKET
1st
368 AC MacLaren & RH Spooner v Gloucs, Liverpool 1903
350* C Washbrook & W Place v Sussex, Old Trafford 1947
2nd
371 FB Watson & Ernest Tyldesley v Surrey, Old Trafford 1928
363 AC MacLaren & AG Paul v Somerset, Taunton 1895
3rd
364 MA Atherton & NH Fairbrother v Surrey, The Oval 1990
306 E Paynter & N Oldfield v Hants, Southampton 1938
4th
324 AC MacLaren & JT Tyldesley v Notts, Trent Bridge 1904
300 Ernest Tyldesley & J Iddon v Leics, Leicester 1928
5th
249 B Wood & A Kennedy v Warwicks, Edgbaston 1975
235* N Oldfield & AE Nutter v Notts, Old Trafford 1939
6th
278 J Iddon & HRW Butterworth v Sussex, Old Trafford 1932
260 AC MacLaren & R Whitehead v Worcs, Worcester 1910
260 K Cranston & A Wharton v Warwicks, Edgbaston 1948
7th
245 AH Hornby & J Sharp v Leics, Old Trafford 1912
206 AH Hornby & WR Cuttell v Somerset, Old Trafford 1904
8th
158 J Lyon & RM Ratcliffe v Warwicks, Old Trafford 1979
150 A Ward & CR Hartley v Leics, Leicester 1900
9th
142 LOS Poidevin & A Kermode v Sussex, Eastbourne 1907
141 JD Tyldesley & W Huddleston v Yorks, Sheffield 1914

10th
141 JT Tyldesley & W Worsley v Notts, Trent Bridge 1905
131 Ernest Tyldesley & R Whitehead v Warwicks, Edgbaston 1914

INDIVIDUAL BATTING

OVER 8000 CHAMPIONSHIP RUNS IN COUNTY CAREER

		Inns	NO	Runs	HS	Avge	100s
Ernest Tyldesley	1909-36	782	87	31903	256*	45.90	85
JT Tyldesley	1895-1923	774	50	30865	295*	42.63	73
C Washbrook	1933-59	669	86	24177	251*	41.46	48
JWH Makepeace	1906-30	702	60	23599	203	36.75	40
J Sharp	1899-1925	735	67	21080	211	31.55	35
FB Watson	1920-37	601	46	20889	300*	37.63	45
J Iddon	1924-39	615	80	20517	217*	38.34	45
C Hallows	1914-32	513	57	17981	233*	39.43	44
KJ Grieves	1949-64	613	58	17408	150*	31.36	19
D Lloyd	1965-83	555	60	16139	195	32.60	34
A Wharton	1946-60	508	50	15544	199	33.93	20
AC MacLaren	1890-1914	472	35	14895	424	34.08	30
E Paynter	1926-39	397	45	14629	322	41.55	31
G Pullar	1954-68	455	40	13849	165*	33.37	26
JL Hopwood	1923-39	511	46	13807	220	29.69	23
H Pilling	1962-80	480	55	13557	149*	31.89	21
A Ward	1890-1903	460	38	13323	185	31.57	21
W Place	1937-55	386	35	12783	226*	36.41	31
JT Ikin	1939-57	382	47	12753	154	38.06	20
GA Edrich	1946-58	420	50	12608	167*	34.07	17
CH Lloyd	1969-86	312	40	12192	217*	44.82	29
B Wood	1966-79	383	47	11283	198	33.58	20
G Fowler	1979-90	326	21	11209	226	36.75	24
JD Bond	1955-72	478	66	10293	157	24.98	11
FC Hayes	1970-83	308	40	10224	157*	38.14	20
RH Spooner	1899-1921	259	12	9367	247	37.92	25
NH Fairbrother	1982-90	260	33	9340	366	41.14	18
J Abrahams	1973-88	367	49	9219	201*	28.99	10
DP Hughes	1968-90	528	100	9102	153	21.26	5
AH Hornby	1899-1914	404	39	9044	125	24.77	8
PT Marner	1952-64	343	28	8760	142*	27.80	7
J Simmons	1968-89	507	135	8394	112	22.56	5

MOST RUNS IN A SEASON

Runs	(Avge)		Season
2605	(60.58)	JT Tyldesley	1901
2403	(68.65)	FB Watson	1928
2365	(69.55)	Ernest Tyldesley	1926
2356	(58.90)	E Paynter	1937
2261	(55.14)	J Iddon	1934
2253	(66.26)	C Hallows	1928
2237	(69.90)	JT Tyldesley	1904
2227	(57.10)	Ernest Tyldesley	1934
2130	(78.88)	Ernest Tyldesley	1928
2100	(50.00)	JWH Makepeace	1926
2064	(44.86)	A Wharton	1959
2026	(49.41)	Ernest Tyldesley	1922
2023	(63.21)	W Place	1947
1976	(50.66)	JWH Makepeace	1923
1962	(51.63)	Ernest Tyldesley	1932
1961	(49.02)	JT Tyldesley	1910
1959	(41.68)	J Sharp	1911
1938	(52.37)	C Hallows	1925
1930	(48.25)	E Paynter	1936
1889	(69.96)	C Hallows	1928
1873	(60.41)	E Paynter	1938
1873	(46.82)	JT Tyldesley	1906
1853	(41.17)	JWH Makepeace	1922
1816	(44.29)	FB Watson	1929

1811 (54.87) Ernest Tyldesley 1930
1801 (39.15) JT Tyldesley 1898
1800 (40.90) FB Watson 1934

JT ('Johnnie') Tyldesley topped the batting averages in 1910 and was a county stalwart for nearly 30 years. His career total is beaten only by brother Ernest among Lancashire batsmen (Allsport)

DOUBLE CENTURIES
424 AC MacLaren v Somerset, Taunton 1895
366 NH Fairbrother v Surrey, Oval 1990
322 E Paynter v Sussex, Hove 1937
300* FB Watson v Surrey, Old Trafford 1928
295* JT Tyldesley v Kent, Old Trafford 1906
291 E Paynter v Hampshire, Southampton 1938
272 JT Tyldesley v Derbyshire, Chesterfield 1919
266 E Paynter v Essex, Old Trafford 1937
256* GE Tyldesley v Warwickshire, Old Trafford 1930
253 JT Tyldesley v Kent, Canterbury 1914
251* C Washbrook v Surrey, Old Trafford 1947
250 JT Tyldesley v Nottinghamshire, Trent Bridge 1905
249 JT Tyldesley v Leicestershire, Leicester 1899
248 JT Tyldesley v Worcestershire, Liverpool 1900
247 RH Spooner v Nottinghamshire, Trent Bridge 1903
244 AC MacLaren v Kent, Canterbury 1897
244 GE Tyldesley v Warwickshire, Edgbaston 1920
243 JT Tyldesley v Leicestershire, Leicester 1908
242 GE Tyldesley v Leicestershire, Leicester 1928

240 RH Spooner v Somerset, Bath 1906
239 GE Tyldesley v Glamorgan, Cardiff 1934
236 GE Tyldesley v Surrey, Oval 1923
236 FB Watson v Sussex, Hove 1928
234 A Hartley v Somerset, Old Trafford 1910
233* C Hallows v Hampshire, Liverpool 1927
232 C Hallows v Sussex, Old Trafford 1928
227 C Hallows v Warwickshire, Old Trafford 1921
226* AC MacLaren v kent, Canterbury 1896
226* W Place v Nottinghamshire, Trent Bridge 1949
226 GE Tyldesley v Sussex, Old Trafford 1926
226 G Fowler v Kent, Maidstone 1984
225 JT Tyldesley v Nottinghamshire, Trent Bridge 1904
225 GE Tyldesley v Worcestershire, Worcester 1932
224 RH Spooner v Surrey, Oval 1911
223 FB Watson v Northamptonshire, Old Trafford 1928
222 J Iddon v Leicestershire, Liverpool 1929
222 E Paynter v Derbyshire, Old Trafford 1939
221 JT Tyldesley v Nottinghamshire, Trent Bridge 1901
220 FH Sugg v Gloucestershire, Bristol 1896
220 JL Hopwood v Gloucestershire, Bristol 1934
219* C Washbrook v Gloucestershire, Bristol 1938
217* J Iddon v Worcestershire, Old Trafford 1939
217* CH Lloyd v Warwickshire, Old Trafford 1971
215 RH Spooner v Essex, Leyton 1904
211* C Washbrook v Somerset, Old Trafford 1952
211 J Sharp v Leicestershire, Old Trafford 1912
210 JT Tyldesley v Somerset, Bath 1904
210 JT Tyldesley v Surrey, Oval 1913
209* C Washbrook v Warwickshire, Edgbaston 1951
209 JT Tyldesley v Warwickshire, Edgbaston 1907
208* E Paynter v Northamptonshire, Northampton 1935
207 FB Watson v Worcestershire, Worcester 1929
204* J Iddon v Warwickshire, Edgbaston 1933
204* C Washbrook v Sussex, Old Trafford 1947
204 AC MacLaren v Gloucestershire, Liverpool 1903
203* GD Mendis v Middlesex, Old Trafford 1987
203* NH Fairbrother v Warwickshire, Coventry & NW 1990
203 JWH Makepeace v Worcestershire, Worcester 1923
201* J Abrahams v Warwickshire, Nuneaton, G & C 1984
201 J Iddon v Sussex, Old Trafford 1932
200* RH Spooner v Yorkshire, Old Trafford 1910
200* JWH Makepeace v Northamptonshire, Liverpool 1923
200* J Iddon v Nottinghamshire, Old Trafford 1934
200 JT Tyldesley v Derbyshire, Old Trafford 1898
200 W Place v Somerset, Taunton 1948
200 C Washbrook v Hampshire, Old Trafford 1948

The evocatively named Winston Place – he could have been nothing but a Northern opening bat – formed a stunningly prolific opening partnership with Cyril Washbrook (Hulton Picture Company)

INDIVIDUAL BOWLING

OVER 400 CHAMPIONSHIP WICKETS IN COUNTY CAREER

		Runs	Wkts	Avge
JB Statham	1950–68	25537	1683	15.17
AW Mold	1890–1901	19945	1300	15.34
RK Tyldesley	1919–31	21902	1297	16.88
H Dean	1906–21	21723	1169	18.58
J Briggs	1890–1900	17529	1070	16.38
R Tattersall	1948–60	17774	1056	16.83
EA McDonald	1924–31	20494	998	20.53
K Higgs	1958–69	21656	961	22.53
R Pollard	1933–50	20242	940	21.53
J Simmons	1968–89	24860	914	27.19
FM Sibbles	1925–37	18626	862	21.60
CH Parkin	1914–26	13045	818	15.94
MJ Hilton	1946–61	15053	802	18.76
LW Cook	1907–23	16760	791	21.18
WR Cuttell	1896–1906	14111	715	19.73
W Brearley	1902–11	12363	669	18.47
W Huddleston	1899–1914	11361	649	17.50
P Lever	1961–76	15911	647	24.59
T Greenhough	1951–66	13588	617	22.02
JL Hopwood	1923–39	12896	599	21.52
DP Hughes	1968–90	16815	557	30.18
PJW Allott	1978–90	12490	522	23.92
WE Phillipson	1933–48	12098	491	24.63
J Iddon	1924–39	12232	481	25.43
PG Lee	1972–82	10898	459	23.74
K Shuttleworth	1964–75	9961	436	22.84
J Sharp	1899–1925	11337	417	27.18
FS Booth	1927–37	9730	400	24.32

MOST WICKETS IN A SEASON

Wkts	(Avge)		Season
182	(13.71)	AW Mold	1895
182	(18.37)	EA McDonald	1925
178	(19.34)	EA McDonald	1928
176	(14.90)	CH Parkin	1923
175	(17.52)	H Dean	1911
172	(16.52)	CH Parkin	1922
169	(13.37)	CH Parkin	1924
163	(12.19)	R Tattersall	1950
163	(19.04)	EA McDonald	1926
150	(14.96)	LW Cook	1920
148	(15.27)	W Brearley	1908
144	(11.36)	AW Mold	1894
143	(21.94)	LW Cook	1921
143	(23.62)	EA McDonald	1927
140	(21.52)	EA McDonald	1929
140	(16.38)	J Briggs	1897
139	(21.12)	R Pollard	1938
136	(15.91)	RK Tyldesley	1929
136	(19.43)	LW Cook	1922
136	(22.66)	LL Wilkinson	1938
135	(14.00)	RK Tyldesley	1924
133	(15.21)	H Dean	1910
131	(17.85)	SF Barnes	1903
131	(18.52)	R Pollard	1947
130	(17.20)	AW Mold	1896
130	(17.39)	R Tattersall	1952
128	(14.17)	MJ Hilton	1956
125	(15.04)	MJ Hilton	1950
125	(15.20)	RK Tyldesley	1926
124	(12.41)	JB Statham	1965
124	(16.16)	H Dean	1920
124	(18.66)	H Dean	1908
122	(16.43)	R Tattersall	1953
122	(17.94)	R Tattersall	1957
122	(17.44)	FM Sibbles	1932
122	(19.77)	J Briggs	1896
121	(14.73)	RK Tyldesley	1930
121	(18.64)	W Brearley	1905
121	(20.79)	CH Parkin	1925
120	(17.45)	J Briggs	1900

NINE OR MORE WICKETS IN AN INNINGS

10–55 J Briggs v Worcs, Old Trafford 1900
10–102 R Berry v Worcs, Blackpool 1953

9–29 AW Mold v Kent, Tonbridge 1893
9–31 H Dean v Somerset, Old Trafford 1909
9–32 CH Parkin v Leics, Ashby-de-la-Zouch 1924
9–33 JL Hopwood v Leics, Old Trafford 1933
9–35 H Dean v Warwicks, Liverpool 1909
9–36 W Huddleston v Notts, Liverpool 1906
9–37 J Hallows v Gloucs, Gloucester 1904
9–40 R Tattersall v Notts, Old Trafford 1953
9–41 AW Mold v Yorks, Huddersfield 1890
9–42 J Iddon v Yorks, Sheffield 1937
9–43 JS Heap v Northants, Northampton 1910
9–44 F Harry v Warwicks, Old Trafford 1906
9–46 H Dean v Derbys, Chesterfield 1907
9–47 W Brearley v Somerset, Old Trafford 1905
9–62 AW Mold v Kent, Old Trafford 1895
9–62 H Dean v Yorks, Liverpool 1913
9–69 JL Hopwood v Worcs, Blackpool 1934
9–77 J Sharp v Worcs, Worcester 1901
9–77 H Dean v Somerset, Bath 1910
9–80 W Brearley v Yorks, Old Trafford 1909
9–109 H Dean v Leics, Leicester 1912

FIFTEEN OR MORE WICKETS IN A MATCH

17–137 W Brearley v Somerset, Old Trafford 1905
16–103 H Dean v Somerset, Bath 1910
16–111 AW Mold v Kent, Old Trafford 1895
15–70 F Harry v Warwicks, Old Trafford 1906
15–85 AW Mold v Notts, Trent Bridge 1895
15–87 AW Mold v Sussex, Hove 1894
15–89 JB Statham v Warwicks, Coventry 1957
15–95 CH Parkin v Glamorgan, Blackpool 1923
15–108 H Dean v Kent, Old Trafford 1912
15–108 JB Statham v Leics, Leicester 1964
15–112 JL Hopwood v Worcs, Blackpool 1934
15–131 AW Mold v Somerset, Taunton 1891
15–154 EA McDonald v Kent, Old Trafford 1928

Jimmy Hallows, a 'shooting star' whose poor health saw early retirement and premature death, showed outstanding all-round form. His nephew, Charles Hallows, was the top Lancashire batsman of the 1920s (Hulton Picture Company)

WICKET-KEEPING

MOST DISMISSALS IN AN INNINGS
7 (6ct 1st) W Farrimond v Kent, Old Trafford 1930
7 (7ct) WK Hegg v Derbys, Chesterfield 1989

MOST DISMISSALS IN A MATCH
11 (11ct) WK Hegg v Derbys, Chesterfield 1989
9 (8ct 1st) G Clayton v Gloucs, Gloucester 1959
9 (8ct 1st) C Maynard v Somerset, Taunton 1982

MOST DISMISSALS IN A SEASON
91 (63ct 28st) G Duckworth, 1928
82 (76ct 6st) G Clayton, 1962

MOST CAREER DISMISSALS
825 (561ct 264st) G Duckworth, 1923–38

LEICESTERSHIRE

Formed: 24 March 1879
Entered official Championship: 1895
Winners: 1975

INNINGS TOTALS

HIGHEST BY THE COUNTY
701–4 dec v Worcestershire, Worcester 1906
609–8 dec v Sussex, Leicester 1900
551–7 dec v Worcestershire, Kidderminster 1929
547 v Sussex, Hastings 1947
541–4 dec v Derbyshire, Glossop 1901

HIGHEST AGAINST THE COUNTY
761–6 dec by Essex, Chelmsford 1990
739–7 dec by Nottinghamshire, Trent Bridge 1903
686–8 by Sussex, Leicester 1900
673 by Essex, Leicester 1899
660 by Yorkshire, Leicester 1896

LOWEST BY THE COUNTY
25 v Kent, Leicester 1912
26 v Kent, Leicester 1911
33 v Lancashire, Leicester 1925
33 v Glamorgan, Ebbw Vale 1965
34 v Yorkshire, Headingley 1906

LOWEST AGAINST THE COUNTY
24 by Glamorgan, Leicester 1971
35 by Northamptonshire, Northampton 1907
36 by Glamorgan, Leicester 1925
36 by Derbyshire, Chesterfield 1905
40 by Worcestershire, Worcester 1971

PARTNERSHIPS

COUNTY BEST FOR EACH WICKET
1st
390 B Dudleston & JF Steele v Derbys, Leicester 1979
380 CJB Wood & H Whitehead v Worcs, Worcester 1906
2nd
289* JC Balderstone & DI Gower v Essex, Leicester 1981
287 W Watson & A Wharton v Lancs, Leicester 1961
3rd
316* W Watson & A Wharton v Somerset, Taunton 1961
305 JC Balderstone & BF Davison v Notts, Leicester 1974
4th
290* P Willey & TJ Boon v Warwicks, Leicester 1984
273* P Willey & PD Bowler v Hants, Leicester 1986
5th
233 NE Briers & RW Tolchard v Somerset, Leicester 1979
226* R Macdonald & F Geeson v Derbys, Glossop 1901
6th
262 AT Sharp & GHS Fowke v Derbys, Chesterfield 1911
237* BJ Booth & RW Tolchard v Surrey, Leicester 1971
7th
206 B Dudleston & J Birkenshaw v Kent, Canterbury 1969
194 WW Odell & H Whitehead v Essex, Leicester 1905
8th
164 MR Hallam & CT Spencer v Essex, Leicester 1964
150 G Geary & TE Sidwell v Surrey, Oval 1926
9th
160 WW Odell & RT Crawford v Worcs, Leicester 1902
133 AE Knight & AE Davis v Sussex, Hove 1905
10th
228 R Illingworth & K Higgs v Northants, Leicester 1977
157 WH Marlow & WE Astill v Gloucs, Cheltenham 1933

INDIVIDUAL BATTING

OVER 8000 CHAMPIONSHIP RUNS IN COUNTY CAREER

		Inns	NO	Runs	HS	Avge	100s
LG Berry	1924–51	969	46	27942	232	30.27	41
MR Hallam	1950–70	827	52	21922	210*	28.28	27
JH King	1895–1925	834	61	21343	227*	27.61	30
CJB Wood	1896–1922	699	47	20344	225	31.20	33
WE Astill	1906–39	957	120	18683	164*	22.32	12
M Tompkin	1938–56	563	23	17235	175*	31.91	25
NF Armstrong	1919–39	589	55	17188	186	32.18	37
BF Davison	1970–83	441	46	16789	184	42.50	33
JC Balderstone	1971–86	482	50	16014	181*	37.06	27
AE Knight	1895–1912	595	31	15851	229*	28.10	27
S Coe	1896–1923	709	65	15747	252*	24.45	15
H Whitehead	1898–1922	617	23	13875	174	23.35	12
VE Jackson	1946–56	508	44	13479	170	29.04	21
AW Shipman	1920–36	607	67	12398	226	22.95	15
RW Tolchard	1966–83	551	145	12144	120*	29.91	10
NE Briers	1976–80	425	38	12067	201*	31.18	17
CH Palmer	1950–59	384	25	11804	201	32.88	23
CC Inman	1963–71	375	35	11538	178	33.93	18
G Lester	1937–58	602	49	11387	143	20.59	6
JF Steele	1970–83	453	56	11051	195	27.83	17
G Geary	1912–38	664	104	10941	122	19.53	6
B Dudleston	1967–80	385	40	10687	202	30.97	24
J Birkenshaw	1961–80	526	98	9985	131	23.32	4
FT Prentice	1935–51	390	21	9934	191	26.92	10
DI Gower	1975–89	274	29	9339	228	38.11	21
BJ Booth	1964–73	359	31	9003	171*	27.44	11
JJ Whitaker	1983–90	255	34	8856	200*	40.07	20

Despite some inconsistency, Maurice Hallam was always an opener with big scoring potential. Against Glamorgan in 1959 he became only the second batsman in the Championship to follow a double century with a score of more than 150 in the same match (Hulton Picture Company)

MOST RUNS IN A SEASON

Runs	(Avge)		Season
2245	(51.02)	LG Berry	1937
2017	(54.51)	W Watson	1959
1903	(38.06)	LG Berry	1933
1896	(41.21)	NF Armstrong	1933
1865	(38.85)	M Tompkin	1955
1847	(38.47)	M Tompkin	1953
1846	(46.15)	NE Briers	1990
1822	(39.60)	MR Hallam	1961
1819	(34.98)	CH Palmer	1952

David Gower's languid style was a feature of one of the most talented of modern batsmen. He enjoyed an excellent run in 1981, but never quite achieved the expected consistency (Allsport/Russell Cheyne)

DOUBLE CENTURIES

252* S Coe v Northamptonshire, Leicester (AR) 1914
232 LG Berry v Sussex, Leicester (AR) 1930
229* AE Knight v Worcestershire, Worcester 1903
228 DI Gower v Glamorgan, Leicester (GR) 1989
227* JH King v Worcestershire, Coalville 1914
226 AW Shipman v Kent, Tonbridge 1928
225 CJB Wood v Worcestershire, Worcester 1906
217* W Watson v Somerset, Taunton 1961
216 AT Sharp v Derbyshire, Chesterfield 1911
210* MR Hallam v Glamorgan, Leicester (GR) 1959
207 LG Berry v Worcestershire, Ashby-de-la-Zouch 1928
205 JH King v Hampshire, Leicester (AR) 1923
203* MR Hallam v Sussex, Worthing 1961
202 B Dudleston v Derbyshire, Leicester (GR) 1979
201* NE Briers v Warwickshire, Edgbaston 1983
201 CH Palmer v Northamptonshire, Northampton 1953
200* CJB Wood v Hampshire, Leicester (AR) 1905
200* MR Hallam v Nottinghamshire, Trent Bridge 1962
200* MR Hallam v Derbyshire, Leicester (GR) 1959
200* JJ Whitaker v Nottinghamshire, Leicester (GR) 1986

AR = Aylestone Road   GR = Grace Road

INDIVIDUAL BOWLING

OVER 400 CHAMPIONSHIP WICKETS IN COUNTY CAREER

		Runs	Wkts	Avge
WE Astill	1906–39	46369	2029	22.85
G Geary	1912–38	32536	1669	19.49
CT Spencer	1952–74	33149	1244	26.64
JE Walsh	1938–56	25326	1057	23.96
JH King	1895–1925	25498	1008	25.29
HA Smith	1925–39	25682	1004	25.57
VE Jackson	1946–56	20751	875	23.71
J Birkenshaw	1961–80	21494	804	26.73
JS Savage	1954–66	18059	728	24.80
JP Agnew	1978–90	16472	581	28.35
A Skelding	1912–29	13771	556	24.76
AW Shipman	1920–36	13775	541	25.40
WW Odell	1902–08	12728	525	24.24
PB Clift	1976–87	12899	521	24.75
T Jayes	1903–11	11650	489	23.82
BS Boshier	1953–64	10643	465	22.88
LB Taylor	1978–90	11408	458	24.90
J van Geloven	1956–65	12832	450	28.51
J Sperry	1937–52	12740	444	28.69
GD McKenzie	1969–75	9571	429	22.31

MOST WICKETS IN A SEASON

Wkts	(Avge)		Season
157	(19.24)	JE Walsh	1948
152	(20.25)	WE Astill	1921
143	(18.16)	HA Smith	1935
143	(20.19)	JE Walsh	1946
142	(22.80)	JE Walsh	1947
138	(16.64)	G Geary	1929
136	(18.80)	WE Astill	1922
127	(28.26)	JE Walsh	1949

NINE OR MORE WICKETS IN AN INNINGS

10–18 G Geary v Glamorgan, Pontypridd 1929
9–33 G Geary v Lancs, Ashby-de-la-Zouch 1926
9–41 WE Astill v Warwicks, Edgbaston 1923
9–63 CT Spencer v Yorkshire, Huddersfield 1954
9–70 JP Agnew v Kent, Leicester 1985
9–78 T Jayes v Derbys, Leicester 1905
9–83 W Shipman v Surrey, Oval 1910
9–89 GC Gill v Warwicks, Edgbaston 1905

FIFTEEN OR MORE WICKETS IN A MATCH

16–96 G Geary v Glamorgan, Pontypridd 1929
15–100 JE Walsh v Sussex, Hove 1948
15–164 JE Walsh v Notts, Loughborough 1949

WICKET-KEEPING

MOST DISMISSALS IN AN INNINGS

6 (4ct 2st) P Corrall v Sussex, Hove 1936
6 (3ct 3st) P Corrall v Middlesex, Leics 1949
6 (6ct) RW Tolchard v Yorks, Headingley 1973
6 (6ct) RW Tolchard v Hants, Southampton 1980

MOST DISMISSALS IN A MATCH

10 (7ct 3st) P Corrall v Sussex, Hove 1936
8 (3ct 5st) J Firth v Kent, Folkestone 1952
8 (7ct 1st) J Firth v Essex, Colchester 1953
8 (8ct) RW Tolchard v Middlesex, Leicester 1979
8 (8ct) P Whitticase v Derbys, Derby 1987
8 (8ct) P Whitticase v Northants, Leicester 1988
8 (8ct) PA Nixon v Warwicks, Hinckley 1989

MOST DISMISSALS IN A SEASON

82 (57ct 25st) J Firth, 1952
71 (65ct 6st) R Julian, 1961

MOST CAREER DISMISSALS

798 (700ct 98st) RW Tolchard, 1965–83

MIDDLESEX

Formed: 2 February 1864
Entered official Championship: 1890
Winners: 1903, 1920, 1921, 1947, 1949 (joint),
          1976, 1977 (joint), 1980, 1982, 1985,
          1990

INNINGS TOTALS

HIGHEST BY THE COUNTY
642–3 dec v Hampshire, Southampton 1923
637–4 dec v Leicestershire, Leicester 1947
634–7 dec v Essex, Chelmsford 1983
632–8 dec v Sussex, Hove 1937
623–5 dec v Worcestershire, Worcester 1949

HIGHEST AGAINST THE COUNTY
582– dec by Surrey, Oval 1919
579–5 dec by Surrey, Lord's 1926
578 by Hempshire, Southampton 1925
575–7 dec by Yorkshire, Bradford 1899
561–4 dec by Nottinghamshire, Trent Bridge 1933

LOWEST BY THE COUNTY
29 v Derbyshire, Chesterfield 1957
41 v Surrey, Oval 1910
41 v Sussex, Lord's 1924
41 v Leicestershire, Lord's 1974
44 v Kent, Lord's 1891

LOWEST AGAINST THE COUNTY
31 by Gloucestershire, Bristol 1924
33 by Gloucestershire, Bristol 1909
35 by Somerset, Lord's 1899
35 by Hampshire, Portsmouth 1922
40 by Nottinghamshire, Lord's 1895

PARTNERSHIPS

COUNTY BEST FOR EACH WICKET
1st
367* GD Barlow & WN Slack v Kent, Lord's 1981
361 IJF Hutchinson & DL Haynes v Kent, Uxbridge 1989
2nd
380 FA Tarrant & JW Hearne v Lance, Lord's 1914
324 SM Brown & WJ Edrich v Warwicks, Edgbaston 1954
3rd
424* WJ Edrich & DCS Compton V Somerset, Lord's 1948
375 JWHearne & EH Hendren v Hants, Southampton 1923
4th
325 JW Hearne & EH Hendren v Hants, Lord's 1919
304 DCS Compton & FG Mann v Surrey, Lord's 1947
5th
338 RS Lucas & TC O'Brien v Sussex, Hove 1895
332 EH Hendren & WFF Price v Worcs, Dudley 1933
6th
212 GOB Allen & JHA Hulme v Glamorgan, Lord's 1934
211 GOB Allen & JHA Hulme v Worcs, Lord's 1936
7th
271* EH Hendren & FT Mann & Notts, Trent Bridge 1925
220* JT Murray & D Bennett v Yorks, Headingley 1964
8th
182* MHC Doll & HR Murell v Notts, Lord's 1913
136 JM Sims & BL Muncer v Kent, Folkestone 1934
9th
160* EH Hendren & FJ Durston v Essex, Leyton 1927
152 E Martin & HR Murrell v Essex, Leyton 1919
10th
230 RW Nicholls & W Roche v Kent, Lord's 1899
130 GW Beldam & C Headlam v Surrey, Lord's 1902

INDIVIDUAL BATTING

OVER 8000 CHAMPIONSHIP RUNS IN COUNTY CAREER

		Inns	NO	Runs	HS	Avge	100s
EH Hendren	1907–37	859	110	37475	301*	50.3	113
JW Hearne	1909–36	683	68	25819	285*	41.98	70
JDB Robertson	1938–50	675	36	24890	331*	38.95	54
WJ Edrich	1937–58	605	55	23643	267*	42.98	56
CT Radley	1964–87	747	124	21828	200	35.03	36
WE Russell	1956–72	658	46	20913	193	34.17	34
DCS Compton	1936–58	455	45	20254	252*	49.40	62
PH Parfitt	1956–72	614	75	19191	200*	35.60	39
PF Warner	1894–1920	545	45	18565	197*	37.13	42
HW Lee	1911–34	605	41	16970	243*	30.08	34
MJ Smith	1959–80	611	67	16969	181	31.19	33
FJ Titmus	1949–82	867	156	15832	120*	22.26	4
MW Gatting	1975–90	366	54	15548	258	49.83	39
JM Brearley	1961–83	447	61	14642	173*	37.93	27
JT Murray	1952–75	701	95	13866	132*	22.88	9
SM Brown	1938–55	496	36	13137	232*	28.55	18
FA Tarrant	1905–14	325	24	11679	250*	38.80	26
NE Haig	1912–34	578	36	11517	137	21.24	10
GD Barlow	1969–86	354	53	11131	160*	36.98	23
WN Slack	1977–88	318	33	10833	248*	38.01	19
RA Gale	1956–65	370	12	10389	200	29.01	4
RO Butcher	1974–89	340	30	10008	197	32.28	17
FT Mann	1909–31	441	41	9923	194	24.80	8
D Bennett	1950–68	536	108	9068	117*	21.18	4
RWV Robins	1925–51	357	24	8938	137	26.84	5
NG Featherstone	1969–79	312	31	8294	147	29.51	8

Bill Edrich maintained an admirable consistency for Middlesex as well as captaining the county with considerable ability (Hulton Picture Company)

MOST RUNS IN A SEASON

Runs	(Avge)		Season
2479	(63.56)	EH Hendren	1933
2471	(77.21)	EH Hendren	1928
2452	(61.30)	JDB Robertson	1951
2263	(87.03)	EH Hendren	1923
2257	(77.82)	WJ Edrich	1947
2214	(65.11)	JDB Robertson	1947
2122	(60.62)	EH Hendren	1931
2050	(43.61)	WE Russell	1964
2036	(63.62)	DL Haynes	1990
2033	(96.80)	DCS Compton	1947
1998	(66.60)	MW Gatting	1984
1963	(47.87)	EH Hendren	1936
1948	(52.64)	WJ Edrich	1939
1922	(60.06)	EH Hendren	1925
1881	(47.02)	JW Hearne	1932
1875	(72.11)	EH Hendren	1927
1860	(44.28)	PH Parfitt	1966
1856	(42.18)	JDB Robertson	1946
1855	(54.44)	JDB Robertson	1948
1853	(61.76)	DCS Compton	1939
1852	(37.79)	JDB Robertson	1957
1840	(61.33)	DCS Compton	1946
1823	(67.72)	EH Hendren	1920
1814	(37.79)	PH Parfitt	1957
1812	(75.50)	EH Hendren	1922

DOUBLE CENTURIES

331* JDB Robertson v Worcestershire, Worcester 1949
301* EH Hendren v Worcestershire, Dudley 1933
285* JW Hearne v Essex, Leyton 1929
277* EH Hendren v Kent, Lord's 1922
267* WJ Edrich v Northamptonshire, Northampton 1947
257 WJ Edrich v Leicestershire, Leicester 1947
258 MW Gatting v Somerset, Bath 1984
255* DL Haynes v Sussex, Lord's 1990
252* DCS Compton v Somerset, Lord's 1948
250* FA Tarrant v Essex, Leyton 1914
245* JW Hearne v Gloucestershire, Bristol 1927
245 WJ Edrich v Nottinghamshire, Lord's 1938
244 CM Wells v Nottinghamshire, Trent Bridge 1899
243* HW Lee v Nottinghamshire, Lord's 1921
240 EH Hendren V Kent, Tonbridge 1925
235 DCS Compton v Surrey, Lord's 1946
234* JW Hearne v Somerset, Lord's 1911
234 EH Hendren v Worcestershire, Lord's 1925
232* SM Brown v Somerset, Lord's 1951
232 EH Hendren v Nottinghamshire, Lord's 1920
232 JW Hearne v Hampshire, Southampton 1923
232 EH Hendren v Nottinghamshire, Trent Bridge 1931
229 JDB Robertson v Hampshire, Lord's 1947
225 HW Lee v Surrey, Oval 1929
225 WJ Edrich v Warwickshire, Edgbaston 1947
224 SW Scott v Gloucestershire, Lord's 1892
223* JW Hearne v Somerset, Taunton 1928
222* EH Hendren v Essex, Leyton 1933
222* WJ Edrich v Northamptonshire, Northampton 1946
221* HW Lee v Hampshire, Southampton 1920
221* JW Hearne v Warwickshire, Edgbaston 1922
221 AE Stoddart v Somerset, Lord's 1900
220* DL Haynes v Essex, Ilford 1990
218* JW Hearne v Hampshire, Lord's 1919
215* JW Hearne v Warwickshire, Edgbaston 1920
214* DCS Compton v Derbyshire, Lord's 1939
213 EH Hendren v Yorkshire, Lord's 1926
211 WJ Edrich v Essex, Lord's 1953
210 MW Gatting v Nottinghamshire, Lord's 1988
209* EH Hendren v Warwickshire, Edgbaston 1928
208* WJ Edrich v Derbyshire, Chesterfield 1956
207* FA Tarrant v Yorkshire, Bradford 1911
206* EH Hendren v Nottinghamshire, Trent Bridge 1925
206* DL Haynes v Kent, Uxbridge 1989
206 ET Killick v Warwickshire, Lord's 1931
204 J Douglas v Gloucestershire, Bristol 1903
203 EH Hendren v Northamptonshire, Lord's 1931
202 TC O'Brien v Sussex, Hove 1895
202 JW Hearne v Warwickshire, Edgbaston 1921
201* EH Hendren v Essex, Leyton 1924
201* JDB Robertson v Somerset, Taunton 1951
201* JDB Robertson v Essex, Lord's 1957
201 EH Hendred v Hampshire, Lord's 1919
201 JW Hearne v Gloucestershire, Gloucester 1922
200* EH Hendren v Essex, Leyton 1923
200* PH Parfitt v Nottinghamshire, Trent Bridge 1964
200* KR Brown v Nottinghamshire, Lord's 1990
200 FA Tarrant v Worcestershire, Lord's 1914
200 EH Hendren v Hampshire, Lord's 1928
200 SM Brown v Kent, Canterbury 1949
200 RA Gale v Glamorgan, Newport 1962
200 CT Radley v Northamptonshire, Uxbridge 1985

INDIVIDUAL BOWLING

Wayne Daniel was a fearsome-looking pace bowler who played a large part in the county's championship successes. One of the longest-serving overseas players, his meagre Test career was poor reward for a high-class and respected cricketer (Allsport/Michael King)

OVER 400 CHAMPIONSHIP WICKETS IN COUNTY CAREER

		Runs	Wkts	Avge
FJ Titmus	1949–82	46931	2170	21.62
JT Hearne	1890–1914	36999	2032	18.20
JW Hearne	1909–36	31012	1356	22.87
JM Sims	1929–52	28995	1168	24.82
JA Young	1933–56	20928	1120	18.68
FJ Durston	1919–33	23631	1076	21.96
AE Moss	1950–63	20522	1053	19.48
FA Tarrant	1905–14	16664	952	17.50
AE Trott	1898–1910	19578	905	21.63
NE Haig	1912–34	22531	881	25.57
PH Edmonds	1971–87	19335	819	23.60
JE Emburey	1973–90	19309	802	24.07
JSE Price	1961–75	15724	702	22.39
WW Daniel	1977–88	14899	673	22.13
JJ Warr	1949–60	13398	666	20.11
D Bennett	1950–68	17513	662	26.45
CIJ Smith	1934–39	11378	641	17.75
JT Rawlin	1890–1909	12788	624	20.31
RWV Robins	1925–51	13947	616	22.64
LH Gray	1934–51	13367	568	23.53
MWW Selvey	1972–82	14370	551	26.07
IAR Peebles	1928–46	10431	543	19.20
RW Hooker	1956–69	12403	463	26.78
DCS Compton	1936–58	13209	450	29.35
NG Cowans	1981–90	9558	446	21.43

MOST WICKETS IN A SEASON

Wkts	(Avge)		Season
154	(19.85)	AE Trott	1900
146	(15.69)	AE Trott	1899
142	(19.63)	JM Sims	1939
139	(17.31)	CIJ Smith	1934
137	(15.14)	FJ Titmus	1955
137	(16.04)	JT Hearne	1893
137	(20.47)	JA Young	1952
127	(19.55)	JA Young	1951
125	(14.76)	JT Hearne	1898
125	(17.65)	JA Young	1949
125	(20.20)	RWV Robins	1929
123	(15.82)	FA Tarrant	1910
123	(21.58)	FJ Titmus	1961
122	(15.81)	JA Young	1947

*Fred Titmus, the long serving off-spinner who effectively
sealed one end for the county* (Hulton Picture Company)

NINE OR MORE WICKETS IN AN INNINGS

10–40	GOB Allen v Lancs, Lord's 1929
10–42	AE Trott v Somerset, Taunton 1900
9–32	JT Hearne v Notts, Trent Bridge 1891
9–41	FA Tarrant v Gloucs, Bristol 1907
9–54	FA Tarrant v Lancs, Old Trafford 1906
9–57	FA Tarrant v Yorks, Headingly 1906
9–57	FJ Titmus v Lancs, Lord's 1964
9–59	FA Tarrant v. Notts, Lord's 1907
9–61	JW Hearne v Derbys, Chesterfield 1933
9–61	WW Daniel v Glamorgan, Swansea 1982
9–65	JJ Warr v Kent, Lord's 1956
9–68	JT Hearne v Lancs, Old Trafford 1898
9–78	JT Hearne v Yorks, Bradford 1908
9–82	JW Hearne v Surrey, Lord's 1911
9–92	JM Sims v Lancs, Old Trafford 1934
9–105	FA Tarrant v Lancs, Old Trafford 1914

FIFTEEN OR MORE WICKETS IN A MATCH

16–114	JT Hearne v Lancs, Old Trafford 1898
16–176	FA Tarrant v Lancs, Old Trafford 1914
15–47	FA Tarrant v Hants, Lord's 1913
15–93	JT Hearne v Somerset, Lord's 1904
15–95	FJ Titmus v Somerset, Bath 1955
15–154	JT Hearne v Notts, Trent Bridge 1893
15–187	AE Trott v Sussex, Lord's 1901
15–189	AR Litteljohn v Lancs, Lord's 1911

WICKET KEEPING

MOST DISMISSALS IN AN INNINGS

7	(7ct)	WFF Price v Yorks, Lord's 1937
6	(4ct 2st)	HR Murrell v Gloucs, Bristol 1926
6	(6ct)	WFF Price v Warwicks, Lord's 1938
6	(4ct 2st)	LH Compton v Essex, Lord's 1953
6	(6ct)	PR Downton v Notts, Lord's 1981

MOST DISMISSALS IN A MATCH
9 (8ct 1st) JT Murray v Hants, Lord's 1965

MOST DISMISSALS IN A SEASON
91 (87ct 4st) JT Murray 1960
79 (55ct 24st) WFF Price 1937

MOST CAREER DISMISSALS
1125 (955ct 170st) JT Murray 1952–75

*An early photograph of John Murray, who enjoyed an
admirable career as wicket-keeper/batsman for the county*
(Hulton Picture Company)

NORTHAMPTONSHIRE
Formed: 1820
Entered official Championship: 1905
Highest placing: 2nd in 1912, 1957, 1965, 1976

INNINGS TOTALS

HIGHEST BY THE COUNTY
636–6 dec v Essex, Chelmsford 1990
592–6 dec v Essex, Northampton 1990
557–6 dec v Sussex, Hove 1914
539 v Essex, Kettering 1933
532–6 v Essex, Northampton 1952

HIGHEST AGAINST THE COUNTY
670–9 dec by Sussex, Hove 1921
631–4 dec by Sussex, Northampton 1938
619–5 dec by Surrey, Northampton 1920
616–5 dec by Surrey, Oval 1921
604–7 dec by Essex, Northampton 1921

LOWEST BY THE COUNTY
12 v Gloucestershire, Gloucester 1907
15 v Yorkshire, Northampton 1908
27 v Yorkshire, Northampton 1908
27 v Yorkshire, Kettering 1933

LOWEST AGAINST THE COUNTY
33 by Lancashire, Northampton 1977
43 by Leicestershire, Peterborough 1968
44 by Essex, Colchester 1986
46 by Derbyshire, Northampton 1912
49 by Leicestershire, Northampton 1909

PARTNERSHIPS

COUNTY BEST FOR EACH WICKET
1st
293 C Milburn & RM Prideaux v Essex, Clacton 1966
278 G Cook & W Larkins v Yorks, Middlesbrough 1982
2nd
344 G Cook & RJ Boyd-Moss v Lancs, Northampton 1986
342 W Larkins & RG Williams v Lancs, Northampton 1983
3rd
398 A Fordham & AJ Lamb v Yorks, Headingly 1990
281 L Livingston & R Subba Row v Notts, Trent Bridge 1955
4th
370 RT Virgin & P Willey v Somerset, Northampton 1976
273 Mushtaq Mohammed & W Larkins V Essex, Chelmsford 1975
5th
347 D Brookes & DW Barrick v Essex, Northampton 1952
236 GJ Thompson & RA Haywood v Yorks, Dewsbury 1911
6th
376 R Subba Row & A Lightfoot v Surrey, Oval 1958
259 D Brookes & EE Davis v Leics, Leicester 1947
7th
229 WW Timms & FI Walden v Warwicks, Northampton 1926
222 GJ Thompson & RA Haywood v Gloucs, Northampton 1911
8th
155 FR Brown & AE Nutter v Glamorgan, Northampton 1952
146* AE Thomas & PA Wright v Essex, Northampton 1923
9th
156 R Subba Row & S Starkie v Lancs, Northampton 1955
137 JE Timms & RJ Partridge v Worcs, Stourbridge 1934
10th
148 BW Bellamy & JV Murdin v Glamorgan, Northampton 1925
 87 JE Timms & EW Clark v Sussex, Hove 1936

Freddie Brown's captaincy saw to it that Northants maintained steady progress in the early fifties. A top class all-rounder, he was almost worthy of a Test place in his forties (Hulton Picture Company)

INDIVIDUAL BATTING

OVER 8000 CHAMPIONSHIP RUNS IN COUNTY CAREER

		Inns	NO	Runs	HS	Avge	100s
D Brookes	1934–59	820	63	26627	257	35.17	60
G Cook	1971–90	669	62	19526	203	32.16	30
JE Timms	1925–49	790	25	18924	213	24.73	28
W Larkins	1972–90	575	35	18766	252	34.75	41
BL Reynolds	1950–70	689	61	17325	169	27.58	19
DS Steele	1963–84	627	89	16620	140*	30.89	22
Mushtaq Mohammed	1966–77	425	45	15037	204*	29.57	32
CN Woolley	1912–31	627	33	14731	204*	24.79	13
AJ Lamb	1978–90	306	58	13670	235	55.12	37
PJ Watts	1959–80	566	85	13207	145	27.45	9
VWC Jupp	1924–38	460	29	13117	197	30.43	15
AH Bakewell	1928–36	398	19	12849	257	33.90	27
RM Prideaux	1962–70	397	39	12833	176*	35.84	21
L Livingston	1950–57	306	33	12363	210	45.28	28
P Willey	1966–83	482	67	11992	227	28.89	18
D Barrick	1949–60	409	50	11525	211	32.10	16
A Lightfoot	1953–70	460	51	11052	122*	27.02	11
RG Williams	1975–90	382	52	9884	175*	29.50	13
RJ Bailey	1982–90	269	38	9466	224*	40.97	24
MEJC Norman	1956–65	342	17	9412	152	28.96	13
BW Bellamy	1920–37	602	64	8903	168	16.54	4
C Milburn	1961–74	310	24	8879	203	31.04	16
N Oldfield	1948–54	252	22	8739	168	37.99	19
BS Crump	1960–72	450	103	8133	133*	23.43	5
RA Haywood	1910–26	291	14	8116	198	29.29	20

Long-serving opening bat Geoff Cook (Allsport/Adrian Murrell)

MOST RUNS IN A SEASON

Runs	(Avge)		Season
2114	(50.33)	N Oldfield	1949
1991	(47.40)	D Brookes	1952
1965	(67.75)	RJ Bailey	1990
1962	(65.40)	AJ Lamb	1981
1957	(42.54)	L Livingston	1955
1932	(56.82)	D Brookes	1946
1925	(49.35)	AH Bakewell	1933
1912	(54.62)	L Livingston	1954
1887	(43.88)	RA Haywood	1921
1846	(48.57)	L Livingston	1956
1845	(59.51)	RT Virgin	1974
1819	(58.67)	F Jakeman	1951
1806	(44.04)	D Brookes	1949
1805	(46.28)	L Livingston	1950

DOUBLE CENTURIES
300 R Subba Row v Surrey, Oval 1958
260* R Subba Row v Lancashire, Northampton 1955
258* F Jakeman v Essex, Northampton 1951
257 AH Bakewell v Glamorgan, Swansea 1933
257 D Brookes v Gloucestershire, Bristol 1949
252 W Larkins v Glamorgan, Cardiff 1983
246 AH Bakewell v Nottinghamshire, Northampton 1933
241* AH Bakewell v Derbyshire, Chesterfield 1936
237 PC Davis v Somerset, Northampton 1947
236 W Larkins v Derbyshire, Derby 1983
235 AJ Lamb v Yorkshire, Headingley 1990
234 RA Harper V Gloucestershire, Northampton 1986
230* WH Denton v Essex, Leyton 1913
227 P Willey v Somerset, Northampton 1976
224 RJ Bailey v Glamorgan, Swansea 1986
213 JE Timms v Worcestershire, Stourbridge 1934
211 DW Barrick v Essex, Northampton 1952
210* D Brookes v Somerset, Northampton 1954
210 D Brookes v Leicestershire, Leicester (GR) 1947
210 L Livingston v Somerset, Weston-super-Mare 1951
208 HM Ackerman v Leicestershire, Leicester (GR) 1970
207* L Livingston v Nottinghamshire, Trent Bridge 1954
207 W Larkins v Essex, Northampton 1990
206* A Fordham v Yorkshire, Headingley 1990
204* CN Woolley v Worcestershire, Northampton 1921
204* D Brookes v Somerset, Northampton 1954
204* Mushtaq Mohammed v Hampshire, Northampton 1976
204* RJ Bailey v Sussex, Northampton 1990
204 SG Smith v Gloucestershire, Northampton 1910
204 AH Bakewell v Somerset, Bath 1930
203* D Brookes v Somerset, Taunton 1956
203 C Milburn v Essex, Clacton 1966
203 G Cook v Yorkshire, Scarborough 1988
200* RJ Bailey v Yorkshire, Luton 1986
200 HC Pretty v Derbyshire, Chesterfield 1906
200 D Brookes v Worcestershire, Kidderminster 1946
200 L Livingston v Kent, Maidstone 1954

INDIVIDUAL BOWLING

OVER 400 CHAMPIONSHIP WICKETS IN COUNTY CAREER

		Runs	Wkts	Avge
EW Clark	1922–47	22463	1048	21.43
GJ Thompson	1905–22	19157	1029	18.61
VWC Jupp	1924–38	23037	1023	22.51
GE Tribe	1952–59	19562	970	20.16
AE Thomas	1920–33	17819	783	25.31
BS Crump	1960–72	18829	759	24.80
W Wells	1905–26	15649	729	21.46
RJ Partridge	1929–48	18639	602	30.96
ADG Matthews	1928–36	14034	536	26.18
Mushtaq Mohammed	1966–77	12283	513	23.94
FH Tyson	1953–60	10451	509	20.53
V Broderick	1939–57	13186	501	26.31
JDF Larter	1960–69	8896	495	17.97
Sarfraz Nawaz	1970–82	11390	488	23.34
W East	1905–14	9659	475	20.33
SG Smith	1909–14	8156	462	17.65
RW Clarke	1947–57	15761	459	34.33
JV Murdin	1913–27	11633	436	26.68
DS Steele	1963–84	10540	420	25.09
JS Manning	1956–60	8531	415	20.55
P Willey	1966–83	12064	415	30.37
MHJ Allen	1956–63	8679	412	21.06
AE Nutter	1948–52	10277	411	25.00
BJ Griffiths	1974–86	11888	408	29.13
ME Scott	1960–69	10079	407	24.76

MOST WICKETS IN A SEASON

Wkts	(Avge)		Season
169	(18.66)	GE Tribe	1955
138	(17.50)	GJ Thompson	1913
135	(19.11)	EW Clarke	1929
133	(19.74)	GE Tribe	1954
124	(16.70)	GE Tribe	1957
122	(18.82)	GE Tribe	1956
122	(19.02)	VWC Jupp	1928

NINE OR MORE WICKETS IN AN INNINGS
10-127 VWC Jupp v Kent, Tunbridge Wells 1932
9–30 AE Thomas v Yorks, Bradford 1920
9–35 V Broderick v Sussex, Horsham 1948
9–43 GE Tribe v Worcs, Northampton 1958
9–45 GE Tribe v Yorks, Bradford 1955
9–64 GJ Thompson v Derbys, Northampton 1906
9–66 RJ Partridge v Warwicks, Kettering 1934

FIFTEEN OR MORE WICKETS IN A MATCH
15–31 GE Tribe v Yorks, Northampton 1958
15–52 VWC Jupp v Glamorgan, Swansea 1925
15–75 GE Tribe v Yorks, Bradford 1955
15–167 GJ Thompson v Leics, Northampton 1906

WICKET KEEPING

MOST DISMISSALS IN AN INNINGS
7 (7ct) KV Andrew v Lancs, Old Trafford 1962
6 (6ct) KC James v Glamorgan, Swansea 1937
6 (5ct 1st) LA Johnson v Warwicks, Edgbaston 1965
6 (6ct) DA Ripley v Sussex, Northampton 1988

MOST DISMISSALS IN A MATCH
10 (10ct) LA Johnson v Sussex, Worthing 1963
10 (8ct 2st) LA Johnson v Warwicks, Edgbaston 1965

MOST DISMISSALS IN A SEASON
87 (81ct 6st) KV Andrew 1962
72 (66ct 6st) DA Ripley 1988

MOST CAREER DISMISSALS
766 (624ct 142st) KV Andrew 1953–66

NOTTINGHAMSHIRE

Formed: March/April 1841
Entered official Championship: 1890
Winners: 1907, 1929, 1981, 1987

INNINGS TOTALS

HIGHEST BY THE COUNTY
739-7 dec v Leicestershire, Trent Bridge 1903
726 v Sussex, Trent Bridge 1895
674 v Sussex, Hove 1893
662-8 dec v Essex, Trent Bridge 1947
661 v Derbyshire, Derby 1901

HIGHEST AGAINST THE COUNTY
706-4 dec by Surrey, Trent Bridge 1947
643-5 dec by Gloucestershire, Bristol 1946
636 by Gloucestershire, Trent Bridge 1904
634 by Gloucestershire, Bristol 1898
627 by Lancashire, Trent Bridge 1905

LOWEST BY THE COUNTY
13 v Yorkshire, Trent Bridge 1901
34 v Warwickshire, Nuneaton 1964
35 v Lancashire, Trent Bridge 1895
38 v Yorkshire, Trent Bridge 1893
39 v Yorkshire, Sheffield (BL) 1905

LOWEST AGAINST THE COUNTY
30 by Derbyshire, Chesterfield 1913
30 by Hampshire, Southampton 1932
32 by Derbyshire, Chesterfield 1904
37 by Lancashire, Liverpool 1907
38 by Northamptonshire, Trent Bridge 1920

George Gunn (left) and brother John, two members of the four-pronged Notts 'Battery', talk over old times at Trent Bridge (Hulton Picture Company)

PARTNERSHIPS

COUNTY BEST FOR EACH WICKET

1st
391 AO Jones & A Shrewsbury v Gloucs, Bristol 1899
318 RT Simpson & WW Keeton v Lancs, Old Trafford 1949
2nd
398 A Shrewsbury & W Gunn v Sussex, Trent Bridge 1890
333 AW Carr & GM Lee v Leics, Trent Bridge 1913
3rd
369 W Gunn & JR Gunn v Leics, Trent Bridge 1903
266 CB Harris & J Hardstaff jnr v Gloucs, Trent Bridge 1936
4th
361 AO Jones & JR Gunn v Leics, Trent Bridge 1903
345 M Newell & DW Randall v Derbys, Trent Bridge 1988
5th
247 J Hardstaff jnr & A Staples v Middlesex, Trent Bridge 1937
246* MJ Smedley & GS Sobers v Glamorgan, Swansea 1971
6th
303* FH Winrow & PF Harvey v Derbys, Trent Bridge 1947
270 RT Simpson & A Jepson v Worcs, Trent Bridge 1950
7th
204 MJ Smedley & RA White v Surrey, Oval 1967
201 RH Howitt & R Bagguley v Sussex, Trent Bridge 1895
8th
220 GFH Heane & R Winrow v Somerset, Trent Bridge 1935
167 WRD Payton & TW Oates v Kent, Trent Bridge 1920
167 A Staples & F Barratt v Surrey, Trent Bridge 1928
9th
131 WRD Payton & AW Hallam v Surrey, Oval 1907
10th
152 EB Alletson & W Riley v Sussex, Hove 1911
140 SJ Staples & TL Richmond v Derbys, Worksop 1922

INDIVIDUAL BATTING

OVER 8000 CHAMPIONSHIP RUNS IN COUNTY CAREER

		Inns	NO	Runs	HS	Avge	100s
George Gunn	1902–32	874	73	29522	220	36.85	52
WW Keeton	1926–52	598	39	22729	242	40.66	53
J Hardstaff, jnr	1930–55	592	63	22585	266	42.69	59
RT Simpson	1946–63	594	42	21708	243*	39.32	45
JR Gunn	1896–1925	718	87	21588	294	34.21	37
WRD Payton	1905–31	708	113	20500	169	34.45	37
WW Whysall	1920–30	527	42	18944	248	39.05	45
DW Randall	1972–90	561	49	18898	237	36.91	29
AO Jones	1892–1914	594	32	18888	296	33.60	28
CB Harris	1928–51	568	59	17734	239*	34.84	29
CJ Poole	1948–62	586	38	17392	219	31.73	22
AW Carr	1910–34	584	39	17292	206	31.72	39
W Walker	1913–37	568	57	16678	165*	32.63	28
CEB Rice	1975–87	437	64	16459	246	44.12	37
MJ Smedley	1964–79	555	67	15263	149	31.27	26
J Iremonger	1899–1914	464	54	14927	272	36.40	29
JB Bolus	1963–72	451	39	14388	202*	34.92	24
J Hardstaff, snr	1903–24	517	65	14126	213*	31.25	21
MJ Harris	1969–82	402	38	13950	201*	38.32	33
B Hassan	1967–85	503	45	13161	182*	28.73	12
NW Hill	1953–68	477	31	12798	201*	28.69	21
RT Robinson	1978–90	357	46	12726	220*	40.91	28
W Gunn	1890–1904	338	24	12437	273	39.60	30
A Staples	1924–38	462	52	11087	131	27.04	10
A Shrewsbury	1890–1902	291	32	11079	267	42.77	29
FW Stocks	1946–57	411	43	10742	166	29.19	12
JD Clay	1948–61	379	17	9609	192	26.54	11
B Lilley	1921–37	464	75	9433	124	24.24	5
GV Gunn	1928–50	358	38	9300	147*	29.06	9
BC Broad	1984–90	236	17	9006	227*	41.12	20
M Hill	1953–65	375	32	8677	-137*	25.29	7

Joe Hardstaff followed his father as a Notts and England batsman; his early form confirmed his ability to hold his own with the very best in county cricket (Hulton Picture Company)

MOST RUNS IN A SEASON

Runs	(Avge)		Season
2458	(54.62)	WW Whysall	1928
2230	(69.68)	J Hardstaff, jnr	1947
2226	(54.29)	BC Broad	1990
2079	(54.71)	WW Whysall	1929
2033	(52.12)	JB Bolus	1970
2029	(47.18)	WW Keeton	1933
1977	(50.69)	MJ Harris	1971
1977	(50.69)	DW Randall	1985
1954	(45.44)	WW Keeton	1946
1948	(39.75)	NW Hill	1959
1944	(55.54)	WW Keeton	1949
1906	(68.07)	RT Simpson	1949
1889	(44.97)	WW Keeton	1937
1873	(85.13)	RT Simpson	1950
1872	(69.33)	J Hardstaff, jnr	1949
1866	(47.84)	WW Whysall	1930
1866	(43.39)	CB Harris	1937
1860	(41.33)	RT Simpson	1959
1851	(43.04)	WW Whysall	1926
1845	(41.93)	MJ Harris	1970
1834	(39.02)	NW Hill	1961
1826	(45.65)	WW Whysall	1927
1818	(55.09)	J Hardstaff, jnr	1939
1815	(56.71)	RT Simpson	1953
1815	(53.38)	AW Carr	1925
1813	(40.28)	CB Harris	1934
1812	(60.40)	J Iremonger	1904
1802	(66.74)	J Hardstaff, jnr	1937
1802	(46.20)	WW Keeton	1934
1802	(42.90)	George Gunn	1928

DOUBLE CENTURIES
312* WW Keeton v Middlesex, Oval 1939
296 AO Jones V Gloucestershire, Trent Bridge 1903
294 JR Gunn v Leicestershire, Trent Bridge 1903
274 AO Jones v Essex, Leyton 1905
273 W Gunn v Derbyshire, Derby 1901
272 J Iremonger v Kent, Trent Bridge 1904
268* JA Dixon v Sussex, Trent Bridge 1897
267 A Shrewsbury v Sussex, Trent Bridge 1890
266 J Hardstaff jnr v Leicestershire, Leicester AR 1937
261 WW Keeton v Gloucestershire, Trent Bridge 1934
250 AO Jones v Gloucestershire, Bristol 1899
249 AO Jones v Sussex, Hove 1901
248 WW Whysall v Northamptonshire, Trent Bridge 1930
247 J Hardstaff jnr v Northamptonshire, Trent Bridge 1951
246 CEB Rice v Sussex, Hove 1976

244 WW Whysall v Gloucestershire, Trent Bridge 1929
243* RT Simpson v Worcestershire, Trent Bridge 1950
243 J Hardstaff jnr v Middlesex, Trent Bridge 1937
242 WW Keeton v Glamorgan, Trent Bridge 1932
239* CB Harris v Hampshire, Trent Bridge 1950
239 J Iremonger v Essex, Trent Bridge 1905
238 RT Simpson v Lancashire, Old Trafford 1949
237 DW Randall v Derbyshire, Trent Bridge 1988
236* W Gunn v Surrey, Oval 1898
234 CB Harris v Middlesex, Trent Bridge 1933
230* RT Simpson v Glamorgan, Swansea 1950
230 W Gunn v Derbyshire, Trent Bridge 1897
227* BC Broad v Kent, Tunbridge Wells 1990
223 WW Keeton v Worcestershire, Worksop 1934
221* J Hardstaff jnr v Warwickshire, Trent Bridge 1947
220 G Gunn v Derbyshire, Trent Bridge 1923
219 W Gunn v Sussex, Trent Bridge 1895
219 CJ Poole v Derbyshire, Ilkeston 1952
216 RT Simpson v Sussex, Trent Bridge 1952
214* J Hardstaff jnr v Somerset, Trent Bridge 1937
213* J Hardstaff snr v Sussex, Hove 1913
213* CEB Rice v Lancashire, Trent Bridge 1978
213 CEB Rice v Glamorgan, Swansea 1978
212 RT Simpson v Essex, Clacton 1951
212 A Shrewsbury v Middlesex, Lord's 1892
210* RJ Hadlee v Middlesex, Lord's 1984
210 J Iremonger v Kent, Trent Bridge 1903
210 WW Keeton v Yorkshire, Sheffield (BL) 1949
209 WW Whysall v Essex, Leyton 1926
209 DW Randall v Middlesex, Trent Bridge 1979
208 WW Keeton v Glamorgan, Trent Bridge 1949
207* W Gunn v Derbyshire, Derby 1896
207 RT Robinson v Warwickshire, Trent Bridge 1983
206 AW Carr v Leicestershire, Leicester (AR) 1925
204* FH Winrow v Derbyshire, Trent Bridge 1947
204* DW Randall v Somerset, Trent Bridge 1976
204 AW Carr v Essex, Leyton 1921
203* M Newell v Derbyshire, Derby 1987
202* JB Bolus v Glamorgan, Trent Bridge 1963
202 J Hardstaff jnr v Worcestershire, Dudley 1947
201* NW Hill v Sussex, Shireoaks 1961
201* MJ Harris v Glamorgan, Trent Bridge 1973
201 RT Simpson v Warwickshire, Trent Bridge 1946
200* J Iremonger v Gloucestershire, Trent Bridge 1906
200* GM Lee v Leicestershire, Trent Bridge 1913
200* J Hardstaff jnr v Somerset, Trent Bridge 1947
200* RT Simpson v Surrey, Trent Bridge 1949
200 RT Simpson v Warwickshire, Trent Bridge 1952

Walter Keeton, whose innings of 312 not out against Middlesex at the Oval in 1939 is still a record for the county. Ten years later, Keeton scored a double century aged 44 – the oldest age for a Notts player (Hulton Picture Company)

INDIVIDUAL BOWLING

OVER 400 CHAMPIONSHIP WICKETS IN COUNTY CAREER

		Runs	Wkts	Avge
TG Wass	1897–1920	30790	1517	20.29
W Voce	1927–52	27087	1218	22.23
SJ Staples	1920–34	26820	1184	22.65
H Larwood	1924–38	18855	1157	16.29
F Barratt	1914–31	25218	1119	22.53
TL Richmond	1912–28	22262	1094	20.34
JR Gunn	1896–1925	25643	1061	24.16
A Jepson	1938–59	29248	1016	28.78
HJ Butler	1933–54	21265	900	23.62
B Dooland	1953–57	13653	741	18.42
EE Hemmings	1979–90	20193	735	27.47
W Attewell	1890–99	12435	726	17.12
AW Hallam	1901–10	13163	684	19.24
C Forbes	1961–72	16267	649	25.07
KE Cooper	1976–90	17833	645	27.64
RA White	1966–80	19586	639	30.65
RJ Hadlee	1978–87	8748	603	14.50
B Stead	1965–76	15988	569	28.09
A Staples	1924–38	16924	569	29.74
J Iremonger	1899–1914	12352	556	22.21
IJ Davison	1959–66	14385	498	28.88
MNS Taylor	1964–72	13751	493	27.89
CEB Rice	1975–87	10875	453	24.00

MOST WICKETS IN A SEASON

Wkts	(Avge)		Season
179	(14.58)	B Dooland	1954
169	(13.48)	TL Richmond	1922
153	(11.78)	AW Hallam	1907
152	(16.06)	B Dooland	1953
146	(20.69)	TL Richmond	1926
145	(13.57)	TG Wass	1908
145	(19.20)	TL Richmond	1920
142	(22.15)	B Dooland	1955
141	(11.62)	H Larwood	1932
139	(18.61)	B Dooland	1956
138	(15.32)	TG Wass	1902
133	(21.19)	W Voce	1935
129	(22.22)	B Dooland	1957
127	(19.83)	W Voce	1936
124	(24.83)	TL Richmond	1921
123	(22.61)	SJ Staples	1927

NINE OR MORE WICKETS IN AN INNINGS
10–66   K Smales v Gloucs, Stroud 1956
9–21   TL Richmond v Hants, Trent Bridge 1922
9–41   H Larwood v Kent, Trent Bridge 1931
9–50   FC Matthews v Northants, Trent Bridge 1923
9–54   RJ Mee v Sussex, Trent Bridge 1893
9–55   TL Richmond v Northants, Trent Bridge 1925
9–67   TG Wass v Derbys, Blackwell 1911
9–91   TG Wass v Surrey, Oval 1902
9–141   SJ Staples v Kent, Canterbury 1927

FIFTEEN OR MORE WICKETS IN A MATCH
17–89   FC Matthews v Notts, Trent Bridge 1923
16–69   TG Wass v Lancs, Liverpool 1906
16–83   B Dooland v Essex, Trent Bridge 1954
16–103   TG Wass v Essex, Trent Bridge 1908
15–193   B Dooland v Kent, Gravesend 1956

WICKET KEEPING

MOST DISMISSALS IN AN INNINGS
6 (6ct)   TW Oates v Middlesex, Trent Bridge 1906
6 (6ct)   TW Oates v Leices, Leicester 1907
6 (6ct)   B Lilley v Somerset, Taunton 1932
6 (5ct 1st)   EA Meads v Derbs, Ilkeston 1948
6 (5ct 1st)   EA Meads v Kent, Trent Bridge 1949
6 (5ct 1st)   G Millman v Northans, Trent Bridge 1959
6 (6ct)   BN French v Essex, Trent Bridge 1982
6 (6ct)   BN French v Somerset, Taunton 1984
6 (6ct)   BN French v Derbys, Trent Bridge 1985

MOST DISMISSALS IN A MATCH
10 (9ct 1st)   TW Oates v Middlesex, Trent Bridge 1906
10 (10ct)   CW Scott v Derbys, Derby 1988

MOST DISMISSALS IN A SEASON
80 (51ct 29st) B Lilley 1926
74 (71ct   3st) G Millman 1961

MOST CAREER DISMISSALS
915 (702ct 213st) TW Oates 1897–1925

SOMERSET
Formed: 18 August 1875
Entered official Championship: 1891
Highest placing: 3rd in 1892, 1958, 1963, 1966, 1981

INNINGS TOTALS

HIGHEST BY THE COUNTY
675–9 dec v Hampshire, Bath 1924
630 v Yorkshire, Headingley 1901
592 v Yorkshire, Taunton 1892
584–8 dec v Sussex, Eastbourne 1948
566–5 dec v Warwickshire, Taunton 1985

HIGHEST AGAINST THE COUNTY
811 by Surrey, Oval 1899
801 by Lancashire, Taunton 1895
692 by Essex, Taunton 1895
672–7 dec by Hampshire, Taunton 1899
642–9 dec by Hampshire, Taunton 1901

LOWEST BY THE COUNTY
25 v Gloucestershire, Bristol 1947
31 v Lancashire, Old Trafford 1894
31 v Gloucestershire, Bristol 1931
33 v Lancashire, Liverpool 1908
35 v Yorkshire, Bath 1898
35 v Middlesex, Lord's 1899
35 v Derbyshire, Derby 1935

LOWEST AGAINST THE COUNTY
22 by Gloucestershire, Bristol 1920
25 by Gloucestershire, Cheltenham 1891
35 by Surrey, Oval 1937
37 by Gloucestershire, Taunton 1907
37 by Derbyshire, Bath 1919

PARTNERSHIPS

COUNTY BEST FOR EACH WICKET
1st
346 HT Hewett & LCH Palairet v Yorks, Taunton 1892
273* NA Felton & PM Roebuck v Hants, Taunton 1986
2nd
290 JCW MacBryan & MD Lyon v Derbys, Buxton 1924
251 JCW MacBryan & A Young v Glamorgan, Taunton 1933
3rd
319 PM Roebuck & MD Crowe v Leics, Taunton 1984
300 GG Atkinson & PB Wight v. Glamorgan, Bath 1960
4th
310 PW Denning & IT Botham v Gloucs, Taunton 1980
251 IVA Richards & PM Roebuck v Surrey, Weston-super-Mare 1977
5th
235 JC White & CCC Case v Gloucs, Taunton 1927
227 IVA Richards & DB Close v Yorks, Harrogate 1975
6th
265 WE Alley & KE Palmer v Northants, Northampton 1961
213 ND Burns & GD Rose v Gloucs, Taunton 1990
7th
240 SMJ Woods & VT Hill v Kent, Taunton 1898
189 JC White & RA Ingle v Hants, Southampton 1935
8th
172 IVA Richards & IT Botham v Leics, Leicester 1983
143* EF Longrigg & CJP Barnwell v Gloucs, Bristol 1938
9th
183 CMH Greetham & HW Stephenson v Leics, Weston-super-Mare 1963
179* NFM Popplewell & D Breakwell v Kent, Taunton 1980
10th
143 JF Bridges & AHD Gibbs v Essex, Weston-super-Mare 1919
139 PR Johnson & RC Robertson-Glasgow v Surrey, Oval 1926

The granite-like Brian Close kept his adopted county firmly on its way towards cricket's top echelons. A legend in his own lifetime, his years of service with Yorkshire and Somerset were punctuated by disputes, but he was a doughty competitor and a natural winner (Hulton Picture Company)

INDIVIDUAL BATTING

OVER 8000 CHAMPIONSHIP RUNS IN COUNTY CAREER

		Inns	NO	Runs	HS	Avge	100s
H Gimblett	1935–54	568	28	19966	310	36.97	45
PB Wight	1954–65	535	48	15964	222*	32.78	25
WE Alley	1957–68	567	54	15584	221*	30.37	23
FS Lee	1929–47	556	35	14624	162	28.06	22
RT Virgin	1957–72	534	23	14570	179*	28.51	20
MF Tremlett	1947–60	594	43	14540	185	26.38	15
PM Roebuck	1974–90	442	64	14418	221*	38.14	26
IVA Richards	1974–86	300	17	14275	322	50.44	46
MJ Kitchen	1960–79	566	37	14226	161*	26.89	16
GG Atkinson	1954–66	453	29	13569	190	32.00	20
LCH Palairet	1891–1909	373	14	12898	292	35.92	26
A Young	1911–33	517	22	12884	198	26.02	11
SMJ Woods	1891–1910	479	18	11654	215	25.27	17
BC Rose	1969–87	386	41	11638	205	33.73	22
E Robson	1891–1923	688	43	11491	111	17.81	4
LC Braund	1900–20	480	33	11198	257*	25.05	11
JC White	1909–37	646	71	10878	192	18.91	6
AW Wellard	1929–50	593	39	10863	112	19.60	2
PW Denning	1969–84	418	40	10547	184	27.90	8
HTF Buse	1929–53	495	50	10044	132	22.57	7
PR Johnson	1902–27	397	16	9870	164	25.90	17
JL Daniel	1898–1927	468	47	9387	174*	22.29	8
VJ Marks	1975–89	374	75	9232	134	30.87	4
RA Ingle	1923–39	479	17	8682	119*	18.79	9
J Lawrence	1946–55	472	47	8585	122	20.20	2
IT Botham	1974–86	248	19	8262	228	36.07	16
CCC Case	1925–35	400	32	8032	155	21.82	9

MOST RUNS IN A SEASON

Runs	(Avge)		Season
2532	(56.26)	WE Alley	1961
2432	(76.00)	SJ Cook	1990
2223	(47.29)	RT Virgin	1970
2173	(62.08)	SJ Cook	1989
2090	(67.41)	IVA Richards	1978
2086	(40.11)	PB Wight	1960
2068	(39.76)	H Gimblett	1952
2018	(38.80)	MF Tremlett	1951
2015	(46.86)	FS Lee	1938
1951	(35.87)	GG Atkinson	1962
1892	(37.84)	GG Atkinson	1961
1839	(42.76)	H Gimblett	1949
1836	(76.50)	IVA Richards	1985
1836	(40.80)	H Gimblett	1953
1830	(33.88)	MF Tremlett	1955

DOUBLE CENTURIES
322 IVA Richards v Warwickshire, Taunton 1985
313* SJ Cook v Glamorgan, Cardiff 1990
310 H Gimblett v Sussex, Eastbourne 1948
292 LCH Palairet v Hampshire, Southampton 1896
264 MM Walford v Hampshire, Weston-super-Mare 1947
257 LC Braund v Worcestershire, Worcester 1913
241* IVA Richards v Gloucestershire, Bristol 1977
231 H Gimblett v Middlesex, Taunton 1946
228 IT Botham v Gloucestershire, Taunton 1980
222* PB Wight v Kent, Taunton 1959
221* WE Alley v Warwickshire, Nueaton (G&C) 1961
221* PM Roebuck v Nottinghamshire, Trent Bridge 1986
219 MD Lyon v Derbyshire, Burton-on-Trent 1924
219 CJ Tavare v Sussex, Hove 1990
217* IVA Richards v Yorkshire, Harrogate 1975
216 IVA Richards v Leicestershire, Leicester (GR) 1983
215 SMJ Woods v Sussex, Hove 1895
215 PB Wight v Yorkshire, Taunton 1962
210 MD Lyon v Gloucestershire, Taunton 1930
206* MD Crowe v Warwickshire, Edgbaston 1987
205 EF Longrigg v Leicestershire, Taunton 1930
205 BC Rose v Northamptonshire, Weston-super-Mare 1977
204 IVA Richards v Sussex, Hove 1977
204 IVA Richards v Surrey, Weston-super-Mare 1977
203 LCH Palairet v Worcestershire, Worcester 1904
202* RJO Meyer v Lancashire, Taunton 1936
201* PM Roebuck v Worcestershire, Worcester 1990

201 AE Lewis v Kent, Taunton 1909
201 HT Hewett v Yorkshire, Taunton 1892

B Cranfield	1897–1908	13001	523	24.85
FE Rumsey	1966–78	9745	503	19.37
SMJ Woods	1891–1910	12278	503	24.40
HR Moseley	1971–82	12246	502	24.39
AE Lewis	1899–1914	11548	495	23.32
JW Lee	1927–36	13866	471	29.43
IT Botham	1974–86	12186	460	26.49
GI Burgess	1966–78	12518	433	28.90
WT Greswell	1908–30	-9271	420	22.07
CH Dredge	1976–88	12669	420	30.16

MOST WICKETS IN A SEASON

Wkts	(Avge)		Season
167	(18.59)	AW Wellard	1938
149	(14.63)	JC White	1929
146	(14.60)	JC White	1922
141	(15.43)	JC White	1923
138	(22.87)	AW Wellard	1937
137	(15.56)	JC White	1921
135	(14.34)	JC White	1924
134	(18.17)	AW Wellard	1936
131	(19.45)	WHR Andrews	1937
130	(14.45)	JC White	1920
128	(19.15)	JC White	1928
128	(20.36)	JC White	1931
127	(19.08)	JC White	1926
122	(21.27)	WHR Andrews	1938
121	(16.00)	KE Palmer	1963
121	(16.53)	JC White	1925

NINE OR MORE WICKETS IN AN INNINGS

10–49 EJ Tyler v Surrey, Taunton 1895
10–76 JC White v Worcs, Worcester 1921
9–26 BA Langford v Lancs, Weston-super-Mare 1958
9–33 EJ Tyler v Notts, Taunton 1892
9–38 RC Robertson-Glasgow v Middlesex, Lord's 1924
9–41 LC Braund v Yorks, Sheffield 1902
9–46 JC White v Gloucs, Bristol 1914
9–51 JC White v Glamorgan, Bath 1932
9–51 AA Jones v Sussex, Hove 1972
9–57 KE Palmer v Notts, Trent Bridge 1963
9–58 JC White v Warwicks, Edgbaston 1922
9–62 WT Greswell v Hants, Weston-super-Mare 1928
9–71 JC White v Sussex, Eastbourne 1931
9–83 EJ Tyler v Sussex, Hastings 1907

FIFTEEN OR MORE WICKETS IN A MATCH

16–83 JC White v Worcs, Bath 1919
15–54 BA Langford v Lancs, Weston-super-Mare 1958
15–71 LC Braund v Yorks, Sheffield 1902
15–78 EP Robinson v Sussex, Weston-super-Mare 1951
15–95 EJ Tyler v Sussex, Taunton 1895
19–96 EJ Tyler v Notts, Trent Bridge 1892
15–96 JC White v Glamorgan, Bath 1932
15–101 AW Wellard v Worcs, Bath 1947
15–175 JC White v Worcs, Worcester 1921

Maurice Tremlett, originally a pace bowler of promise, then a fine, forcing batsman, became skipper of Somerset and took them off the bottom of the table in 1956, after four seasons in 17th place. Tremlett's four-year reign saw great improvement for the side (Hulton Picture Company)

INDIVIDUAL BOWLING

OVER 400 CHAMPIONSHIP WICKETS IN COUNTY CAREER

		Runs	Wkts	Avge
JC White	1909–37	37184	2082	17.85
AW Wellard	1929–50	34614	1415	24.46
BA Langford	1953–74	32633	1346	24.24
E Robson	1891–1923	28057	1039	27.00
HL Hazell	1929–52	21335	905	23.57
KE Palmer	1955–69	16763	801	20.92
EJ Tyler	1891–1907	17747	799	22.21
J Lawrence	1946–55	18431	745	24.73
WE Alley	1957–68	15673	720	21.76
VJ Marks	1975–89	22957	704	32.60
WHR Andrews	1930–47	16504	701	23.54
JF Bridges	1911–29	16693	647	25.80
LC Braund	1900–20	18007	643	28.00
HTF Buse	1929–53	18394	637	28.87

WICKET KEEPING

MOST DISMISSALS IN AN INNINGS

6 (5ct 1st) HW Stephenson v Glamorgan, Bath 1962
6 (6ct) G Clayton v Worcs, Kidderminster 1965
6 (6ct) DJS Taylor v Essex, Taunton 1981
6 (6ct) DJS Taylor v Hants, Bath 1982

MOST DISMISSALS IN A MATCH

9 (6ct 3st) AE Newton v Middlesex, Lord's 1901
9 (8ct 1st) HW Stephenson v Yorks, Taunton 1963

MOST DISMISSALS IN A SEASON

85 (71ct 14st) G Clayton 1965
83 (49ct 34st) HW Stephenson 1954
83 (73ct 10st) G Clayton 1966

MOST CAREER DISMISSALS

945 (656ct 289st) HW Stephenson 1948–64

SURREY

Formed: 22 August 1845
Entered official Championship: 1890
Winners: 1890, 1891, 1892, 1894, 1895, 1899,
1914, 1950 (joint), 1952, 1953. 1954.
1955, 1956, 1957, 1958, 1971

INNINGS TOTALS

HIGHEST BY THE COUNTY
811 v Somerset, Oval 1899
742 v Hampshire, Oval 1909
707-9 dec v Lancashire, Oval 1990
706-4 dec v Nottinghamshire, Trent Bridge 1947
634 v Lancashire, Oval 1898

HIGHEST AGAINST THE COUNTY
863-9 dec by Lancashire, Oval 1990
705-8 dec by Sussex, Hastings 1902
704 by Yorkshire, Oval 1899
616-5 dec by Essex, Oval 1904
600-7 dec by Sussex, Oval 1903

LOWEST BY THE COUNTY
14 v Essex, Chelmsford 1983
35 v Somerset, Oval 1937
50 v Glamorgan, Cardiff 1948
58 v Northamptonshire, Oval 1913

LOWEST AGAINST THE COUNTY
25 by Worcestershire, Oval 1954
26 by Yorkshire, Oval 1909
27 by Lancashire, Old Trafford 1958
31 by Glamorgan, Oval 1957
32 by Northamptonshire, Oval 1905

Andrew Sandham was doomed to spending much of his
career in the shadow of Jack Hobbs at the Oval. However, as
his record shows, he was a fine batsman in his own right
(Hulton Picture Company)

PARTNERSHIPS

COUNTY BEST FOR EACH WICKET
1st
379 R Abel & W Brockwell v Hants, Oval 1897
364 R Abel & DLA Jephson v Derbys, Oval 1900
2nd
371 JB Hobbs & EG Hayes v Hants, Oval 1909
344 A Sandham & RJ Gregory v Glamorgan, Oval 1937
3rd
353 A Ducat & EG Hayes v Hants, Southampton 1919
317 A Ducat & TF Shepherd v Essex, Leyton 1928
4th
448 R Abel & TW Hayward v Yorks, Oval 1899
334 R Abel & TW Hayward v Somerset, Oval 1899
5th
208 JN Crawford & FC Holland v Somerset, Oval 1908
288 HA Peach & A Ducat v Northants, Northampton 1920
6th
298 A Sandham & HS Harrison v Sussex, Oval 1913
294 DR Jardine & PGH Fender v Yorks, Bradford 1928
7th
262 CJ Richards & KT Medlycott v Kent, Oval 1987
200 TF Shepherd & JW Hitch v Kent, Blackheath 1921
8th
205 IA Greig & MP Bicknell v Lancs, Oval 1990
204 TW Hayward & LC Braund v Lancs, Oval 1898
9th
168 ERT Holmes & EWJ Brooks v Hants, Oval 1936
161 GJ Whittaker & WS Surridge v Glamorgan, Oval 1951
10th
173 A Ducat & A Sandham v Essex, Leyton 1921
172 A Needham & RD Jackman v Lancs, Old Trafford 1982

INDIVIDUAL BATTING

OVER 8000 CHAMPIONSHIP RUNS IN COUNTY CAREER

		Inns	NO	Runs	HS	Avge	100s
JB Hobbs	1905–34	860	69	38707	316*	48.93	130
TW Hayward	1893–1914	804	64	30971	315*	41.85	78
A Sandham	1911–37	738	65	28961	292*	43.03	68
JH Edrich	1958–78	637	71	25740	226*	45.47	67
EG Hayes	1896–1919	693	38	21706	276	33.13	41
MJ Stewart	1954–72	727	76	20905	227*	32.11	40
A Ducat	1906–31	577	49	19738	290*	37.38	45
LB Fishlock	1933–52	514	36	19228	253	40.22	45
R Abel	1890–1904	471	34	19085	357*	43.67	52
HS Squires	1928–49	553	37	16129	236	31.25	31
RJ Gregory	1925–47	533	70	15848	243	34.22	30
KF Barrington	1953–68	477	81	15789	207	39.87	33
TH Barling	1927–48	509	43	15662	269	33.60	26
TF Shepherd	1919–32	447	53	15622	277*	39.64	34
B Constable	1939–64	570	67	14953	205*	29.72	19
GRJ Roope	1965–82	516	110	14842	171	36.55	20
AR Butcher	1972–86	446	40	13224	188	32.57	24
Younis Ahmed	1967–78	410	57	13020	183*	36.88	17
PGH Fender	1914–35	506	49	12688	189*	27.76	15
MA Lynch	1977–90	381	47	12257	172*	36.69	27
JF Parker	1932–52	452	60	12120	204*	30.91	16
EA Bedser	1946–61	551	66	11720	163	24.16	5
DGW Fletcher	1947–61	409	30	11657	194	30.75	18
PBH May	1950–63	278	42	11440	211*	48.47	30
GS Clinton	1979–90	375	48	10993	192	33.61	18
W Brockwell	1890–1903	388	41	9969	225	28.72	17
SJ Storey	1960–74	417	50	9487	164	25.85	10
TH Clark	1947–59	356	30	9433	191	28.93	8
AJW McIntyre	1938–63	456	63	9289	143*	23.63	6
MJ Edwards	1961–74	374	19	9090	121	25.60	8
GP Howarth	1972–84	301	19	8590	183	30.46	17
FC Holland	1895–1908	361	25	8355	153	24.80	10
RDV Knight	1968–84	275	27	8127	142	32.77	11
AJ Stewart	1981–90	233	28	8032	206*	39.18	14

Tom Hayward, whose 2814 runs in a season for Surrey constituted a Championship record which lasted for 22 years. He was originally regarded as an all-rounder (Allsport)

MOST RUNS IN A SEASON

Runs	(Avge)		Season
2814	(70.35)	TW Hayward	1906
2499	(62.47)	JB Hobbs	1914
2264	(50.31)	R Abel	1901
2238	(52.04)	JB Hobbs	1913
2134	(64.66)	R Abel	1899
2084	(61.29)	JB Hobbs	1925
2077	(47.20)	LB Fishlock	1950
2074	(50.58)	TW Hayward	1904
2056	(57.11)	A Sandham	1925
2039	(58.25)	TW Hayward	1901
2038	(56.61)	A Sandham	1929
2026	(46.04)	LB Fishlock	1949
1968	(63.48)	JB Hobbs	1922
1963	(50.33)	TW Hayward	1911
1963	(50.33)	LB Fishlock	1946
1935	(53.75)	JB Hobbs	1920
1913	(56.26)	A Sandham	1928
1913	(46.65)	JH Edrich	1966
1889	(49.71)	RJ Gregory	1937
1884	(50.91)	A Sandham	1930
1880	(58.75)	R Abel	1900
1874	(46.85)	TW Hayward	1908
1850	(50.00)	TW Hayward	1900
1844	(39.23)	EG Hayes	1909
1843	(76.79)	DM Ward	1990

1835	(50.97)	RJ Gregory	1934
1833	(50.91)	R Abel	1897
1832	(57.25)	R Abel	1898
1826	(55.33)	A Sandham	1921

DOUBLE CENTURIES

357* R Abel v Somerset, Oval 1899
316* JB Hobbs v Middlesex, Lord's 1926
315* TW Hayward v Lancashire, Oval 1898
292* A Sandham v Northamptonshire, Oval 1921
291 IA Greig v Lancashire, Oval 1990
290* A Ducat v Essex, Leyton 1921
282* A Sandham v Lancashire, Old Trafford 1928
277* TF Shepherd v Gloucestershire, Oval 1927
276 EG Hayes v Hampshire, Oval 1909
273* EG Hayes v Derbyshire, Derby 1904
273 TW Hayward v Yorkshire, Oval 1899
271 A Ducat v Hampshire, Southampton 1919
269 TH Barling v Hampshire, Southampton 1933
263 DM Ward v Kent, Canterbury 1990
253 LB Fishlock v Leicestershire, Leicester (GR) 1948
250 R Abel v Warwickshire, Oval 1897
248* A Sandham v Glamorgan, Cardiff 1928
243 RJ Gregory v Somerset, Oval 1938
239 A Sandham v Glamorgan, Oval 1937
236 HS Squires v Lancashire, Oval 1933
235 A Ducat v Leicestershire, Oval 1926
234 C Baldwin v Kent, Oval 1897
233* HT Barling v Nottinghamshire, Oval 1946
232 JN Crawford v Somerset, Oval 1908
231 R Abel v Essex, Oval 1896
230 A Sandham v Essex, Oval 1927
229* TW Hayward v Derbyshire, Derby 1896
227* MJ Stewart v Middlesex, Oval 1964
226* JH Edrich v Middlesex, Oval 1967
226 JB Hobbs v Nottinghamshire, Oval 1914
225 W Brockwell v Hampshire, Oval 1897
221 R Abel v Worcestershire, Oval 1900
221 TE Jesty v Essex, Oval 1986
219 R Abel v Kent, Oval 1898
219 TW Hayward v Northamptonshire, Oval 1906
218 A Ducat v Nottinghamshire, Trent Bridge 1930
217 R Abel v Essex, Oval 1895
216 JH Edrich v Nottinghamshire, Trent Bridge 1962
215 R Abel v Nottinghamshire, Oval 1897
215 JB Hobbs v Essex, Leyton 1914
215 JB Hobbs v Warwickshire, Edgbaston 1925
215 A Sandham v Somerset, Taunton 1932
213 DLA Jephson v Derbyshire, Oval 1900
212 TF Shepherd v Lancashire, Oval 1921
212 FR Brown v Middlesex, Oval 1932
211 PBH May v Nottinghamshire, Trent Bridge 1954
210* TF Shepherd v Kent, Blackheath 1921
210 HS Squires v Derbyshire, Oval 1949
210 LB Fishlock v Somerset, Oval 1949
209* A Sandham v Somerset, Oval 1921
208 TW Hayward v Warwickshire, Oval 1906
208 A Ducat v Essex, Leyton 1928
207* TF Shepherd v Kent, Blackheath 1925
207 KF Barrington v Nottinghamshire, Oval 1964
206* AJ Stewart v Essex, Oval 1989
206 ERT Holmes v Derbyshire, Chesterfield 1935
205* R Abel v Middlesex, Oval 1901
205* B Constable v Somerset, Oval 1952
205* JH Edrich v Gloucestershire, Bristol 1965
205 JB Hobbs v Hampshire, Oval 1909
204* TW Hayward v Warwickshire, Oval 1909
204* A Ducat v Northamptonshire, Northampton 1921
204* JF Parker v Derbyshire, Oval 1947
204 JB Hobbs v Somerset, Oval 1929
204 A Sandham v Warwickshire, Edgbaston 1930
203* JB Hobbs v Nottinghamshire, Trent Bridge 1924
203 A Ducat v Sussex, Oval 1920
202 EG Hayes v Middlesex, Oval 1907
202 TW Hayward v Derbyshire, Oval 1911
202 JB Hobbs v Yorkshire, Lord's 1914
201* A Jeacocke v Sussex, Oval 1922
200* HA Peach v Northamptonshire, Northampton 1920
200* JB Hobbs v Warwickshire, Edgbaston 1928
200* MJ Stewart v Essex, Oval 1962
200 A Sandham v Essex, Leyton 1923
200 JB Hobbs v Hampshire, Southampton 1926

INDIVIDUAL BOWLING

OVER 400 CHAMPIONSHIP WICKETS IN COUNTY CAREER

		Runs	Wkts	Avge
T Richardson	1892–1904	27371	1531	17.87
PGH Fender	1914–35	34669	1479	23.44
GAR Lock	1946–63	25255	1458	17.32
PI Pocock	1964–86	33752	1297	26.02
AR Gover	1928–47	30091	1291	23.30
AV Bedser	1946–60	23753	1241	1914
JC Laker	1947–59	20480	1201	17.05
WS Lees	1896–1911	24510	1149	21.33
RD Jackman	1966–82	25349	1124	22.55
JW Hitch	1907–25	23686	1096	21.61
WH Lockwood	1890–1904	18395	1001	18.37
PJ Loader	1951–63	17134	897	19.10
WC Smith	1900–14	14790	892	16.58
T Rushby	1903–21	16902	851	19.86
HA Peach	1919–31	17723	692	25.61
GG Arnold	1963–77	13656	691	19.76
EA Bedser	1946–61	15891	660	24.07
EA Watts	1933–49	16292	635	25.65
ST Clarke	1979–88	11022	578	19.06
Intikhab Alam	1969–81	15806	540	29.27
GA Lohmann	1890–96	6213	480	12.94
D Gibson	1957–69	9997	458	21.82
JF Parker	1932–52	12775	454	28.13
JN Crawford	1904–19	7982	421	18.95
WS Surridge	1947–56	12053	416	28.97
DAD Sydenham	1957–67	8062	408	19.75
W Brockwell	1890–1903	10218	409	24.98
EG Hayes	1896–1919	10957	400	27.39

MOST WICKETS IN A SEASON

Wkts	(Avge)		Season
238	(14.23)	T Richardson	1897
237	(13.89)	T Richardson	1895
215	(12.56)	WC Smith	1910
191	(15.46)	T Richardson	1896
171	(15.42)	AR Gover	1936
169	(17.01)	WS Lees	1905
154	(19.31)	JW Hitch	1913
154	(20.25)	WS Lees	1906
153	(11.58)	GAR Lock	1957
152	(19.24)	WC Smith	1911
152	(12.34)	GAR Lock	1955
143	(19.49)	PGH Fender	1922
142	(14.54)	JC Laker	1950
139	(18.88)	AR Gover	1937
136	(18.44)	PGH Fender	1923
132	(10.65)	GA Lohmann	1891
126	(19.76)	JW Hitch	1914
126	(21.29)	T Richardson	1898
124	(18.39)	WS Lees	1907
124	(20.46)	PGH Fender	1925
123	(21.87)	T Rushby	1911
120	(11.31)	T Richardson	1894
120	(19.57)	RG Harman	1964
120	(20.17)	WS Lees	1909

NINE OR MORE WICKETS IN AN INNINGS

10–43	T Rushby v Somerset, Taunton 1921
10–54	GAR Lock v Kent, Blackheath 1956
10–67	EA Watts v Warwickshire, Edgbaston 1939
9–17	PJ Loader v Warwicks, Oval 1958
9–28	PJ Loader v Kent, Blackheath 1953
9–31	WC Smith v Hants, Oval 1904
9–47	JW Sharpe v Middlesex, Oval 1891
9–47	T Richardson v Yorks, Sheffield 1893
9–49	T Richardson v Sussex, Oval 1895
9–57	PI Pocock v Glamorgan, Cardiff 1979
9–59	WH Lockwood v Essex, Leyton 1902
9–70	T Richardson v Hants, Oval 1895
9–70	DAD Sydenham v Gloucs, Oval 1964
9–81	WS Lees v Sussex, Eastbourne 1905
9–94	WH Lockwood v Essex, Oval 1900
9–105	WH Lockwood v Gloucs, Cheltenham 1899

FIFTEEN OR MORE WICKETS IN A MATCH

16–83	GAR Lock v Kent, Blackheath 1956
15–83	T Richardson v Warwicks, Oval 1898
15–113	T Richardson v Leices, Oval 1896
15–154	T Richardson v Yorks, Headingley 1897
15–155	T Richardson v Hants, Oval 1895
15–182	GAR Lock v Kent, Blackheath 1958
15–184	WH Lockwood v Gloucs, Cheltenham 1899

WICKET KEEPING

MOST DISMISSALS IN AN INNINGS
7 (7ct)   A Long v Sussex, Hove 1964

MOST DISMISSALS IN A MATCH
11 (11ct)   A Long v Sussex, Hove 1964
11 (11ct)   AJ Stewart v Leics, Leicester 1989

MOST DISMISSALS IN A SEASON
79 (60ct 19st) AJW McIntyre 1949
77 (66ct 11st) A Long 1962

MOST CAREER DISMISSALS
1132 (963ct 169st) H Strudwick 1902–27

Tom Richardson's wickets total was a Championship record for over 30 years. A lion-hearted pace man, his exertions saw early burn-out and premature death from a heart attack (Hulton Picture Company)

CAPTAIN STUART SURRIDGE

Whether Walter Stuart Surridge was the *best* county captain is arguable; a good captain can always improve a team's performance, and lack of leadership can pull good players down, but no-one can make something out of nothing. The most gifted of leaders will fail to deliver when the material is lacking.

So, it cannot be proved whether or not Surridge was the best captain but he was certainly the most successful. Quite simply, Surridge skippered Surrey for five seasons from 1952 to 1956, and they were champions every time. In 1951 they had finished sixth.

The county's season-by season record makes for compelling reading.

Season	P	W	L	D
1952	28	20	3	5
1953	27	13	4	10
1954	26	15	3	8
1955	28	23	5	0
1956	26	15	5	6
Total	135	86	20	29

Under Surridge's leadership a remarkable 63.7 per cent of all matches were won outright. Almost as remarkably, only just over one in five of the games were drawn, in an age when drawn games were becoming a problem. Their 1955 record was most amazing of all. Their number of wins had been baeten only by Yorkshire – in 32 matches – in 1923, while they were the first side to win the title without suffering a drawn match.

Surridge's secrets certainly did not include leadership by example in batting or bowling, though he was often worth a few runs, and some valuable wickets. He inspired in the field however, with his total of 230 catches during his captaincy stint strong evidence of his ability and dedication in this department.

Mainly, however, it was inspiration by attitude. Surridge went out to win every match, right from the start, and only when a win was impossible would he countenance the draw. His stated formula was, 'Attack all the time, whether batting, bowling or fielding', and for once in cricket, enterprise and aggression within the Law brought its just rewards. Would it were always thus.

Surrey retained the title under Peter May in 1957 and 1958, but already a tailing off was in evidence which saw them gradually sink back into the pack. The players were the same, the side remained successful. The difference? There was no Surridge.

(Below): *Surrey, 1952 – County Champions in the first season of Stuart Surridge's leadership and four times under him thereafter* (Hulton Picture Company)

SUSSEX

Formed: 1 March 1839
Entered official Championship: 1890
Highest placing: 2nd in 1902, 1903, 1932,
1933, 1934, 1953, 1981

INNINGS TOTALS

HIGHEST BY THE COUNTY
705–8 dec v Surrey, Hastings 1902
686–8 v Leicestershire, Leicester 1900
670–9 dec v Northamptonshire, Hove 1921
631–4 dec v Northamptonshire, Northampton 1938
611 v Essex, Leyton 1905

HIGHEST AGAINST THE COUNTY
726 by Nottinghamshire, Trent Bridge 1895
681–5 dec by Yorkshire, Sheffield (BL) 1897
674 by Nottinghamshire, Hove 1893
642–7 dec by Nottinghamshire, Hove 1901
640–8 dec by Lancashire, Hove 1937

LOWEST BY THE COUNTY
20 v Yorkshire, Hull 1922
23 v Warwickshire, Worthing 1964
24 v Lancashire, Old Trafford 1890
29 v Lancashire, Liverpool 1907
35 v Glamorgan, Horsham 1946

LOWEST AGAINST THE COUNTY
35 by Kent, Catford 1894
37 by Gloucestershire, Clifton 1891
39 by Gloucestershire, Hove 1935
40 by Leicestershire, Hove 1960
41 by Middlesex, Lord's 1924
41 by Glamorgan, Hove 1925

Don Smith, a forcing, opening left-hand bat and a useful
bowler of left-arm seam (Hulton Picture Company)

PARTNERSHIPS

COUNTY BEST FOR EACH WICKET
1st
490 EH Bowley & John Langridge v Middlesex, Hove 1933
368 JH Parks & EH Bowley v Gloucs, Hove 1929
2nd
385 EH Bowley & MW Tate v Northants, Hove 1921
349 CB Fry & EH Killick v Yorks, Hove 1901
3rd
298 KS Ranjitsinhji & EH Killick v Lancs, Hove 1901
294 JM Parks & James Langridge v Kent, Tunbridge Wells
      1951
4th
326* James Langridge & G Cox v Yorks, Headingley 1949

303* AP Wells & CM Wells v Kent, Hove 1987
5th
297 JH Parks & HW Parks v Hants, Portsmouth 1937
246 A Collins & KS Ranjitsinhji v Kent, 1Hove 1900
6th
255 S Duleepsinhji & MW Tate v Northants, Hove 1930
226 G Cox & G Potter v Worcs, Worcester 1954
7th
344 KS Ranjitsinhji & W Newham v Essex, Leyton 1902
218 TER Cook & AF Wensley v Worcs, Eastbourne 1933
8th
229* CLA Smith & G Brann v Kent, Hove 1902
209 G Stannard & HE Roberts v Worce, Hove 1920
9th
178 AF Wensley & HW Parks v Derbys, Horsham 1930
160* KS Ranjitsinhji & FW Tate v Surrey, Hastings 1902
10th
130 G Stannard & GR Cox v Essex, Hove 1919
113 GR Cox & HR Butt v Hants, Chichester 1901

INDIVIDUAL BATTING

OVER 8000 CHAMPIONSHIP RUNS IN
COUNTY CAREER

		Inns	NO	Runs	HS	Avge	100s
John Langridge	1928–55	866	57	30340	250*	37.50	67
JM Parks	1949–72	877	124	27233	205*	36.16	37
KG Suttle	1949–71	953	79	26588	204*	30.42	43
Jas Langridge	1924–53	861	125	25893	167	35.18	35
EH Bowley	1912–34	703	35	22921	283	34.31	40
J Vine	1896–1922	762	60	21399	202	30.48	31
HW Parks	1926–48	666	89	19471	200*	33.74	38
G Cox	1931–60	655	47	19351	232	31.31	40
CB Fry	1894–1908	349	23	18471	244	56.65	62
TE Cook	1922–37	671	55	18420	278	29.90	31
ASM Oakman	1947–68	769	65	17952	229*	25.50	17
JH Parks	1924–39	640	54	17874	197	30.50	36
AE Relf	1900–21	641	52	16557	189*	28.11	20
KS Ranjitsinhji	1895–1920	297	36	16194	285*	62.04	50
EH Killick	1893–1913	659	43	16001	200	25.97	17
MW Tate	1912–37	704	62	15298	203	23.82	16
DV Smith	1946–62	536	55	13891	206*	28.87	12
PWG Parker	1976–90	41	60	13432	140	35.25	32
GR Cox	1898–1928	858	172	12588	107*	18.34	2
RR Relf	1906–21	440	15	11977	272*	28.18	20
LJ Lenham	1956–70	488	41	11531	191*	25.79	7
CM Wells	1979–90	375	57	10709	203	33.67	19
GD Mendis	1974–85	331	30	10464	209*	34.76	21
MA Buss	1961–78	477	41	10182	159	23.35	7
PJ Graves	1965–80	428	44	9885	145*	25.74	9
C Oakes	1935–54	413	40	9297	160	24.92	13
AF Wensley	1922–36	499	55	8824	140	19.87	7
JRT Barclay	1970–86	397	38	8777	119	24.44	7
AP Wells	1982–90	286	47	8387	150*	35.099	13
G Brann	1891–1904	320	26	8341	159	28.37	20
DS Sheppard	1947–62	215	22	8329	204	43.15	22
AW Greig	1967–78	312	18	8206	226	27.91	12
ER Dexter	1957–68	225	20	8178	203	39.89	23
KS Duleepsinhji	1926–32	161	7	8170	333	53.05	31

MOST RUNS IN A SEASON

Runs	(Avge)		Season
2578	(50.54)	JH Parks	1937
2563	(85.43)	KS Ranjitsinhji	1900
2441	(65.97)	John Langridge	1949
2413	(80.43)	CB Fry	1903
2382	(74.43)	CB Fry	1901
2376	(79.20)	CB Fry	1904
2364	(43.77)	John Langridge	1937
2302	(47.95)	John Langridge	1938

2285 (76.26) KS Ranjitsinhji 1899
2130 (43.46) EH Bowley 1928
2106 (41.29) John Langridge 1939
2082 (53.58) JM Parks 1959
2072 (56.00) TER Cook 1934
2067 (76.55) KS Ranjitsinhji 1901
2057 (38.81) KG Suttle 1962
2028 (56.33) KS Duleepsinhji 1929
2007 (48.95) John Langridge 1934
2000 (36.36) EH Bowley 1923
1982 (55.50) DS Sheppard 1953
1954 (33.68) ASM Oakman 1961
1934 (47.17) VWC Jupp 1961
1912 (86.90) CB Fry 1905
1888 (41.04) John Langridge 1947
1885 (33.66) LJ Lenham 1961
1884 (43.81) EH Bowley 1929
1882 (57.03) EH Bowley 1927
1873 (40.71) John Langridge 1950
1861 (43.27) JM Parks 1957
1850 (57.81) KS Duleepsinhji 1931
1835 (37.44) EH Bowley 1921
1831 (45.77) John Langridge 1933
1830 (63.10) CB Fry 1900
1830 (38.93) KG Suttle 1960
1817 (42.25) John Langridge 1951
1814 (36.28) HW Parks 1947
1813 (50.36) G Cox 1950
1803 (38.36) John Langridge 1935

217* VWC Jupp v Worcestershire, Worcester 1914
215 John Langridge v Glamorgan, Eastbourne 1938
214 CB Fry v Worcestershire, Hove 1908
214 TE Cook c Worcestershire, Eastbourne 1933
213* HP Chaplin v Nottinghamshire, Hove 1914
212* G Cox v Yorkshire, Headingley 1949
211 CB Fry v Hampshire, Hove 1904
210 RR Relf v Kent, Canterbury 1907
209* GD Mendis v Somerset, Hove 1984
209 CB Fry v Yorkshire, Hove 1901
207* KS Ranjitsinhji v Lancashire, Hove 1904
206* DV Smith v Nottinghamshire, Trent Bridge 1950
205* G Cox jnr v Glamorgan, Hove 1947
205* JM Parks v Somerset, Hove 1955
204* KG Suttle v Kent, Tonbridge 1962
204 KS Ranjitsinhji v Lancashire, Hove 1901
204 KS Ranjitsinhji v Surrey, Oval 1903
204 DS Sheppard v Glamorgan, Eastbourne 1949
204 GD Mendis v Northamptonshire, Eastbourne 1980
203 MW Tate v Northamptonshire, Hove 1921
203 ER Dexter v Kent, Hastings 1968
203 CM Wells v Hampshire, Hove 1984
202 KS Ranjitsinhji v Middlesex, Hove 1900
202 J Vine v Northamptonshire, Hastings 1920
202 KS Duleepsinhji v Essex, Leyton 1929
202 John Langridge v Leicestershire, Hastings 1939
201* W Newham v Somerset, Hove 1896
201* CB Fry v Nottinghamshire, Hove 1905
200* HW Parks v Essex, Chelmsford 1931
200 EH Killick v Yorkshire, Hove 1901
200 CB Fry v Surrey, Hastings 1903
200 KS Ranjitsinhji v Surrey, Oval 1908
200 John Langridge v Derbyshire 1951

Genial George Cox, a high quality batsman who maintained his good humour throughout some very bleak spells. He was also a respected and sympathetic coach (Hulton Picture Company)

DOUBLE CENTURIES
333 KS Duleepsinhji v Northamptonshire, Hove 1930
285* KS Ranjitsinhji v Somerset, Taunton 1901
283 EH Bowley v Middlesex, Hove 1933
280* EH Bowley v Gloucestershire, Hove 1929
278 TE Cook v Hampshire, Hove 1930
275 KS Ranjitsinhji v Leicestershire, Leicester (AR) 1900
272* RR Relf v Worcestershire, Eastbourne 1909
254 KC Wessels v Middlesex, Hove 1980
250* John Langridge v Glamorgan, Hove 1933
246 KS Duleepsinhji v Kent, Hastings 1929
244 CB Fry v Leicestershire, Leicester (AR) 1901
241 John Langridge v Somerset, Worthing 1950
234* KS Ranjitsinhji v Surrey, Hastings 1902
234* John Langridge v Derbyshire, Ilkeston 1949
234 CB Fry v Yorkshire, Bradford 1903
233 CB Fry v Nottinghamshire, Trent Bridge 1905
232* John Langridge v Northamptonshire, Peterborough 1934
232 G Cox jnr v Northamptonshire, Kettering 1939
230 KS Ranjitsinhji v Essex, Leyton 1902
229* ASM Oakman v Nottinghamshire, Worksop 1961
229 CB Fry v Surrey, Hove 1900
229 CB Fry v Yorkshire, Hove 1904
228 EH Bowley v Northamptonshire, Hove 1921
227 John Langridge v Northamptonshire, Northampton 1938
226 CB Fry v Derbyshire, Hove
226 AW Greig, Warwickshire, Hastings 1975
225 RR Relf v Lancashire, Eastbourne 1920
222 KS Ranjitsinhji v Somerset, Hove 1900
220 KS Ranjitsinhji v Kent, Hove 1900
220 RA Young v Essex, Leyton 1905
220 EH Bowley v Gloucestershire, Hove 1927
220 TE Cook v Worcestershire, Worcester 1934
219 KS Ranjitsinhji v Essex, Hove 1901

KS Ranjitsinhji, the first coloured cricketer to establish himself on the world stage, established a reputation as a batsman of magical gifts and fearsome single-mindedness. (Hulton Picture Company)

INDIVIDUAL BOWLING

OVER 400 CHAMPIONSHIP WICKETS IN COUNTY CAREER

		Runs	Wkts	Avge
MW Tate	1912–37	35415	2019	17.54
GR Cox	1898–1928	37294	1658	22.49
NI Thomson	1952–72	29091	1431	20.32
AE Relf	1900–21	30015	1428	21.01
Jas Langridge	1924–53	27750	1257	22.07
FW Tate	1891–1905	22157	1062	20.86
JH Cornford	1931–52	25186	961	26.20
AF Wensley	1922–36	24471	921	26.57
A Buss	1958–74	22148	886	24.99
JA Snow	1961–77	17784	821	21.66
AE James	1948–60	20082	755	26.59
DL Bates	1950–71	19258	747	25.78
JH Parks	1924–39	18983	723	26.25
RG Marlar	1951–68	16196	677	23.92
EH Killick	1893–1913	17421	630	27.65
AER Gilligan	1920–32	12454	604	20.61
ASM Oakman	1947–68	16464	601	27.39
EH Bowley	1912–34	15129	597	25.34
DJ Wood	1937–55	15982	520	30.73
J Vine	1896–1922	15405	518	29,73
CE Waller	1974–85	14913	489	30.49
ACS Pigott	1978–90	14428	476	30.31
AW Grieg	1967–78	12560	439	28.61

CHG Bland	1897–1904	11133	428	26.01
J Spencer	1969–80	11500	411	27.98
MA Buss	1961–78	22148	408	31.07
Imran Khan	1977–88	7969	400	19.92

MOST WICKETS IN A SEASON

Wkts	(Avge)		Season
194	(133.44)	MW Tate	1925
179	(13.10)	MW Tate	1923
154	(21.40)	GR Cox	1905
153	(14.28)	FW Tate	1902
139	(12.61)	MW Tate	1924
139	(14.38)	AER Gilligan	1923
138	(18.39)	GR Cox	1907
137	(19.00)	MW Tate	1934
136	(15.50)	James Langridge	1933
128	(19.99)	AE Relf	1910
127	(18.51)	MW Tate	1928
126	(20.00)	FW Tate	1901
124	(15.58)	MW Tate	1932
124	(21.21)	NI Thomson	1961
123	(15.91)	NI Thomson	1958
122	(16.43)	WA Humphreys	1893
122	(19.04)	NI Thomson	1954
120	(21.32)	NI Thomson	1959

NINE OR MORE WICKETS IN AN INNINGS

10–48	CHG Bland v Kent, Tonbridge 1899
10–49	NI Thomson v Warwicks, Worthing 1964
9–34	James Langridge v Yorks, Sheffield 1934
9–35	JEBBPQC Dwyer v Derbys, Hove 1906
9–44	JEBBPQC Dwyer v Middlesex, Hove 1906
9–46	RG Marlar v Lancs, Hove 1955
9–50	GR Cox v Warwicks, Horsham 1926
9–53	JH Cornford v Northants, Rushden 1949
9–60	AE James v Yorks, Hove 1955
9–71	MW Tate v Middlesex, Lord's 1926
9–73	FW Tate v Leics, Leicester 1902
9–95	AE Relf v Warwicks, Hove 1910
9–114	EH Bowley v Derbys, Hove 1929

FIFTEEN OR MORE WICKETS IN A MATCH

17–106	GR Cox v Warwicks, Horsham 1926
16–100	JEBBPQC Dwyer v Middlesex, Hove 1906
15–68	FW Tate v Middlesex, Lord's 1902
15–72	AE Relf v Leics, Hove 1912
15–75	NI Thomson v Warwicks, Worthing 1964
15–98	FH Parris v Gloucs, Bristol 1894
15–119	RG Marlar v Lancs, Hove 1955
15–133	RG Marlar v Glamorgan, Swansea 1952
15–161	J Vine v Notts, Trent Bridge 1901
15–193	WA Humphreys v Somerset, Taunton 1893

WICKET KEEPING

MOST DISMISSALS IN AN INNINGS

6	(6ct)	HR Butt v Gloucs, Bristol 1899
6	(6ct)	HR Butt v Hants, Hove 1901
6	(6ct)	HR Butt v Leics, Hove 1909
6	(3ct 3st)	RT Webb v Notts, Hove 1955
6	(6ct)	JM Parks v Worcs, Dudley 1959
6	(6ct)	RT Webb v Somerset, Hove 1960
6	(6ct)	MG Griffith v Essex, Clacton 1964

MOST DISMISSALS IN A MATCH

8	(8ct)	HR Butt v Kent, Tonbridge 1899
8	(8ct)	HR Butt v Somerset, Hove 1900
8	(7ct 1st)	GB Street v Worcs, Hastings 1923
8	(4ct 4st)	WL Cornford v Worcs, Worcester 1928
8	(8ct)	RT Webb v Somerset, Hove 1960
8	(8ct)	A Long v Kent, Hove 1976

MOST DISMISSALS IN A SEASON

85	(79ct 6st)	JM Parks 1959
81	(66ct 15st)	HR Butt 1905

MOST CAREER DISMISSALS

1044 (807ct 237st) HR Butt 1890–1912

Alan Oakman enjoyed a long career as batsman, bowler and brilliant catcher. After his retirement from playing, 'Oaky' was on the Warwickshire staff for many years (Hulton Picture Company)

WARWICKSHIRE

Formed: 8 April 1882
Entered official Championship: 1895
Winners: 1911, 1951, 1972

INNINGS TOTALS

HIGHEST BY THE COUNTY
657–6 dec v Hampshire, Edgbaston 1899
645–7 dec v Worcestershire, Dudley 1914
635 v Derbyshire, Edgbaston 1900
614–8 dec v Essex, Edgbaston 1904

HIGHEST AGAINST THE COUNTY
887 by Yorkshire, Edgbaston 1896
656–3 dec by Northamptonshire, Coventry 1928
634 bySurrey, Oval 1906
633 by Worcestershire, Worcester 1906
616–7 dec by Hampshire, Portsmouth 1920

LOWEST BY THE COUNTY
16 v Kent, Tonbridge 1913
28 v Derbyshire, Derby 1937
35 v Yorkshire, Sheffield (D) 1979
35 v Yorkshire, Edgbaston 1963
36 v Hampshire, Portsmouth 1927

LOWEST AGAINST THE COUNTY
15 by Hampshire, Edgbaston 1922
23 by Sussex, Worthing 1964
34 by Nottinghamshire, Nuneaton, 1964
40 by Glamorgan, Cardiff 1929
42 by Kent, Edgbaston 1925
44 by Nottinghamshire, Edgbaston 1989

PARTNERSHIPS

COUNTY BEST FOR EACH WICKET

1st
377* NF Horner & Khalid Ibadulla v Surrey, Oval 1960
333 JF Byrne & S Kinneir v Lancs, Edgbaston 1905
2nd
465* JA Jameson & RB Kanhai v Gloucs, Edgbaston 1974
344 JHG Devey & S Kinneir v Derbys, Edgbaston 1900
3rd
327 S Kinneir & WG Quaife v Lancs, Edgbaston 1901
282 J Whitehouse & AI Kallicharran v Northants, Northampton 1979
4th
470 AI Kallicharran & GW Humpage v Lancs, Southport 1982
402 RB Kanhai & Khalid Ibadulla v Notts, Trent Bridge 1968
5th
268 WG Quaife & W Quaife v Essex, Leyton 1900
266 RES Wyatt & AJ Croom v Somerset Edgbaston 1928
6th
220 HE Dollery & J Buckingham v Derbys, Derby 1938
204 WG Quaife and ACS Glover v Worcs, Worcester 1908
7th
250 HE Dollery & JS Ord v Kent, Maidstone 1953
244 TW Cartwright & QC Smith v Middlesec, Nuneaton 1962
8th
228 AJW Croom & RES Wyatt v Worcs, Dudley 1925
203 GW Humpage & WA Bourne v Sussex, Edgbaston 1976
9th
154 GW Stephens & AJW Croom v Derbys, Edgbaston 1925
126 FR Santall & W Sanders v Notts, Edgbaston 1930
10th
128 FR Santall & W Sanders v Yorks, Edgbaston 1930
126 RES Wyatt & JH Mayer v Surrey, Oval 1927

INDIVIDUAL BATTING

OVER 8000 CHAMPIONSHIP RUNS IN COUNTY CAREER

		Inns	NO	Runs	HS	Avge	100s
DL Amiss	1960–87	854	86	31617	232*	41.16	70
WG Quaife	1895–1928	1018	162	31476	255*	36.77	68
MJK Smith	1957–75	669	87	24393	200*	41.91	41
HE Dollery	1934–55	638	60	22617	212	39.12	49
RES Wyatt	1923–39	599	99	20814	232	41.62	50
LTA Bates	1013–35	712	49	18434	211	27.80	20
NF Horner	1952–65	600	32	16841	203*	29.64	24
AI Kallicharran	1972–90	445	51	16824	243*	42.70	47
AJW Croom	1924–39	592	62	16809	211	31.71	23
FR Santall	1920–39	756	79	16787	201*	24.79	20
GW Humpage	1975–90	513	66	16095	254	36.00	16
FC Gardner	1947–60	538	56	15646	215*	32.46	25
N Kilner	1926–37	516	34	15452	228	32.05	23
EJ Smith	1904–30	718	64	15348	177	23.46	20
JH Parsons	1910–34	477	46	14992	225	34.78	33
JA Jameson	1962–76	500	39	14869	240*	32.35	23
S Kinneir	1898–1914	467	42	13834	268*	32.55	25
TA Lloyd	1977–90	422	32	13481	208*	34.56	26
C Charlesworth	1898–1921	594	24	13477	216	23.64	15
Khalid Ibadulla	1957–72	548	58	12396	170*	25.59	13
WJ Stewart	1955–69	410	43	12262	182*	33.41	19
RT Spooner	1948–59	485	54	11658	168	27.04	11
AFA Lilley	1895–1911	435	25	11365	171	27.71	15
AVG Wolton	1948–60	428	53	11156	165	29.74	9
A Townsend	1948–60	518	62	11035	154	24.19	4
RE Hitchcock	1950–64	456	61	11034	153*	27.93	13
RB Kanhai	1968–77	258	44	10883	253	50.85	32
JS Ord	1933–53	422	31	10666	156*	27.27	13
TW Cartwright	1952–69	509	64	9464	210	21.26	4
CS Baker	1905–20	340	40	8781	155*	29.27	9

Alvin Kallicharran enjoyed many a fine season with Warwickshire, his adopted county; he finally became a 'home' player with a permanent residence in the county (Allsport/ Adrian Murrell)

MOST RUNS IN A SEASON

Runs	(Avge)		Season
2169	(63.79)	MJK Smith	1959
2137	(57.75)	DL Amiss	1984
2118	(68.32)	AI Kallicharran	1982
2107	(47.88)	N Kilner	1933
2100	(42.85)	WJ Stewart	1962
2036	(42.41)	HE Dollery	1952
2020	(63.12)	RES Wyatt	1928

2012	(47.90)	AI Kallicharran	1984
2009	(41.85)	MJK Smith	1961
2001	(55.58)	DL Amiss	1978
1988	(44.17)	MJK Smith	1962
1040	(55.42)	RES Wyatt	1929
1919	(45.69)	HE Dollery	1949
1871	(46.77)	HE Dollery	1953
1867	(47.87)	MJK Smith	1960
1863	(32.68)	Khalid Ibadulla	1962
1857	(33.76)	NF Horner	1960
1813	(49.00)	GW Humpage	1984
1807	(54.75)	RES Wyatt	1937
1801	(48.67)	FC Gardner	1950

RES Wyatt's excellent batting form and useful bowling were unable to give Warwickshire the long-desired uplift in the late twenties. In 1930, he added the county captaincy to his other roles (Allsport)

DOUBLE CENTURIES

305* FR Foster v Worcestershire, Dudley 1914
268* SP Kinneir v Hampshire, Edgbaston 1911
255* WG Quaife v Surrey, Oval 1905
254 GW Humpage v Lancashire, Southport 1982
253 RB Kanhai v Nottinghamshire, Trent Bridge 1968
246 JHG Devey v Derbyshire, Edgbaston 1900
243* AI Kallicharran v Glamorgan, Edgbaston 1983
240* JA Jameson v Gloucestershire, Edgbaston 1974
235 AI Kallicharran v Worcestershire, Worcester 1982
232* DL Amiss v Gloucestershire, Bristol 1979
232 RES Wyatt v Derbyshire, Edgbaston 1937
230* RB Kanhai v Somerset, Edgbaston 1973
230* AI Kallicharran v Lancashire, Southport 1982
228 N Kilner v Worcestershire, Worcester 1935
225 JH Parsons v Glamorgan, Edgbaston 1927
224* AJ Moles v Glamorgan, Swansea 1990
223* WG Quaife v Essex, Leyton 1900
222 JF Byrne v Lancashire, Edgbaston 1905
216 C Charlesworth v Derbyshire, Blackwell College 1910
215* SP Kinneir v Lancashire, Edgbaston 1901
215* FC Gardner v Somerset, Taunton 1950
213* RB Kanhai v Gloucestershire, Edgbaston 1974
212 HE Dollery v Leicestershire, Edgbaston 1952
211 LTA Bates v Gloucestershire, Gloucester 1932
211 AJW Croom v Worcestershire, Edgbaston 1934
210 TW Cartwright v Middlesex, Nuneaton (G&C) 1962
210 AI Kallicharran v Leicestershire, Leicester (GR) 1982
209* AI Kallicharran v Lancashire, Edgbaston 1983
209 FS Gough-Calthorpe v Hampshire, Edgbaston 1921
208* TA Lloyd v Gloucestershire, Edgbaston 1983
207* WG Quaife v Hampshire, Edgbaston 1899
206 C Charlesworth v Yorkshire, Dewsbury 1914
205 GW Humpage v Derbyshire, Chesterfield 1984
203* NF Horner v Surrey, Oval 1960
202* DA Reeve v Northamptonshire, Northampton 1990
201* FR Santall v Northamptonshire, Northampton 1933
201* RES Wyatt v Lancashire, Edgbaston 1937
200* WG Quaife v Essex, Edgbaston 1904
200* MJK Smith v Worcestershire, Edgbaston 1959
200* AI Kallicharran v Northamptonshire, Edgbaston 1984
200 FR Foster v Surrey, Edgbaston 1984
200 LTA Bates v Worcestershire, Edgbaston 1928
200 HE Dollery v Gloucestershire, Gloucester 1949

INDIVIDUAL BOWLING

OVER 400 CHAMPIONSHIP WICKETS IN COUNTY CAREER

		Runs	Wkts	Avge
WE Hollies	1932–57	42826	2105	20.34
S Santall	1895–1914	26754	1125	23.78
JH Mayer	1926–39	24727	1108	22.31
JD Bannister	1950–68	24304	1085	22.40
TW Cartwright	1952–69	18709	1002	18.67
GAE Paine	1929–47	20659	905	22.82
EF Field	1897–1920	21330	905	23.34
DJ Brown	1961–82	22266	889	25.04
H Howell	1913–28	17631	875	20.14
WG Quaife	1895–1928	22914	842	27.21
S Hargreave	1899–1909	16528	767	21.54
CW Grove	1938–53	14525	649	22.38
TL Pritchard	1947–55	14746	636	23.18
RES Wyatt	1923–39	20439	634	32.13
FR Foster	1908–14	11625	571	20.35
GC Small	1980–90	14074	510	27.59
FSG Calthorpe	1919–30	14332	486	29.48
RG Thompson	1949–62	9705	419	23.16

MOST WICKETS IN A SEASON

Wkts	(Avge)		Season
175	(15.16)	WE Hollies	1946
163	(17.47)	TL Pritchard	1948
152	(19.92)	H Howell	1923
150	(16.80)	GAE Paine	1934
145	(17.69)	WE Hollies	1951
132	(15.84)	TW Cartwright	1967
132	(17.50)	H Howell	1920
129	(18.48)	GAE Paine	1932
128	(13.78)	TW Cartwright	1964
128	(18.30)	WE Hollies	1948
128	(20.30)	WE Hollies	1949
127	(18.91)	WE Hollies	1935
123	(12.17)	S Hargreave	1903
123	(18.84)	LR Gibbs	1971
123	(19.35)	WE Hollies	1957
122	(16.00)	H Howell	1924
122	(19.48)	EF Field	1911
121	(22.12)	JH Mayer	1929

NINE OR MORE WICKETS IN AN INNINGS

10–49 WE Hollies v Notts, Edgbaston 1946
10–51 H Howell v Yorks, Edgbaston 1923
9–32 H Howell v Hants, Edgbaston 1925
9–35 S Hargreave v Surrey, Oval 1903
9–35 H Howell v Somerset, Taunton 1924
9–35 JD Bannister v Yorks, Sheffield 1955
9–39 CW Grove v Sussex, Edgbaston 1952
9–56 WE Hollies v Northants, Edgbaston 1950
9–65 RG Thompson v Notts, Edgbaston 1952
9–93 WE Hollies v Glamorgan, Edgbaston 1939
9–104 EF Field v Leics, Leicester 1899
9–118 FR Foster v Yorks, Edgbaston 1911

FIFTEEN OR MORE WICKETS IN A MATCH

15–76 S Hargreave v Surrey, Oval 1903
15–89 TW Cartwright v Glamorgan, Swansea 1967

WICKET KEEPING

MOST DISMISSALS IN AN INNINGS
7 (4ct 3st) EJ Smith v Derbys, Edgbaston 1926
6 (4ct 2st) AFA Lilley v Worcs, Edgbaston 1906
6 (5ct 1st) J Buckingham v Sussex, Edgbaston 1939
6 (6ct) RT Spooner v Notts, Edgbaston 1957
6 (6ct) AC Smith v Derbyshire, Derby 1970
6 (5ct 1st) KJ Piper v Somerset, Weston 1990

MOST DISMISSALS IN A MATCH
8 (8ct) AFA Lilley v Kent, Edgbaston 1897
8 (8ct) EJ Smith v Derbys, Edgbaston 1926
8 (7ct 1st) EJ Smith v Worcs, Edgbaston 1930
8 (8ct) RT Spooner v Lancs, Edgbaston 1989
8 (8ct) GW Humpage v Lancs, Edgbaston 1989

MOST DISMISSALS IN A SEASON
77 (54ct 23st) JA Smart 1932
77 (74ct 3st) AC Smith 1962

MOST CAREER DISMISSALS
771 (639ct 132st) EJ Smith 1904–30

WORCESTERSHIRE

Formed: 5 March 1865
Entered official Championship: 1899
Winners: 1964, 1965, 1974, 1988, 1989

INNINGS TOTALS

HIGHEST BY THE COUNTY
633 v Warwickshire, Worcester 1908
628–7 dec v Somerset, Taunton 1988
627–9 dec v Kent, Worcester 1905
590 v Somerset, Worcester 1903
578–6 dec v Warwickshire, Edgbaston 1909

HIGHEST AGAINST THE COUNTY
701–4 dec by Leicestershire, Worcester 1906
645–7 dec by Warwickshire, Dudley 1914
625–6 dec by Gloucestershire, Dudley 1934
623–5 dec by Middlesex, Worcester 1949
603–9 dec by Warwickshire, Edgbaston 1920

LOWEST BY THE COUNTY
24 v Yorkshire, Huddersfield 1903
25 v Yorkshire, Hull 1906
25 v Surrey, Oval 1954
25 v Kent, Tunbridge Wells 1960
28 v Yorkshire, Bradford 1907

LOWEST BY THE COUNTY
30 by Hampshire, Worcester 1903
31 by Hampshire, Bournemouth 1965
47 by Sussex, Worcester 1903
50 by Northamptonshire, Northampton 1946
50 by Kent, Dover 1955

PARTNERSHIPS

COUNTY BEST FOR EACH WICKET
1st
309 HK Foster & FL Bowley v Derbys, Derby 1901
306   FL Bowley & FA Pearson v Gloucs, Worcester 1913
2nd
287* TS Curtis & GA Hick v Glamorgan, Neath 1986
276 TS Curtis & GA Hick v Hants, Worcester 1988
3rd
314 MJ Horton & TW Graveney v Somerset, Worcester 1962
306 LG Crawley & WV Fox v Northants, Worcester 1923
4th
281 JA Ormrod & Younis Ahmed v Notts, Trent Bridge 1979
277 HHI Gibbons & BW Quaife v Middlesex, Worcester 1931
5th
393 EG Arnold & WB Burns v Warwicks, Edgbaston 1909
261 HHI Gibbons & CH Palmer v Northants, Dudley 1939
6th
265 GA Hick & SJ Rhodes v Somerset, Taunton 1988
226 DB D'Oliveira & SJ Rhodes v Lancs, Old Trafford 1990
7th
205 GA Hick & PJ Newport v Yorks, Worcester 1988
197 HHI Gibbons & R Howorth v Surrey, Oval 1938
8th
177* GA Hick & RK Illingworth v Somerset, Taunton 1988
145* F Chester & WH Taylor v Essex, Worcester 1914
9th
181 JA Cuffe & RD Burrows v Gloucs, Worcester 1907
141 WV Fox & CV Tarbox v Warwicks, Edgbaston 1929
10th
119 WB Burns & GA Wilson v Somerset, Worcester 1906
 94 RD Burrows & EW Bale v Yorks, Worcester 1906

INDIVIDUAL BATTING

OVER 8000 CHAMPIONSHIP RUNS IN COUNTY CAREER

		Inns	NO	Runs	HS	Avge	100s
D Kenyon	1946–67	969	48	31375	259	34.06	64
GM Turner	1968–82	464	59	20736	311*	51.70	67
JA Ormrod	1962–83	726	78	19711	204*	30.41	28
HHI Gibbons	1927–46	628	54	19524	212*	34.01	42
FL Bowley	1899–1923	667	23	19355	276	30.05	34
RGA Headley	1958–74	658	50	18679	187	30.72	29
FA Pearson	1901–26	747	36	17644	167	24.81	22
MJ Horton	1952–66	595	39	15782	233	28.38	19
PA Neale	1975–90	512	77	15777	167	36.26	25
G Dews	1946–61	579	44	14717	139	27.50	17
DW Richardson	1953–67	572	48	14074	169	26.85	15
HK Foster	1899–1925	397	14	13637	216	35.60	24
L Outschoorn	1947–59	519	47	13293	215*	28.16	21
EG Arnold	1899–1913	483	50	13158	200*	30.38	19
E Cooper	1937–51	415	28	12508	216*	32.32	18
BL D'Oliveira	1965–80	392	58	12128	227	36.31	24
TW Graveney	1962–70	323	59	11892	164*	45.04	24
RG Broadbent	1950–63	474	45	11309	155	26.36	9
GA Hick	1985–90	191	25	10859	405*	65.41	38
TS Curtis	1980–90	292	41	10340	197*	41.19	19
R Howorth	1934–51	523	47	9592	114	20.15	2
SH Martin	1932–39	379	26	9482	191*	26.86	13
R Booth	1956–70	562	102	8849	113*	19.23	2
EJO Hemsley	1966–82	352	47	8614	176*	28.24	4
DN Patel	1976–86	329	26	8573	153	28.29	13
RO Jenkins	1938–58	480	100	8286	109	21.80	1
BW Quaife	1928–37	428	40	8085	136*	20.83	2

MOST RUNS IN A SEASON

Runs	(Avge)		Season
2452	(54.48)	HHI Gibbons	1934
2443	(76.34)	GA Hick	1988
2346	(61.73)	GM Turner	1970
2273	(90.92)	GA Hick	1990
2271	(55.39)	TW Graveney	1964
2165	(51.54)	CF Walters	1933
2138	(53.45)	D Kenyon	1954
2082	(44.29)	HHI Gibbons	1938
2063	(47.97)	D Kenyon	1953
2043	(56.75)	GM Turner	1981
2002	(44.48)	D Kenyon	1950
1978	(41.20)	D Kenyon	1952
1934	(64.46)	GA Hick	1986
1924	(32.61)	RGA Headley	1961
1903	(43.25)	D Kenyon	1951
1896	(35.77)	D Kenyon	1962
1872	(46.80)	E Cooper	1949
1868	(53.37)	GA Hick	1987
1847	(38.47)	D Kenyon	1957
1832	(41.63)	MJ Horton	1959
1832	(37.38)	MJ Horton	1962
1822	(37.18)	PE Richardson	1953
1802	(41.90)	D Kenyon	1956

DOUBLE CENTURIES
405* GA Hick v Somerset, Taunton 1988
311* GM Turner v Warwickshire, Worcester 1982
276 FL Bowley v Hampshire, Dudley 1914
262* M Nichol v Hampshire, Bournemouth 1930
259 D Kenyon v Yorkshire, Kidderminster 1956
253* D Kenyon v Leicestershire, Worcester 1954
252* GA Hick v Glamorgan, Abergavenny 1990
246* RE Foster v Kent, Worcester 1905
238* D Kenyon v Warwickshire, Worcester 1953

233 MJ Horton v Somerset, Worcester 1962
231* Nawab of Pataudi v Essex, Worcester 1933
229 D Kenyon v Hampshire, Portsmouth 1959
228* GM Turner v Gloucestershire, Worcester 1980
227* GA Hick v Northamptonshire, Worcester 1986
227 BL D'Oliveira v Yorkshire, Hull 1974
226 CF Walters v Kent, Gravesend 1933
224* Nawab of Pataudi v Kent, Worcester 1933
222 Nawab of Pataudi v Somerset, Weston-super-Mare
     1933
221* Younis Ahmed v Nottinghamshire, Trent Bridge 1979
219* GA Hick v Glamorgan, Neath
217 FL Bowley v Leicestershire, Stourbridge 1905
216* E Cooper v Warwickshire, Dudley 1938
216 HK Foster v Somerset, Worcester 1903
215* L Outschoorn v Northamptonshire, Worcester 1949
215 HK Foster v Warwickshire, Worcester 1908
214* Nawab of Pataudi v Glamorgan, Worcester 1934
212* HHI Gibbons v Northamptonshire, Dudley 1939
212 MJ Horton v Essex, Leyton 1959
212 GA Hick v Lancashire, Old Trafford 1988
204* JA Ormrod v Kent, Dartford 1973
202* D Kenyon v Hampshire, Portsmouth 1954
202* GM Turner v Warwickshire, Edgbaston 1978
201 FL Bowley v Gloucestershire, Worcester 1913
201 D Kenyon v Glamorgan, Stourbridge 1960
200* EG Arnold v Warwickshire, Edgbaston 1909
200* D Kenyon v Nottinghamshire, Worcester 1957
200* JA Ormrod v Gloucestershire, Worcester 1982

Graeme Hick, the Zimbabwean batting giant now qualifed for England (Allsport/Ben Radford)

INDIVIDUAL BOWLING
OVER 400 CHAMPIONSHIP WICKETS IN
COUNTY CAREER

		Runs	Wkts	Avge
RTD Perks	1930–55	47931	2009	23.85
N Gifford	1960–82	33372	1485	22.47
JA Flavell	1949–67	29736	1397	21.28
CF Root	1921–32	27580	1352	20.39
R Howorth	1934–51	24888	1170	21.27
PF Jackson	1929–50	28022	1061	26.41
RO Jenkins	1938–58	23930	1005	23.81
LJ Coldwell	1955–69	19758	931	21.22
RD Burrows	1899–1914	21810	829	26.30

EG Arnold	1899–1913	19440	797	24.39
FA Pearson	1901–26	22736	761	29.87
MJ Horton	1952–66	18070	667	27.09
JA Cuffe	1905–14	16478	646	25.50
GA Wilson	1899–1906	15361	612	25.09
VA Holder	1968–80	12524	549	22.81
AP Pridgeon	1972–89	16048	485	33.08
RGM Carter	1962–72	12359	475	26.01
BM Brain	1959–75	11106	459	24.19
JD Inchmore	1973–86	13222	455	29.05
GW Brook	1930–35	12108	441	27.45
NV Radford	1985–90	10911	437	24.96
SH Martin	1932–39	12573	432	29.10
DNF Slade	1958–71	9541	418	22.82
BL D'Oliveira	1965–80	9998	408	24.50

MOST WICKETS IN A SEASON

Wkts	(Avge)		Season
196	(17.46)	CF Root	1925
165	(20.21)	CF Root	1923
147	(16.00)	CF Root	1924
146	(21.72)	CF Root	1929
145	(17.91)	CF Root	1927
143	(19.76)	RTD Perks	1939
140	(19.88)	RO Jenkins	1949
139	(17.99)	JA Flavell	1961
135	(14.00)	JA Flavell	1966
135	(19.11)	LJ Coldwell	1961
132	(14.99)	JA Flavell	1965
132	(18.18)	LJ Coldwell	1962
132	(23.59)	RTD Perks	1938
129	(22.10)	CF Root	1930
128	(21.41)	GW Brook	1930
123	(15.93)	CF Root	1931
122	(21.98)	RTD Perks	1937
121	(18.80)	RTD Perks	1936
121	(18.94)	R Howorth	1935
121	(19.69)	JA Flavell	1960
120	(18.80)	R Howorth	1936

NINE OR MORE WICKETS IN AN INNINGS
9–23   CF Root v Lancs, Worcester 1931
9–30   JA Flavell v Kent, Dover 1955
9–38   JA Cuffe v Yorks, Bradford 1907
9–38   AJ Conway v Gloucs, Moreton-in-Marsh 1914
9–40   CF Root v Essex, Worcester 1924
9–40   RTD Perks v Glamorgan, Stourbridge 1939
9–42   RTD Perks v Gloucs, Cheltenham 1946
9–45   PF Jackson v Somerset, Dudley 1935
9–56   JA Flavell v Middlesex, Kidderminster 1964
9–70   NV Radford v Somerset, Worcester 1986
9–81   CF Root v Kent, Tunbridge Wells 1930
9–122 JA Flavell v Sussex, Hastings 1954

FIFTEEN OR MORE WICKETS IN A MATCH
15–87   AJ Conway v Gloucs, Moreton-in-Marsh 1914
15–106 RTD Perks v Essex, Worcester 1937
15–122 RO Jenkins v Sussex, Dudley 1953
15–142 GA Wilson v Somerset, Taunton 1905

WICKET KEEPING

MOST DISMISSALS IN AN INNINGS
6 (4ct 2st) GW Gaukrodger v Kent, Tunbridge Wells 1907
6 (3ct 3st) H Yarnold v Hants, Worcester 1949
6 (6ct)   GR Cass v Essex, Worcester 1973
6 (6ct)   HG Wilcock v Hants, Portsmouth 1974
6 (6ct)   SJ Rhodes v Sussex, Kidderminster 1988
6 (6ct)   SJ Rhodes v Warwicks, Edgbaston 1989

MOST DISMISSALS IN A MATCH
9 (5ct 4st) H Yarnold v Hants, Worcester 1949
9 (9ct)   SJ Rhodes v Sussex, Kidderminster 1988

MOST DISMISSALS IN A SEASON
96 (80ct 16st) R Booth 1960
95 (53ct 42st) H Yarnold 1949
95 (81ct 14st) R Booth 1962
95 (88ct 7st) R Booth 1964

MOST CAREER DISMISSALS
970 (831ct 139st) R Booth 1956–70

YORKSHIRE
Formed: 8 January 1863
Entered official Championship: 1890
Winners: 1893, 1896, 1898, 1900, 1901, 1902,
1905, 1908, 1912, 1919, 1922, 1923,
1924, 1925, 1931, 1932, 1933, 1935,
1937, 1938, 1939, 1947, 1949, 1959,
1960, 1962, 1963, 1966, 1967, 1968

INNINGS TOTALS

HIGHEST BY THE COUNTY
887 v Warwickshire, Edgbaston 1896
704 v Surrey, Oval 1899
681–5 dec v Sussex, Sheffield 1897
662 v Derbyshire, Chesterfield 1898
660 v Leicestershire, Leicester 1896

HIGHEST AGAINST THE COUNTY
630 by Somerset, Headingley 1901
592 by Somerset, Taunton 1892
574 by Gloucestershire, Cheltenham 1990
566 by Sussex, Sheffield (BL) 1937
560–5 dec by Sussex, Hove 1901
560–6 dec by Surrey, Oval 1933

LOWEST BY THE COUNTY
23 v Hampshire, Middlesbrough 1965
26 v Surrey, Oval 1909
31 v Essex, Huddersfield 1935
33 v Lancashire, Headingley 1924
35 v Gloucestershire, Bristol 1959

LOWEST AGAINST THE COUNTY
13 by Nottinghamshire, Trent Bridge 1901
15 by Northamptonshire, Northampton 1908
20 by Sussex, Hull 1992
20 by Derbyshire, Sheffield (BL) 1939
23 by Derbyshire, Hull 1921

PARTNERSHIPS

COUNTY BEST FOR EACH WICKET
1st
555 P Holmes & H Sutcliffe v Essex, Leyton 1932
554 JT Brown snr & J Tunnicliffe v Derbys, Chesterfield 1898
2nd
346 W Barber & M Leyland v Middlesex, Sheffield 1932
333 P Holmes & E Oldroyd v Warwicks, Edgbaston 1922
3rd
323* H Sutcliffe & M Layland v Glamorgan, Huddersfield 1928
301 H Sutcliffe & M Leyland v Middlesex, Lord's 1939
4th
312 D Denton & GH Hirst v Hants, Southampton 1914
299 P Holmes & R Kilner v Northants, Harrogate 1921
5th
340 E Wainwright & GH Hirst v Surrey, Oval 1899
329 F Mitchell & E Wainwright v Leics, Leicester 1899
6th
276 M Leyland & Emmott Robinson v Glamorgan, Swansea 1926
233 MW Booth & GH Hirst v Worcs, Worcester 1911
7th
254 W Rhodes & DCF Burton v Hants, Dewsbury 1919
247 P Holmes & W Rhodes v Notts, Trent Bridge 1929
8th
292 R Peel & Lord Hawke v Warwicks, Edgbaston 1896
192* W Rhodes & GG Macaulay v Essex, Harrogate 1922
9th
192 GH Hirst & S Haigh v Surrey, Bradford 1898
176* R Moorhouse & GH Hirst v Gloucs, Bristol 1894
10th
149 G Boycott & GB Stevenson v Warwicks, Edgbaston 1982
148 Lord Hawke & D Hunter v Kent, Sheffield 1898

INDIVIDUAL BATTING

OVER 8000 CHAMPIONSHIP RUNS IN COUNTY CAREER

		Inns	NO	Runs	HS	Avge	100s
H Sutcliffe	1919–39	721	74	32814	313	50.71	96
G Boycott	1962–86	607	101	29485	260*	58.27	94
D Denton	1895–1920	890	50	28291	221	33.67	50
GH Hirst	1891–1921	869	106	27314	341	35.79	50
W Rhodes	1898–1930	1020	136	26859	267*	30.38	38
P Holmes	1913–33	591	60	22680	315*	42.71	55
M Leyland	1920–46	600	73	21871	263	41.50	51
JH Hampshire	1961–81	654	83	19548	183*	34.23	31
L Hutton	1934–55	420	48	19361	280*	52.04	63
DB Close	1949–70	683	83	18425	198	30.70	24
DEV Padgett	1951–71	648	61	16860	146	28.72	26
J Tunnicliffe	1891–1907	622	54	16597	243	29.22	21
JV Wilson	1946–62	600	58	16326	230*	30.12	22
PJ Sharpe	1908–74	574	60	15114	172*	29.40	19
A Mitchell	1922–39	452	55	14531	189	36.60	33
E Oldroyd	1910–31	445	55	14096	194	36.14	33
W Barber	1926–46	400	40	12763	255	35.45	24
DL Bairstow	1970–90	566	100	12371	145	26.54	9
JT Brown, snr	1890–1904	432	34	12340	311	31.00	18
W Watson	1939–57	357	55	12198	214*	40.39	24
R Illingworth	1951–83	556	116	12144	150	27.60	10
R Kilner	1911–27	416	39	11511	206*	30.53	13
K Taylor	1953–68	448	32	11123	203*	26.73	13
FA Lowson	1949–58	329	26	10799	259*	35.64	22
RG Lumb	1970–84	370	27	10682	165*	31.14	20
JD Love	1975–89	369	54	9657	170*	30.65	11
NWD Yardley	1936–55	351	42	9578	183*	30.00	14
S Haigh	1895–1913	575	95	9514	159	19.82	3
MD Moxon	1981–90	271	20	9475	218*	37.74	16
FS Jackson	1890–1907	283	17	8955	160	33.66	18
EI Lester	1946–56	271	19	8847	186	35.10	20
P Carrick	1970–90	459	77	8711	131*	22.80	3
Lord Hawke	1890–1909	471	62	8630	166	21.10	7
E Wainwright	1890–1901	378	24	8294	228	23.42	14
E Robinson	1919–31	392	70	8210	135	25.49	7

MOST RUNS IN A SEASON

Runs	(Avge)		Season
2624	(87.46)	H Sutcliffe	1932
2197	(109.85)	G Boycott	1971
2167	(60.19)	L Hutton	1939
2137	(85.48)	H Sutcliffe	1928
2123	(62.44)	P Holmes	1925
2098	(63.57)	L Hutton	1949
2049	(97.57)	H Sutcliffe	1931
2029	(54.83)	P Holmes	1920
1969	(56.25)	M Leyland	1933
1966	(59.57)	H Sutcliffe	1935
1963	(46.73)	D Denton	1905
1941	(55.45)	G Boycott	1983
1913	(61.70)	G Boycott	1982
1891	(72.73)	G Boycott	1975
1882	(60.70)	P Holmes	1928
1872	(38.20)	PJ Sharpe	1962
1854	(50.10)	AA Metcalfe	1990
1848	(51.33)	GH Hirst	1904
1831	(53.85)	D Denton	1912
1822	(45.55)	H Sutcliffe	1937

DOUBLE CENTURIES
341 GH Hirst v Leicestershire, Leicester (AR) 1905
315* P Holmes V Middlesex, Lord's 1925

313 H Sutcliffe v Essex, Leyton1932
311 JT Brown v Sussex, Sheffield (BL) 1897
302* P Holmes v Hampshire, Portsmouth 1920
300 JT Brown v Derbyshire, Chesterfield 1898
285 P Holmes v Nottinghamshire, Trent Bridge 1929
280*L Hutton v Hampshire, Sheffield (BL) 1939
277* P Holmes v Northamptonshire, Harrogate 1921
275 P Holmes v Warwickshire, Bradford 1928
271* L Hutton v Derbyshire, Sheffield (BL) 1937
270* L Hutton v Hampshire, Bournemouth 1947
270 H Sutcliffe v Sussex, Headingley 1932
269* L Hutton v Northamptonshire, Wellingborough 1949
267* W Rhodes v Leicestershire, Headingley 1921
263 M Leyland v Essex, Hull 1936
260* G Boycott v Essex, Colchester 1970
259* FA Lowson v Worcestershire, Worcester 1953
255* H Sutcliffe v Essex, Southend
250 P Holmes v Warwickshire, Edgbaston 1931
248 W Barber v Kent, Headingley 1934
247 M Leyland v Worcestershire, Worcester 1928
243 J Tunnicliffe v Derbyshire, Chesterfield 1898
235 H Sutcliffe v Middlesex, Headingley 1925
234* H Sutcliffe v Leicestershire, Hull 1939
233 G Boycott v Essex, Colchester 1971
232* GH Hirst v Surrey, Oval 1905
232 H Sutcliffe v Surrey, Oval 1922
230 H Sutcliffe v Kent, Folkestone 1931
230 JV Wilson v Derbyshire, Sheffield (BL) 1952
228 E Wainwright v Surrey, Oval 1899
228 H Sutcliffe v Sussex, Eastbourne 1928
224* P Holmes v Essex, Leyton 1932
221 D Denton v Kent, Tunbridge Wells 1912
220* P Holmes v Warwickshire, Huddersfield 1922

220* G Boycott v Northamptonshire, Sheffield (BL)1967
218* MD Moxon v Sussex, Eastbourne 1990
218 GH Hirst v Sussex, Hastings 1911
216* AA Metcalfe v Middlesex, Lord's 1988
214* W Watson v Worcestershire, Worcester 1955
214* G Boycott v Nottinghamshire, Worksop 1983
214 GH Hirst v Worcestershire, Worcester 1901
213 H Sutcliffe v Somerset, Dewsbury 1924
212 H Sutcliffe v Leicestershire, Leicester (AR) 1935
211* M Leyland v Lancashire, Headingley 1930
210* R Peel v Warwickshire, Edgbaston 1896
210* M Leyland v Kent, Dover, 1933
210 MW Booth v Worcestershire, Worcester 1911
209* D Denton v Worcestershire, Worcester 1920
209 P Holmes v Warwickshire, Edgbaston 1922
208 BB Wilson v Sussex, Bradford 1914
206* R Kilner v Derbyshire, Sheffield (BL) 1920
206 H Sutcliffe v Warwickshire, Dewsbury 1925
205 H Sutcliffe v Warwickshire, Edgbaston 1933
204* M Leyland v Middlesex, Sheffield (BL) 1927
204* G Boycott v Leicestershire, Leicester (GR) 1972
204* RJ Blakey v Gloucestershire, Headingley 1987
203* K Taylor v Warwickshire, Edgbaston 1961
203 JT Brown v Middlesex, Lord's 1896
203 H Sutcliffe v Surrey, Oval 1934
202 H Sutcliffe v Middlesex, Scarborough 1936
201* G Boycott v Middlesex, Lord's 1975
201 W Rhodes v Somerset, Taunton 1905
201 L Hutton v Lancashire, Old Trafford 1949
200* D Denton v Warwickshire, Edgbaston 1912
200* H Sutcliffe v Worcestershire, Sheffield (BL) 1935
200 H Sutcliffe v Leicestershire, Leicester (AR) 1926

David Denton was a batsman legendary for his 'luck', which lasted 22 season and saw him through more than 28 000 runs and 50 centuries! (Hulton Picture Company)

INDIVIDUAL BOWLING

OVER 400 CHAMPIONSHIP WICKETS IN COUNTY CAREER

		Runs	Wkts	Avge
W Rhodes	1898–1930	48911	3112	15.71
GH Hirst	1891–1921	37917	2095	18.09
S Haigh	1895–1913	24685	1571	15.77
GG Macaulay	1920–35	26295	1551	16.95
FS Trueman	1949–68	25341	1488	17.03
H Verity	1930–39	17216	1304	13.04
JH Wardle	1946–58	22797	1280	17.81
WE Bowes	1929–47	18850	1240	15.20
R Illingworth	1951–83	22142	1206	18.35
D Wilson	1957–74	18614	917	20.29
P Carrick	1970–90	25756	828	31.10
DB Close	1949–70	19501	817	23.86
E Robinson	1919–31	17179	811	21.18
AG Nicholson	1962–75	15707	809	19.41
R Kilner	1911–27	12893	785	16.42
A Waddington	1919–27	14416	762	18.91
E Wainwright	1890–1901	12671	746	16.98
R Peel	1890–97	10529	678	15.52
TF Smailes	1932–48	13215	629	21.00
EP Robinson	1934–49	12150	601	20.21
CM Old	1966–82	12277	586	20.95
GA Cope	1966–80	14279	562	25.40
R Appleyard	1950–58	8316	540	15.40
A Sidebottom	1973–90	13376	539	24.81
MW Booth	1908–14	10087	507	19.89
GB Stevenson	1973–86	12956	446	29.04
FS Jackson	1890–1907	8311	431	19.28
RA Hutton	1962–74	9629	417	22.22
A Coxon	1946–50	7774	405	19.19
A Drake	1909–14	7159	402	17.80

MOST WICKETS IN A SEASON

Wkts	(Avge)		Season
206	(12.29)	W Rhodes	1900
196	(13.59)	W Rhodes	1901
182	(14.84)	GH Hirst	1906
176	(15.21)	GG Macaulay	1925
169	(13.93)	R Appleyard	1951
169	(13.98)	WE Bowes	1932
165	(12.69)	H Verity	1936

161	(13.63)	H Verity	1935
159	(11.73)	GC Macaulay	1924
158	(17.13)	JH Wardle	1952
158	(19.03)	MW Booth	1913
157	(14.45)	H Verity	1937
156	(12.44)	GH Hirst	1908
153	(11.93)	H Verity	1933
153	(12.69)	H Verity	1936
149	(13.34)	GG Macaulay	1923
145	(14.16)	S Haigh	1900
144	(15.84)	JH Wardle	1950
143	(12.90)	W Rhodes	1920
143	(14.72)	W Rhodes	1903
142	(12.42)	W Rhodes	1919
141	(16.41)	W Rhodes	1907
141	(18.28)	MW Booth	1914
140	(12.48)	W Rhodes	1902
140	(15.21)	GH Hirst	1907
139	(11.41)	R Kilner	1923
138	(12.34)	H Verity	1931
138	(13.18)	WE Bowes	1935
138	(13.53)	S Haigh	1906
137	(16.35)	A Waddington	1920
136	(14.80)	R Peel	1895
135	(13.74)	H Verity	1932
135	(16.36)	A Drake	1914
135	(16.75)	GH Hirst	1901
134	(15.05)	GH Hirst	1910
133	(14.86)	JH Wardle	1955
132	(12.79)	FS Trueman	1960
130	(16.93)	GH Hirst	1895
129	(14.03)	EP Robinson	1946
129	(15.66)	W Rhodes	1899
129	(17.62)	JH Wardle	1948
127	(14.35)	R Appleyard	1954
127	(15.40)	A Waddington	1922
126	(13.84)	W Rhodes	1898
126	(15.76)	W Rhodes	1905
126	(15.79)	GG Macaulay	1926
123	(11.99)	S Haigh	1902
123	(17.39)	WE Bowles	1933
120	(11.27)	W Rhodes	1923
120	(13.31)	GG Macaulay	1922

NINE OR MORE WICKETS IN AN INNINGS

10–10 H Verity v Notts, Headingley 1932
10–35 A Drake v Somerset, Weston-super-mare 1914
10–36 H Verity v Warwicks, Headingley 1931
10–47 TF Smailes v Derbys, Sheffield 1939
 9–12 H Verity v Kent, Sheffield 1936
 9–22 R Peel v Somerset, Headingley 1895
 9–23 GH Hirst v Lancs, Headingley 1910
 9–25 S Haigh v Gloucs, Headingley 1912
 9–25 JH Wardle v Lancs, Old Trafford 1954
 9–28 W Rhodes v Essex, Leyton 1899
 9–29 AC Williams v Hants, Dewsbury 1919
 9–36 Emmott Robinson v Lancs, Bradford 1920
 9–39 W Rhodes v Essex, Leyton 1929
 9–41 GH Hirst v Worcs, Worcester 1911
 9–42 R Illingworth v Worcs, Worcester 1957
 9–43 H Verity v Warwicks, Headingley 1937
 9–43 MJ Cowan v Warwicks, Edgbaston 1960
 9–44 H Verity v Essex, Leyton 1933
 9–45 GH Hirst v Middlesex, Sheffield 1907
 9–48 H Verity v Essex, Westcliff 1936
 9–48 JH Wardle v Sussex, Hull 1954
 9–59 H Verity v Kent, Dover 1933
 9–60 H Verity v Glamorgan, Swansea 1930
 9–62 AG Nicholson v Sussex, Eastbourne 1967
 9–66 E Wainwright v Middlesex, Sheffield 1894
 9–121 WE Bowes v Essex, Scarborough 1932

FIFTEEN OR MORE WICKETS IN A MATCH

17–91 H Verity v Essex, Leyton 1933
16–35 WE Bowes v Northants, Kettering 1935
16–112 JH Wardle v Sussex, Hull 1954
15–38 H Verity v Kent, Sheffield 1936
15–50 R Peel v Somerset, Headingley 1895
15–51 A Drake v Somerset, Weston-super-Mare 1914
15–56 W Rhodes v Essex, Leyton 1899
15–63 GH Hirst v Leices, Hull 1907
15–100 H Verity v Essex, Westcliff 1936
15–123 R Illingworth v Glamorgan, Swansea 1960

WICKET KEEPING

MOST DISMISSALS IN AN INNINGS
7 (7ct) DL Bairstow v Derbys, Scarborough 1982

MOST DISMISSALS IN A MATCH
11 (11ct) DL Bairstow v Derbys, Scarborough 1982
 9 (8ct 1st) A Dolphin v Derbys, Bradford 1919
 9 (9ct) DL Bairstow v Lancs, Old Trafford 1971
 9 (9ct) RJ Blakey v Sussex, Eastbourne 1990

MOST DISMISSALS IN A SEASON
96 (88ct 8st) JG Binks 1960
82 (70 ct 12st) JG Binks 1961

MOST CAREER DISMISSALS
957 (709ct 248st) D Hunter 1890–1909

Maurice Leyland, always the archetype Yorkshireman, whose left-handed batting proved to be the bastion of the county's middle order for more than a decade (Hulton Picture Company)

6

POSTSCRIPT

Qualification and Other Matters

When the Championship was officially recognised in 1890 the rules were, in the main, still those drawn up in 1873. In brief, no player, whether amateur or professional, was allowed to play for more than one county per season; at the season's start, each player was to choose his county, qualifying either birth or 'residence'; the latter constituted an unbroken period of two years or a family home of longer standing, though while serving out his period of 'residence', a player was able to play for the county of his birth.

In the spring of 1899 the MCC, having been given sole responsibility in this field, drew up new rules to come into force in 1900. Again, no player could play for more than one county in a season; he could always play for the county of his birth, place of residence norwithstanding; residential qualification came after 24 months' continuous residence. A cricketer who played for a county for five consecutive years was qualified for that county for all time, or until he played for another county. A cricketer could play for his old county while qualifying for another. Finally, a cricketer qualified for one county who wished to play for another had to give his present county notice in writing before commencing residence in his 'new' county. Likewise a county wishing to sign a player qualified for another were obliged to inform the present county in writing before commencing negotiations with the player.

Minor amendments took place in the next few seasons,but in December 1906 an advisory meeting of county representatives at Lord's voted that all players should be registered by MCC, with the qualifications of each player approved by Lord's after their first championship appearance.

An interesting amendment to the qualification rules was approved in 1908, stating that no cricketer could play for more than one county in the same *calendar year*, on pain of two years' disqualification. A Brit-

ish colony, dependency or state was regarded as a 'county', and the main reason for the new amendment was to prevent Frank Tarrant of Middlesex playing for his native Australian state, Victoria, during the close season!

In March 1910 an advisory committee meeting at Lord's approved the proposition that any Serviceman posted abroad who had been qualified for a county for at least two seasons should retain his qualification on his return home. Covering of bowlers' run-ups and the creases at certain periods during a match was approved, and most importantly umpires were required to award six runs for any hit over the ropes or boundary fence on any ground.

A number of new regulations were introduced for the re-start of County Championship cricket in 1919, the most drastic being that every match should be limited to two days, with extended playing hours. Predictably this arrangement lasted only one season. A new form of qualification was introduced; officers, NCOs and men who were serving in 1919,and would be serving in 1920, in a county Regiment, would be qualified in 1920 for that county, providing they had not already played for another county.

A new set of qualification rules was drawn up in 1924, the first of which stated that each county should fill in a form for each player at the start of a season, sending the original to MCC, and duplicates to each county. Another new rule concerned players who were resident in England but not qualified by birth for any of the first-class counties. These were now enabled to play for the county whose capital (or county town) was closest to his place of birth, or residence. Little else was done with regard to qualifications until 1937, when a new rule was confirmed stating that a player who had not played for any county or state for 24 months might be qualified for a county on 12 months' residence.

In 1939, new conditions were agreed for special

registration of players. It was stated that a player could go from one county to another on special registration, on any of the following conditions:
1. The player is not required by any county for which he is qualified.
2. He is a recognised English amateur returning from overseas.
3. The player has special connections with a county – e.g., his father played for more than five years, or there is a well-established family home in the county.
4. The cricketer resides permanently in the United Kingdom but has no qualification for any county.

In the years following the Second World War there was a great deal of tinkering with the rules of county cricket in an effort to arrest the decline in spectator interest, and the qualification rules did not escape.

In 1951 there was a general tightening up in this department. A limit of 10 specially-registered players – and 8 professionals – was established, with only two special registrations per year allowed, on three-year contracts. Players born abroad had to live in the United Kingdom for three years before registration. However, county players were now enabled to play for state teams, under local rules.

In 1954 it was stated that overseas players had to live in the United Kingdom for 10 years before qualifying for special registration, while an overseas player qualifying outright for a county had to live there for three years without playing any cricket outside the county. In 1957 it was agreed that each county be limited to two overseas players, but only from 1962!

With county cricket continuing to fall in public esteem – 1961 saw total attendances fall below one million for the first time since the war – various gimmicks were tried to revive interest Bonus points were introduced, as described in Chapter Two. Other ideas included the abolition in 1961 of the follow-on rule for the first time since 1900; supposedly, the new rule would encourage early declarations and give sides batting second more chance. The new-ball rule was also amended; instead of being available after 75 overs or 200 runs, the rule was now 85 overs. Fast and true wickets were pleaded for, and a faster over-rate (at least 20 per hour) suggested.

For 1962, qualification rules for overseas players were relaxed – two years' residence, not three, was now required. For 1963, the distinction between amateurs and professionals was abolished, and the follow on re-introduced. For 1964, residential qualification for a player not needed by his former county was reduced to one year; and in 1965, an overseas player could play Tests without breaking his county qualification. A 75-yard boundary, mandatory since 1957, was now optional and a second innings could be forfeited.

What did all this tinkering achieve? Some of the decisions were very subtle; for instance the shrewd move to abolish the distinction between amateurs and professionals seems to have been far too subtle for many observers, and completely irrelevant to the troubles then afflicting the county cricket scene!

Over-rates continued to plummet, along with spectator attendance; innumerable options were discussed and, occasionally, acted upon. Sunday play was

legitimised in 1966; May 15 of that year saw play on the Sabbath for the first time, at Ilford for Essex v Somerset. But more revolutionary, and far-reaching, was the decision, for the 1968 season, that each county could register and play one overseas player *without any qualification*, After five seasons, these players would be regarded as 'English'. Soon, two were to be allowed; but with the belief that it was too much of a good thing, 1991 saw a reversion to a single overseas registration.

The new limited-overs tournaments in the 1960s and 1970s probably stimulated a general interest in county cricket, but have had little effect on attendances in the County Championship. The changes to regulations with regard to covering of pitches, overs and fielding limitations and player qualification seem to have been infinite in their number and variety yet their effect seems to have been inconsequential.

New depths were plumbed in the sophistication of tactics aimed at reducing action in championship matches, as defensive bowling and field-placing resulted in fewer runs, wickets and results. Some apparently drastic remedies were tried, but even fines for tardy over-rates achieved only limited success after the inevitable loop-holes were explored.

A genuine effort to ensure production of fair, if not good, wickets by a system of docking points was introduced, and its first effect was to rob a side of a possible Championship title. Manifestly the scheme was effective; the howls of protest were therefore all the more distasteful. As ever, the cynicism of short-term self-interest reared its ugly head, and sadly achieved a large measure of general support. A new regulation actually possessed teeth; we could not have that!

The official County Championship completed its 100th year reasonably strong financially, but otherwise chaotic. Future viability is an improbable ideal; the competition may continue into the foreseeable future as a training ground for the rigours of five and six-day Test matches, with perhaps 17 four-day matches. So poor are wickets throughout the country that only the introduction of a flat-seamed ball in 1990 made it possible for some matches to last even *three* days, while the probable reduction of potential cricket-playing days in future, with the almost inevitable loss of local festivals which are part of the cricketing traditions of many counties, would appear to make the four-day idea counterproductive.

In the meantime, past form suggests that we will see an ever decreasing tempo so that what is now squeezed into three days will be spread over four. Even where safeguards are introduced, ways will be found to circumnavigate them.

To the aficionado, the English County Cricket Championship remains the most riveting and relevant of all cricket competitions; it has produced the best cricket, the best performances and, unarguably, the best umpires. With all its faults, its deficiencies, its anachronistic situation, it is the nonpareil. Yet its ultimate demise is inevitable, possibly sooner rather than later. Some current enthusiasts may see it out, but the eventual outcome is certain. County cricket – the traditional form played over four innings and several days – is dying. The verdict – suicide.

INDEX

Page references in *italics* denote illustrations